Also by Sven Birkerts

An Artificial Wilderness:
Essays on Twentieth-Century Literature

The Electric Life:
Essays on Modern Poetry

AMERICAN ENERGIES

Essays on Fiction

Sven Birkerts

WILLIAM MORROW AND COMPANY, INC.

New York

Library of Congress Cataloging-in-Publication Data

Birkerts, Sven.
    American energies : essays on fiction / Sven Birkerts.
      p.   cm.
    Includes bibliographical references and index.
    ISBN 0-688-10612-9
    1. American fiction—20th century—History and criticism.
  I. Title.
  PS379.B56   1992
  813'.509—dc20   91-36814
                                       CIP

Printed in the United States of America

First Edition

1 2 3 4 5 6 7 8 9 10

BOOK DESIGN BY MARIA EPES

To the true readers . . .

Preface

This is one of those books that knew its title before it knew its contents. The two words—*American Energies*—clicked together one day when my back was turned, and I have trusted their convergence ever since. Or tried to. I have to admit to a few moments of wavering. For as the essays accumulated and the book began to outgrow its file folders, I began to wonder if those seven syllables were not misleadingly optimistic. Indeed, I fairly often caught myself making large-scale assessments about our literature that had more to do with entropy than energy. And during one brief interlude the manuscript even bore the experimental title, "The Death of the American Novel."

A contradiction? It would seem so, and interpreted one way it could suggest a vacillating confusion on the part of the critic. But no, there is a way to make sense of it. The terms of the contradiction are not the sort that cancel each other out. And much as I have stared and pondered, I have not felt the least impulse to bring the two views—call them the *optimistic* and the *pessimistic*—into line. Rather, I have studied to understand how they live side by side in the same critical sensibility. I ask myself, How can I write so many essays and reviews that praise the work of individual American writers and then turn around and write reflections that in one way or another argue that our fiction is floundering? Can one have it both ways?

As you will see, *American Energies* tries to do exactly that. I insist throughout that vital and ambitious novels and stories *are* being written, published, and read. But I also insist that our cultural climate, the atmospheric medium within which meanings are discovered and passed along, is in a perilous condition. The social and private power of the written word is rapidly waning. For a great many reasons—and these will be taken up in the essays that follow—the activities of the novelist and short-story writer have become a flutter at the margins of the culture. Though works of beauty and imagination are created every season, nothing seems to stick. There is no *burr* quality, no grip, and the fault is partly the writer's, partly society's. One can, however, comment on the brilliance of the plays, even as one suspects that the game may be lost.

But there is also another reason for the twin perspectives, this having to do with the divergent aspects of the critic's job description. Simply, one writes and thinks differently depending on the task at hand: The lenses I don to evaluate a single book are not the same ones I use when the subject is larger trends and connections.

The vocational bread-and-butter work, at least for me, involves encountering books before they are officially books. They arrive for preview in the generic form of bound galley proofs; they are still in the last part of the publishing birth canal, not yet "out." And I can never begin reading a new novel or collection without an excited tensing-up. *This* may be the one, the work—the vision—that catches our moment, that gathers what we are and gives it an unforgettable shape. This may be a book that changes lives.

Nearly always, of course, the anticipation is chased by a sagging sense of collapse. Nevertheless, where the effort has been sincere, the reviewer tries to work for the positives. The fiction writer is working to express something, is acting as if the whole business truly mattered. The least that the critic can do is to respond in kind and assume that matters of the highest importance are really at stake. Through such collaborations illusions may come to look like realities.

·   ·   ·

But the critic also lives in the world. I have eyes in my head. I see over and over how these books, begotten out of passion and private mission, matter not a fig to 99 plus percent of the population. I survey the postmodern mayhem of a culture split from itself, dissolving among its competing images and manias, and I have to ask about the relevance of the literary. What *are* these novels and stories giving us? How are they making sense of what is happening? Could it be that they are so very little read because, despite the versions of life they offer, they are not offering the *essential* things, whatever those may be? These are the questions that vex me and give rise to the darker perspectives that I invoke. I do find myself writing increasingly dire-sounding reflections on the state of the art. But be assured that they are not obituaries—they are calls to arms. The other pieces assert it clearly enough: We have the necessary energies in abundance. What we need are bold acts of connection.

American Energies, then, embodies the two extreme poles of my critic's nature. The book does not, however, take the shape of a diptych; it is conceived, rather, as a kind of funnel, with ever-narrowing apertures of focus. The first section, "Backgrounds," is made up of general essays. These are my nonliterary readings of the cultural trends that have everything to do with the way literature gets written and received. I take up the "postmodern" questions, looking at the status of the printed word before an encroaching electronic tide, at the breakdown of artistic hierarchies, at the situation in the classroom where the word is taught, and so on.

"American Fiction," the second section, includes a number of essays that try to get a fix on how it is with the contemporary novel and story. Here I project the trends discussed above upon the practice of our writers. Two pieces in particular, "The Talent in the Room" and "Paranoids and Intellectuals," attempt to crystallize the problem and make a gesture toward solutions. The other pieces, written over a period of several years, vary in scope and urgency but reflect the same obsessions. What is our fiction telling us about our lives? How is it helping us, and how is it failing us? What next?

The last long section is entitled "American Writers" and it breaks the preceding aerial maps down into a sequence of specific engagements. These are close-focus pieces on individual writers. Some try to draw the arc of a career, others to direct a beam at a single book.

.   .   .   .

They were all written to deadline, usually with fairly generous length allotments, but sometimes not. I have resisted polishing, or adding, or—horrors!—revising estimates. Even where I might have changed my view, I have let the earlier reaction stand. For each piece is the result of a fresh encounter, a meeting of reader and printed page that took place before the votes were tallied and the consensus declared. The reader will note, I think, that resonances pass between the reflective meditations and the more targeted discussions. This is as it should be. Even though the critic's sensibility may look like a spectrum, with different and seemingly distinct bands, it is finally *one* sensibility—and indeed, at closer inspection the colors are seen to dissolve imperceptibly one into the next.

I owe thanks to the generosity, intelligence, and tact of a number of editors: Leon Wieseltier and Ann Hulbert at *The New Republic*; Caroline Fraser, Harriet Brown, and Lex Kaplen at *WigWag* (a wonderful episode in American magazine publishing); Elizabeth Pochoda, formerly of *The Nation*; Pat Towers, Adele Sulcas, and Amy Gross at *Mirabella*; Herb Leibowitz at *Parnassus*; Jack Beatty at *The Atlantic*; Gerald Marzorati at *Harper's*; Evelyn Renold at *Lear's*; Margaret Ann Roth and Sophie Glazer at *The Boston Review*; Michael Lerner at *Tikkun*; Askold Melnyczuk at *Agni*; Nancy Kline, formerly of the Expository Writing Program at Harvard; William Phillips and Rosanna Warren at *Partisan Review*; Michael Dirda and Nina King at *The Washington Post Book World*; Maura High at *NER/BLQ*: Dianne Donovan at *The Chicago Tribune*; John Ferguson, formerly of *The Boston Phoenix*; Henry Louis Gates at *Transition*; Robert Wilson at *USA Today*; Jeffery Paine at *The Wilson Quarterly*; and Alida Becker at *The New York Times Book Review*. A debt of gratitude, as well, to Maria Guarnaschelli, my editor at William Morrow and Company, and to Helen Pratt, my agent.

Contents

AMERICAN WRITERS

· · · ·

Contents

. . . .

Contents

BACKGROUNDS

Postmodernism:
Bumper-Sticker Culture

You would have to have been in a coma in Bali not to know that this summer marked the twentieth anniversary of the Woodstock music festival. If you missed it on the cover of *Life* or on *20/20*, your nightly entertainment reporter must have filled you in. You could not turn around, really, without being assailed by the anthropological wonder of it all. Not only did people then wear long hair and dress oddly, but they acted and spoke in ways that now seem entirely foreign. The era was all like some long, preternaturally vivid dream collectively experienced. And like a dream, that whole period seems to have vaporized upon our awakening. None of the bright concept people, or commentators, or TV anchors, knew how to connect the past with the present, except to keep harking back to some variation on "the times they are a-changin' . . ."

My thoughts last summer were on the subject of postmodernism; rather, they were *supposed* to be there, for I had promised to write a piece of cultural reflection. But into that oyster there crept an irritant. I found my thoughts slipping away from questions about our culture at present and returning continually to the mystery of that foreignness. Why was it so difficult to talk or write in a believable way about the counterculture of the late sixties? What were the obstacles preventing intelligent evaluation? Clichés and quotations from rock songs seemed to be all the response that anyone could manage—or else a kind of peppy, breathless idealism that retrospectively poisoned the era. It was only very recently that the jagged belt of cartoon lightning hit me: I realized that this failure has a great deal to do with postmodernism. My topic and the formerly ulterior question suddenly fused together.

Gratifying though such a bonding of thoughts may be, it has not made anything easier. But it has changed the agenda and forced me to pitch my thoughts in a specific direction: the background to postmodernism and the characterization of its aesthetic strategies must now hook up to a consideration of this dream interlude in our recent history.

The path, as I begin to make it out, moves through the vast lowlands of postmodernism first, only later linking up with the six-ties. But it cannot *begin* with postmodernism. Indeed, what I face, if I am strict about it, is a regression that could take me back to Plato. Somewhat arbitrarily, therefore, in order to have a place to launch from, I pick up a cue from the word *postmodernism*: to get to the *post,* it seems essential to make a few observations about the other half of the word—*modernism.*

In October 1929, the year of the international stock-market crash, in the heyday of modernism, W. H. Auden wrote a peculiar, syntacti-cally dissonant sonnet—"Sir, no man's enemy, forgiving all"—in which he, in effect, called upon God to remedy a host of modern ailments: the "intolerable neural itch," "the distortions of ingrown virginity," and so on. In the last two lines, quickly upping and lowering the ante, he exhorted: "Harrow the house of the dead; look shining at/ new styles of architecture, a change of heart."

Sixty years later, some parts of his prayer have been answered—if not by God then by history. Though the "intolerable neural itch" is with us worse than ever, we do have new styles of architecture, and music, and painting, and writing . . . And we have our change of heart. Sadly, it does not appear to be a change for the better. What we are experiencing is something more like a *loss* of heart. And the new styles and the loss are linked; they are what we talk about when we talk about postmodernism.

Postmodernism. Post-modernism. We encounter the word everywhere these days. It is like a large decalcomania that has been pressed down over the surface of contemporary life. Postmodernism is a mood, an aesthetic, a perspective, what some have called a "periodizing concept." If it is a label, then it is a label still in transit, for the larger shaping forces are themselves in various stages of momentum. A clear definition is impossible to provide. This is not to say, however, that intellectuals and intellectual faddists on every front are not weighing in with their summations and projections.

Predictably, the range of response has been vast. Frederic Jameson, one of the more astute of these commentators on our inchoate present, has suggested that shifts in the system of world capitalism may be in large part responsible for our postmodern condition: that larger, more fluid networks of commerce are redefining our place in the social order, indeed altering the order itself. The Frenchman Lyotard, who emerged as if out of nowhere to don the guru's mantle, cites for causes the collapse of defining metanarratives—our religious and secular belief systems—coupled with the fundamental transformation of information and knowledge that is being wrought by the new computer technologies. Others, like Jean Baudrillard, argue that the image, or "simulacra," has supplanted the thing itself and that the very nature of what we call the "real" has changed.

Whatever the angle of inquiry, though, a consensus has been struck in certain quarters: that in a century of vertiginous changes, some sort of critical mass has been attained in recent decades; that we have moved away from modernism and are now living, for better or worse, in a postmodern era. There is little to be gained at present by vaunting one theory over another—too much is in flux. We would do better to try to gain some purchase on the nature of the overall change, and then to assess some of the possible repercussions in the sphere of the arts.

The logical place to begin, as I suggested earlier, is on the familiar ground of modernism. Now that we are confidently—or nervously—

post it, we should be able to catch a clear picture in the rearview mirror. Besides, we've lived for so long surrounded by its trophies, it should not be too hard to sketch its fundamental precepts.

Briefly, modernism was the cultural response to the enormous social, political, and technological changes that afflicted Western societies in the early decades of our century. Of course, those changes, the forces that determined them, had been proceeding apace long before the century ever rolled over: a steady demographic shift from rural areas to urban centers, intensifying imperialist expansion on the part of the global powers, secularization and the erosion of belief systems, accelerating industrialization, with untold refinements in the technologies of mass production. These factors converged and effected what amounted to a wholesale transformation of life. Historians and memoirists often refer to the unusually temperate summer before the outbreak of the First World War as representing the last glow of the old dispensation. Certainly nothing was ever the same after that war ended.

The litany of modernist masters is familiar to everyone: Eliot, Pound, Joyce, Wyndham Lewis, William Carlos Williams, Gertrude Stein, the Italian futurists, and the Russian constructivists, Stravinsky, Schönberg, Picasso and the Cubists. . . . Art struck at right angles to the reigning modes of nineteenth-century style. Wan Pre-Raphaelitism and the mimetic cult of beauty were set upon with knives and clubs. The new spirit was cosmopolitan; its subjects were often violent or frightening, its attitude angry or despairing; it was fragmented, confusing, aggressively referential. Aesthetic innovation was pushed to the foreground, so much so that it became a conspicuous part of the product. Part of the message was seen to be in the means. As Pound wrote in his celebrated poem "Hugh Selwyn Mauberly": "The age demanded an image/ Of its accelerated grimace." And if there is a single archetype embodying modernist practice, it is probably the Poundian vortex—the shapely swirl of energy holding shattered fragments in place, but only just.

Still, for all their awareness of dispersal and chaos, the early modernists were within shouting distance of the discarded ideals of wholeness and organic completion. Their dissonance played off echoes of remembered harmonies. At the same time, they saw themselves as pioneers; the future was uncertain, to be sure, but it was a terrain to be colonized. The terrible (and exalting) energies of the machine and the mad carnage of international war were carrying the world toward some destination: the idea of an unknown future is deeply figured in their art. Indeed, it was only with the modernists that the notion of the artist as advance runner—as avant-gardist—truly entrenched itself. To be at the front, cutting a path, forging artistic innovations—all this implied that there was a future to move into.

No longer. All has changed—utterly—since then. Now it is modernism that is finished. An inexorable push of forces has again shifted the configuration of things; we stand now in the midst of new conditions. And we find new styles, new ways of registering the world. We may decry the aesthetic, fault the perspective, lament the loss, or repudiate the label that has been attached, but the fact of the change is incontestable.

The shift from modernism to postmodernism is a shift of kind, not degree. But this does not mean that the conditions that spawned modernism have gone away. No, urbanism, societal fragmentation, violence, and the collapse of a sense of transcendent grounding to human affairs are all live components of our late-twentieth-century worldview. But these components have been acted upon and intensified by an array of new forces; the result is what scientists like to call a "paradigm shift." Simply, the recognitions of modernism, for so long an essential part of our equipment for living, no longer address the world as we experience it, not fully. Too many new conditions have emerged.

Three stand out and deserve some comment. First, there is the actual and psychological fact of the nuclear capability of the superpower nations. Modernism took shape in the face of growing international militarization, and the human potential for destruction was seen to be enormous. But the ultimate all-terminating option did not then exist. It does now, and it has made all the difference. Even more than the atrocities of the Nazi death camps, the images of destruction at Hiroshima and Nagasaki—the iconic mushroom cloud—have seeped into the collective psyche, infecting all of us with the anxious knowledge that minutes—*minutes*—separate us from the potential extinction of all biological life. The generations born after 1940 carry as a part of their legacy the understanding that they may be the final witnesses of planetary life. In the face of such a possibility, all human history—its inventions, cathedrals, artworks—seems both unbearably poignant and irrelevant.

The second momentous postwar change has been the all but total societal reorganization caused by the Western world's move from industrial mechanization to information processing. The implementation of computer-based technologies at every level has profoundly modified the ways in which we perceive our world. Machinery, no matter how sophisticated, is in the last analysis solid, opaque. Its processes can be isolated and comprehended, should we care to make the effort. Information processing, on the other hand, is essentially invisible—neural as opposed to mechanical.

And as the patterns of this processing have altered our social behavior, we have had to surrender the older picture of reality. More and more we feel that we are functioning within some larger—and fundamentally inscrutable—circuitry; that signals and information bits are generated, circulated, and stored by power centers that exceed our comprehension and control. Modernism responded to the deadening power of bureaucracy and its total short-circuiting of individual responsibility. But the computer is the abstracted apotheosis of bureaucracy, a depersonalizing force that grows exponentially every time the microchip is further refined. Advances in recent decades have dealt a tremendous blow to the concept of self-reliant individualism.

The third transformation is as profound as the others; it may, indeed, prove to be *the* galvanizing force. I'm referring to the utter saturation of Western societies by the electronic media, principally television. The modernist performed in a world that was still marked by distances and far horizons. Shrinkage had begun, but the planet could yet be counted vast and mysterious. True, there was radio, and high-speed telegraphy, but only since the 1950s, with TV, have we seen the globe turn into a spinning top on the coffee table. A tap of the remote-control panel puts us in the heart of the Brazilian rain forest; electronic images gather and expunge the last earthly mysteries. The generations that have grown up entirely within the force field of TV know a world very different from the world their fathers knew. Not only has distance been breached and psychically collapsed, but the sense of *difference,* too, has fallen away. TV brings us a constant and fluent juxtaposition of kinds of programming and

· · · ·

kinds of images. A typical thirty-minute newscast will show and interpret footage from China, Iran, and the site of some cult slaying; it will intercut its "serious" presentation with ads for ravioli and cat food; it will bring into collision the face of a grieving mother and the happily panting visage of a basketball star. And it will never— *never*—remark on its process. Who can guess what cumulative effects this sort of exposure has on the psyche? What habits are eroded, what others implanted?

One of the most telling effects of the electronic media has been the creation of a persuasive sense of an eternal present, a *Now.* So powerful is the hold of the image and the rapid-shift sequence, so mesmerizing the juxtaposition of contents, that the watcher is gradually seduced away from causal/historical habits of mind. The structure of programming allows absolutely no time for absorption or reflection. Hour upon hour the world's montage is rushed past our eyes. It becomes increasingly difficult, especially for younger minds, to hold intact a historical sense—an understanding of the world as a complex of developmental sequences. It is much easier to think—or simply respond—laterally, across the field of the cultural present, than vertically within a historical context. This situation is exacerbated by the fact that so much of TV programming consists of stylized and decontextualized slices of history. George Washington selling cars; Nazi officers cracking one-liners with Hogan again and again on reruns. As we become glutted with these bits of the past— many of them falsified past recognition—we start to surrender our sense of narrative connection, and any feeling about our own historical place in the world.

There have been any number of related cultural metamorphoses—a more thorough account would deal with them as they deserve—but even this short inspection should suggest the extent to which our lives have been changed since the high heyday of modernism. The psychological consequences are yet untabulated, but the rough outlines are obvious enough. As individuals we have been robbed of our myths and certainties; we have been undermined, and made to feel powerless before the rushing totality of the world. Never before in history, to be sure, has the proverbial man-on-the-street felt less authority or less sense of personal identity. The man-on-the-street won't even go onto the street if he can help it. Frederic Jameson has written at length about what he calls the postmodern "death of the bourgeois subject"—that is, the death of the sense of oneself as an active, empowered agent, as a clearly bounded and particularized being.

With the globe made small, with all distances and wildernesses eliminated (Bill McKibben's recent book, *The Death of Nature,* is an elegy everyone should read), and with a steady collage of the past flowing by us on our screens, we find ourselves planted—marooned—in the Now. We have not only lost our grip on real history, on the past shaping the present, but we have also lost any vital sense of the future. The possibilities are so unnerving, our awareness of our lack of control so paralyzing, and the diet of present-tense stimulus so addicting that we look no further into the calendar than the time we have circled for our next vacation. We no longer think of ourselves as contributing to the making of the world. We are acted upon, and we accept it. Politics, economics, and now ecological determinants will force certain larger courses of action upon all of us. But for the individual the variables are simply too many to be calculated. We take our motto from the popular bumper sticker: SHIT HAPPENS.

With these general speculations on our present condition in mind, we can now start narrowing the aperture for a look at the arts: for while postmodernism is, in the largest sense, societally grounded, its features are most clearly seen as they emerge in our various cultural products. Here we see specific aesthetic features. These differ, naturally, from genre to genre, but distinctive stylistic signatures can be isolated.

1. Postmodernism abandons the traditional (and, later, modernist) stance of high seriousness in terms of its regard for its subject. In the perceived absence of valid "metanarratives" or any ground of historical continuity, meaning—the old vice of "high" art—becomes a provisional affair. More often than not it is ribbed, tickled, and mocked—as is the reader's or viewer's expectation. The postmodernist work announces to its audience that the time-honored distinctions of high and low no longer apply, that the reference base will henceforth include the full continuum of cultural signs. A novel like Thomas Pynchon's *V*—a paradigmatic postmodernist work—freely interrupts its more traditionally ordered scenes with episodic absurd-

ities and farcical interludes. The language switches constantly from an archly *moderne* idiom to a bop-inspired street vernacular. The performances of Laurie Anderson or Spalding Gray are smartly orchestrated collages mixing anxious cultural commentary with surprise silliness.

The point is that the old "high" art proposes life as a deep and difficult problem. Its very approach suggests that there is some place, existentially speaking, to *get to*. The essence of postmodernism is, by contrast, a concern with style and surface. The frontal, devotional posture is replaced with an ironic obliquity. The new message: there is nowhere to get to, so let's just play the game as a game. Most contemporary practitioners, be they writers, filmmakers, painters, or performance artists, would probably agree with Oscar Wilde that there is nothing so profound as appearances.

2. In postmodern expression, historical awareness is replaced by historical referentiality. Where the contract with past and future has been broken, a vertigo-inducing freedom of appropriation results. The past becomes a kind of keyboard on which the postmodernist performs. E. L. Doctorow, in *Ragtime,* takes license to rewrite the past as fantasy, playing fast and loose with real-life figures like Jung, Freud, and the architect Stanford White. Similarly, in his novel *Libra*, Don DeLillo reenacts the Kennedy assassination, contriving a possible scenario from the archive of "what ifs," and making his variation more persuasively live than our legacy of statistics and memories. Contriving meaningful sequences or accurate judgments is not, for these artists, the main point. The goal is, rather, to seize the past as an arena for free play, and to conjure with it an unnerving and edgy fluidity. Political accountability is beside the point here, for that would, by definition, require a resurrection of the past; indeed, of the whole conception of a forward-moving time-line and a worldview shaped by ideas of cause and consequence. Postmodernism locates itself in posthistory.

3. Postmodernism, as an aesthetic, abjures continuity; it thrives instead on juxtaposition and combination. The electronic media have schooled us all in quick-flash perception; we are connoisseurs of the blip. Again, limitless freedom. As all images and concepts—all references—are drawn from the pool of the Now, anything can sit alongside anything else. Boundaries are not nonexistent, but they

exist mainly to be mocked and flouted. They are to the highest degree porous. And just as "high" and "pop" culture signs live together, so do genres cross-pollinate. Songs from the 1960s turn up on TV shows; Herriman's cartoon creatures become protagonists in Jay Cantor's novel *Krazy Kat*; historical moments are staged and posed as if for photographs in Robert Wilson's *Civil Wars*. So, too, we find philosophers like Umberto Eco writing learned essays on subjects like Disneyland. And when the old dividing walls have been torn down, all expressions will perhaps be subsumed within a single oceanic category. At which point, of course, the very idea of category will have become superfluous.

Here I might point out the deep congruity that exists between the postmodern aesthetic and the academic discipline of deconstruction. Deconstruction has as one of its goals the total dissolution of textual authority; it seeks to undermine the ideological bases of its target texts by exposing the "privileged" terms upon which such bases must rest. One of the many consequences is that formerly freestanding disciplines like philosophy, history, sociology, and so on, cede their autonomy, becoming part of a larger unstructured entity known simply as "theory."

Another of the effects of the deconstructionist enterprise has been the dethroning of the authority of any single textual voice. Texts (etymologically "weavings") are shown to be polyvalent entities, less the singular products of intending individual authors, more components in a grand and complex tapestry of other texts. Postmodernist works, if they do not necessarily grow out of deconstructionist tenets, nevertheless show the influence of those tenets in their anticipatory attitudes. That is, they fend off potential attack by avoiding the kinds of claims to integrity that would mark them out as targets. They do so, in part, by donning the prophylactic of irony. Irony is the sovereign preemptive strategy. It says: "I don't take this completely seriously, so why should you?"

Some examples might help to bring these general assertions into sharper relief. As it happens, Todd Gitlin has already assembled a broad and suggestive inventory (in "Hip-Deep in Post-Modernism," *The New York Times Sunday Book Review,* November 6, 1988). In the spirit of postmodernism, let me weave a paragraph from his text into mine: One postmodernist trope is the list, as if culture were a garage

. . . .

sale, so it is appropriate to evoke postmodernism by offering a list of examples, for better and for worse:

> Michael Graves's Portland Building, Philip Johnson's A T & T, and hundreds of more or less skillful derivatives; Robert Rauschenberg's silk screens, Warhol's multiple-image paintings, photorealism, Larry Rivers's erasures and pseudo-pageantry, Sherrie Levine's photographs of "classic" photographs; Disneyland, Las Vegas, suburban strips, shopping malls, mirror-glass office building facades; William Burroughs, Tom Wolfe, Donald Barthelme, Monty Python, Don DeLillo, Isuzu "He's lying" commercials, Philip Glass, *Star Wars,* Spalding Gray, David Hockney ("Surface is illusion, but so is depth"), Max Headroom, David Byrne, Twyla Tharp (choreographing Beach Boys and Frank Sinatra songs), Italo Calvino, *The Gospel at Colonus,* Robert Wilson, the Flying Karamazov Brothers, George Coates, the Kronos Quartet, Frederick Barthelme, MTV, "Miami Vice," David Letterman, Laurie Anderson, Anselm Kiefer, John Ashbery, Paul Auster, the Pompidou Center, the Hyatt Regency, *The White Hotel,* E. L. Doctorow's *Book of Daniel, Less Than Zero,* Kathy Acker, Philip Roth's *Counterlife* (but not *Portnoy's Complaint*), the epilogue to Rainer Werner Fassbinder's *Berlin Alexanderplatz,* the "language poets"; the French theorists Michel Foucault, Jacques Lacan, Jacques Derrida, and Jean Baudrillard; television morning shows; news commentary cluing us in to the image-making and "positioning" strategies of candidates; remote-control-equipped viewers "grazing" around the television dial.

I would add, from a recent issue of *USA Today* (itself a postmodernist collage of the world), the following trends: syndicated Nintendo TV shows that will "wrap live action around cartoon adventures" and feature so-called "camp cameos" by Vanna White, Elvira, and Magic Johnson; entertainment shows that search for real criminals and news programming that carries acted "recreations" of newsworthy events; and the new pop music mode of "sampling," or mixing bits of old hits into new songs.

Gitlin's garage-sale inventory catches beautifully the heteroclite character of the postmodern aesthetic. Reading across the examples, we see—if we know some of the references—the commonalities.

They are all "cutting edge" productions: they are hip, the latest thing, Zeitgeist. It could be that taken together they give us a picture of our time that can be gotten nowhere else, in no other way. Certainly they share many of the characteristics that I enumerated: in the main they are playful, ironic; they fuse genres, set pop-culture resonances against the old expectations of "high" culture. They are, without exception, stylized, packaged for consumption. In none of these examples do we detect even a glimmer of the kind of seriousness of approach that distinguished modernist works by writers like Woolf and Eliot, composers like Schönberg or Webern, painters like Kline, Kandinsky, or Kokoschka.

Are we then at the end of "high" or "serious" culture? Is the making of meaning no longer a function of the arts? Or could it be that *meaning,* as such, is a prison from which we are finally being released?

The postmodernist would probably answer as follows: that artistic meaning as we have been taught to think of it is a chimera. It may have had—did have—a place in a different world, a world of closed hierarchies and fixed value systems. But these hierarchies and value systems were themselves illusory, willed into place by ruling elites. Meaning—certainly meaning as a result or consequence of art—must now be seen as a sop thrown to the audience. To have such meaning, we must believe that our lives, and the history that we are part of, have a purpose, an end. But the chaos of late modernity has shown clearly that there is no such thing: all is open, in process, disconnected. The character of contemporary life is fluid, complex, without center. We cannot move *forward,* but we can move. We can station ourselves in the flux of the present and enjoy the collisions and discontinuities; we can look at life as a spectacle.

Postmodernism is, in this sense, the very apotheosis of aestheticism. Enjoy the play of surface, never mind the depths. There *are* no depths. Notions of profundity, cravings for connection and significance, must be jettisoned. Needless to say, the postmodernist view does not sit easily with those who still think of life—personal and collective—as a search for some ultimate understanding or truth: it is not Judeo-Christian. But these retrograde dissenters are in an unfortunate position just now. What can they say or do? For rage, protest, exhortations about the noble purposes for which we are born—holdover ideas from the pre-secular eras—seem clumsy and excessive before the polished pastel surfaces of the Now. Raising a cry, one comes perilously close to sounding like that most extinct of all creatures—the socially conscious, committed sixties activist: the hippie, the flower child; the . . . burnout.

Here the path bends around to connect with my second subject: the counterculture of the late sixties and early seventies and the absolute foreignness of its dominant impulses and expressions to our present-day culture. Truly it is a puzzle to be contemplated. How just twenty years ago this country—and the West in general—witnessed the sudden outburst of a youth movement that proclaimed as its guiding values sincerity, organicism, political accountability, spirituality, material asceticism . . . Values that, quite obviously, run counter to our present postmodern "spirit" at every level. And it should be emphasized that this was not a local, factional outburst, but a weather that moved over the whole landmass, quickly carrying along a great many people from all sectors of the population.

That the counterculture should have erupted so suddenly and sweepingly is perplexing enough. More perplexing still is the fact that it came about just when the vast complex of forces was pushing our society onto its present postmodern track. Logically speaking, the late sixties should not have happened. The so-called "youth revolution" of that time was initiated and perpetuated by a generation that had come of age in the postwar fifties—the first generation to have soaked itself since childhood in the rays of the cathode tube: the unlikeliest generation of all.

Received wisdom has it that the escalating U.S. involvement in Vietnam was the precipitating factor—that fear and anger galvanized an otherwise docile crop of affluent baby boomers. But this is simplistic. For one thing, protest was only a small part of what the counterculture was about. Over and above protest, this period represents an attempted revolution in values. It was as if the lid had been wrenched off some great vat boiling with unauthorized impulses and feelings. A simple recognition—*that things did not have to be this way*—flashed through the whole culture. Or, rather, through that part of the culture that henceforth became the "subculture." The eruption took the explosive form it did because the contents—those boiling impulses and feelings—were contained under a great pressure. Not just a pressure of authority—parental or governmental—but also a pressure from the direction of the future. Was it not clear to everyone with a gram of intuition where the world was heading? Consider the image of the dying ember blazing up one last time. It may be trite, but it gives the idea: that this Western youth movement was the final flaring up of a romantic worldview in a society that was fast becoming entrenched in a new worldview, that of postmodernism.

Why did this flare-up not come sooner? Any attempt to answer brings us up against the overwhelming complexity of historical causation. A vast complex of social forces converged to make the summer of 1968 a watershed. I won't rehearse them at great length. Vietnam, the draft; the sharp political polarization between hawks and doves; the legacies of civil-rights activism and post-Beat protest; the spectacular growth of the popular-music industry . . . But there was something else, too, and to explain that, I have to reach for another analogy.

The generation that made the counterculture was, as I have said, the first generation to have grown up in an all-surrounding media environment. From earliest childhood on, its members watched the same TV shows, listened to the same music, first on AM, then FM, radio. Earlier generations had experienced some of this connectedness via radio, but not nearly to the same extent. *This* was the generation that, while still in grade school and early high school, saw Kennedy assassinated; its members sat through the long weekend of replayed images—our first electronic wake. These were the kids who watched *Leave It to Beaver* and *My Three Sons,* and later, the Beatles on *The Ed Sullivan Show.* When this population came of age, when it reached the hormonally volatile years of late adolescence, it suddenly grasped itself as a collectivity. Millions of teens looked into the mirror of TV and rock and roll and saw not their frightful conformity, but their power. Numbers. No generation in history has ever had such a mirror to look into. The result was a shocking explosion of adolescent narcissism.

This moment of recognition—1968, let's say—was twisted into its particular historical form by the explicit circumstances of the period. Had the members of this generation grown up the same way—with rock and TV—but in different conditions (in tranquil peacetime, say), the eruption might still have come, but it would have had a different character. I hesitate to make any projections about what might have been.

The first instance of collective self-recognition, then, also proved to be the last large-scale flowering of certain impulses and values. The immediate consequence of this recognition of numerical power was the proclamation of utopia, a place outside of time (and away from progress). Communes flourished. Hippies banded together into large, free-floating households and attempted to live by sharing. The work of the world (the work of progress) was abjured for contemplation and getting high; it was an era of useless activity and endless free time. Simplicity was an ideal, fantasies were rural. People voiced notions of freedom, of spiritual connection to more enduring—and saving—values.

I don't need to spell out the fine points. But I will remark again how astonishing it is that these choices were espoused even as the larger drift of society was toward computerization, media-saturation, consumerism, and a bewitchment with surfaces—the materialism that now defines our situation was lurking in the wings. And when the counterculture fell in upon itself, as it did just a few years later (brought down by excess and impracticality, and by a sharply tightened economy), the reaction—the claiming of these other options—was overwhelming.

The era of the counterculture is gone, hauntingly gone. We have nothing but our response to its slogans, artifacts, and music to bring it back, for the spirit of that time seems to elude language. Every descriptive phrase sounds so wrong, so impossibly idealistic. Look how garish and fumbling were the efforts of the media to review the legacy of Woodstock this past summer. The attempts, and their failure, may well be the most telling way of measuring what our culture has since come to. Cynicism and irony—everything living, certainly everything that espouses a frank ideal, withers in their glare. I wonder if even the most articulate of the many icon figures of the sixties could survive the arched eyebrow of a Dave Letterman.

The point I'm making is finally this: that the sixties youth culture was a surprise warning bell run through our society, a preemptive outburst that sought to swerve us off the path that we were already embarked on. Never mind that one of its many causes was a collective narcissism: its effects far transcended that origin. The postures and slogans of that movement sound foolish today because we have resumed that path, because we *need* to see them as foolish lest we reproach ourselves too severely for the choices we have made. The deep postmodernist current contained a slight, but breathtakingly potent, countercurrent, a genuine romanticism that in many ways reflected what was best in us. The collapse of the counterculture into folk myth—and, worse, into the stuff of ridicule—shows how eager we were to be rid of that part of ourselves. For with that utopian dream came a different sort of responsibility, one that we were obviously not ready for.

The Totalized World:
A Note

I have recently been having an argument through the mails with a
writer friend. An argument about reading. I maintain that we
cannot be said to be reading unless we actually hear the sounds
words make in what T. S. Eliot called our "auditory inwardness." My
friend, a poet, contends that conditions have changed and that most
reading is now carried on with the eyes alone—he cites speed-
reading and the split-second scanning of newspaper pages.

I come back at him with an analogy: A Mahler symphony is on
the turntable in the next room—we either hear the sounds as a
backdrop to whatever else we are doing, or we *listen*. I say that if we
gut the daily paper in a matter of minutes, we are not so much
reading the words as stripping the signs of their designatory sense.
That, the poet says, is what we must now call reading. I fire back
that without hearing the sounds, we deprive ourselves not only of
the rhythmic value of the language, but of the cumulative sense of
context as well. We are less likely to retain what we have not heard.
We do not receive the words as they were meant to be received; we
get information, but we cannot get meaning. I say that where there

is no contract with meaning, there is no reading. The poet calls me an idealist. We exchange epistolary sighs.

What has this to do with our political being-in-the-world? A great deal, I think. To begin with, few people would deny that where politics is concerned, we are now living in what Marshall McLuhan long ago christened "the global village." The electronic net now extends over every wrinkle of our troubled sphere; its access and influence grow at a frightening rate. Round-the-clock television news channels bring us uninterrupted flickers of footage—from Iran, Berlin, Vilnius, London, Israel, Guatemala. . . . The daily press is like a spinning dial, and the revolutions have accelerated to the point where we can scarcely see the numbers. And Ted Koppel is there every night, presiding over the day's crisis like some Druid priest.

One profound consequence is that we—those of us who care to live in the world, or who cannot seem to do otherwise—live with a split. Inner double vision has become all but second nature. We walk the dog on Elm Street, but at the same time we dwell anxiously on the decimation of the Brazilian rain forest. Our sense of enmeshment and implication extends around the whole planet. Moreover, we have gradually—during the last quarter-century—internalized the knowledge that the web in which we perch is being rewoven incessantly. And that nothing we think, say, or do is going to change that.

The awareness of totality brings paralysis, for what energy we have is directed toward the internal balancing of foreground and background. Our very sanity depends upon our ability to hold bits of information in their appropriate matrices. The gas bill is due tomorrow, the Soviet Union is collapsing as a world empire. . . .

Politics, for those of us not directly involved in government, is information. And there is now more information than a human being can possibly digest. Indeed, our world environment is nothing *but* information. Equilibrium is perpetually threatened and must be perpetually restored. Indeed, what *is* sanity if not the effective management of information?

Over the past few decades our place in the human collective has been redefined for us. We are now, whether we wish it or not, citizens of the world; everything is connected, and the fine filament of responsibility extends between all sentient individuals. Or so we have come to believe. The song says: "We are the world." The bumper

. . . .

SVEN BIRKERTS

sticker says: "Think globally, act locally." The new science of Chaos proposes that a butterfly flapping its wings in China affects the weather pattern over Oklahoma.

Our technology has fit us—cognitively and psychologically—into a new system, a new evolutionary magnitude. In what feels like the blink of an eye, our environment has been changed. Where once the gaze was arrested by the horizon, it now penetrates every physical barrier. But even so, our biological endowment imposes its limits: we simply cannot process all the information we would have to in order for our global citizenship to have meaning. We are therefore torn. We feel guilty when we lower the gates, when we reject information that we know is probably significant. But then *all* information is probably significant.

If we attempt to keep up, on the other hand, then we pledge ourselves to a kind of insanity. We speed-read. Not just newspapers, but the world itself. Skimming over the words without hearing them, however, is not reading—it gives sense but not meaning. Absorbing information without substantive context, without awareness of the local, human rhythms that give true shape to the deeds and pronouncements, is compulsive and debilitating. It paralyzes the will to action.

What shall we do? Shall we discipline ourselves to be less aware? Dismantle the technology, the densely imbricated electronic systems? We won't. Should we then exert ourselves to learn everything? It's impossible, of course. But we will try, and we will in the process sacrifice what was formerly—and for millennia—the human scale of our sentience. We will, further, redefine our notions of what is sane and what is not: we will learn to think of our anxious and untethered state as home.

·   ·   ·   ·
The Totalized World: A Note

The Nostalgia Disease

Once there was another city here, and now it's gone.
There are almost no traces of it anymore, but millions of
us know it existed, because we lived in it: the Lost City of
New York.

It was a city, as John Cheever once wrote, that "was still
filled with river light, when you heard the Benny Goodman
quartets from a radio in the corner stationery store, and
when almost everybody wore a hat." In that city, the taxi-
cabs were all Checkers, with ample room for your legs, and
the drivers all knew where Grand Central was and always
helped with the luggage. In that city, there were apartments
with three bedrooms and views of the river. You hurried
across the street and your girl was waiting for you under
the Biltmore clock, with snow melting in her hair.

—Pete Hamill, "The New York We've Lost"

M y subject here is not the great, perhaps vanished, city of New
York, but rather nostalgia, that peculiar condition wherein
memory fuses with desire to create a pain that is very nearly pleasur-
able. Or a pleasure verging upon pain. I picked the opening passage of
the lead essay from a special issue of *New York* magazine (December
1987—entitled "You Must Remember This") to identify a particular
frequency or tone. But almost any passage from any of the other

essays could have served as well, so limited are the options of the mode. The writer assembles luminous details from the archive of the remembered—or fantasied—past. The details declare an order that was once natural and whole, against which the present is viewed as hopelessly fallen. And it works. Even though I had no experience of the city in those storied times, I felt a bittersweet pang. Like everyone, I have my own New Yorks, my own lost better days.

I cited the Hamill passage, too, because it was handy—I'd saved the magazine to brood over. But in truth I could have lowered my net almost anywhere: our culture is awash as never before in repackaged bits of the past. We find them on screen and radio, in books and magazines, even in the posturing about patriotism and "family values" that so recently confused our electoral process. Our appetite for the stuff is bottomless. We have just emerged from eight years of a nostalgia presidency—a grand, collective bathing in the images and pieties of an earlier, less cynical and compromised era (what an irony: here was the most ruthless cynicism, here were the gravest compromises!)—and there is no sign that the impulse is slackening. Indeed, nostalgia now threatens to become a permanent feature of our cultural life, a kind of ground bass against which we play our changing ideals and aspirations.

Consider just a few of its recent manifestations. On television, the closest thing we have to a national psyche, we not only have shows like *thirtysomething, Wonder Years, China Beach,* and *Almost Grown,* but every second commercial comes wrapped in the musical and visual tissue of the past. The radio dial lands on oldies and rock "classics" with each turn of the wrist. Or else it gets stuck on yet another repeat broadcast of one of Garrison Keillor's down-home Lake Wobegon monologues. Recent movies that have more or less successfully mined the vein include *1969, Eight Men Out, Bull Durham* (an odd instance of nostalgia filtered through the present), *Tucker, Stand by Me, Everybody's All-American,* and *Imagine: John Lennon,* to name just a few. And wherever we look, we see headlines beaming the return of Elvis, or yet another anniversary special on JFK, Marilyn, or 1968. . . . The barons of midcult have grasped the formula for success. Processions of what we've some-how lost—once we've been tipped off that that's what they are—are as irresistible as sex and scandal. It appears that our desire for the clarity and certainty of the imagined past will batten repeatedly on certain surefire images. Country roads, weathered barns, city scenes with fedoras and oldfangled cars, beaded hippies flashing peace signs: all that matters is that these emblems tell us how we were before self-consciousness and fragmentation afflicted us. Before everything changed.

Some might argue that nostalgia has always been with us, that we find the longing for a better past in Sappho and Homer, as well as in Norman Rockwell and Currier & Ives. And to be sure, all of us, as individuals, experience nostalgia sharply at times—more sharply, I think, as we grow older. This was as true of our great-grandparents as it is now of us. But something is different. The impulse has deepened and strengthened; it has become commodified. Where once it may have waxed and waned in the self and the culture, it is now a constant—we live by looking over our shoulders. The reasons for this are many. But chief among them is the fact that we now have a technology for collective cultural experience that did not exist even fifty years ago. Pulsations did not then move through the whole of the body politic, certainly not at such a rate or intensity. We were not joined, as we are now, by a finely meshed electronic net. We were not then alerted at every instant to the universalized state of things. We brooded over the disappearing past privately, more fitfully.

Technology and media are part of the equation; changing historical circumstances are another. Nostalgia could not have thrived so vigorously in an an earlier day because people were not so mesmerized by the past. Present and future held too strong a claim on the attention—there was too much to be done just to survive, to inch forward into the future. No longer. In the past few decades everything about the way life is lived has altered. At some point in the post–World War II period, technological and societal changes attained critical mass. Suddenly (at least from a historical vantage point), the bedrock certainties about our experience of reality shifted and assumed new configurations. We are now squarely—and perhaps irrevocably—stuck in a fragmented and self-conscious condition that some have labeled "postmodernism" (I will take this up shortly). And nostalgia is now no longer an occasional fibrillation in the psyche—it is more akin to the persistent sensation felt by the amputee in his or her "phantom" limb.

The reasons for this change are fairly obvious, at least on the surface. We are, psychologically, all creatures of habit, programmed to desire constancy and security. But it happens that we now find ourselves in a world that is locked into an ever-intensifying spiral of change. One could argue that our fundamental modes and rhythms have been altered more since the 1940s than during all the millennia that came before. Until then—and I must generalize—we lived in relation to an ancient and familiar paradigm of country and city. True, we had mass-production industries and air travel. But most individuals could, if pressed, have found the continuity between their way of life and the age-old human pattern.

Things are radically different now. For most of our hundreds of millions of citizens, the city-country distinction has been exploded into the anonymous surround of the megasuburb. We can no longer just look around to see where we fit into the scheme. Analogously, the physical ties of family and community have come unraveled, only partly replaced by the pseudoimmediacy of telephone communications. And how we do what we do—not to mention the *what* itself— has been revolutionized past recognition. Information crisscrosses the country on screens and via fax machines; business gets conducted from terminal to terminal. We look up from the panel just long enough to see whether we need our galoshes or sunglasses. And at the end of the day we cushion our spent selves with vivid washes of music and the numbing flicker of televised images.

I exaggerate, of course. But it is to make a point: that our private and public worlds are changing faster than our response mechanisms can cope. Change itself is changing, upping its rate with merciless regularity. And the threat of the world—headlined by AIDS, drugs, political corruption, nuclear arms, environmental panic, and violent crime—looms larger than ever before. On top of this, there is now the sense that the changes are final, that we are not going to rouse ourselves and go back to old ways. The momentum is too great; it is beyond the control of any government or organization. If once we moved expectantly into the future, we now cower before it. What we hope, above all else, is to squeak through without getting hurt too badly.

· · · ·

The Nostalgia Disease

Our longing for what we perceive as the certainties of the past is, of course, only partly conscious. We carry it around as a need, as something akin to a biological drive. Or a defense, a place to run to. Or a mode of orientation. Our picture of the past, preserved, amplified by the incessant images that envelop us, becomes an internal compass; the more lost we feel, the more often we need to refer to it. A fact, as I have suggested, that is hardly lost on our politicians and image-brokers. Their instincts zero in on the true condition of the populace more quickly and accurately than any market survey could hope to. As our need intensifies—it does so daily—so does the purveying of packaged offerings. More and more every day, the past is being offered to us as a commodity for consumption. We learn to react to our sense of loss by taking out our pocketbooks.

Nostalgia is the easy response of the individual who feels cut off from the past, from the secure continuity of tradition. It is a compensatory reflex before the anxiety of disconnectedness. The psyche avoids the hard work of mourning and tries to fill its void with a set of images. Here I should clarify one thing: that these are almost never images of the real thing. For the real thing, truly recalled, places one in danger of grief. Nostalgia is the response elicited by the simplified and stylized image—the general store, the old porch swing, Grandma handing out lemonade. The more stylized it gets, the closer we are to kitsch. Nostalgia is a look at the past, an attempted emotional connection, that comes *after* desire has falsified and colorized it. There is little or no true relation to the event as we might have experienced it while embedded in the then-uncertain present.

This brings us, in not all that roundabout fashion, to a consideration of the so-called postmodern condition. Postmodernism, as Todd Gitlin pointed out in a recent essay in *The New York Times Book Review* ("Hip-Deep in Post-Modernism," November 6, 1988), has become the buzzword of the late 1980s. Pundits invoke the term to explain anything from shifts in the styles of art to all-embracing transformations in the world at large. The sifting of applications will go on for some time. Still, a general ground of assumptions, or contentions, can be identified.

Briefly, postmodernism espouses the view that a permanent

change has taken place in Western culture in the past few decades. The time-line, which was the indicator of progress, of directional movement into the future, has shattered. The great eras of growth and innovation are ended. We are postindustrialist, posteverything; there are no more terrestrial frontiers. What's more, cultural energies (like our natural resources) are depleted. The kinds of transformations that now lie in store for us are mainly organizational—they involve new distribution of information and refined modes of processing (computerization), as well as a more thorough saturation of every societal sphere by the electronic media. In the arts, the subject of so much postmodernist theorizing, we no longer look to an avant-garde pushing its vector into the unknown; we no longer think of art as discovery. Instead, we have an aesthetics of combination, the presentation of old materials.

Gitlin sums up this aesthetic quite concisely in his essay:

> Post-modernism . . . is indifferent to consistency and continuity altogether. It self-consciously splices genres, attitudes, styles. It relishes the blurring or juxtaposition of forms (fiction-nonfiction), stances (straight-ironic), cultural levels (high-low). It disdains originality and fancies copies, repetition, the recombination of hand-me-down scraps. It neither embraces nor criticizes, but beholds the world blankly, with a knowingness that dissolves feeling and commitment into irony. It pulls the rug out from under itself, displaying an acute self-consciousness about the work's constructed nature. It takes pleasure in the play of surfaces and derides the search for depth as mere nostalgia for an unmoved mover.

Among the proponents of this aesthetic, Gitlin cites artists like David Byrne, Robert Wilson. John Ashbery, Laurie Anderson, Spalding Gray, David Hockney, Italo Calvino, and Don DeLillo. Of the "vision" itself he writes:

> In effect, post-modernism expresses the spiritless spirit of a global class linked via borderless mass media with mass culture, omnivorous consumption and easy travel. Their experience denies the continuity of history; they live in a perpetual present garnished by nostalgia binges. Space is not real, only time.

. . .

The Nostalgia Disease

I would disagree only with the last sentence. A sense of time wherein all events and products can be viewed as contemporaneous is hardly "real." The whole point of the postmodern project is to affirm that our connection to history has been ruptured. We have left the old perspective—which saw styles and expressions as naturally bound to their times—and have embraced a perspective of hyper-conscious pluralism. Overrun with information and stimulus, we have lost a distinct sense of what our time means or how it differs from (and grows out from) former times. We respond to our confusion by browsing freely and indiscriminately among the relics and styles of the past. Everything flows together, unsutured by any sense of causal connection or sequence. And when there are no laws about how things fit together, irony—bemused detachment—is the inevitable consequence.

Nostalgia, the word, comes from the Greek *nostos,* which means "to return home and survive." *Webster's Third New International Dictionary* gives the archaic definition as "a severe melancholia caused by a protracted absence from home." The more current meaning given is "a wistful or excessively sentimental . . . yearning for return to or return of some real or romanticized period or irrecoverable condition or setting in the past." This nostalgia, this longing for connection that is projected upon falsified images, increasingly replaces what were once natural linkages emerging from an understanding of the progression of experience. The more that the objects of our nostalgia become calculated media commodities, the further we get from being able to grasp our condition.

The yearning itself is authentic, I have no doubt, but as the object and the indulgence are generally false, the process can only be debilitating. Nostalgia, fostered by the products of our popular culture, sets us ever more deeply into a schizophrenic relation to ourselves. When we discharge our pain and sadness at the loss of meaningful parts of the past by consuming manufactured images, we break contact with ourselves and with the truth of that past. Such nostalgia short-circuits the mourning process. And where mourning lets us lay the past to rest and get on with things, the bathos of nostalgia keeps us floating in a perpetual illusion about an attainable or renewable past. By immersing ourselves in the afterglow of our own history—the seductive, doctored afterglow—we lose the initiative to keep making history. That is, to perform freely and unselfconsciously in the face of the present.*

The self-consciousness, which goes hand in hand with the distanced perception of irony, is the most insidious aspect of the nostalgia transaction. Heightening and sentimentalizing the images allows for safe consumption; it shields us from the pain of the genuine. Irony, incorporating the attitude of knowing, of being "wised-up," anticipates and preempts true response. We are rendered passive. When Garrison Keillor delivers his Lake Wobegon stories, his tone and arch pauses do the work of distancing. His every vocal gesture is telling us that, hey, this is cute and folksy, that we ought to be comfortably amused by the doings of these dear, benighted small-town folks. What was once in earnest exists now to be chuckled over. The truth has not come closer—it has receded. And when one of the characters on *thirtysomething* launches into yet another paean to the lost ideals of the sixties, it is always with a grimace that derides the very clichés that are being vented. Again, the matter of the past is hedged around with the quotation marks of our supposed superiority. The net effect is the divestiture of the past: we can't find our way back to it because its soul has been leached away.

Prepackaged nostalgia builds easy bridges to what is finally a dream about how things were. The more that such bridges are built, and the more that we use them in our daily traffic, the more likely it is that the truth about the past will slip away. That truth is complex and difficult. It reflects to us images of the present that are not always

---

*One might, of course, uphold the opposite case: that we take our bearings for the future from the fond ideals—and idealizations—of the past; and indeed, that to uphold a sense of purpose a nation must look back upon something brighter and nobler than the history that revisionists would offer us. What could have been more nostalgic, in this sense, than Ronald Reagan's farewell address to the nation, his invocation of John Winthrop's "city upon a hill"? I would not want to argue that we should do away with the heightenings and distortions that must attend such a vision. But I would point out that even the president—the prince of nostalgia—warned in the same speech against "an eradication of the American memory that could result, ultimately, in an erosion of the American spirit." Though his exhortation was for all Americans to learn the *patriotic* facts, he, too, was aware of the dangers of memory gone awry. The drive to nostalgia must be recognized for what it is, and it must be tempered consistently with the complicated truth. Otherwise we are condemned to keep dreaming.

.   .   .   .

The Nostalgia Disease

pleasing. It posits the ongoing work of culture as a massive task. Postmodernism, by contrast, offers simple, even inviting, views. We can venture into a bazaar of images and attitudes that lay no claim on us: its ironies feel cool, fashionable. But until we can break out of the cage we have made for ourselves, those ironies and the self-consciousness that attends them will be our fate.

And here is the demonic irony at the root of all others: that the quality we most prize in all of these trumped-up images of the past is the *lack* of irony and self-consciousness. We long for nothing so much as a time when people did things out of simple necessity and desire, when everything was not tainted by self-awareness, when the guy running to meet his girl under the Biltmore clock was not simultaneously watching himself running to meet his girl under the Biltmore clock.

The Second Time
Around

I n our culture, the lag between a sound and its answering echo—an event and its resurrection in the collective memory—is, roughly speaking, twenty years. A generation. I don't know whether this has been true in other times and places, but somehow I think not. Did 1934 bring before the public eye a reassessment of 1914? Not that I've ever heard. For that matter, there was really no such thing as "the public eye" back then, certainly not in the sense that we have one at present.

Now, though, in the golden age of the electronic media, we have got very big on the twenty-year anniversary—on hearing how it was that Sgt. Pepper got the band to play. In the last few years, we've been through the intense public reprise of three assassinations (the two Kennedys and King), the death of Marilyn Monroe, the 1968 Columbia uprising, Woodstock.

Part of the blame can, of course, be directed at the media; in their constant search for material that will play, they are forced to keep spading up the past. But there is another logic here as well: the logic of how things do in fact become interesting with the passing of time. Nothing is duller, they say, than yesterday's paper. A distance of ten years makes for some change of perspective, but not quite enough. We have not yet cleansed ourselves of the event's afterimages; our emotions have not fully cooled. But at the remove of two decades everything is changed again. By then we've slipped free of our attachments. It is possible to *see* certain things again, to hold them clearly in recollection, to revisit. Twenty years gives us not just the event but also the former self to return to.

Richard Goldstein begins his introduction to *Reporting the Counterculture*—a collection of twenty-seven commentaries he wrote for the *Village Voice* between 1966 and 1971—by reflecting on how what went around is now coming around. He tells of finding among his things a "torn and long neglected" tie-dyed shirt—a shirt he'd worn on assignment, dropped acid in, even made love in. It is his *petite madeleine,* flinging the past in his face. He understands that what used to be the incandescent—or Day-Glo—present has soaked up into the shirt's swirls and stains. And he is left with a question: what to do with the damned thing?

He ends up stuffing the shirt back into the jumble of a drawer. End of story, almost. That very night, he reports, he chanced to see a shirt very much like his, only "bolder and more lurid," on the back of Al Bundy's teenage daughter on *Married . . . with Children.* Goldstein salutes the irony with a quip: "Those who do not understand history are forced to wear it." Touché. Wit, I think, is our only recourse against the bafflement of postmodern replay.

Goldstein's book is in itself a kind of tie-dyed artifact. Had these columns been reprinted ten years back, I would not have thought to read them; and had I read them, I might have shrugged and yawned. But now, suddenly, they are of compelling interest—and I don't think just to me. The interest is not because of any special insights or observations, really, and not because of any special excellence of style (though Goldstein was a lively and observant counterculture journalist), but simply because of the resurfacing of echoes and figments from the era itself. Goldstein wrote the language of the day, and hearing that language again—its pauses, poses, and coinages— sets the memory reels turning.

Goldstein has divided his collection into three sections, entitled The Music, The Movers, and The Madness. The arrangement is thematic, of course, but it is also calculated to mark out a precise trajectory. We move from the heady, wide-open early days, when "for a time, it really seemed as if the old order was crumbling and each of us could expand to fill the void," to the latter days, when hype and co-optation blew stale cynicism over everything. The sequence also tracks Goldstein's own changing attitudes and vantages—from celebrant to critic, from watcher to participant. Journalism and generational self-definition become, for a time, one and the same thing.

Compressed in these pages, then, is the whole unfolding and withering down of hope. The author had no such intention, naturally, over the week-by-week course of writing to deadline, but it emerges as a retrospective effect. And I suspect that this effect—this larger resonance—is what convinced Goldstein that he had a book.

Let me plot three points on this generational parabola. First, here is Goldstein writing in 1968 about his 1967 interview with Janis Joplin and her band, Big Brother and the Holding Company:

> I first met them last year in San Francisco. In a ranch house with an unobstructed view of ticky tack. They were assembled for an interview on hippie culture, and I began with a nervous question about turning on. In answer, somebody lit up and soon the floor was hugging-warm. I glanced down at my notes as though they had become hieroglyphics (which they had). When it was time to split, and everyone had boarded a paisley hearse, I muttered something like, "We shouldn't be interviewed. We should be friends." And the car drove away laughing, with long hair flying from every window.

Then, from Chicago in 1968:

> I slipped out and walked across the street, shaking. I sat for 10 minutes with a girl who had been unconscious. We watched the medical crews covering their faces. And when the tear gas came, we ran away. On Michigan Avenue, I sat in the street, and ripped away the remnants of my press cards. I whooped the way they did in *The Battle of Algiers,* and chanted the way they did in *La Chinoise,* and I raised my hands in a television "V" at the flag they had lowered to half mast.

Finally, from 1971, from a piece entitled "Love and Money and the Shootout in Marin":

> Last August 7, a young man with tawny skin walked into the Marin County Civic Center with three guns inside his coat. He walked into court. He said, "This is it." He gave the guns away. Three crowded men held them over five country people: the judge, the assistant district attorney, and three female jurors. They walked into the sunlight. They climbed inside a yellow van. They started the motor up. There was some confusion. The judge died in his robes. The young man died in his tawny skin. Two convicts died in their courtroom fatigues. The jurors lived. The young D.A. lived, his spine severed. The third con, shot bad in the stomach, lived to be accused.

Tone and diction tell the story here: the third citation could have come from last week's *Village Voice*; the first two might just as well have come from Crete in the Minoan period.

This is not the place to analyze the manifold complexities of societal change. Something utterly raw and new grew old; fast-buck artists moved in like sharks; the plug was yanked, and the electricity went shuddering back into its hold. The fascination of a book like this lies less in its reflections on the hows and whys of change, more in the unexpected glimpses it gives of life on the other side of the wall, before everything turned.

I am convinced that something rare and miraculous took place back in the late sixties. So many pressures came from so many directions, such a diversity of currents ran through the body politic all at once, that the traditional frame—the expectations we shared about time and its nature—collapsed. For a short interval our sense of history, of living on a time-line, was short-circuited. How to explain this?

In Robert Musil's novel *Young Törless*, the hyperreflective hero has an epiphany in the course of an argument with a friend. "Things just happen: that's the sum total of wisdom," he exclaims, liberated briefly from the imprisoning sense that everything both *has* and *is* a cause. *Things just happen*. That, I think, was it: the feeling that so many of us had for a short time. Things were just happening, in our private lives and in the culture at large. There seemed to be no obvious path from yesterday to today, and no way of guessing what might come next. And, indeed, if things just happened, then anything could happen. We imagined ourselves in a realm of freedom and pure potentiality.

No doubt this is what the writer Geoffrey O'Brien was after when he titled his subjective memoir of the period *Dream Time* (Goldstein cites the epithet approvingly in his introduction). For in dreams—and surely nowhere else—things do just happen. Or seem to. The future, the next image sequence, is entirely unknown. "Dream time" brings surprise. And sometimes it also brings terrible things.

Ah, but we are all now children of Freud. We know that nothing in dreams is really accidental. The contents are precisely determined—by our psychic structures and by the stored messages of our experience. Our dreams project the real shape of our fears and desires. Was not the same true, finally, of the sixties, even the early glory days? We were dreaming our desires, and soaking ourselves in the sweet sensations of release. Outside the dream, pressing right up against its bubble skin, was the real. Waiting.

Reporting the Counterculture. Richard Goldstein. 208 pp. Unwin Hyman. 1990. $24.95

. . . .

The Second Time Around

The Boomers
Go Bust

There is in New York, where all things are possible, a group of the young and disaffected that calls itself the Vile Body—in homage, I presume, to the legendarily crotchety conservative Evelyn Waugh. The members (their average age is thirty-five) meet once a month, in the words of Terry Teachout, "to drink, eat stale popcorn and pretzels, and talk endlessly about whatever happens to be on our minds." Why their popcorn should be stale, I don't know. I do know, however, that many of the group members are contributors to right-leaning journals like *Commentary* and *The New Criterion*. They have now gathered their ideas and opinions into the fifteen essays packaged as *Beyond the Boom: New Voices on American Life, Culture, and Politics*. Writes editor Teachout: "We believe ourselves to be the true voices of our generation. We represent the vast majority of baby boomers, the ones who gladly put the '60s behind them without a second thought."

A generation book, then—one introduced by no less a personage than Tom Wolfe, who appears to be a sort of guru-in-residence for the group. The collective intent of these essays is to draw a line in the dust, to announce: That was then, this is now. And to make a splash, of course. The consensus of the contributors is that the youth culture of the sixties was a complete bust, and that the conservative backswing that began with Reagan's 1980 presidential campaign represents a grand awakening on the part of young Americans. The essays fall into groupings that reflect sociological, then cultural, then personal perspectives.

Defining and giving voice to a whole generation is no small task; problems will crop up. For starters, the ringing call of unanimity in Teachout's foreword proves somewhat hard to sustain. What emerges, if anything, is a sense of profound generational ambivalence; righteousness and self-hatred are locked in a bitter tug-of-war.

The first signs of this are seen in the nervousness around nomenclature. The fact that, according to Teachout, everyone born between the years 1946 and 1964 is, statistically speaking, a "boomer" creates some small confusion. The writers solve this by designating "older" and "younger" boomers. The former—the older brothers and sisters who took the road of drugs, rock and roll, and sexual liberation—were hippies. They are mocked and derided throughout the book. But then there is the somewhat stickier matter of the yuppies. Though more than a few hippies crossed over and became yuppies, the term is generally associated with the younger set. And any self-respecting younger boomer knows that the Y-appellation wears about as well as a pair of cast-iron Nikes. What to do?

The first essays in *Beyond the Boom* expend considerable ingenuity in contending with the yuppie label. Alas, often as not the writers are working at cross-purposes, consequently strengthening the impression of ambivalence at the generational core. Interestingly, the greatest polarization is found between husband-and-wife boomers Richard and Susan Vigilante. In her essay "The Drunks Shall Inherit the Earth," Susan Vigilante links the proliferation of AA and similar twelve-step rehabilitation programs with the fact that a great many younger boomers (read yuppies) have "tried to 'enrich' their lives with booze and drugs and sex." She cites a chilling spiritual impoverishment as probable cause but manages to end on the most muted note of optimism: "Are the baby boomers a generation of jerks? Perhaps. But for every baby boomer who enters a twelve-step program and sticks with it, the number of jerks drops by one."

. . . .

The Boomers Go Bust

Husband Richard rejects all such apologetics. The object of his screed, "The War Against the Yuppies," is to save the beleaguered creatures and the values they uphold. "We are the first generation in American history," grieves Vigilante, "that is despised for trying to establish homes, families, careers, businesses, and identities." His argument, roughly, is that yuppies incarnate what might also be called the bourgeois virtues, and that these—"future-directedness, personal discipline, self-reliance, prudence, thrift, diligence, and honesty"—are the very foundation of a healthy society. Ergo, stop the bashing. "Yuppies of the world, unite" is Vigilante's final cry. "You have nothing to lose but that stupid name."

If the first essays create a somewhat confused picture, the more intellectually and aesthetically oriented pieces redress the balance. The totality of boomers may be an amorphous entity, but there is no doubt whatsoever about the cultural politics of this self-appointed vanguard. They are conservative. I don't mean just ordinary stand-up-for-values conservative. I mean prickly, humorless, pious, very nearly Commie-sniffing conservative. Roger Kimball, who leads off the cultural section with "Requiem for the Critical Temper," would have it that the American university has been thoroughly infiltrated by radicals; that the values of the sixties, dead everywhere else, live on in the enclaves of the tenured professoriat. "College curricula," he fumes, "are increasingly being determined by radical political imperatives." He adduces as evidence a series of new courses that have replaced traditional requirements at Stanford, courses where "freshmen watch movies, read the writings of the Algerian revolutionary Frantz Fanon, and attend classes with inspiring titles like 'Our Bodies, Our Sheep, Our Cosmos, Ourselves.'" I wonder if Kimball would be so kind as to send me a course catalog care of this magazine. Given the near universal triumph of the Reagan revolution cited by most of the contributors, one might ask: Who are the students obediently taking notes on the need for armed insurrection? They must all be in California, for on our other coast the stacks of Fanon stand untouched in the bookstore bins.

In other culturally oriented contributions, Donna Rifkind tilts against the literary careerism of the McInerney pack (a windmill if ever there was one); Andrew Ferguson goes after the specter of revisionism, arguing that our tenured radicals are bent upon teaching

.   .   .

SVEN BIRKERTS

us that everything we thought we knew—about George Washington, the heroes of the Wild West, the Bible—is wrong ("Watch for a biography asserting that Ringo was the genius behind the Beatles," quips Ferguson); and Bruce Bawer goes mawkish over the decline of American movies, once again contriving to pin the blame on that malevolent epoch known as the sixties. So far, *Beyond the Boom* is pretty tame stuff—no trenchant political or aesthetic analyses, nothing for the unregenerate oldsters (those of us born before, say, 1954) to get alarmed about. Indeed, in tone and level of discourse the pieces are middlebrow journalese, quickly skimmed and just as quickly forgotten. What little psychological meat there is between the covers is to be found in the handful of more personal essays that round out the anthology. Here we heed a more strident and, well, frightening set of voices. And if I were a younger boomer, I would be more than a little worried about what my representative spokespeople were saying.

Lisa Schiffren is a case in point. Her contributor's note identifies her as a "Special Assistant in the Department of Defense Office of Special Operations/Low Intensity Conflict," whatever that is, and adds, "The opinions expressed in this essay are her own and do not necessarily reflect official Defense Department policy." Good thing, I say, though that "necessarily" gives me momentary pause. In "A Whiff of Grapeshot," Schiffren stands up tall to ask: "What happens to a society so far from nature and human nature that its men do not know how to use guns or kill, and have no concrete, rooted idea of what they are defending?" This is, we learn, the society dreamed of by the older boomers, those who "rejected the test" of Vietnam, "then justified their rejection convincingly enough to sway the society itself . . . to their way of thinking."

Here, at last, is a clear position. One whole generation is indicted for its cowardice. Another—Schiffren's—is deemed fit to meet the moral challenge:

> I suspect we would rise [to] a real threat. I'd guess that many of us would eagerly leave our fast-track careers and insulated lives for the chance of a real test, given half an excuse. In fact, the dirty secret of my generation is a resurgent fascination with guns and war—in books, in movies, in video games. Yuppies

stalk each other with dart guns and amuse themselves with the novels of Tom Clancy as if the peace movement of the '60s had never happened. Who doubts that they would find the real thing no less seductive?

How proud Schiffren is of that "dirty secret" and her boldness in telling it! With what glee her yuppies wield their dart guns; how briskly the peace movement of the sixties is brushed away! That such a person should have a niche, however unimportant, in the halls of power is cause for alarm. Should we assume that some such rage percolates under the vestments of all those upright citizens celebrated by Richard Vigilante?

Terry Teachout's concluding essay, "A Farewell to Politics," confirms such a notion. The man can scarcely contain his bile. "I was fascinated by the '60s," he announces, "as a fly is fascinated by a spider." Though too young to be a full-fledged hippie, Teachout spent his adolescence in confused mimicry of his elders. But something was not right. The heady potion of marijuana, rock and roll, and laid-back spirituality was not to his liking. His dissatisfaction intensified until it brought him to a crossroads: "The boomers just older than me were busy listening to Philip Glass and reading Ann Beattie; the boomers just younger than me were busy changing the world. I didn't want to be left behind. So I switched sides."

At this point the skeptical older boomer might sit up and pay attention. *Changing the world?* After all the smirks and swipes directed against the counterculture comes a promise of substance. But Teachout, backing away, offers nothing more than a volley of praise for the hands-on activism of the editors of the *Dartmouth Review* (whose basic agenda, you may recall, was the terrorizing of minorities). So much for politics and so much for the plus side of the tally sheet.

Teachout ends his coming-of-age saga by justifying his own turning away from politics. He states his belief that "the great battles of the '90s will be fought in another arena: that of culture." Our last image is of our editor staring at the screen of his word processor, dreaming about the book he is writing, a book "about what it was like to grow up in a small midwestern town in the '60s and '70s, a book that contains not a trace of politics in it, that is all about home and family and the more abundant life." A lovely sentiment. But coming as it does after two-hundred-some pages of righteousness and reaction, that picture of home and family starts to look like something out of David Lynch.

Teachout is right about one thing: that the great battles of the nineties will be fought in the "arena of culture." Indeed, they have already commenced. The much-publicized controversy surrounding NEA funding is just a preliminary skirmish, but it gives a hint about the stakes involved. Art wants to breathe the oxygen of freedom, and the conservatives cannot bear that it should. Why? Because a free art tells truths about our souls and our social institutions, and gives the lie to the systems of order and repression that the right would espouse. The art these politicians and their constituents fear carries a message of individual liberty, which was, beneath the media hype, also the message of the social initiatives of the sixties. Slight though the polemics of the Vile Body are, they supply an important litmus test of values and attitudes. These boomers may meet only to munch popcorn and exchange views, but their seniors are trying to impose their agendas on our cultural life.

I can understand how the pendulum swings back and forth through history, creating cycles. I can understand too the age-old battle between fathers and sons. What I cannot fathom is how youth has managed to turn upon itself. Was the Aquarian project of social liberation—misguided as it was in some ways—so offensive, so terrifying to the generation just coming up? If so, then we older boomers ended up destroying our deepest ideals. We chased away all spirit, spontaneity, enthusiasm, and experiment, and left in our wake a new way of being young—a way that formerly belonged just to the embittered old. I can only hope that Teachout is wrong about these being the "true voices" of a generation.

Beyond the Boom: New Voices on American Life, Culture, and Politics. Terry Teachout, ed. 243 pp. Poseidon Press. 1990. $18.95

．　．　．

The Boomers Go Bust

The Hipness
unto Death

At some point in the 1950s, television ceased to be just an odd-looking gizmo—a radio running a picture track—and entered the bloodstream of our culture. The culture must have been ready, for as soon as it lodged, the medium flourished as few things beneficent ever do: growing, improving, widening its empery until now, only a few decades later, it is one—very likely the *only*—thing we all have in common. Daily and nightly we gather in front of the glass, arrested by the forms our collective dreaming takes.

The statistics are boggling. Average daily watching time is routinely placed between four and six hours per person. *Per person!* That means, of course, that there have to be millions and millions of people who do nothing but watch. Which in turn means . . . Well, it may mean any number of different things. To the stolid nonalarmists it means little—they call it a harmless pleasure and point back to the mass spectatorship at gladiator fights. Educators, however, make a connection to falling SAT scores and burgeoning illiteracy. A few worried souls go still further. They see in our prostration before the electronic altar the direst of portents: that the race has given up on ideals of individual attainment and is slipping backward into an oceanic state of mass passivity.

Mark Crispin Miller, an essayist and television critic, takes up his post somewhere near the latter end of the spectrum. While those at the opposite end might brand him a TV "crank," the tag hardly sticks to a thinker as lucid and witty as Miller. Indeed, these virtues will make *Boxed In: The Culture of TV* a threat to all shrugging equanimity. Miller's essays are the most provocative writing on the subject since Marshall McLuhan first made it a subject.

Miller's subtitle is an elegant contrivance, oxymoronic in playing off "culture" and "TV," and suggestive in its activation of a secondary meaning—a culture as a bacterial growth that can be studied. But where the scientist makes use of slides and high-powered microscopes, Miller relies on more speculative equipment. Essentially, he applies the close-reading skills he learned in academia (he now professes film criticism in the Writing Seminars at Johns Hopkins University) to the sprawling but finally closed (hence "boxed in") system of the media. And though he might cringe at any close association with the chic discipline of deconstruction—his prose, happily, is jargon-free—his procedure does involve a kindred disinterring of paradoxes and concealed contradictions. Miller's aim is to expose the mendaciousness behind the blithe facade, the skull beneath the skin.

Television, as Miller asserts in "The Hipness unto Death," his sharply argued introduction, has finally swamped us. By the late 1970s almost all protest and outcry had died out. "Here was the completion of an enormous transformation," he writes, "all the more striking for the fact that no one was struck by it." And this saturation, which Miller sees as an implicit vanquishing of dissent, was precisely what our advertising conglomerates had been striving to achieve. For they had long since grasped that the medium was the ultimate selling machine. Not just because images and product pitches could be directed at a passive watcher, but—even more insidious—because exposure to a seamless, hypnotic, self-referential world wore away at all scruples and inhibitions. It turned everyone, however briefly, into the child at the toy-store window.

Programming *programs*—the principle is that simple. And pro-

.   .   .

The Hipness unto Death

gramming in America, Miller insists, serves the imperatives of capital at every turn. "Advertising executives," another television critic has said, "like to say that television shows are the meat in a commercial sandwich." Sadly, these bosses further dictate that the meat will be nothing but baloney and more baloney. They have seen to it that network programming has steadily purged itself of everything that might remind the viewer that there is still a world outside TV: they would create "a site secured against all threatening juxtaposition." Miller refuses the traditional perspective—that network television is simply giving the public what it wants. His overriding vision requires that he argue the reverse, even if it leads him to an occasional improbable hypothesis. Miller writes, for instance, that those old prime-time standbys, the westerns, were phased out because the independent ethos of the solitary frontiersman was just too much at odds with the kind of herd docility that advertising would foster. The point makes sense logically. But Miller underestimates the degree to which content depends upon context. If these brokers can get the Beatles' "Revolution" to sell running shoes, then they can surely co-opt the iconic lone cowpoke on his horse. It could just be that natural selection—that is, the shifting of viewer tastes—finished off the western.

In Miller's scheme, the greatest potential threat to TV's sly blandishments is the unassimilated watcher—the detached mocker who might spot the subtle coercion of the sales pitch and balk. But here, as elsewhere, the medium is ahead of its audience.

Most ads and shows have incorporated, in defense, a "hip," winking attitude. "TV preempts derision," Miller writes, "by itself evincing endless irony. . . . TV protects its ads from mockery by doing all the mocking, thereby posing as an ally to the incredulous spectator."

Miller's analysis, be assured, is not a conspiracy theory. He fingers no Madison Avenue cabals or boardroom villains. Those days are gone. What Miller suggests is that the fundamentally commercial nature of TV works to make it a self-regulating system. That is, the ultimate logic of consumer advertising would have all watchers be led to think in the same ways, and thus want the same things. Members of the media work force don't need orders from above any longer. They know what makes ratings, and they push their pitches accordingly. "More disquieting even than the old nightmare of conspiracy," the author says, "is the likelihood that no conspiracy is needed." He reverts to this idea in a more sustained way at the end of the book.

The first dozen essays, composing a section titled What's on TV, are model subversions. Miller, like Roland Barthes before him, proves that popular culture yields wonders when subjected to academic modes of scrutiny. In each instance he isolates a particular TV narrative—thereby breaking the contextual spell—and then reads its images to uncover the underlying structure. Since everything on TV is calculated to sway and *sell,* results are guaranteed—there are always subliminal messages. Drawing from a wide sample—he looks at ads, game shows, documentaries, newscasting, and prime-time offerings—Miller ends up making a comprehensive inquiry into what might be called the televisual psyche. If it's true that we become what we behold, then we are in serious trouble.

In "Massa, Come Home," for instance, Miller unpacks the well-known "Come to Jamaica" commercial until the play of its master-slave archetypes is fully visible. Dismantling the ad frame by frame, he shows how the carefully juxtaposed images both cancel all fears about violent or uppity natives—fears prompted by reports of real unrest—and affirm the place of those same natives as cheerful domestics.

> The opening shot presents an image of impending violence converted into recreation. A group of blacks, wearing helmets, waving sticks, gallop on horseback toward the camera. One of them pulls ahead of the others, swinging his instrument down like a sabre, and strikes—a polo ball. It is an archetypal vision of imminent destruction (there are, in fact, four horsemen here), but the martial implication is simultaneously denied, as if to say, "You expect to be killed by our natives? Sit back and relax! This is only an athletic display!"

By the time he's finished, Miller has exposed the covert racism in every last image. The lulling, enticing narrative will never seem anything but pernicious now.

Miller's other analyses are no less eye-opening. "Getting Dirty," his reading of a deodorant-soap ad, wittily discovers a subtext of slippery sexual innuendos all orchestrated along "pseudofeminist"

. . .

The Hipness unto Death

lines to flatter the female consumer with references to her sexual and—implicitly—financial power. "Virtù, Inc." examines the carefully projected images of the Reagan presidency. Miller finds that they neatly reflect the tenets enumerated by Machiavelli in *The Prince*, only modernized for a media age. Reagan, who is for Miller "an anthology of the worst of popular culture, edited for television," has parlayed gestures and postures into the enormous power of mandate.

But even the president is subject to the media, "which sets him up and breaks him down according to its own implicit schedule—he thrives only as a novelty, then turns at once into a joke or a nostalgia item." Miller's essay "A Viewer's Campaign Diary, 1984" goes behind the scenes to show just how this kind of setting up and breaking down actually happens.

Miller's mode of close reading gets us in behind the programming facade, convincing us, finally, that every instant, every televised image, is the function of a baser calculation. But while this approach effectively strips the content, it gives no purchase on the form—the technology—itself. The kinds of questions that Marshall McLuhan raised back in the sixties are still with us. The steady interaction of viewer psyche and medium has to result in profound reorganizations within that psyche. What about induced passivity, shortened attention spans, and impaired reality-testing? "What's on TV" tells part of the story, but "What's TV?" would tell another part.

Miller might, for example, usefully glance at the impact that the medium has had in an avowedly noncapitalistic country like the Soviet Union. Image production there is nowhere near our standard of sophistication, nor is it subject to the same *sell* imperatives, but the bottom-line effect on viewers is not so different. As Ellen Mickiewicz reports in her study *Split Signals: Television and Politics in the Soviet Union,*

> The television viewer is very much the consumer . . . no longer the *Homo faber* that Marx envisioned. . . . The "new Soviet man" is now in the armchair in front of the television set, and so is the rest of the family.

Advertising may well be bending us to its will, but it can do so because of the form, the very *structure,* of the medium.

* * *

After two short sections that detour into other realms of popular culture—rock and roll and cinema—Miller returns to his central subject. Only now he is gazing from a higher and more frightening altitude. "Big Brother Is You, Watching," an essay written to mark the arrival of the Orwell year, brings news every bit as chilling as what we find in *1984*.

Miller begins by establishing a strong connection between Orwell's vision of Oceana and the radical critique of the Enlightenment carried out by Max Horkheimer and T. W. Adorno. For those two thinkers, the Enlightenment ideal was responsible for the crisis of modernity. Its ultimate program, as they wrote in their *Dialectic of Enlightenment,* was "the disenchantment of the world; the dissolution of myths and the substitution of knowledge for fancy." But what began as the desire for the rational mastery of nature led, in Pandora's box fashion, to the mass extermination of human beings and the atomic bomb. Once unleashed, the impulse to control and dominate could not be contained.

Orwell's Oceana is, for Miller, the apotheosis of these deeper tendencies of the Enlightenment. Rational understanding has become the tool of authority. In Oceana, he writes, "the Party sees through anyone who would see through the Party, because the Party has seen through itself already. . . ." Its impulse is to totality, and to the erasing of all individual subjectivity in the interests of absolute control. One of its most powerful devices, and defenses, is the promulgation of "relentless irony."

Now comes the leap. Television, Miller insists, makes use of the same strategy for the same end: to flatten all resistance, to enlist all would-be opponents, to achieve total domination through identification. Because the medium is deeply iconoclastic—capable of seeing through all behaviors and reducing all differences—it ceaselessly cuts away at independent subjectivity. The viewer is finally brought to inhabit a condition of "hip inertia."

Once again, Miller is not blaming the machinations of media elites. This silent transformation is coming about through the logic at the very heart of consumer advertising, which is the logic at the heart of capitalism. The viewer will in time become kin to Orwell's Winston Smith: "In too many ways, the ex-hero of this brilliant,

. . . .

dismal book anticipates those TV viewers who are incapable of read-ing it: 'In these days he could never fix his mind on any one subject for more than a few moments at a time.' " Miller adds, "At this moment, Winston Smith is, for the first time in his life, not under surveillance." Simply, when enough of the subliminal structure has been internalized, no control from without is needed: "As you watch, there is no Big Brother out there watching you—not because there isn't a Big Brother, but because Big Brother is you, watching." If you can get to the end of this essay, this book, without feeling a chill, you may be beyond reclamation.

Though he is often incisively humorous, Miller is ultimately pessimistic in his vision. The reader looks for signs of hope, for averting turns that might still be made; none are given. Maybe the one bright spot is the example of Miller himself. After all, here is a man who has put in countless hours before the set but remains brilliantly sane. He is himself an advertisement for critical conscious-ness in the face of all-but-irresistible seduction—an Odysseus smart enough to tie himself to the mast. His *Boxed In* is the kind of criticism we will need in ever-greater supply, lest we drown in the effluence of popular "culture."

Boxed in: The Culture of TV. Mark Crispin Miller. 349 pp. Northwestern University Press. 1988. $39.95

Amusing Ourselves
to Death

Publishers' blurbs notwithstanding, topical books are not all "timely" or "prophetic." Neil Postman's *Amusing Ourselves to Death,* which draws part of its inspiration from the prognostications of Orwell and Huxley, comes—if its argument is taken with full seriousness—too late. Malignant cells, each in the familiar iconic shape of a television screen, have already lodged themselves in the vital organs of our culture, and their metastasis can no longer be checked.

Postman—an educator, communications theorist, and author of some fifteen previous books, including the controversial *Teaching as a Subversive Activity*—is hardly the first television basher to have come along. Every few years, it seems, some civic-minded humanist rears up to decry the dangers posed by our national pastime, by its pervasiveness, its triviality, and its shameless sponsorship of violence, greed, and sexual promiscuity. Most of these critics, however, lay their emphasis on the contents of network programming; they would solve the problem by upgrading the quality of the shows we watch. Not Postman. "The best things on television," he writes, "are its junk, and no one and nothing is seriously threatened by it. . . . Television is at its most trivial and, therefore, most dangerous when its aspirations are high, when it represents itself as a carrier of important cultural conversations." The trouble begins, according to Postman, when the line between amusement and discourse disappears—and in his view it largely has.

Postman is not much concerned with the old argument over TV's content. Acknowledging his debt to Marshall McLuhan, he urges that the most significant thing about television is the *fact* of it. What's on the tube matters far less than our staggering statistical presence in front of it. Varying McLuhan's old tag slightly; he maintains that "the medium is the metaphor." And though his explanation has a journalistic simplicity about it ("We do not see nature or human motivation or ideology as "it" is but only as our languages are. And our languages are our media. Our media are our metaphors. Our metaphors create the content of our culture."), the implication arrests the hand on its way to the dial: our new collective metaphor is turning the natural life of American culture into one big entertainment.

Before launching into his major diatribe, Postman steps back to get some historical perspective. He finds, from our Colonial Period to the late nineteenth century, a society shaped predominantly by the ways of the book. Evidence would suggest, for example, that between 1640 and 1700 "the literacy rate for men in Massachusetts and Connecticut was somewhere between 89 percent and 95 percent, quite probably the highest concentration of literate males to be found anywhere in the world at the time." Where the printed word was the paradigm for discourse, social and political life were bound to sustain a high level of rationality and responsibility.

And indeed, Postman goes on to argue that the descendants of these men—descendants of both genders—participated with informed enthusiasm in the public events of their day. The strenuous debates between Abraham Lincoln and Stephen Douglas not only called upon their auditors to sit in place for more than three hours at a stretch, but also demanded from them a close attention to the intricate syntax of the argumentation. Lincoln's public, insists Postman, was interested in his points and in his skill at putting them across; how his hair was styled was rightfully irrelevant. Just how did everything change?

A key transition in the life of public discourse, Postman asserts, came with the invention of the telegraph:

> Telegraphy gave a form of legitimacy to the idea of context-free information; that is, to the idea that the value of information need not be tied to any function it might serve in social and political decision-making and action, but may attach merely to its novelty, interest, and curiosity. The telegraph made information into a commodity, a "thing" that could be bought and sold irrespective of its uses or meaning.

As wire-service-fed newspapers rushed to bring their readers the world, whether they needed it or not, the ancient bond between information and use, word and deed, became attenuated. The subsequent implementation of the photographic image all but snapped it. Visuals provided a "pseudo-context" and legitimized dissociated coverage: "For countless Americans, seeing, not reading, became the basis for believing."

Television, for Postman, is only the latest development in this process. But it is in television that the tendencies to fragmentation, abstraction, superficiality, and decontextualization find their apotheosis. Postman calls it "the peek-a-boo-world," and in the second half of the book he tells us in no uncertain terms how we are being seduced into idiocy.

"Now . . . This," his chapter on news reporting, savages the process by which the networks feed us the world in upbeat montages of "bite-sized" bits. The actuality of events is travestied; worse, the purpose is clearly to entertain rather than to inform. The moguls behind the scenes grasped long ago that it was more important to hold the viewer than to tell him anything meaningful. Thus:

> A suspected killer being brought into a police station, the angry face of a cheated consumer, a barrel going over Niagara Falls (with a person alleged to be in it), the President embarking from a helicopter on the White House lawn—these are always fascinating or amusing, and easily satisfy the requirements for an entertaining show.

. . . .

Amusing Ourselves to Death

Postman's real worry is not so much that we are being deprived of information as that "we are losing our sense of what it means to be well informed."

Next on the agenda is an examination of the ways in which the television "metaphor" has distorted our public perception of politics and religion. By this point most readers will have picked up the pattern and will be able to second-guess the argument. The savvy custodians of our common weal have increasingly come to tailor their "truths," the ultimate criterion no longer being the objective status of what they say—or, in the case of religious programming, the sacral resonance of church space and ritual—but rather its suitability for media transmission. Anyone who followed the news broadcasts of the "historic" Geneva summit will have to cede Postman's point; certainly the most frightening "star wars" were the ones going on in front of the video monitors.

On the mark though they are, these chapters finally tell you little that you did not already know. Politicians and evangelist hucksters have been selling snake oil since the time of the first snake; the idiot box is the natural extension of the soapbox, and most of what comes from either is bubbles. The real horripilations are to be found in Postman's penultimate chapter. "Teaching as an Amusing Activity." Here again, the point is simple, even obvious, but the implications for the future bring on the night sweats.

Children now, almost without exception, are growing up in front of the television screen. Many of them are getting their first taste of education (sometimes, indeed, even learning their first words) from programs like *Sesame Street.* Postman's vision does not allow him to accept the usual pieties about these shows:

> *Sesame Street* appeared to be an imaginative aid in solving the growing problem of teaching Americans how to read, while, at the same time, encouraging children to love school. . . . We now know that *Sesame Street* encourages children to love school only if school is like *Sesame Street.* Which is to say, we now know that *Sesame Street* undermines what the traditional idea of schooling represents.

Postman then documents some of the ways in which progressive-minded (or defeated) educators have tried to bring their curricula into line with the watching habits of students. One representative instance of the tail wagging the dog is the "Voyage of the *Mimi*" project, sponsored by the U.S. Department of Education, the Bank Street College of Education, PBS, and the publishers Holt, Rinehart and Winston: $3.65 million was put up to finance a twenty-six-part television package about a whale-research laboratory. Dramatic episodes featuring young people were linked with picture books and computer games in order to teach "map and navigation skills, whales and their environment, ecological systems, and computer literacy." Obviously, observes Postman, someone up top had been asking: "What is television good for?, not What is education good for?" Which is not to imply, of course, that map and navigation skills and knowledge of whales should not be among our priorities.

No surprise, then, that this writer is not sanguine about the fate of our culture. Where McLuhan took the exalted view—our media, he said, were creating a "global village," restoring us to an interactive intimacy lost since the invention of the printing press—Postman sees little but intellectual and moral deterioration. His concluding chapter, The Huxleyan Warning, suggests that we will be overcome not from without, as Orwell feared, but from within. *Brave New World,* not *1984,* ought to be our minatory parable. "Big Brother does not watch us, by his choice. We watch him, by ours." If there is any solution—and the author confesses that he feels obliged, for form's sake, to extend *some* thread of hope—it is to make the understanding and criticism of television a central part of the educational process. But he is not specific on this score. The impression persists that in his heart of hearts Postman believes we are too far gone.

Amusing Ourselves to Death has taken on many of the attributes of its subject matter. It is, like so much that passes before us on the screen, glib and easy to engage. Although its contents—its messages—are appalling, the presentation itself is quite entertaining: statistics are quickly glossed, anecdotal material is planted every few pages lest the attention wander, and the few key points are repeated over and over like the litany in some detergent ad. I found myself longing for the subtle and sustained discussion that the print medium is so perfectly suited for. But I still couldn't brush Postman's fundamental indictment aside. If only a fraction of what he says is true, the time is nigh for a squad of Carrie Nations to set to work. Do take a few hours out from your favorite prime-time divertissement to read this book. Behold what we become as we become what we behold.

Amusing Ourselves to Death: Public Discourse in the Age of Show Business. Neil Postman. 184 pp. Viking. 1986. $15.95

. . . .

SVEN BIRKERTS

Objections Noted:
Word Processing

P eople ask me why I refuse to use a word processor. I tell them because it feels like a typewriter with a condom over it. The very sight of one of those sculpted plastic instruments with its pert ticket-counter "everything's under control" screen depresses me beyond measure. It makes me feel how close the final victory of technology over spirit really is. Hell, it *is* the victory of technology over spirit.

Neither can I bear the chirping good humor with which owners talk about their disks and programs.

The word-processor argument. Most people, I'm sure, maintain that there *is* no word-processor argument. Indeed, I hardly ever meet anyone who writes who isn't using one—a few poets, maybe . . . Louis Simpson . . .

Lemmings!

Literature has got lightweight and modular enough without writers all shifting their idly fluffed-together paragraphs around. If you can't organize it in your head, it's not ready to be organized.

The WP is a death-ray directed at the last remnants of the prophetic soul.

The word processor is just a tool, they say. Just a tool. Just a tool. Never mind that it's an ugly tool, utterly alien from anything relating to spirit. (Would you paint with a steel-handled brush?) Never mind that the machine you work on changes the compositional process, changes you. It's just a tool.

Like any tool, the WP came into being to meet a need. Writers were tired of wadding up sheets of paper, of playing cut-and-paste with paragraphs, of drawing lines to bridge one part of a text to another. The technology was there to bring the material/production side of writing in line with the rest of the twentieth century. The quasi-"intelligence" of the computer was put into the service of the infinitely complex intellectual/psychological operation of writing.

Given that so many writers profess themselves to be iconoclasts, sturdy individualists, etc., the rate of defection from paper and metal to plastic and electricity is nothing short of astonishing.

These are the same people who love the old game of baseball and scream at any move to modernize or streamline its immemorial rituals.

But the lemmings did line up to leap. Why?

They say it's because the user can *quickly* make changes, corrections, erasures, rearrangements. Because he can try things out and then get rid of them. Because he has more access to his text, more control, a sense of mastery. Because the WP vanquishes fear, eliminates the block-inducing threat that the white page seems to hold.

I've heard it said that now *everyone* can become a writer.

Hot dog.

I think the real reason for the rush to molded plastic, the deep-down unacknowledged reason, is that the apparatus confers a feeling of power, of being plugged in to something. For we all know, in that same deep-down place, that the writer, the thinker, the person who would speak up for spirit, has never had less power. Ever. Has never been such a zero. Why not a humming bright unit that allows the user to say, "I, too, belong to the modern world. You can see screens just like this at the airport, on Wall Street, in the offices on Madison Avenue."

·   ·   ·

SVEN BIRKERTS

* * *

The word processor has, among other things, made the word more susceptible to the directives of the will. The ruling paradigm is now one of change, of changeability. The writer says, with Valéry, that the work is never finished. Clearly demarcated draft stages have been superseded by a single stage—the unstable, open, "in-process" stage. Writing is closer to becoming that unfixed play of signifiers celebrated by French literary theoreticians. Literary morticians. Indeed: writing has been brought many steps closer to resembling the mutability of thought itself—which never rests, except in the crystallizations of written language.

The stability of the word—epitomized by the independent, fixed, *printed* sign—has been correspondingly undermined.

Writing on the word processor: it's like eating those force-fed new chickens that have never seen sunlight. Like eating fish bred in indoor pools.

Word "processing": In the sixties the word "processed" was a term of fierce derision. Blacks called a brother "processed" when they wanted to mark him as a "Tom."

The shift from manual writing to the typewriter to the word processor roughly corresponds to the shift from walking to riding in a carriage to riding in a car. In both cases, the progression is toward ease and facilitation. But, we might ask, what has become of our ancient relationship to land, to sky, to time itself?

A flat, opaque two-sided sheet of paper is replaced by an electronic screen of indeterminate depth. Where a black mark was conspicuously *imposed* upon the white surface, we now find a green mark elicited from the humming green screen. The broken-up left-to-right linearity is replaced, for the writer, by what *feels* like an unbroken continuity (the apparatus does the lineation). The static character of the typed sign gives way to the fluid, provisional character of the processed sign. The composition blocks—sentences, paragraphs— are no less fluid.

If the movement from speech to writing was, in part, an attempt to impose fixity upon the fleeting, then might we not in some sense be moving back toward the laxity of the impromptu—at least on the level of conception, where everything exists under the aspect of replaceability?

Writing on a word processor: the principle of Don Juanism projected upon the sentence. The writer is more likely to be haunted by the thought that there is a better word than this, a better sentence, a more interesting ordering of paragraphs.

Writing by hand, even typewriter, inevitably results in visible corrections, in drafts. These are, in effect, the record of the evolution of the thought and its expression. The WP handily eliminates every trace. The writer never has to look over his shoulder and see what a botch he's made of things. Less conscience, less sense of consequence.

As Louis Simpson wrote: "If I think I can easily change the next word and there's nothing final about what I'm writing, then the nature of my writing changes."
How would you live if you knew you could live forever?
The ideal of *le mot juste* is vaporized; the new ideals are of plurality and provisionality.

I've noticed that I read a word-processed page differently—more casually—than a typewritten page. Could the mode of writing significantly influence the mode of reading? Maybe. When everybody becomes a writer, no one will read.
The difference between seeing your words drawn forth from the depths of a screen versus seeing them planted on the page through the mechanical action of a key is enormous. The screen, with its electrical "live" humming and its impatiently pulsing cursor, represents (much like TV) a quasi-consciousness. Does the writer feel just the slightest bit less responsible?

Speaking for myself: writing is very much a matter of drafts, *distinct* written drafts. I believe that prose is produced as much by the body, the rhythmic sense, as it is by intellect and verbal imagination. It wants to build up a certain musculature on the page. The instant correctability afforded by the WP allows for cosmetic alterations that are often quite adequate. But *merely* adequate. My experience has shown me that the best writing comes when I am forced to type over something that I've already deemed to be finished. My impatience— not to mention the new rhythmic state I'm in—forces me to push the language further. In the process of retyping the text, I reach more deeply into it. Later, the words give me the impression of having been handled, worn smooth.

Even simple mistakes can be read as signs, parapraxias signaling the incompleteness of an expression. When a page of prose is done, I no longer make typos.

Already it's getting hard to find ribbons. The people who used to repair typewriters are retiring, dying off. The day will come—soon— when journals will accept only disk submissions.

There . . . I've succeeded in depressing myself. All of a sudden my desk looks like a museum: the beautiful pencil, the sharpener, the pens, the stack of paper like a street of dreams. The Olivetti clattering as I type this: sad hoofbeats of a retreating army . . .

. . . .

The Orwell
Mystique

Working with an archivist's patient rigor and the tenacity customarily ascribed to powerful burrowing creatures, John Rodden has put together an astonishingly thorough study showing how personal, political, institutional, and media-related factors combined to create the public phenomenon of George Orwell. I don't know that any writer's career has been scrutinized through such an array of lenses. Exhaustive approaches, naturally, have their hazards: Rodden's assiduous handling of detail quite often leads him into repetitiveness and argumentative overkill. But the book's achievement transcends its flaws. *The Politics of Literary Reputation: The Making and Claiming of "St. George" Orwell* is a necessary contribution both to Orwell studies and to an assessment of the interdependence of culture and communications.

Though he cuts his path through an ideological minefield, Rodden remains effectively nonpartisan. He tells us in his preface that he is a "left of center white male of working-class origins, a post-Vatican Catholic liberal." He does not, however, get livid about the neoconservatives' effort to set Orwell up as one of their founding fathers; neither is he soft on the methods and motives of liberals of the Lionel Trilling stripe. He is firm and tactful—the scholar in him always tempers the would-be polemicist.

The core argument of the book is fairly simple: that George Orwell, universally admired as a literary figure and a moral and political authority, did not come to be canonized on the strength of his achievements alone. No one, argues Rodden, wins cultural eminence where there is not some engine of Rube Goldberg complexity clattering in the background. The popular image of Orwell— the virtuous, ascetic, engaged, iconoclastic, totalitarian-scourging, windowpane stylist—is very much the product of sustained and selective media presentations. From the very start of his career, Orwell's literary and political persona was refracted to the public through reviews, articles, books, radio and television presentations, and mass-circulation magazines—until, at some point, the name became its associations in the free air of the public domain. Orwell today is the Abraham Lincoln of the written word.

Rodden, let me hasten to say, is not out to undercut Orwell's real contributions. Rather, he wants to discover why and how his accomplishment could be packaged for sale in so many different cultural supermarkets, while the comparable attainments of a Koestler, Silone, or Malraux could not. The making and "claiming" of Orwell, then, is very much about specific webs of circumstance in midcentury England and America. It is as much the story of individual desires and projections as it is an anatomical exploration of our diverse institutional bodies. Rodden is alert to the significance of power and power vacuums: If Orwell had not come along, the collective force of our need might well have spontaneously generated someone else for the post.

But Orwell did come along. Eric Blair emerged from St. Cyprian's and Eton in the early 1920s determined to make himself into a writer of consequence. He dreamed of the embossed spines of his eventual collected works; he suffered through a lonely exile in the civil service in Burma; and he returned to become George Orwell.

Rodden tracks the progress of Orwell's public reception by breaking apart his eventual image into what he sees as its four principal components and discussing each in turn. These "faces"—the Rebel, the Common Man, the Prophet, and the Saint—are seen as sequential developments, with certain inevitable overlaps. Thus, the Orwell that first captured the imagination of a small sector of the British intelligentsia was the public-school boy who had, as one memorable epithet had it, "gone native" in his own country. This first Orwell—author of a slim documentary memoir called *Down and Out in Paris and London* (1933)—was the tramp-outsider who scorned the chase for the glittering prizes and cast his lot with the laboring poor. The image would soon enough bleed over into that of the writer as Common Man. Orwell's *The Road to Wigan Pier* (1937) and *Homage to Catalonia* (1938) confirmed that his dissent was something more than a romantic pose; his engagement in social and political causes appeared entirely selfless. The prophetic Orwell only appeared in later years, after publication of the satirical allegory *Animal Farm* (1945) and *1984* (1949). And his secular sainthood has been largely a posthumous honor, representing a peculiar magnification of perceived and invented virtues.

Orwell was fortunate from the first in winning the adoration of a great many of the leading intellectuals of his time—figures from all parts of the political spectrum. Rodden's sampling is startling:

> Characterizations of Orwell by Anglo-American intellectuals of the Left and Right—to Lionel Trilling the figure of "the man who tells the truth," to Irving Howe an "intellectual hero," to T. R. Fyvel a "literary hero," to Angus Wilson "one of my great heroes," to John Atkins a "social saint," to Stephen Spender "an example of the 'lived truth,' " to George Woodcock a "conscience," to Alfred Kazin "a hero whom I shall always love," to Joseph Epstein and Malcolm Muggeridge a "hero of our time," to Richard Rees a "spiritual hero," to John Wain a "moral hero"—indicate that for many intellectuals, regardless of their politics or even generation, Orwell has stood for nothing less than an heroic model and ethical guide.

Rodden later adds the names of Edmund Wilson, Raymond Williams, Norman Podhoretz, Christopher Hitchens, V. S. Pritchett, and a dozen others. The mystery, of course, is how—and why—one mere man could come to be all things to all people.

. . . .

SVEN BIRKERTS

* * *

The Orwell phenomenon is, as Rodden shows, an exceedingly complex business. There is no disputing that Orwell's particular combination of virtues—his devotion to the downtrodden, his polemical fervor, his easily worn man-in-the-street persona, his lean, angular physiognomy (would we cherish an Orwell who looked like Alfred Hitchcock?), his readiness to plunge into action, his apparent modesty in the face of growing influence and popularity—proved attractive to intellectuals of every political coloration. But the surprising thing is that these men (women, other than Mary McCarthy and Sonia Orwell, play almost no part in this account) were not boosting Orwell *in spite of* their politics—it was always *because* of, and by way of. They claimed him as their spokesman-hero because they saw their own ambitions and political ideals incarnated in his image. How can this be?

In the thirties, there was no great conflict or contradiction of values. Orwell was, like every other self-respecting intellectual, a man of the Left. It was only with the stirrings of the European war and the clashes over Stalinism that the fracturing of leftist allegiances began. Orwell's fierce anti-Stalinism dates from the early months of 1937 when he witnessed the Communist party's attempted suppression of revolutionary parties in Spain. But on June 8 of that same year, he wrote to Cyril Connolly: "I . . . at last really believe in Socialism, which I never did before." Orwell never made any clear repudiation of that assertion before his death in 1950.

This fact has not prevented innumerable attempts to hie the man into every conceivable political corral. Indeed, the circumstances of Orwell's later years—and of his death—made such wrangling all but inevitable. Orwell himself did not help matters. Throughout the postwar years, he scrupulously avoided all overt political affiliation. He stayed within the perimeters of the Left, but he kept his declarations artfully unbinding. He was, as Rodden shows, a master of compartmentalization, keeping his various friends and associates from meeting one another. After his death it came out that he had moved like a wraith through half a dozen seemingly exclusive political and social factions. There is no consensus among his surviving friends as to what his true persuasions might have been. Nor does any reading of Orwell's last major testament, *1984,* supply clear answers. The work has been read in different ways by different constituencies: as a straight-on anti-Communist tract; as a satire of the same; and as a warning about emerging strains in the Western political system. Orwell died before he could hang out a placard confirming or denying any particular intent—not that he would ever have done so.

The timing of Orwell's death put the seal on the mystery. As Rodden writes:

> [H]e died at precisely the 'right' historical moment. Indeed, if Orwell had lived until 1955 or certainly into the 1960s, he would not have been spared the agony of taking sides on numerous political issues: the Cold War, McCarthyism, de-Stalinization, Hungary, Suez, Algeria, the Campaign for Nuclear Disarmament, the New Left, Vietnam, the student movement. Inevitably, as happened with Bertrand Russell, Koestler, Sartre, Camus and others in the 1950s and 1960s, his positions (or lack thereof) on such issues would have compromised him in the eyes of some groups which today claim him as a patron saint. . . . Never could he have won or maintained his current stature on so many fronts.

Orwell remains, then, a blank screen for others to scribble their wishes on. Some members of the Left, such as Christopher Hitchens, would bear him aloft over the divisive conflicts of recent decades; they would resurrect the committed Socialist in the present. Others, like Podhoretz and Kristol, engage in active projective identification: they assume that Orwell would have turned when they did, following the same branching paths into the stony redoubt of the neoconservatives. "If Orwell were alive today . . ." is the customary polemical gambit. Well, if Orwell were alive today he wouldn't be Orwell— and where would that leave us?

So long as he lived, Orwell won and held the esteem of most of the leading intellectuals of the West. This esteem, ramified through thousands of appreciative-to-adulatory reviews, citations, and studies, paved the way toward his eventual assumption into the general stratosphere of renown. Rodden gives fascinating accounts of how such influential figures as Trilling, Woodcock, Podhoretz, and Raymond Williams advanced Orwell's standing while using him to buttress their own positions. He finds a close connection, for instance, between Trilling's presentation of Orwell in his well-known introduction to *Homage to Catalonia* and his own efforts to define himself as an engaged intellectual, an image that cut sharply against the grain of his detached, contemplative character. To identify himself with Orwell's authority, Trilling had in part to create it.

Ultimately, though, it was not until the mass media caught hold of him that Orwell pushed past the localized celebrity of intellectual circles and became public property. This might never have happened as it did—or happened at all—had not the rippling anxieties of the Cold War come when they did. The dark fantasy of *1984* was camera-ready—the perfect propaganda tool. And Henry Luce's publications lost no time in trumpeting Orwell as the prophet of the totalitarian menace. Television and radio coverage followed. For a period in the 1950s, there was a new TV adaptation of the novel every year. The long countdown to 1984 was under way.

At some point the inevitable happened: the image and the truth about the man-behind-the-image parted company. The posthumous career of George Orwell has had very little to do with anything that Orwell really wrote, said, or did. The simplified contents of *1984* have floated free of their covers and now move like decorative dirigibles through the public arena, the sad consequence of the packaging of ideologies for mass consumption. Orwell, as author, shares very nearly the same fate. To the man-in-the-street and to the writer of the late-night term paper, he is some mustachioed road-warrior, anti-Communist avatar supreme.

Rodden's book, for all its density of documentation, will provoke the attentive reader. There is much in these pages about infighting within political cenacles, about hype and packaging, about the contrast between the intellectual's "reception" of ideas and the public's ravenous consumption of simplified images, and about our professed fears and longings.

As for me, I was less perplexed by the way our media machines have made Orwell into a household cartoon—nothing surprises me on that front—than by his investiture by the intellectual establishment. Let's face it: Orwell, and only Orwell, bears this near-ecclesiastical authority in our culture. And the sense of the man as the very *fons et origo* of righteous enlightenment deepens daily, even now. It pushes into every crevice: Orwell is presented as the father of the virtuous prose style, of documentary reportage, of media criticism. Very soon it will be Orwell as the father of environmental awareness. I'm not joking. Recently, in a single afternoon's reading, I found Wendell Berry (in *Harper's*) citing Orwell in an essay on global thinking and Bill McKibben doing the very same thing in his *New Yorker* essay "The Death of Nature." In both instances, the use of the Orwell quotation was a rhetorical ploy; it was a way of injecting authority at a critical point in the presentation. It was the appeal to Scripture all over again.

My question isn't "Why Orwell?" but "Why *still* Orwell, and why *only* Orwell?" Are we that hero-starved? Can it be that our intellectual culture has produced no one of comparable worth in four decades? It seems not. Whom could we name? Titans of the intellect we may have, but they don't look like titans. For we expect something more. And that something more is not just political engagement: it is a moral sureness, a natural distribution of attributes leading to a naturalness of response, a heart and mind unbothered by the temptations of the main chance. That in our age Orwell alone is seen to possess such characteristics says something devastating about our situation. The degree to which we venerate the man as a figure for our times, and our future, is the degree to which we are failing ourselves.

The Politics of Literary Reputation: The Making and Claiming of 'St. George' Orwell. John Rodden. 478 pp. Oxford University Press. 1989. $27.50

.   .   .   .

SVEN BIRKERTS

Highbrow/
Lowbrow

E very critic, I suspect, is afflicted now and then by the itch to meddle with his subject's work. Not necessarily to improve what's *on* the page, but rather to raise a baton and redirect the traffic of ideas—even when the ideas before him are good ones, necessary ones. He sees what he perceives to be roads not taken, grand opportunities lost. The impulse is undeniably grandiose. But it is also, in the last analysis, critical; therefore it is part of the job description.

Lawrence Levine's *Highbrow/Lowbrow: The Emergence of Cultural Hierarchy in America* has affected me in just this way. Thoughtful, probing, packed through its rifts with provocative lore, the book is in many ways exemplary—it is even written with grace and care. And yet, when I set it aside, I felt a most ungrateful twinge of disappointment. It was as if Levine had been building steadily toward what Prufrock called an "overwhelming question"—or connection— only to veer sharply to the side when the moment of truth arrived.

But first, about the book and its successes. As the subtitle indicates, *Highbrow/Lowbrow* traces the process whereby an open and pluralistic American culture—*culture* used here primarily in its artistic sense—became, over the course of the nineteenth century, stratified according to class and perceived value distinctions. Levine's lengthy opening chapter looks closely at changes in the performance and reception of Shakespeare's plays in 1800s America. Subsequent chapters demonstrate that the very same kinds of shifts were taking place with respect to opera, classical music, and art, accompanied by an increasingly rigid definition of "high" and "low" culture. The epilogue addresses itself, if glancingly, to debates being waged in our culture today, most notably the controversy surrounding Allan Bloom's *The Closing of the American Mind.*

Shakespeare was not always the exclusive property of self-flattering elites. We know, of course, that aristocrats and common folk stood elbow to elbow in the Globe Theatre in Elizabeth's day. Levine convinces us that this was true as well in the cities and pioneer towns of late eighteenth- and early nineteenth-century America. Audiences representing a full cross section of the population jammed theaters of every description to see the plays performed. Shakespeare was, he asserts, more popular here for a time than in England. The documentation is as amusing as it is instructive:

> In 1816 in Lexington, Kentucky, Noah Ludlow performed *The Taming of the Shrew, Othello,* and *The Merchant of Venice* in a room on the second floor of an old brewery, next door to a saloon, before an audience seated on backless cushionless chairs. In the summer of 1833, Sol Smith's company performed in the dining room of a hotel in Tazewell, Alabama . . . His "heavy tragedian" Mr. Lyne attempted to recite the "Seven Ages of Man" from *As You Like It* while "persons were passing from one room to the other continually and the performer was obliged to move whenever anyone passed."

These were boisterous audiences—heckling, applauding, calling for favorite scenes to be reprised—but they were not altogether ignorant. They knew at least enough to hoot at puns and one-liners and to hiss in anticipation of upcoming villainy. Certainly they were no less boisterous in responding to the other offerings on the bill: the plays were often sandwiched between song-and-dance routines, bawdy farces, and juggling acts. "[T]he play may have been the thing," quips Levine, "but it was not the only thing."

By the middle of the nineteenth century, however, this democratic pluralism began to yield to the pressures of stratification. Shakespeare's plays were gradually uprooted from the soil of competing popular entertainments; performances were cleansed of "low" effects and were more and more often given in separate theaters. And as the Bard came to be seen as one of "theirs," working-class audiences stuck with the burlesques and music halls. An aura of sanctity soon enveloped Shakespeare and his works.

Levine finds a number of reasons for this transformation. For one thing, massive immigration from non-English-speaking countries was changing the character of the working classes—fewer and fewer people were able to parse out the lines. Growing literacy, too, exerted a paradoxical impact; it "encroached upon the pervasive oral culture that had created in nineteenth-century America an audience more comfortable with listening than reading." But suggestive as this is, one wonders what actual effect "letters" were having on the defecting constituency.

The real momentum for change was, as Levine points out, rooted in a more fundamental play of historical forces:

> The process that had seen the noun "class" take on a series of hierarchical adjectives—"lower," "middle," "upper," "working"—in the late eighteenth and early nineteenth centuries was operative for the noun "culture" a hundred years later. Just as the former development mirrored the economic changes brought about by the Industrial Revolution in England, so the latter reflected the cultural consequences of modernization.

An increasingly powerful elite, in other words, began to look for ways to mark out its superiority—it claimed the Bard and defined the new terms for his appreciation.

The argument of *Highbrow/Lowbrow* is carried out mainly by way of carefully marshaled examples. And by the time Levine has discussed the parallel sacralization of the other arts, there is no gainsaying his underlying thesis: that culture is not an absolute, but a production of multiple social forces. The "classic" is a chameleon

· · · ·

entity, adapting to the pressures of its lobbyists; it is an exclusionary barrier lowered against the masses by elites, a tool of image enhancement. Levine's documented assertions may give some pause to those presently defending the immutable sancity of the "canon."

The presentation is not without its problems, however. Chief among these is Levine's refusal to draw what has to be a crucial distinction—that between "culture" and "entertainment." The images we get of working men and women stomping and catcalling through a performance of, say, *Othello* do not give us a sense of culture spreading its beams across lines of class. They suggest, rather, that the play is being brought down to the level of the farcing and banana juggling that follow it. We have to ask, pressing the relativist's case, whether culture might not inhere less in the artifact than in the uses it is put to. If *Othello* did not impinge meaningfully on the inwardness of its viewers—it may not have—then what did it do? But then, the question itself, assuming Arnoldian criteria of meaning and inwardness, takes an elitist vantage. Levine needs to bring these kinds of distinctions into the light.

We might also question the validity of building an argument about high and low culture primarily on the reception of Shakespeare's plays. Shakespeare must be seen as something of a special case; he clearly wrote to offer something to viewers of every level of class and education. The broad appeal of his plays, in other words, says more about the plays than about the tastes of the populace at large. We are left wondering whether the stratification of early nineteenth-century American society was not a bit more pronounced than Levine allows.

A final frustration—to me, the major one—is that Levine has appended to *Highbrow/Lowbrow* an epilogue that would draw some connections between his findings and our contemporary situation. But as he refuses to grapple with the major issues, the section is *sans* teeth. Levine tilts only timidly against the so-called "Bloom thesis," its Platonist assumption that eternal verities undergird all culture, and that these are embodied in a handful of sovereign masterpieces. If Levine's findings lead him into the relativist's corner, then he ought to press his case more explicitly. Stepping back from the elitist-relativist debate, Levine writes:

· · · ·

SVEN BIRKERTS

If the debate is to be fruitful it needs to be rooted not merely in the web of our immediate aesthetic and social predilections but in the matrix of history, which can allow us to perceive more clearly what shapes culture has assumed in the American past, which may in turn allow us to understand better both the possibilities and the effects of the types of cultural boundaries we embrace.

Coming in the penultimate paragraph of his epilogue, this expression seems unnecessarily rhetorical and evasive.

But the real weakness of the concluding section lies in its avoidance of the question of postmodernism. For what is postmodernism in our present-day culture but a concerted attack upon hierarchy, an attempted shattering of the high/low distinctions that have been applied to genres and cultural products? Andy Warhol, Robert Venturi, Philip Glass, Don DeLillo, Thomas Pynchon, Robert Wilson, and a throng of others have in the last decades worked to sabotage the very alignments that Levine has been tracking so carefully. To conclude such a stimulating excursus with thoughts about the present state of things while ignoring this latest current-shift is to deprive oneself—and one's readers—of resolution. Levine has a fine eye for cultural nuance and for the sweep of larger historical dynamics. He should look more searchingly at the present to see how his saga continues.

Highbrow/Lowbrow: The Emergence of Cultural Hierarchy in America. Lawrence W. Levine. 320 pp. Harvard University Press. 1990. $29.95

Teaching
in a Video Age

The assumption that I operate under in this piece is a sad one. To me, at least. It is that we are rapidly and remorselessly leaving behind the age of the book—of the printed page, the written record—and are entering upon something that might be designated "the media age."

I have been teaching one of the required writing courses to Harvard freshmen for five years now (and similar courses elsewhere before that). I have been present to watch a tendency start to turn into a condition. At first a few students, then some, then most. My syntax accelerates the momentum of the change, but never mind. Let me try to explain what I mean.

To begin with, I would emphasize that I am in no way disputing the brightness or seriousness of my students. No, one has only to step into the classroom on the first day of school to feel their keenness. Fifteen sets of eyes flash to the door to check out the new teacher. They are alert, curious, ready to begin. Sometimes it seems that everything else moves and changes over the years—that only those eyes remain constant. Certainly they are an important part of what teaching is all about.

But if the eyes are changeless, then what is different? It has to be something there *behind* that bright display of energy—the cognitive makeup, the fundamental relation to the world and to history. In these students, I find a whole new set of aptitudes and responses, an altered dispositional alignment. I'll try to describe it. For starters, one can't help but notice that these kids are quicker—more restless in posture and demeanor, more neural. Certain of their reflexes have been honed to a disconcerting pitch of readiness. They have been programmed to perform, and they can scarcely wait to begin. At the same time, they seem blanker, shallower, than their predecessors. And while I'm sure that seventeen- and eighteen-year-olds have always been oriented toward the present—in their lives, in the culture—the extent to which they are cut off from the past, from an encompassing sense of history, is startling. Indeed, I would say that the scope of their ignorance proves the prophet false—it *is* something new under the sun.

What am I saying? That these young people are all dressed up with no place to go. That they are formidably trained and "psyched," but that they have little knowledge or understanding to put to use. The engine is sophisticated, but the tank is nearly empty. Choose your own metaphor. The point is that they are appallingly without the kinds of context required for any significant exchange of ideas.

This recognition overtakes me every term, usually right away. For it is my habit to stop and ask for explanations whenever certain words, names, or references come up. I watch as those clear, focused gazes cloud over, again and again. "Can anyone tell me who Sigmund Freud was?" Pause. You can almost *feel* the urgent ransacking of fifteen memory banks. When was the French Revolution? *What* was the French Revolution? Who was Karl Marx? And so on. They just don't know. Most of them, that is. And if they do have some inkling, then they have a hard time formulating a coherent answer. They lack the means, the language. "He's the guy . . . you know, Freudian slip?"

I realize that this gripe has a familiar, even fashionable, sound to it. All of a sudden everybody is talking about "cultural literacy," about shared information, about the woeful inadequacy of high school curricula, etc. And I, too, have been reading E. D. Hirsch's book of that title. But I do not think that this is mainly, centrally, a curriculum-related problem. In fact, it is something much larger, and much more difficult to remedy. What Hirsch has identified is just one of the consequences of this profound cultural shift—the shift from print as a cognitive base to one shaped by a range of electronic media. A massive collective rewiring is under way.

Hirsch is, of course, right to be alarmed. The problems are very real and very pressing. Americans *are* increasingly isolated from one another because they lack a common set of associations, of usable cultural counters. But where Hirsch's analysis stops, the crisis begins. What would people communicate about once they had these common references? The Gettysburg Address? Carbon dioxide? Would the discourse of the nation become a grand game of Trivial Pursuit? The real point is that we lack the substance *behind* those names, dates, and tag lines. We have lost a sense of the past, a historical grounding; we are without a working knowledge of ideas and philosophies; we have lost our feeling for language as a living, supple, delighting, and generative entity. And no fiddling with curricula is going to restore these things to us.

I was most struck in my reading of Hirsch by how little he discussed reading, and how seldom he mentioned TV. Television was brought up only twice in his text, and then just in passing. Yet I would argue that these two activities—their essentially inverse relation to one another—must form the very axis of the debate. Not in a simplistic way. Not in the sense that time spent watching is seen merely as time spent away from books. No, more in the sense that TV (I use TV here as a shorthand for a whole set of new technologies, including VCR movies, video games, portable cassette players, word processors programmed to check spelling and do God knows what else . . .) works to create an ambience, a new synaptic patterning, a persuasive sense of a collectively shared "now," all of which cut against reading and what it represents. For reading is stillness, absorption, the forging and sustaining of mental perspectives; it is active, difficult; it opens upon density and diversity. And it is also listening: to voices, sounds, rhythms, and articulations of otherness. To read is to situate oneself in some relation to a heritage; to watch is to surrender passively to a churning of images.

. .   .   .

SVEN BIRKERTS

I'm not saying that my students do nothing but watch TV, listen to tapes, and play video games. But I do believe that their inner dispositions, their sensibilities, have been formed—more than those of any generation in human history—by those activities, those forces. They are at large in our culture. One doesn't have to watch television to be affected by its ubiquity. The fact of it, the fact that our obscure but omnipresent Zeitgeist is conditioned by it and everywhere alludes to it, makes it harder than ever to venture the independent act of reading a book. Reading becomes a struggle because the prevailing attitude is that it is an odd, asocial activity. An eccentricity. I don't mean reading for school, and I don't mean "beach" reading. I mean the serious, private, self-generated interaction with books that forms the main path toward inner cultivation.

Almost none of my students read independently. I know this because I ask them. On the first day of class I request written answers to certain questions. About their backgrounds, their experience with high school English. And about their reading. How much they read outside of school, what they read, their favorite books, and so on. The responses are heartbreaking. Nearly every student admits— some of them sheepishly, others not—that reading is a problem. "Too busy." "I wish I had the time!" "I've always had a hard time with books that are supposed to be good for me." And then, proudly: "If I have the time, I like to relax with Stephen King." I can't tell you how many of my best and brightest have written that sentence. Stephen King, Stephen King, Stephen King. How rarely will someone cite a reputable "serious" book—by Milan Kundera, Vladimir Nabokov, Walker Percy, Anne Tyler, *anyone*. Nonfiction—history, politics, social history, psychology—is a terra incognita. But there they have an excuse: they will have to *study* the stuff.

Fine, so kids don't read anymore. Will the world of the future be different, worse, because people can't pass the time discussing Eudora Welty and Heinrich Böll? Well, yes. I fear it will be much worse. Not because certain plots, characters, inventions, or themes won't be assessed. To focus on those elements overlooks the other, perhaps *deeper,* functions of reading. I mean: the way that the reading of serious books teaches one constantly (often unconsciously) about the world. The reader cross-references information about everything from dates and places to speech patterns to social mores. We are

· · ·

Teaching in a Video Age

more apt to know about the French Revolution from having come across references to it in a dozen contexts than from having studied a textbook back in the tenth grade. But even more important is the way that reading keeps the language alive in us. Not just words and their uses, but a feeling for the syntactic masonry required by different kinds of expression. Exposure to language on the page—the kind of hearing that goes on over thousands and thousands of pages—enlarges the inner reach. It teaches what can be expressed and how it can be expressed. It gives a feeling for the growth and movement of ideas, and alerts us to the full range of positions, tones, and possibilities. The reader learns a healthy distrust of appearances—for what are most novels but penetrations and reversals of our preconceptions about character and situation? He learns, too, to search out the opacities and secrets of other lives, and to hold complex orders of experience in his head. Will the world be different if people stop reading? Very likely it will once again be flat.

So much for students and their reading habits. The fact remains that my course (Expository Writing: Literature) is supposed to teach them to *write*. Clearly and expressively, subtly, and with depth and dimension. I have eleven or twelve weeks, two 50-minute classes a week, plus three private conferences. Where to begin?

I believe—as must be obvious—that one cannot write well if one does not read. Or, at the very least, if one does not have the soul, the inner resources, of a reader. I believe that writing that is clear and varied, capable of sustained exposition as well as of detail and discrimination, cannot happen where there is not a sensibility equipped to generate it. And such a sensibility cannot exist without the kind of auditory inwardness that reading cultivates. For writing is so much more than just the transmission of ideas or information. Writing—effective, memorable writing—depends upon the writer hearing the language. One balances sounds, their values and meanings; one holds in readiness clauses and word-chains; one speeds up and slows down according to the needs of the expression. The ear does the brain's fingertip work—it joins and adjusts, adds and subtracts. It hears the rightness of a phrase, rejects a dissonance. If you can't hear words and their arrangements—the music that accompanies and enforces meaning—then you can't write. Certainly not well.

But as I have indicated, these students are not eager readers. The printed page taxes and wearies them; they find little pleasure there. What hope does a teacher have for getting them to write well? Initially, I confess, I always despair. I read through their first papers—so neatly word-processed, so proudly titled with the boldfaced curlicues that the technology makes possible—and my heart sinks. The writing is almost always flat, monotonous, built up of simple units. Immigrant prose. But no, immigrant prose, clumsy though it may be, is often alert to the textures and imagistic possibilities of the language. This writing is bland and slippery, unpressurized by mind. It shows, if anything, the influence of rhetoric and televised banality. "The controversy surrounding the use of steroids is a heated one. Should an athlete be allowed to take drugs to improve performance? Or should these drugs be outlawed? The recent case of Olympic athlete Ben Johnson . . ." Simple units. Where there is a compound sentence, it is, more often than not, a creation made up of two short declarations joined by a comma or a conjunction. "These drugs must be outlawed and athletes must follow the law." The prose has little or no musicality and lacks any depth of field; it is casually associative in movement, syntactically inert, and barren of interesting reference. Complexity is nonexistent. Some sort of communication has been ventured, but only a paid reader—that is, a teacher—would read more than a few lines. If I exaggerate, it's only slightly.

The problem is immediately obvious. There is, however, no real dilemma. I must do what I can in the time I have to change this state of affairs. As I cannot undo the effects of years and years of not reading, I must do the next-best thing. I must teach them to listen, to make hearing the core of their writing process. I must give them a good solid dose of close reading.

Close reading, as I understand it, is really nothing more than paying attention to a text. The difficulties are not in the conception, but in the doing. To close-read a page of prose, a poem, anything, is to create a receptivity, a silence, in yourself so that the work can leave an impression. Just as you cannot race past a painting in a museum and call that "seeing" the art, so you cannot move your eyes rapidly over a page and imagine that you have "read" it. The goal of close reading might be stated as follows: to hear the language on the page as intensely as the writer heard it in the process of composition, and to feel its rhythms, hesitations, and pauses. The only talent required is a talent for focus and deceleration. To read anything in a meaningful way, you must push through the shallow-field perceptual mode that modern life makes habitual. The operation is not nearly as simple as it sounds. The eye has been taught to speed across word clusters. The sound in the ear, which lags behind the eye, is usually a noise, like the garbling that comes when tape gets dragged across the magnetic heads. That garble has to be slowed, at the very least to normal-speech tempo. The harder it is for a reader to slow the pace, the more vital it is that he learn how to.

What procedure I have for teaching my writing course has been slow to evolve. For while I sensed the nature of the problem early on, it took me a good long time to plant my response at the core of my pedagogy. At first I was busy obeying what I saw as the three-part requirement of the course: I assigned a variety of readings in the anthology, careful to provide examples of the main literary genres (short story, essay, poetry, and drama); I asked for a set number of papers, most of which were to deal with themes from the reading; and I arranged a schedule of private conferences. Conference time was used for going over finished work. I would point out mistakes, make suggestions for the future. And, I have to say, my students did improve. Their work at the end of the course was always more polished and confident than it had been at the start.

But something was wrong. I could sense it. The kinds of improvements that were being registered were of degree, not kind. The prose was better, but most of the progress was attributable to practice, to the fact that they were writing on a weekly schedule. The fundamental flaws—stylistic simplicity, glibness, and so on—were all still there. I was sending these students out with a nod and a good grade, but I did not have the feeling that I had really made a difference to their writing.

The first breakthrough came with the decision to make one of their assignments a personal essay. It seemed like a natural way to break the monotony of literary topic papers, and it sorted well with the essay portion of the course. After all, we were reading Annie Dillard, George Orwell, Loren Eiseley, and others—why not get them to try something in a similar vein? I was startled by the results. Not only were the essays themselves more interesting than anything I had received before, but the writing was better. Dramatically so. I suddenly found stylistic variety, precision, a willingness to be expressive. I kept shaking my head. What could I conclude but that when the topic was something that concerned them—a person, an activity, an episode from their lives—then they cared much more about how their prose sounded. They *wanted* to get something across; they wanted it to be interesting. What's more, they knew their subject— its details and intricacies—and they felt more confident about making use of what they knew. The potential, in other words, was there.

It was not long before I followed this lead and started to experiment. For one thing, I positioned the personal-essay assignment closer to the beginning of the course (before it had been a reward, a chance for release given late in the term). I reasoned that if the students could feel the satisfactions of depth, detail, and stylistic care, then they might try to achieve similar results in their nonpersonal writing. Here I met with disappointment. The students saw the personal essay as a "fun" assignment—once the fun was over, the drudgery could begin. I could not sell them on the notion that the other assignments offered kindred pleasures.

Possibly for this reason—I can't remember now—I decided to build upon the personal-essay assignment. Under the new dispensation, I treated the first submission as a rough draft (without telling the students this beforehand: the words "rough draft" are the kiss of death in a writing class). I then based a full thirty- to forty-minute conference on a discussion of the piece. *Discussion* is not quite apt. The meetings were more like cheerful police interrogations. I cast myself in the role of their ideal—if bullying—listener; I questioned them relentlessly, flattering, wheedling, pushing for data. "But what was it *like* to be six years old and studying the violin? Where did you stand? How long? How did you hold the thing? Can you remember what you played, how it sounded? Did you hate your parents for making you do this? *Why* did they make you do this?" Whatever their topic, I pressed. And of course there was always much more to be learned. As often as not, the student arrived by himself at the core of interest, at the real topic that the first version had somehow masked. "Well, why didn't you say *that*? That's the most interesting

· · · ·

Teaching in a Video Age

thing you've said. If you were making an all-night confession to your best friend, how would you describe what happened? Would you pick these same details?"

My goal was to get the student to leave the conference with a clear sense of what was interesting about his subject—indeed, with a clear sense that I was interested in hearing every last detail. I filled them up with question marks and then turned them loose.

And the writing improved further. I started getting wonderfully evocative—and searching and hilarious—essays on every topic under the sun. I could scarcely believe the change I was seeing. When they wrote for themselves, about themselves, they *listened*. And they took pains to make their prose sound good.

Still, this was a writing course in literature, and the question remained: could I get them to transfer these skills, if not the enthusiasm, to subjects they deemed less exciting or relevant? I would be lying if I said yes. Some difference was felt, sure. Now there was an extra measure of confidence, a kind of self-momentum that carried over. But I could not rely on it. And several years later, I still cannot. Personal writing by itself is not a magic solution. But it points the way to a valuable tactic that I had long overlooked.

My experience with teaching the personal essay—especially with the now-obligatory interrogatory conference—showed me something that holds out genuine hope for the cause. It is, in fact, what decided me on writing this piece. To put it simply: I discovered that my students were not only tolerant, or patient, with detail—they were fascinated by it. And I don't just mean details and sense memories from their own lives. I mean detail for itself, as a category of magnitude. It was as if the general principles that they were forced to master in high school—combined with the fact that most of them had never given reading a chance—had left them with an enormous cognitive vacuum. They were so obviously avid for brass tacks, for concrete instances and precise distinctions. I had long assumed the opposite, that nothing was so boring to them as "nitpicking," or going over a text or a topic with attentive care. I was wrong. They loved it. And this extended not only to the fine points of essays and stories, but also to the subtleties of writing styles—their own and those of others. What an eye-opening discovery—that here, in an era of rhetoric and appearances, in a climate characterized by the evanescent images on the TV screen and the impatient pulsing of the personal computer, was a desire, a positive *relish,* for intricacy and detail. How to explain it? Was it that the world of the daily news was just too much with them—does an overwhelmingly complex macroreality make them crave what they can manipulate and master? I don't know. But this recognition changed my teaching completely.

Where formerly I rushed from genre to genre, basing nearly all in-class discussion around themes and concepts—because I thought this would keep them interested, and if they were interested, they would write better—now I've all but thrown the switch into reverse. If we used to cover four genres, we now cover two, with maybe just a nod toward a third. Instead of discussing four short stories, we're lucky to finish with two. But what a difference! At times now I feel like we're a team of mechanics working on an engine. The engagement is intense; the give-and-take is focused, often excited. I don't flatter myself that I'm some sort of superteacher, nor do I believe that the gods keep sending me the very best students. I think I know what's making the change. These students are getting a taste of what reading—and writing—really are, many of them for the first time ever. They're finding out how much a text can hold, and be.

A typical session might go something like this. Let's say that I've asked everyone to read George Orwell's essay "On Shooting an Elephant." In giving the assignment, I've done nothing more than stress that they should read slowly and carefully. Now we begin.

The first thing I do, always, is to ask them to keep their books closed and listen while I read the opening, in this case the first paragraph:

> In Moulmein, in Lower Burma, I was hated by large numbers of people—the only time in my life that I have been important enough for this to happen to me. I was sub-divisional police officer of the town, and in an aimless, petty kind of way anti-European feeling was very bitter. No one had the guts to raise a riot, but if a European woman went through the bazaar alone somebody would probably spit betel juice over her dress. As a police officer I was an obvious target and was baited whenever it seemed safe to do so. When a nimble Burman tripped me up

on the football field and the referee (another Burman) looked the other way, the crowd yelled with hideous laughter. This happened more than once. In the end the sneering yellow faces of the young men that met me everywhere, the insults hooted after me when I was at a safe distance, got badly on my nerves. The young Buddhist priests were the worst of all. There were several thousands of them in the town and none of them seemed to have anything to do except stand on street corners and jeer at Europeans.

I stop. I've tried to read slowly and expressively. When I've let the word-sounds die off, when I'm certain of the attention of my students, I start to ask questions. Simple, factual questions. For if I've learned anything from teaching literature, it's this: assume nothing. We'll get nowhere so long as individuals in the class have blind spots and unanswered questions.

First things first. Where is Burma? Many blank looks. But one or two hands go up, and we establish the geographical site. Now, what is Orwell, the presumed narrator, doing there? That is, why is he a subdivisional police officer? When? The same thing happens—slowly. But by degrees, as they pool their remembered facts, the overall context is set out. British imperialism. The Raj. The empire on which the sun never sets . . . And what is betel juice—where does it come from, what color is it? Football? No, he means soccer, of course. And who knows anything about Buddhism? Okay . . . what is a bazaar?

At this point, I'm still insisting that they keep their books closed. I read the passage again. But the questions I ask afterward are of a different sort. I say: "If you had nothing but this passage to go by, what could you tell me about the person who is speaking? Age, personality, anything. Do you like him or dislike him? Do you trust his perspective? Why?" There are long silences. With only their memories to check, they are not sure what to say at first. But opinions do begin to surface. Assertions and counterassertions. Inevitable disagreements. I have to keep punctuating these with my stock "Why do you say that? Where do you get that?" What emerges from the process is finally this: that they have retained nearly all of the information; that most of them can give at least some part of the passage verbatim. I push at this, and they are intrigued enough to oblige. In a matter of minutes, working together, we have pretty much reconstituted the order of the sentences, a good deal of the wording. They have astonished themselves.

Now we switch again. I ask them to account for what happens to them when they read. Do they see pictures in their minds, do they hear a voice? They nod: pictures. We talk about whether these are clear or blurry, general or precise. Depends, they say. I ask them which images are vivid, and why. Then I reframe the question: "If you had to open a film on the basis of this first paragraph—remaining faithful to what has been given—how would you do it?" Here is a question they can respond to. They like to think in terms of film— they grasp the problematic instantly. I get sophisticated suggestions about close-ups, cuts, camera movements, and so on. But when this threatens to become a separate game, I force another change of subject. "If we had nothing but the first paragraph to go by, what would we guess that the essay will be about?" I allow them to open their books. They comb the sentences looking for clues. As they already know where the essay will go, they are gratified to find the oppositions and tensions spelled out right on top of the narrative surface. Combining these hints with what we've already determined about the character and attitude of the narrator, they make good progress reconstructing the moral resolution.

I've touched on the avidness that these students display for detail. Let me add to this. I have noticed, for one thing, that the impulse, or aptitude, comes to life most quickly when the task can be posed as a challenge, a detection problem. Can anyone find . . . ? If they believe that there is an answer to be got, they will exercise remarkable ingenuity in searching—and they appear to enjoy the process. My second observation—or suggestion—is that the close-reading process never be allowed to overwhelm everything else. The students respond well to sudden changes in magnitude. I like to switch from the most microscopic of inspections—comparing sentence rhythms, say—to the most broadly thematic questions. Like: how do these very subtle contrasts find their way into the big picture? Why would an author expend so much care on his prose—what is he trying to communicate that is so important?

As you can see, there is enough in one opening paragraph to

claim the best energies of a class for a whole hour. But what then? Obviously we cannot work through the rest of the piece with the same diligence. I have several follow-up strategies. Sometimes I let *them* choose the focal zone. I simply ask: If you imagine your attention as a kind of gauge, at what point does the needle shoot up most dramatically? Where is the uranium deposit? Different passages are named, and in each case there are opinions about why. Is it the subject matter? The imagery? The use of language? My job is to keep pushing, to get them to make finer and finer discriminations.

Or else I will pluck a particularly well-written section and ask the students to locate the subtlest of its language devices. Again, once they believe that there is an answer waiting at the far end of their search, they will filter the words and sentences through the finest of meshes. For example:

> When I pulled the trigger I did not hear the bang or feel the kick—one never does when a shot goes home—but I heard the devilish roar of glee that went up from the crowd. In that instant, in too short a time, one would have thought, even for the bullet to get there, a mysterious, terrible change had come over the elephant. He neither stirred nor fell, but every line of his body had altered. He looked suddenly stricken, immensely old, as though the frightful impact of the bullet had paralysed him without knocking him down. At last, after what seemed a long time— it might have been five seconds, I dare say—he sagged flabbily to his knees. His mouth slobbered.

In minutes they are bringing forward their trophies. How the inset phrase of the first sentence enacts the sensation of recoil. How the second sentence builds tension by contrasting the speed of the bullet with the slow, almost viscous movement of the narrator's voice. How the s's in the third and fourth sentences contribute to a jagged impression of impact and imminent collapse. How "sagged flabbily" sketches a movement using sound and rhythm (' ' --). And so on. They are happy to keep going.

And the good of all this close reading? Well, to begin with, it gets them interested in prose. As a medium, as an object of study. They see value in reading it carefully. And they have a new respect for its possibilities. The realization dawns that writing technique—

.   .   .

style—is something more than just clear exposition. Syntax and word-sounds, they see, can be manipulated for effect. It's suddenly obvious that reading involves a lot more than moving the eyes back and forth over clusters of key words; that there are instances where every least phrase deserves to be heard and weighed.

We don't, of course, spend all of our time looking at isolated passages from the prose of the masters. As this is a writing course, it is essential that they transfer some of the benefits derived from this kind of reading to their own practice. And one way to make a beginning at this is to get them to level similar attention at their own prose and the prose of their peers. I do this in two ways. First, with in-class exercises. A typical exercise may be assigned as follows: "Take out a sheet of paper. I want you to find a way to characterize your morning thus far. Give us a story, an episode, a dialogue, whatever you like. But it has to be interesting, and it has to win us over. You have fifteen minutes." Or else: "You are a book reviewer for a nationally syndicated radio program, something on the order of *All Things Considered*. You have a two-minute slot in which to render your verdict of [say] Eudora Welty's 'Why I Live at the P.O.' You have to convey something of what the story is like, *and* you have to keep your easily bored listeners from switching the dial."

At the end of fifteen minutes, I collect the papers. I have asked them to work anonymously. I tell them, further, that if they absolutely hate what they have produced, they should write NO on top of the page. Some do. But most are eager to hear their words read aloud.

I then go through the pieces in sequence, reading them and soliciting responses. "Do you want to hear more? Does this work? Is the attention needle moving, twitching, or is it at rest? Why?" Then, working from memory, they have to specify their reactions. Why is it dull? The words, the cadences? Why did you laugh there? Can you remember a sentence, an image? How would you change it to make it better?

A more sustained inspection takes place when student essays are photocopied and passed around (with names excised). As always, they have the option of refusing to have their papers discussed. But most are game. My procedure, then, is to give them ten minutes or so to read the essay and to make notations. In addition, I ask each reader to a) find the very best passage and mark it off and b) to come up with one constructive—and specific—suggestion for the author.

I begin by reading the first paragraph. By now they all know my spiels about how much can be learned from first impressions and about how openings often encode an author's entire agenda. When I have finished reading, I ask for responses based solely upon that first paragraph. What is the voice? The subject? Can we tell from these few sentences where it might go? Do we care? If this writer has won your interest—at least provisionally—then how has he/she managed it? If not, why not? Most writing teachers are familiar with the basic workshop mode, and what I do does not vary significantly. We look for good and bad points; I make every effort to get critics to frame their reservations constructively—not just "This is boring" but "This might be more interesting if . . ." The one way that my approach might differ from some others is in the amount of focus directed at an isolated portion of the text, generally the beginning (though the last paragraph can yield wonders as well). I emphasize the notion of organicism. A sentence or paragraph, I say, can be tested like a tissue culture—it can often tell us essential things about the condition of the rest of the body, and so on. One need only remember not to work the technique (or simile) to death. There is always a right time for switching to the big picture, for asking how the parts cohere, for taking a good, hard look at what the author is saying and what that's worth. But there will come a time—and this is the benchmark of progress—when students will not be able to talk about the *what* without repeated references to the *how*. And *that* is a writer's perception.

I started this essay by pointing to what I see as a genuinely worrisome situation—that we are now witnessing the emergence of generations of students who are not, and have never been, readers; whose habits and reflexes have been conditioned by the media culture they live in. And I expressed alarm, further, at how this conditioning (or, to reverse it, *lack* of conditioning) impoverished their writing. My awakening to a certain potential for change—finding that they can still learn what reading and paying attention are all about and that this can improve their writing—does not entirely vanquish my alarm. While it's true that I note considerable progress in my students' writing, I feel that it has been a progress initiated, not necessarily secured. I fear the gravity pull of old tendencies and the inevitable incursion of academic jargon. Twelve weeks is simply not enough time to drive the nail home.

The improvements? Mainly, I would say, these students have learned something about the value of attention. They have begun to listen and, to greater or lesser degree, they have begun to hear. They have grasped the idea that prose makes a sound, and that the way it sounds matters to its effectiveness. Their work now ventures complexity and stylistic diversity—more concrete nouns, more attempts to pin down exact sensory perceptions. It is also less solipsistic: that is, it reflects consideration for the ear and interest of the potential reader. To be sure, the results are not pure magic. The sow's ear of the given is not yet the silk purse of the desired. But the changes leave me, for the first time, with a sense of job satisfaction. I could here cite any one of the several dozen passages that have begun to restore my faith, but the context forbids it. For each passage, or sentence, is part of a long story; to do it honor, I would have to track the student through the various stages of composition and critique—subject, I think, for another essay.

Suffice it to say, I am not altogether without hope. The wholesale erosion of literacy will not abate, but some of these students will still manage to catch a hint of what it means to read. They will, perhaps, find that there is pleasure to be had in the surmounting of verbal obstacles. Others may discover the peculiar satisfaction that comes as words are fitted together to make meaning, and that there is a release of adrenaline in the throes of composition that is like nothing else. There will be those, too, who will never come close to attaining such realizations and for whom writing will always be a battle. But my fantasy is that even the least committed, least attentive student will have absorbed a portion of what I have offered. Not as knowledge, necessarily, or as a set of skills, but in the form of a voice, a superego. I would hope that even such a student would find it unaccountably harder, and more irksome, to fling together just any old words. There would arise in him, or her, at those moments of temptation, like a dream half-remembered, the image of an expectant but scrupulous reader, one who is just waiting to see what marvels will next be revealed.

AMERICAN
FICTION

The Talent
in the Room/
with Postscript

"The Talent in the Room"—a Note

This essay, originally undertaken as an assignment for a journal, reflects the hazards that accompany all attempts at synoptic evaluation. One reads and ponders and sets down an interpretation. Later, inevitably, one reads other authors and books and finds the contours of judgment shifting. I have been tempted by hindsight to make substantial additions, deletions, and revisions to this essay. If I have finally not done so, it is because I have realized that the alterations would be no less provisional. If I were to rewrite the piece today, I would make a bigger place for John Updike—the power of Rabbit at Rest *forced me to change my thoughts about the whole series of Harry Angstrom novels. I would likewise argue more strenuously for Paul West, whose recent novels have been a revelation of sorts. There would be a dozen other shifts and fidgets. But enough. One says what one can and moves on. New valuations should provide incentive for new essays.*

In his 1959 miscellany, *Advertisements for Myself,* Norman Mailer included a short and scrappy bulletin summarizing his reactions to his generation of novelists. The piece was called "Evaluations—

Quick and Expensive Comments on the Talent in the Room." Quick they were—Mailer's opinions took the short route from gut to pen, without a delaying detour through the precincts of reasoned discrimination. By "expensive" I assume he meant that his temerity in shooting from the hip was likely to cost him dearly in the fraternal back rooms where writers meet to swap drinks and gossip.

And no doubt his judgments—and his near-sadistic glee in delivering them—made for some tough sidewalk encounters in the months and years that followed. Wrote Mailer of his friend James Jones: "What was unique about Jones was that he had come out of nowhere, self-taught, a clunk in his lacks, but the only one of us who had the beer-guts of a broken-glass brawl. What must next be said is sad, for Jones has sold out badly over the years." And of Bellow: "There were some originalities and one or two rich sections to *Augie March* (which is all I know of his work) but at its worst it was a travelogue for timid intellectuals and so to tell the truth I cannot take him seriously as a major novelist."

He continued on, knocking off the stalwarts of a whole generation as if they were so many candlepins, and getting away with the game—if indeed he did—by holding his own performance before the same interrogator's lamp. "When I come to assess myself," he wrote in the adjoining essay, "and try to imagine what chance I have of writing that big book I have again in me, I do not know in all simple bitterness if I can make it. For you have to care about other people to share your perception with them, especially if it is a perception which can give them life, and now there are too many times when I no longer give a good goddam for most of the human race."

Mailer is, of course, Mailer. He has made his place in American letters in part through his great talent, but in part, too, by his willingness to thumb the top of the bottle and shake the mixture inside. The opinions themselves are helter-skelter, skewed on the one hand by his double-dare-you machismo, on the other by his inability to register anything that does not come in on the narrow Mailer frequency. Bellow's ambitiously serious playfulness, for instance. Or women writers (Mailer apologizes in "Evaluations" for his inability to read the other sex, adding: ". . . I doubt if there will be a really exciting woman writer until the first whore becomes a call girl and tells her tale." The distinction, I confess, is lost on me).

Nevertheless, to read "Evaluations"—or any of the prose in the book, for that matter—in our cautious times is to feel a suddenly livening jangle of spirit. I'm not talking about Mailer's bad-boy cleverness, and certainly not about the accuracy of his calls. I mean that larger thing, the sense suffusing the posturing that the game is worth something, that literature matters, that there is that whale known as the Great American Novel to be harpooned, and that, by God, somebody is going to do it.

That time, and that feeling about the novel, are gone now—so far gone that it's impossible even to comment on such notions without wincing smiles and incessantly arched eyebrows. Novels are read, sure, and every so often one gets talked about, but *the novel* does not seem to matter that much anymore. Certainly not as an arena of struggle or as a symbolic enactment of some larger one-on-one with contemporary experience. No, ours is more a time of petitioning congressmen to keep arts funding alive, advancing arguments to prove that art and theater matter to the public. Left and right, our publishers—supposed custodians of our intellectual provender—are knuckling under to corporation bureaucrats. Literacy is dwindling, but not so rapidly as the shared sense of the importance of artistic culture. Free-spoken estimates like Mailer's are unheard of these days.

Or almost. Where the novel is concerned, the single exception would have to be Tom Wolfe's lengthy polemic, "Stalking the Billion-Footed Beast: A Literary Manifesto for the New Social Novel," published in the November 1989 issue of *Harper's*. True, Wolfe was as much proselytizing his own vision as passing judgment on others, but the splash was considerable. Letters of response were printed— applause, outrage—and the editorial pages of the more serious magazines and quarterlies were lit up for a time. The excitement was caused in part by what Wolfe was saying, but even more, I suspect, by the simple fact that somebody was taking the novel seriously.

Well, debate is a sign of life, if not health, and this debate ought to be kept alive for that reason alone. But "Stalking the Billion-Footed Beast" is also a most curious document, one that can tell us a great deal about the failures and attainments of the contemporary American novel. It can tell us even more when it is read with a glance back at Mailer's somewhat more personalized manifesto and its underlying assumptions.

Wolfe's basic pitch goes something like this: that the American novelist, who up through the 1950s had been working in a traditional realist mode, turned tail in the 1960s and allowed the accelerations and complications of the real world to overwhelm his art (again, the masculine pronoun—Wolfe, like Mailer, gives almost no mention to women writers). He cites Philip Roth's observation: "The actuality is continually outdoing our talents, and the culture tosses up figures daily that are the envy of any novelist." The sixties witnessed a dramatic and wholesale swerve away from the high road of tradition and into side-road enterprises like absurdism, magical realism, something called radical disjunction (the list is Wolfe's); and then, with the seventies, came minimalism. Of all deviations, this last gets the fiercest lash from Wolfe's pony whip.

Wolfe then retails his own discovery—how his successes with what has come to be known as the New Journalism (the vividly detailed rendering of the actual) led him to realize that the very same techniques could be applied to fiction. After citing Lionel Trilling's well-known view, that the realistic novel was the product of class-stratified societies and had to expire when the old hierarchical certainties melted down, Wolfe counters:

> . . . I would say that precisely the opposite is the case. If we substitute for *class,* in Trilling's formulation, the broader term *status,* that technique has never been more essential in portraying the innermost life of the individual. This is above all true when the subject is the modern city. It strikes me as folly to believe that you can portray the individual in the city today without also portraying the city itself.

Wolfe lays great stress here, as throughout, on the conjunction between the *real* and the *urban.* Soon after comes the rousing call to arms:

> At this weak, pale, tabescent moment in the history of American literature, we need a battalion, a brigade, of Zolas to head out

into this wild, bizarre, unpredictable, Hog-stomping Baroque country of ours and reclaim it as literary property. Philip Roth was absolutely right. The imagination of the novelist is powerless before what he knows he's going to read in tomorrow morning's newspaper. But a generation of American writers has drawn precisely the wrong conclusion from that perfectly valid observation. The answer is not to leave the rude beast, the material, also known as the life around us, to the journalists, but to do what journalists do, or are supposed to do, which is to wrestle the beast and bring it to terms.

Brave words, and a provocative essay. For all his implicit and explicit self-promotion, Wolfe makes some smart assessments about what elements are lacking in the contemporary novel. Indeed, set beside Mailer's tally-sheet venture, it is a monument of reasoned argumentation. Nevertheless, one is left with an unsettled feeling: it is as though Wolfe were dreaming some bright and excited dream alongside the main struggles of the practicing American novelist. He has shot off a whole row of tin ducks at the shooting gallery, but it's somehow not the right gallery. His battle cry is as far from what is going on now—and why—as Mailer's spirited rabble-rousing is from our cultural climate. Still, his misconceptions, so starkly posed, help to clarify the terms of the discussion.

Wolfe is, it must be said, better as a *provocateur* than as a thinker. To begin with, his move of substituting *status* for *class,* so pivotal to his argument, is specious. It sounds good, but I don't think it can work in practice. The class distinctions that the nineteenth-century realists studied and represented were the very gear mechanism of the societies in question. Status, by contrast, is a fluid entity, a token available to anyone who can amass the necessary cash. While the enumeration of status traits can tell us much that is interesting, even significant, about the state of things in our fiscally porous culture, it cannot serve as a more solid foundation upon which a writer might found a comprehensive societal anatomy. The point is that all that was solid, including the link between social appearance and reality, has melted into air.

Second, there is much that is suspect about Wolfe's easy flitting between genres, his assumption that our writers need only retool to journalistic specifications. Journalism is by definition—even etymologically—of and for the day; it gives us the factual record, the supposedly objective snapshot of the state of things at a given time and in a given place. The novelist operates within a different time frame, and is necessarily concerned to inscribe a deeper, more lasting portrait. The journalist finds the world; the novelist makes one. What resonance the novel achieves is intended, in part, for the listening ear of the future reader; his business, to steal from Ezra Pound, is with news that stays news.

Wolfe repeatedly fuses the idea of the realist aesthetic with something that might be called "urban reportage." His arguments—like his own best example, *The Bonfire of the Vanities*—revolve around the axis-pole premise of New York City. The preoccupation with status and the much-bruited collision of all levels of society (the economic, occupational, and racial) are intimately bound up with his experience of writing about that city. At times it looks as if the whole point of his sloganeering is to persuade his readers that he has taken on one of the few big sociohistorical subjects available to the contemporary novelist. The others—Wolfe enumerates them—are "racial clashes, the hippie movement, the New Left, the Wall Street boom, the sexual revolution, the war in Vietnam."

Now *this* is interesting. For if we take a panoramic scan of the novel of the last decade and a half, we find few—maybe *no*—major urban novels (this in a decidedly urban era); we find next to nothing having to do with racial clashes, the hippie movement, the New Left, the Wall Street boom . . . The sexual revolution has been addressed, mostly obliquely, in terms of its impact on changing mores, and the Vietnam War, subject of half a dozen powerful movies, has been touched upon only glancingly (the most affecting Vietnam novel I've read, Larry Heinemann's *Paco's Story,* approaches its material retrospectively, by way of one vet's delirious flashbacks). Wolfe did not mention Watergate or our undeclared participation in wars the world over, but there again next to nothing turns up in fiction.

Clearly, then, Wolfe is arguing against the evidence. His exhortation flies directly in the face of a grand—and obvious—refusal on the part of American novelists. Though very likely it is not so much that they are *ignoring* the existence of those subjects as affirming that they cannot be given ready novelistic treatment. But Wolfe does not

·   ·   ·   ·

do much with this possibility. He makes out, instead, that our best and brightest are cowed by this "Hog-stomping Baroque country of ours," and elect to break their pencil points over minimalist, or absurdist, or magic-realist diversions.

Actually, nothing could be further from the truth. The powerful central thrust of the contemporary American novel is very much toward realism—only it is a realism altogether unlike what Wolfe would propose. Instead of looking to the present, it harks back to earlier decades; instead of addressing the big societal picture, it looks to the individual, the family, the bounded community; instead of taking on the urban subject, the "billion-footed beast," it is occupied with a decidedly rural and small-town order—an order that our daily news tells us is going the way of the dodo bird. What gives? To answer, we must step back a few paces.

The history of any art, or even any development within an art, is ultimately a complicated case-by-case business, and one generalizes with an uneasy sense of presumptuousness. Still, on that level where certain things are seen to be more true than not, where trends appear like consolidated smoke-shapes out of the burning of separate twigs and branches, some assertions are possible. One: that the post–World War II period saw the emergence of a distinct new incarnation of the American novel. Two: that the prime movers were overwhelmingly male (Mary McCarthy is a notable exception), many of them the sons and grandsons of Jewish immigrants. Three: that these ambitious young men were possessed by the dream of writing the Great American Novel, that elusive, totalizing entity that would register like a faithful mirror the hopes, energies, contradictions, and failings of postwar America. They sought, by and large, the creation of novels of the *Now,* though several would fix their gazes back upon the recent war. A short list, running up to the beginning of the 1960s, would include: Mailer's *The Naked and the Dead, Barbary Shore,* and *The Deer Park;* Bernard Malamud's *The Natural* and *The Assistant;* Saul Bellow's *Dangling Man, The Victim,* and *The Adventures of Augie March;* J. D. Salinger's *The Catcher in the Rye;* Richard Wright's *Native Son;* James Baldwin's *Go Tell It on the Mountain* and *Giovanni's Room;* William Styron's *Lie Down in Darkness;* Joseph Heller's *Catch-22;* John Updike's *Rabbit, Run;* Mary McCarthy's *The Oasis* and *The*

Groves of Academe; John Barth's *The Floating Opera;* Vance Bourjaily's *The Violated;* Philip Roth's *Letting Go;* Jack Kerouac's *On the Road;* and Thomas Pynchon's *V.*

The list is not, of course, exhaustive. Nor was every novelist a young Jewish male. But even those who did not fit the dominant ethnic profile shared certain attributes in their work. They wrote of and for the present, used mainly urban (New York) settings, and often featured an alienated protagonist at odds with the prevailing norms of conformity and consumerism. Rebels and disaffected outsiders included: Holden Caulfield, Yossarian, Rojack, Benny Profane, Harry Angstrom, Augie March, Todd Andrews, Sal Paradise. . . .

This is not a history of the postwar novel, however, and I will not go on at length about this period. My intent is simply to set up a background against which the tendencies of the present may be seen more clearly. For as I've suggested, the contemporary novelist seems to have a very different orientation. The Great American Novel—even the ambition of it—has become a kind of joke. (Maybe everything had changed by 1973, when Philip Roth published a minor piece of fiction entitled *The Great American Novel.*) Its former avatars, most of them grown into and beyond respected middle age, have given up that dream. Bellow writes clattery little novellas, Roth has moved into postmodernist privacies, Heller plies a tired black humor, Mailer shuttles between ancient Egypt and the lowlife of Provincetown. . . . The great majority of serious novels published today say little of the city or the events on our television screens. Young Jewish males are no longer the mainstay of the art—if there has been a dominant emergent force it is women, black and white. All is changed, changed utterly.

What befell the novel was life. The falcon got away from the falconer; the center gave way. In her celebrated essay "Mr. Bennett and Mrs. Brown," Virginia Woolf wrote that ". . . on or about December, 1910, human character changed." I would change *character* to *history,* and assert, further, that at ever-shorter intervals our history—rather, our collective experience of our times—undergoes a major transformation. I don't know about 1910. But surely in about 1968—the year of Chicago, King, Kennedy—we fell together into a phantasmic public dream, which lasted until 1972, or 1973, at which point we woke up to find that the long night had changed everything.

.   .   .   .

SVEN BIRKERTS

For a short time we had a shared sense of urgency, a quickening that came from the illusion that we were making history with our own hands. Then, abruptly, it was over. A vacuum pump drew the charge from the atmosphere, and left behind a sickly dread. The shame of Vietnam, of Watergate, of a presidential resignation, and pardon—even the Beatles broke up. To be sure, there is no accounting for the myriad particulars of public history and their interpenetration. But public history impinges upon private initiative, and the change was all too plain. Out of the dream had come powerful and sui generis extrusions—*Why Are We in Vietnam?*, *Portnoy's Complaint* and *Our Gang*, *Gravity's Rainbow*, *A Hall of Mirrors*, *Slaughterhouse Five*, *them*, and, tardily, *Humboldt's Gift*. Then it was over.

Indeed, to draw the dividing line, we could say that *Humboldt's Gift* (1975) was the last big novel of the old dispensation—the last novel that still assumed a listening culture, that broached serious ideas and played for big stakes. Bellow's subject was, broadly speaking, the place of the artist in an increasingly soulless culture—his Von Humboldt Fleischer was based upon his late friend the poet Delmore Schwartz—but for all his indictments of a civilization gone bankrupt, he ended the novel with the puzzlingly optimistic emblem of the season's first crocus. Probably Bellow intended this hint of renewal to apply only to the fortunes of his narrator; if he was referring more inclusively to artistic culture, I would have to demur. Certainly fiction of the sort he had championed—and practiced—was headed into seasons of drought. The world was now too much with us.

This brings us back to Philip Roth's observation and its appropriation by Wolfe: "The actuality is continually outdoing our talents, and the culture tosses up figures daily that are the envy of any novelist." For Wolfe this circumstance is the perfect justification for the New Journalism, which, in his cosmos, then becomes a template for the future development of the novel. But I would read a different meaning into Roth's statement. He is not merely pointing to the existence of extraordinary, outsized figures on our common public landscape—he is, I think, referring also to the shattering of the context that might explain them. He is saying, in other words, that there is no usable connection between public effects and the causes that have spawned them. The system has, in this sense, broken down. Reality has outstripped the writer in that it has outstripped his assumptions about what makes sense. The real has become surreal. Some bonding element in the social order has crumbled away, shivering our picture of public life into fragments. Watergate long ago proved that the social contract was a tissue of lies and evasions, and that government ran on fear and self-interest; assassinations pointed to the retributive violence alive in the American heart. All heroism leaked out of political life, and with it all confidence in solid goals and purposes. The strain of counterculture solidarity that had run through the liberal-democratic part of the culture gave way to narcissistic self-protection. And on and on.

The rise of the New Journalism—the triumphant application of fictional strategies to the retailing of factual, or actual, matters—coincided directly with the appearance of minimalism. Wolfe: "The Minimalists, also known as the K-Mart Realists, wrote about real situations, but very tiny ones, tiny domestic ones for the most part, usually in Rustic Septic Tank Rural settings, in a deadpan prose composed of disingenuously short, simple sentences—with emotions anaesthetized, given a shot of novocaine." He means, presumably, writers like Ann Beattie, Bobbie Ann Mason, Frederick Barthelme, Barry Hannah, Amy Hempel, Mary Robison, Jay McInerney, and the dozen and a half short-story writers who hastened down the same road.

The reasons for the rise of minimalism seem obvious enough. Where the larger crystal has been shattered, one fastens upon the individual shards. If the culture has become too fragmented and distracted to support the coherent structure necessary for a novel of some scale, then deal with what is there. If the rhythms and recognitions of private life are shaped by television, then present a televisual prose of quips and quick cuts.

But minimalism is so easy to beat up on, and it has pretty much passed from currency. Wolfe wastes far too much energy scoring off easy points at its expense. Indeed, one might say that he has set the trend up as a straw man to avoid confronting the real developments of the last decade. For these, as we shall see, argue strongly against his own prescription for the American novel.

* * *

The received wisdom about American culture and, by extension, the American novel, is that pluralism reigns; that this is, further, partly the natural consequence of a diversified body politic, and partly the fate of all artistic enterprise in a postmodern era. For what is postmodernism but the ongoing wake of all entrenched *isms*? Where there is no God, everything is permitted. Where there is no one necessary artistic style, styles of the possible will flourish. And indeed, at first glance we see no one strain or aesthetic that can be identified as governing the others. Tour the fiction shelves of your local bookstore—every author and trend comes brightly and insistently blurbed. The new this, the most exciting that. Who will choose between the competing covers, between minimalist, regionalist, postmodernist, traditionalist, feminist, and punk authors of genius (I have even seen one young talent touted as a *post*-postmodernist)?

As it happens, the situation is not as impossible as it first appears. A big part of the confusion has to do with the cataract of hype that comes pouring out from the offices of publicists. If we believe what we read in the ads, blurbs, and jacket notes, then the authentic voice of our times has several hundred incarnations and can presently be found lounging in cafés from Baton Rouge to Joliet. But if we are willing to cock a more cynical eye, to ignore the frosting and assume instead that originality and quality are always scarce commodities, if we are willing, that is, to just plunge in and read, a very different picture begins to emerge.

I imagine the report of a literate extraterrestrial who has come to research our culture by reading our novels. His report home might run as follows: "These Americans are a sad and lonely people. They live in small cities and towns and on farms, and they think a great deal about the past. The men work at manual trades. They like to drink and spend their time with other men; they often engage in acts of violence. The women are concerned with families and relationships, and they are not much happier than the men. The American blacks do not have much contact with the white people; they, too, have a great interest in stories about the past. In general, Americans black and white care little about life in other countries, or politics and the processes of government. They are not involved with science; they do not like to talk about ideas. They are very often alone in rooms or else driving in cars. . . ."

And indeed, the most striking—and paradoxical—fact about the American novel since 1975 is that it has almost nothing to do with the cultural life of the present. Most of the novels—the artistically significant novels, that is—could as easily have been written in the 1950s. And even those that *do* situate themselves in the near present, as does a novel like Russell Banks's recent *Affliction,* usually have as settings towns and backwater places that are relatively unscarred by postmodern and postindustrial transformations (Banks's drama is played out in a small New Hampshire town, in a world of bars, pickup trucks, and hunting lodges). How few contemporary works even allude to Vietnam, Watergate, the social upheavals of the late 1960s, international politics, or technological change. Insofar as this literature can be said to represent the collective psyche, we are, as a nation, fully turned away from the agitations of our historical moment.

These novels of our mainstream—I will treat of exceptions later—can be seen to fall into three basic categories. There are, to begin with, the rural, small-town (or small-city) narratives that look back to an earlier time: Larry Woiwode's *Beyond the Bedroom Wall,* Joan Chase's *During the Reign of the Queen of Persia,* William Kennedy's Albany trilogy—*Legs, Billy Phelan's Greatest Game,* and *Ironweed*—Joyce Carol Oates's *You Must Remember This,* Pete Dexter's *Paris Trout,* Alfred Alcorn's *The Pull of the Earth,* Wallace Stegner's *Angle of Repose* and *Crossing to Safety,* Peter Matthiessen's *Killing Mister Watson,* Richard Russo's *Mohawk,* Reynolds Price's *Kate Vaiden,* Douglas Bauer's *Dexterity,* Richard Ford's *A Piece of My Heart,* Larry McMurtry's *Lonesome Dove* and *Texasville,* Jim Harrison's *Dalva.* . . .

Alongside these, similar in retrospective preoccupation but differing in that they take a more panoramically or lyrical-mythic approach: David Bradley's *The Chaneysville Incident* and Toni Morrison's *Sula, Tar Baby, The Song of Solomon,* and *Beloved,* which create often epical narratives out of the tragic history of American blacks; Louise Erdrich's *The Beet Queen* and *Love Medicine,* and T. Coraghessan Boyle's *World's End,* which chronicle the collisions between white and Native American cultures across several generations; and E. L. Doctorow's heightened historical retellings, including *World's Fair* and *Billy Bathgate.*

. . . .

SVEN BIRKERTS

Finally, there are the many works that take families and relationships as their central pivot: Anne Tyler's *Breathing Lessons* and *Dinner at the Homesick Restaurant* (to name just two of her novels), Marilynne Robinson's *Housekeeping*, Alice Walker's *The Color Purple*, Susan Minot's *Monkeys*, Mona Simpson's *Anywhere But Here*, Andre Dubus's *Voices from the Moon*, David Shield's *Dead Languages*, Charles Baxter's *First Light*, Amy Tan's *The Joy Luck Club*, Sue Miller's *The Good Mother* and *Family Pictures*, James Salter's *Light Years*, Lynne Sharon Schwartz's *Rough Strife*, *Disturbances in the Field*, and *Leaving Brooklyn*, and much of the oeuvre of Gail Godwin and Joyce Carol Oates.

Some mention must be made, of course, of the styles and voices of this prose, for the presentation on the page determines what imprint the subject will leave upon the reader. As might be expected, the novelists of the rural-retrospective persuasion favor a straight-on approach, a style of masculine understatement that is the closest thing our literature has to a norm. Commonalities notwithstanding, however, the individual signatures are distinct, with much variation in nuance. An excerpt from Russell Banks's *Affliction*, which occupies the same tonal register as the prose of Kennedy, Russo, Oates, and Matthiessen, shows a hard-working sentence-by-sentence construction that sustains an edge that is Banks's alone:

> He checked the time, ran his tongue across mossy teeth, reached for a cigarette and lit it and lay in bed for a few moments, hands under his head, smoking and running a fragmentary narrative of the end of last night in front of his eyes. Sitting in the dark by the window in his office at the town hall. Driving out to Toby's Inn in his car. Slumping silently in a booth with Jack Hewitt and his girlfriend, Hettie Rogers, and three or four other men and women, and later, his toothache anaesthetized by alcohol, yakking and laughing in a loud hearty voice with one or two kids he knew only vaguely. Then drinking at the bar alone, and at last, just before the sudden blackness at the end of the loop, standing in the parking lot, examining his pale-green car as if it were a stranger's, finding it unaccountably ugly. Then nothing.

The prose is finely constructed, but it *is* constructed. While plot is important, it is not always foremost; it functions also as a kind of frame upon which the writer can hang these moments of verisimilitude. For these novels are as much about the texture of the real as they are about the lives imagined.

The more expansive mythic strain derives directly from the story-telling tradition, having taken on an infusion of energy from the magical-realism mode made popular by Gabriel García Márquez. The tales are often improbable, featuring uncanny coincidences and convergences of fates. In the opening section of Louise Erdrich's *The Beet Queen,* for instance, a young mother abandons her children for good at a small-town fair—she climbs into the stunt pilot's plane and gets lofted away:

> Without a backward look, without a word, with no warning and no hesitation, she elbowed through the people collected at the base of the grandstand and stepped into the cleared space around the pilot. I looked at The Great Omar for the first time. The impression he gave was dashing, like his posters. The orange scarf was knotted at his neck and certainly he had some sort of moustache . . . The plane lurched forward, lifted over the low trees, gained height. The Great Omar circled the field in a low swoop and I saw my mother's long red crinkly hair spring from its tight knot and float free in an arc that seemed to reach out and tangle around his shoulders.

This prose is imaginative in its spinning of narrative threads, but fairly matter-of-fact in its descriptions—as though a sober tone will better persuade us of marvels. It can, however, in the more breathless passages of a David Bradley or Toni Morrison, soar toward lyric crescendo:

> There is a loneliness that can be rocked. Arms crossed, knees drawn up; holding, holding on, this motion, unlike a ship's, smooths and contains the rocker. It's an inside kind—wrapped tight like a skin. Then there is a loneliness that roams. No rocking can hold it down. It is alive, on its own. A dry and spreading thing that makes the sound of one's own feet going seem to come from a far-off place.
>
> —from *Beloved*, by Toni Morrison

The family and relationship novels, meanwhile, concerned as they are with atmospheres and interactions, tend to allow a far greater variety of stylistic approaches. The directness favored by Sue Miller can be contrasted with the poetic impressionism in James Salter or Lynne Sharon Schwartz or the gripping colloquialism of Alice Walker or the more self-consciously literary brooding of a young writer like David Shields:

> I understand that whenever Demosthenes got a little tongue-tied he'd leave Athens to camp out on the Mediterranean coast where, with pebbles in his mouth, he'd rehearse his oration against the sound of the Aegean sea until his rather unGreek diffidence ceased and words became waves within him. Then he'd return to Athens to deliver a very authoritative, unhesitant speech which always concerned the sanctity of the Greek city-state and never received anything less than unrestrained applause from the rude multitude.
>
> —from *Dead Languages*

The determined aversion to the present—which can also be seen as a turn *toward* the past, the domestic, the nonurban—is the salient attribute of the contemporary American novel. This is not just happenstance, any more than it was happenstance that the work of the first postwar generation was so occupied with the cultural moment. For those writers, many of them first-generation Jewish males, that moment was the ground upon which their battle for ascendency was fought. The terrain (the city) and the struggle itself fascinated—obsessed—them; they set out to chart their arrival as provocatively and memorably as they knew how. The much-quoted opening words of Bellow's *The Adventures of Augie March* sound the announcement:

> I am an American. Chicago born—Chicago, that somber city—and go at things as I have taught myself, free-style, and will make the record in my own way: first to knock, first admitted; sometimes an innocent knock, sometimes a not so innocent.

That particular assimilation war is ended, and with it a chapter in our literature. But there have been other wars, most notably those waged by blacks and women. What is so striking is that the literary fruits of these social and political engagements have taken the form of retrospection. Tracing roots, tracing wounds. Striking, too, is that while the black presence in our ranks of leading novelists is significant, it is mainly black women who are committing their visions to the page. Apart from David Bradley, who wrote one very powerful saga, *The Chaneysville Incident,* Charles Johnson, and the prolific John Edgar Wideman (*Damballah, Sent for You Yesterday . . .*), the black male voice is scarcely to be heard; one whole side of the story is going largely unreported. For the narratives that stream forth from the great many gifted black women writers—Toni Morrison, Alice Walker, Toni Cade Bambara, Gloria Naylor, and others—are not only retrospective attempts to come to terms with history and family relations, but they are significantly centered upon female characters. The males are seen as drifters, gamblers, drunks, and abusers—or else they are absent. Women are the wounded builders, grievers, and nesters; they tell the family stories and shape the histories that will be passed along. These are not dominantly novels of violence and protest, elements so central to the black experience of past decades, so much as of bitter witness and accommodation. They do not miscegenate, electing instead to find the terms of a separate peace.

Similarly, the best energies of the women's writing of the past decades have not gone into novels depicting the social and political side of feminist struggle, but rather into the probing of relationships and family structures. The writers would seem to recognize that the private realm is the seedbed for any larger initiative. They look to the past because they seek to trace the roots of their own awareness of oppression. Novelists like Marilynne Robinson, Sue Miller, Mona Simpson, Anne Tyler, Gail Godwin, Susan Minot, and others train their focus upon the family. The injuries they find are not as a rule isolated instances, but systemic behaviors; characters perpetuate what has been inflicted upon them. The power of a novel like Mona Simpson's *Anywhere but Here* has everything to do with the protagonist's determination to break the bewitching spell her mother has cast, to be *different.* The big picture of the world does not matter much in these novels—living rooms and kitchens are arena enough to host the combats and alliances that shape identity. Together these writers can be said to ratify Carol Gilligan's insight about gender differentiation: "Yet in the different voice of women lies the truth of an ethic of care, the tie between relationship and responsibility, and the origins of aggression in the failure of connection." This observation sheds light not only upon the more domestic preoccupations of women, but it explains a great deal about the recurrent violence in so many of the novels authored by men.

But the question is still before us: why is it that the great majority of our most talented writers are refusing the challenge of the present? What we need, wrote Wolfe, is "a battalion, a brigade, of Zolas to head out into this wild, bizarre, unpredictable, Hog-stomping Baroque country of ours and reclaim it as literary property." The need is there because we are doing nothing of the kind.

I would say that there are two main reasons for this. The first has to do with the extraordinary intractability of the present: it does not work well as either subject matter or setting, at least not for novels of traditional ambition. The Wolfe scenario is far too simplistic. His picture of reality assumes essential continuity; that the present is but a fascinatingly compounded variation upon the past. His suggestion to the writer is no less naive: just go out there in the old Zola way, with pad and pencil, and gather up the material. I have to disagree. A detailed transcription of contemporary settings and status symbols does not adequately reckon up the main features of our world, our *experience* of it. The minimalists tried doing brand names and bumper stickers and failed. Maybe Wolfe gives them such a trouncing because their strategy is not so different from his own.

The fact is that at some point in the not too distant past reality changed. Conditions first, then the *feel* of things. The innumerable pressures put on the social fabric by hitherto unknown circumstances and processes—by communications technologies, computers, international financial networks, the failure of old ideologies—have brought us rather abruptly into the postmodern era. As the social fabric has been rewoven, so has the place of the individual in the family, community, and societal totality been altered. The old constants live only vestigially, certainly within our urban and suburban cultures; familiar relationship patterns have either been erased or complicated beyond immediate recognition. So many writers look to small towns and to the past because the conditions of postmodernity make it so hard to create the viable dramatic situations that the novel seems to require.

Simply: the stuff of our daily reality cannot be captured in language as readily or convincingly as the stuff of former times. A *modem* is not a *rake,* a *cooler* is not a *drink,* and a transcontinental phone conversation between a parent and child is not a face-to-face by the kitchen sink. Most of us now pass most of our time at a remove from what might be called the primary props of life. We don't farm, work with our hands, or even engage in comprehensible sorts of occupations. We live in condo units and suburban enclaves that have been carved from the wilds; we spend our hours punching plastic keys on terminals, hiking through malls, or driving along lonely highways in our cars. To set drama in the present, a writer must be able to summon the present to the page. To the degree that Wolfe managed this in *Bonfire,* he did so by simplifying and caricaturing; his New York is an anthology of stage sets, and his characters are types. Whether other writers will, in time, find more searching ways to deal with the diffuse and distracting materials of postmodernity remains to be seen.

The second reason is somewhat more speculative, and for this we need an assist from Henry James. James wrote, in 1879, apropos of Nathaniel Hawthorne: "History, as yet, has left in the United States but so thin and impalpable a deposit that we very soon touch the hard substratum of nature." More than a century old, James's statement might yet prove the defining one for American fiction. For there is still at the core of our republic a powerful tradition vacuum. If we go back three generations, we are with the pioneers. The present may appear all plate glass and molded plastic, but there is a sense that it is yet a frail extrusion. Our writers know this and respond. Many may not write about the present because they don't trust it to be real. Indeed, history has so far outrun our ability to assimilate its changes that art is forced to lag. The old notion of the novel being a mirror held up to society is no longer tenable; a better metaphor is that of the delayed echo.

Our situation is easily expressed: we have a great many writers who can tell us where we've been, and very few who can tell us what is happening now. The few who do, or try, are valuable witnesses;

· · · ·

SVEN BIRKERTS

without their efforts we would lack all purchase on the present, except what is conferred by the popular media.

We might first check in with the senior survivors of the earlier generation of novelists, most of whom at one time or another took a shot at the Great American Novel. The recent returns are, I have to say, disappointing. Saul Bellow, whom I once would have called the undisputed king of the hill, has fallen short in recent novels. *Humboldt's Gift* delivered on all of the promise of the earlier work, but since that novel the Bellow voice has become ever more querulous. The last two novels, *A Theft* and *The Bellarosa Connection,* are wooden in their manipulation of characters and conceits; they lack entirely the hothouse blossoming of ideas that made the earlier work so thrilling. Walker Percy, who was, with Bellow, one of the few American novelists willing to bring ideas into his work, recently passed away—an enormous loss. Norman Mailer, after publishing *Ancient Evenings,* his bombastic novel about dynastic Egypt, and his alimony-maker, *Tough Guys Don't Dance,* has added nothing new to our vision of ourselves in late-century America.

John Updike, ever elegant and thoughtful, and fully capable of catching the present in the nets of his style, has gone too far in the direction of ironic playfulness in recent work. His fiction holds none of the density or weight of his autobiographical reflections. It remains to be seen whether the fourth panel of the Rabbit saga will make a serious finish for his ongoing portrait of Harry Angstrom. Meanwhile, John Barth has surrendered himself entirely to his storytelling muse; his megalithic novels, like *The Tidewater Tales,* spin widening loops out of the present and back into the tradition; we glimpse our times, but they are as a mere shimmer on the scales of some ancient and archetypal creature. Philip Roth? Present, but oddly unaccounted for: the Zuckerman project became a postmodern phantasmagoria of creators becoming characters, and vice versa, while the latest novel, *Deception,* was but a soft play of voices in a carpeted bedroom.

This brings us to our less established novelists of more idiosyncratic bent. The talent pool is enormous, and includes writers like Bruce Duffy, Jay Cantor, Paul West, Susan Daitch, David Leavitt, Paul Auster, David Markson, Nicholson Baker, Larry Heinemann, Brad Leithauser, and others. But while these are all stylists of a high order, none could be said to have grappled face-on with the Zeitgeist.

. . . .

A few have dared approaches. Larry Heinemann gives us bursts of Vietnam, via flashback, in *Paco's Story;* Paul Auster tries to recreate something of the atmosphere of the late sixties in New York in his coming-of-age tale, *Moon Palace.* But most of the other novelists work obliquely, resorting to fictional biographies (like Duffy's Wittgenstein portrait in *The World As I Found It,* Cantor's *The Death of Che Guevara,* West's *Rat Man of Paris* and *The Very Rich Hours of Count von Stauffenberg*), cartoon worlds (like Cantor's *Krazy Kat* or Daitch's *The Colorist,* about a young woman who makes her living filling in cartoon panels), or a postmodern displacement onto other genres (like Auster's existential detective stories in his *New York Trilogy;* Markson's voice collage, *Wittgenstein's Mistress*). Not one of these novelists has yet produced the big synthesis of the present that might throw the shivers of recognition down a reader's spine.

The good news, of course, must wait for the end. There are three novelists currently at work who *are* connecting, who have given—and keep giving—the essential record: Don DeLillo, Thomas Pynchon, and Robert Stone. They are alone. Interestingly, Wolfe mentions only Stone, and then just in passing, in his account. Possibly their work is too threatening to his program, for they accomplish in the old true way—via fictional creation—what he would essay with the tools of journalism.

DeLillo has been publishing his novels for twenty years now, moving his way steadily forward through the ranks. He is a superb mimic, highly adept at catching the voices and manners of latter-day Americans. His earlier novels, like *Ratner's Star, Great Jones Street,* and *Americana,* were too obviously constructed around thematic premises, but with *White Noise* and *Libra* he has made powerful statements about our culture at large. *White Noise* is his best work to date, a sublime farce playing out his characters' fears of death and identity loss against an only slightly amplified present. DeLillo has a sure grasp of the implications of our technologies and bureaucracies, and he can pitch his prose in a way that is at once hilarious and horrifying:

> Steffie took my hand and we walked past the fruit bins, an area that extended about forty-five yards along one wall. The bins were arranged diagonally and backed by mirrors that people

accidentally punched when reaching for fruit in the upper rows. A voice on the loudspeaker said: "Kleenex Softique, your truck's blocking the entrance." Apples and lemons tumbled in twos and threes to the floor when someone took a fruit from certain places in the stacked array. There were six kinds of apples, there were exotic melons in several pastels. Everything seemed to be in season, sprayed, burnished, bright. People tore filmy bags off racks and tried to figure out which end opened. I realized the place was awash in noise. The toneless systems, the jangle and skid of carts, the loudspeaker and coffee-making machines, the cries of children. And over it all, or under it all, a dull and unlocatable roar, as of some form of swarming life just outside the range of human apprehension.

—from *White Noise*

Pynchon shares many of the same preoccupations with DeLillo— he is intent upon finding the black hole at the heart of the contemporary. *Vineland,* while easier and more benevolent than the apocalyptic gargantua *Gravity's Rainbow,* is nonetheless obsessed with the soullessness and distractedness that have overtaken American life. He can deal lightly with our gadgets and malls and video fantasies, but he shows no mercy to bureaucratized evil and our betraying politicians. Pynchon's prose, like DeLillo's, is tuned to the pitch of a changed reality:

"Ooo-wee! No-o-o mercy!" This was their star-and-sidekick routine, going back to when they were little, playing Bionic, Police, or Wonder Woman. A teacher had told Prairie's class once to write a paragraph on what sports figure they wished they could be. Most girls said something like Chris Evert. Prairie said Brent Musberger. Each time they got together, it suited her to be the one to frame and comment on Che's roughhouse engagements with the world, though more than once she'd been called on for muscle, notably during the Great South Coast Plaza Eyeshadow Raid, still being talked about in tones of wounded bewilderment at security seminars nationwide, in which two dozen girls, in black T-shirts and jeans, carrying empty backpacks and riding on roller skates, perfectly acquainted with every inch of the terrain, had come precision whirring and ticking into the giant

Plaza just before closing time and departed only moments later with the packs stuffed full of eyeshadows, mascaras, lipsticks, earrings, barrettes, bracelets, pantyhose, and fashion shades, all of which they had turned immediately for cash from an older person named Otis, with a panel truck headed for a swap meet far away.

The referential swirl is unremitting; the reader gets a ride over the peaks and troughs of the American landscape that no assemblage of monitors could quite duplicate.

Robert Stone is not nearly so tuned to the distractions of the postmodern surface. His eye is fixed upon the deeper—perennial—struggles, and he is determined to find out on what grounds meaning is still possible. The characters in his novels drink, take drugs, and suffer, and, like the characters in Graham Greene's world, whom they at times recall, search for God. Stone is one of the very few who, along with being concerned with ultimates, is also mindful of the larger political reality—with the fact that the United States does not live in the splendid isolation of an earlier era. Stone is a shrewd portrayer of character—he knows the sweats and anxieties of his marginal men and women—and a dramatizer of genuine power. His *A Flag for Sunrise,* an existential-political thriller set in the fictitious Central American country of Tecan, has a range of concern that dwarfs most contemporary efforts. Stone forges a prose that can hug the contours of the daily as well as activate the thoughts and impulses of his characters; when necessary, he will rise toward a more prophetic pitch:

> Holliwell did not sleep although he lay in bed until dawn. In the slant of the new sun he drove to the mission, parked and walked the narrow beach.
>
> The sight of the ocean oppressed him. He was not deceived by its exquisite sportiveness—the lacy flumes of breaking wave, the delicate rainbows in the spray. He knew what was spread out beneath its trivial entertainments. The ocean at its morning business brought cognate visions to his mind's eye; a flower-painted cart hauling corpses, a bright turban on a leper.
>
> Beside the beach at Danang he had seen a leper with a "Kiss

Me" tee shirt. There was nothing to get angry about; some stern wit had made a statement and the leper had got a shirt.

For a long time Holliwell stood by the water. A few yards away under the slate-blue rollers, the universe was being most spontaneously itself. Its play dazzled. It beguiled temporal flesh with promises and it promised all things from petty cheer to cool annihilation.

Here it is, then, the talent in the room. Large mainstream, tiny fringe contingent. I don't think that we need to choose between them, for we cannot do without either. The mainstream writers are plumbing a past—recent yet remote—in which the wild transformations of the present lay dormant. They are creating a tradition and a memory-record without which we would fly away. Because for all of its superficial chaos and glitter, America is still very much the place that Henry James remarked—snatch the topsoil away, and the blank gaze of Nature stares you out. But that chaos of surface is nonetheless real, and the filtering of the present, its deeper currents and tendencies, cannot be left to Hollywood and the nightly news. More of our younger writers need to take the risk of turning their art upon the present. Battalions and brigades would be wonderful. But they would have to do more than inventory our dubious tokens of status. Their job would be to start reassembling the shattered crystal, fitting pieces together to create a whole that matters.

" The Talent in the Room—Postscript"

In reading and reviewing contemporary fiction, I am repeatedly struck by the fact that few—almost none—of the works make any effort to address the phenomenon of the sixties. I mean the counterculture in its various facets—protest, drugs, alternative lifestyles, sexual experimentation, rock and roll . . . No list of components adequately describes what happened, but anyone who had reached the age of sentience by 1968 or thereabouts knows that something remarkable took place within the culture as a whole. We experienced, for better or worse, a sustained tremor of the collective unconscious. Everyone was implicated, those who moved with the surge and those who resisted. To say that "something was in the air" scarcely captures the sensation. For many people it was as if the public order and the private order had converged. Maybe the best analogy would be to that painfully sensitized period that comes in late adolescence when the largest questions of meaning and purpose are suddenly magnified, that period when the individual takes a reading on the future that often proves decisive. The sixties have become such a point of reference for an entire generation, even though many of the habits and attitudes have been repudiated.

It is interesting, then, how few of our writers have turned their attention to the period. Part of the reason, I suspect, is that the inner life of those times is so difficult to register in words. So much of it had to do with the inchoate sensations that were induced by music, drugs, and the camaraderie of quasi-tribal social rituals. The naturalistic transcription of counterculture doings, mostly in movies, has resulted either in parodic kitsch or else something resembling cultural anthropology. The inner magic, and disturbance, are not there.

Among our writers, only Robert Stone, Don DeLillo, and Thomas Pynchon have found ways to incorporate the period, its energies and contradictions, into their fiction. They have all recognized in that brief cultural interlude a condensation of our fundamental nature. The sixties were a vivid and phantasmagoric dream, one that they happen to find relevant to our waking condition. It is no coincidence, either, that each of these writers has what might be called a "paranoid" sensibility. Paranoia is the logical response to a true understanding of power and its diverse pathologies. Paranoia is what happened when the illusions of the counterculture collapsed and the true extent of the political web became apparent. Paranoia is what truth comes to sound like in a society given over to distraction, spectacle, and the bromides of public relations. The work of these three novelists is the thread of sanity that we will need if we are to escape from the labyrinth with our souls intact.

SVEN BIRKERTS

Paranoids
and Intellectuals:
Keepers of the Flame

The reader should be aware that there is a lapse of over a year between the writing of "The Talent in the Room" and "Paranoids and Intellectuals." If allowances are made for certain necessary recurrences in the basic structure of the argument, as well as for the inevitable shifts of perspective that come with additional reading and thinking, then the two can be taken together as the panels of a diptych.

It has become a tiresome subject, and I feel more than a little perverse bringing it up. Still, there is more to be said—much more—so let me begin. American fiction, the genre, is in a muddle. I specify *genre* because the problem does not have to do so much with the works themselves, which are various and often excellent, but with the form itself. And to contain the generalizing impulse, if only slightly, I will specify still further: It is the American *novel* that is in a state of muddle.

How can I say this? How can I, at one and the same time, suggest that there is no shortage of worthy works *and* express concern for the art? In the same way, I suppose, that one can point to the large numbers of affluent citizens and still assert that the economy is in trouble. It is a question of the big picture, the center; it involves the disorientation that every serious novelist must feel when he or she tries to get a fix on the meaning or worth of the novelist's enterprise. Simply, there is a pervasive and anxiety-inducing sense of drift, an awareness on the part of reader and writer alike of an attenuating communication. The reader no longer expects to encounter a challenging vision of life as it is really experienced, and the writer is no longer sure how to present an encompassing and relevant picture of things as they are. The ink on the old contract is fading.

This is not a new or sudden development. My sense is that the current condition has been several decades in the making. As far back as the 1960s we heard laments that the American novel was exhausted, finished; that it had moved into minor and academic modes, had divorced itself from political and social realities, and so on. Indeed, these plaints came at a time when other literatures—Latin American and Eastern European, especially—were bourgeoning. We heard the same song, with slightly different words, during the seventies and eighties, when minimalist modes became the fashion.

The culmination of disaffection was reached two years ago, when Tom Wolfe launched his widely discussed broadside, "Stalking the Billion-Footed Beast: A Literary Manifesto for the New Social Novel," in the pages of *Harper's* magazine. Wolfe declared in no uncertain terms that American fiction writers—he mainly discussed novelists—had capitulated to reality. That the rough and rowdy facts of the world had overpowered them into submission, forcing a retreat into self-reflexive, self-indulgent, and generally self-defeating postures. Our writers had handed over their authority to journalists and other purveyors of the documentary—a major mistake. And Wolfe urged as a solution a return to the example of the nineteenth-century social novel. There he had found inspiration for his own colossally successful *The Bonfire of the Vanities,* and other writers could help themselves to the same well.

Though he was wrong about the solution—and I hope my reasons for saying so will emerge shortly—Wolfe was, I think, right about the problem, which is a problem of representation. How to render in words a convincing picture of reality. The answer, alas, is not to call for more representation. It is reality that has changed. And the problem is that to this day the aesthetic identity of the American novel remains largely tethered to the basic premise of nineteenth-century realism. Though a few brave souls have made a go at incorporating modernist approaches—including fragmented or multiple narratives, interior monologues, ambitious referentiality, and the like—the majority have stayed with the staple orientations of realism. Whether this is owing to some peculiar warp in the collective creative disposition, or is simply a reflection of the demands of the marketplace—give readers what they want or risk failure—is hard to say. But the fact remains that even now, in the early 1990s, our fiction is overwhelmingly realistic in approach. Whatever other ambition a novel may have, its principal means are a development of credibly rounded characters and a narrative that would simulate a coherent-seeming exterior order.

This is not, in and of itself, a problem. There is nothing intrinsically wrong with the realist procedure, and in skilled hands the results can still be persuasive. The problem lies elsewhere. It lies in the fact that our common reality has gradually grown out of the reach of the realist's instruments. We live our late-century lives less and less in the foursquare world of surfaces and bounded events that realism evolved to depict. Our business is increasingly with a new experiential hybrid. We live among signals and impulses and processes that our language has a hard time capturing. Our consciousness is mapped to a new field, and the contours of that field are determined by the way we spend our days. We don't talk over the fence, but over the phone—worse, we leave messages on machines and check in to see if our messages have been returned. Our professional lives are likewise shorn of clear boundaries—most of us interact more with buttons and digits than with people. We drive, park, drive again, surrounding ourselves during bubble time with a distracting environment of music or talk-show barking. Dinner? Often as not we nuke it in the microwave before kicking back with a well-deserved night in front of the VCR.

If I present a caricature, it's to drive home a point: that the ambient drift of our dailyness is not exactly fodder for the novelist. We fight traffic, not duels. An accurate depiction of our doings would involve inordinately extensive descriptions of downtime—outwardly dull and routinized movements. And I don't know how much more of dramatic interest a cutaway view of our inner lives would provide. The spread sheet, worries about the MasterCard bill, a bit of flirtation at the deli counter . . .

What I'm saying is not new or revolutionary, though I don't hear it verbalized all that often. Way back in 1963, in an essay entitled

"Mass Society and Post-Modern Fiction," Irving Howe was quoting critic Stanley Kauffmann as follows:

> When Vittorio de Sica was asked why so many of his films deal with adultery, he is said to have replied, "But if you take adultery out of the lives of the bourgeoisie, what drama is left?" . . . It is the continuing problem of the contemporary writer who looks for great emotional issues to move him greatly. The anguish of the advertising executive struggling to keep his job is anguish indeed, but its possibilities in art are not large-scale. The writer who wants to "let go" has figuratively to leave the urban and suburban and either go abroad, go into the past, or go into those few pockets of elemental emotional life left in this country.

This was written nearly thirty years ago. Urbanization and suburbanization have been supplemented by the rampant incursions of labor-saving technologies and electronic communications. The problem of the writer who would represent the world and do so with some artistic tension has become all but insurmountable. It will only intensify as we march deeper into late modernity (or wherever it is that we are marching). Very few writers have the narrative gifts and perceptual resources to make readable fiction out of the real stuff of our daily experience. John Updike is one of the very few, and it is precisely for this that *Rabbit at Rest* is important—it is a kind of "limit text" for the contemporary realist.

And what of the others, those who lack Updike's special alchemizing gifts? Most of the rest have taken one of the available paths indicated by Kauffmann. They have steered to one side or another of the great challenge—to find a shape for the experiences and sensations of our historical moment—in order to find a way to tell a satisfying story. And while many have succeeded at this, it is fiction itself that has paid a price. Fiction is now just an adjunct to the cultural life, an entertainment or a private vice. It is no longer the powerful medium of exploration and reflection that it used to be. And this is a shame.

The much-maligned movement of minimalism may have been the first real signal of the crisis in the genre. What was, or is, distinctive about minimalism, apart from its fetishistic attention to the brand-

name specifics of our social environment—as if these, properly de-
coded, might tell a story of their own—is the use of the gap. The
unstated. The way of cutting from one rendered moment or situation
to another that would confer some eloquence or suggestiveness to
the absent material. It seems clear now that this was a logical first
response to the elusive and random-feeling materials of modern life.
The plan was to hint the presence of these great zones of the inchoate—the vacancies and anxious spells of distraction—without trying
to pin them down or name them. We should note, by the way, the
difference between the vaporized minimalism of an Ann Beattie and
the laconic repressions of a Hemingway. For the latter, the unstated
was a solid presence, a specific emotion or complex of emotions to
be avoided—he knew, and we know, what was being left out. For
Beattie and her cohort, however, minimalism became a way of not
dealing with that which could not be dealt with—the thousand and
one grades of anomie that may not have existed fifty or a hundred
years ago.

Minimalism, for all the excitement it generated in the workshop
communities of the 1970s and 1980s, failed with readers. While it
did catch something of the *feel* of contemporary experience, it offered
no purchase. It did not clarify life in the least, but simply added its
impressions of muddle to the muddle we were already living in.

At the opposite pole, we have the much-honored conclusion of
the *Rabbit* tetralogy. Updike appeared to exult in the challenge he had
set himself: to fashion resonance from the unremarkable materials of
the cultural present. And to a remarkable degree, he succeeded,
though, interestingly, the power and poignance of *Rabbit at Rest* arise
less from his evocations of the present and much more from their
constant, often implicit, contrast to the way things used to be. Rabbit's appetite for nostalgia is mighty—it is what makes him a poet:

> Rabbit feels betrayed. He was reared in a world where war was
> not strange but change was: the world stood still so you could
> grow up in it. He knows when the bottom fell out. When they
> closed Kroll's, Kroll's that had stood in the center of Brewer all
> those years, bigger than a church, older than the courthouse,
> right at the head of Weiser Square there, with every Christmas
> those otherworldly displays of circling trains and nodding dolls

and twinkling stars in the corner windows as if God Himself put them there to light the darkest time of the year.

The *now* has been annexed, but from an angle. We see it always against Rabbit's private rue at what is gone—it has not been carried, flailing and kicking, into the arena of representation.

But by and large, as I observed, we are back with the options as set out by Stanley Kauffmann in the early 1960s. The vast majority of serious American novels fall into one (or several) of a very few categories. Of course, each category is vital in its own way, but each also represents a strategic way of avoiding head-on confrontation with the present—with the world as it has become. Now—and I jump in ahead of myself—I do *not* mean to suggest that rural or small-town settings are not part of the here and now, or that family relations are not universally contemporary. But I do believe that there are energies and currents that we all understand as more essentially of our moment. These intangible and elusive components of our *Zeitgeist* are what pose the problem. They have everything to do with our present situation and what is likely to arise from it. They are what is largely missing from the novels of our most distinguished writers.

As Kauffmann suggested, the menu of options is finally quite limited. Most of our best novelists are writing about either (a) rural or small-town life, (b) the near past (the last fifty years, say), (c) families, or (d) the historical or mythologized past. Obviously the categories will combine and cross-fertilize, with family novels having rural settings, and so on.

Now consider this list of American novelists: Reynolds Price, Russell Banks, Anne Tyler, Toni Morrison, Wallace Stegner, Larry Woiwode, Joyce Carol Oates, Louise Erdrich, T. Coraghessan Boyle, E. L. Doctorow, Sue Miller, Andre Dubus, William Kennedy, John Barth, Saul Bellow, Marilynne Robinson, Alice Walker, Jane Smiley, Mona Simpson, Pete Dexter, John Casey, Peter Matthiesen, William Styron, James Salter, Evan S. Connell, Lynne Sharon Schwartz, Gail Godwin, David Bradley, Amy Tan, Joan Chase, David Leavitt . . .

I could go on for at least a few more paragraphs, and with every writer I mention I could evoke for myself a particular density and richness of world—Russell Banks's rough and flinty New Hampshire

. . . .

towns, Louise Erdrich's myth-haunted upper Midwest, Toni Morrison's small-town Ohio, etc. But I have to say that when I am disturbed and baffled by the alien structures I glimpse from the car window, or the picture of life I assemble from the evening news, these are not the writers I turn to for understanding. Each presents a world, but none, at least—for me—presents the world as I sense it has become, or is fast becoming. This latter is a world of screens and information vaults, with a population ever more distracted from its cultural roots, ever more alarmed about crime, disease, and security, and uncertain about the meaning of an individual existence in a future that promises to be ruled by the spirits of collectivism and bureaucracy.

In a very real sense, then, our fiction is in retreat, and we have every reason to wonder if authors can, or will, find ways to connect the reader with the dominant forces of the age, most of which threaten our public and private myths of coherence. So long as they do not—or do so only in small numbers—our literature must stand removed from the center of relevance; it must be counted minor.

But of course there are exceptions. Exceptions that, when considered together, give us some warrant for imagining a different future for our fiction, a renewed connectedness. These are writers who have taken the challenge of representing contemporary experience more to heart, and whose art points toward the future in ways which that of their no less gifted peers does not.

The problem, as I have suggested, is not to get the features of present-day reality onto the page—the minimalists accomplished that in their way—but to animate those features and give them some measure of dramatic necessity; to defeat the centrifugal tendency of our postindustrial order. The scatter and distraction of our age are such that even "the anguish of the advertising executive struggling to keep his job" begins to look like a viable subject (at least it has clearly defined contours). The novelists I have in mind have adopted several different strategies for galvanizing the chaos around us. All are ambitious. And they can, with some flourishes of the Procrustean knife, be divided into two groups.

In the first grouping are the novelists I will call, with no pejorative intent, the paranoids. Paranoia, they used to say in the late sixties, is just a heightened state of awareness. These writers find not only a propulsive energy but also a principle of connection, of organization, in their vision of a concealed and dangerous other order. They see behind the random shimmer of surfaces and events a set of vested interests that must advance their ends conspiratorially through political and economic channels. They see the deeper exchanges of our body politic as controlled by the machinations of an elite; the web extends to, and at times embraces, the criminal subculture. And much of the tension in the work of these writers—I am thinking mainly of Robert Stone, Thomas Pynchon, Don DeLillo, and, based on what I've seen so far of his recent magnum opus, Norman Mailer—arises from the contrast between the banal drift of the ordinary and the intuited, or revealed, operations of conspiracy.

To exploit this particular tension, these novelists must create protagonists who somehow encounter the hidden system (which is, I suspect, visualized differently by each writer). Thus, Robert Stone, in A *Flag for Sunrise,* has Frank Holliwell, at once an idle traveler and a reluctant operative, visit Tecan, a fictitious Latin American country that is the site of all the familiar sorts of covert intervention. DeLillo, in *MAO II,* gives us Bill Gray, a reclusive writer who agrees to take part in a hostage-release effort, stirring up a nest of terrorist and antiterrorist intrigue. Pynchon's *Vineland* features a whole gallery of veterans from the counterculture wars of the 1960s, who, working one side of the fence or the other, are still very much caught up in ideological struggles. And Mailer's *Harlot's Ghost,* of course, has the whole CIA family tree shaking in the winds of postwar as well as recent history. Each of these writers, it would seem, has answered the problem of apparent disorder by pushing past the glut of surface signals to claim that whether we know it or not, our fates are significantly controlled by these networks—that they are, in a sense, the deeper reality of the present.

But these are, naturally, very different kinds of writers, with different aims and techniques. DeLillo's sense of conspiracy, for instance—except for *Libra,* his rewriting of the Kennedy assassination—is usually deployed more for impressionistic than investigative or didactic ends. In novels like *White Noise* and *MAO II,* two of his more realized works, the final connections are left dangling; the idea of a hidden order presided over by government cabals and

mysteriously employed free-lancers is there to impart edgy ominous-
ness to the narrative. Interested as he is in secret systems and link-
ups, DeLillo is no less interested in registering the disconnectedness
that comes when sense networks can no longer organize the streams
of oncoming data:

> Then action, bodies moving through the night. Because just as
> she was beginning to doubt and fear and mind-wander, she
> stepped out of the van on a cloud-banded evening and three men
> detached themselves from a playground wall and approached,
> two strangers and her tank-top cousin Rick, a football player
> with a clean-shaven head except for one wavy lock right on top,
> dyed y'know like parrot-green. The other guys wore suits and
> showed a certain weary expertise.

DeLillo is so good at capturing a multiplex culture transected by
obscurely meaningful signals ("a football player with a clean-shaven
head except for one wavy lock right on top . . ."), and so fascinated
by its contemplation, that one begins to suspect that the conspiracy
elements of the narrative may have been woven in mainly to shape
what threatens to become a sprawl of quirkily pointed observations.

Pynchon, especially in *Vineland* (his first novel after a decade
and a half hiatus), seems closer to the DeLillo frequency than the
others. Like DeLillo, Pynchon is mesmerized by the daily surrealism
of our culture. But he is also, as much as or more than DeLillo,
gripped by a vision of the ultimate entwinement of capital, ideology,
technology, and force. A true paranoid, one might say—but only if
one had lived in blissful ignorance of the daily news. Interestingly,
he does not, at least in *Vineland,* make conspiracy his central subject.
He uses it, rather, as the action principle of his narratives—to generate situations and to activate the subtly duplicitous interactions between his main players. But he is always ready to strike away from
the dominant line of the plot and to insert absurd, often truncated
subplots that serve the function of Boschian detail: They augment
the overall impression of reality held in check on the very edge of
hallucination.

Moreover, Pynchon—again like DeLillo—is funny. Indeed, he
is more willing than any of his cohorts to let a perfectly plausible
scene make a sudden U-turn and become preposterous. We can call

this a postmodern playfulness or an uncanny insight into the hidden "logic" of situations. This determination to have it both ways is Pynchon's trademark. Though his final ambition may well be to penetrate the underside of modernity and expose its darkest tendencies, he consistently breaks up his hyperrealistic scenarios with passages of comic-book excess:

> He taught her the Chinese Three Ways, Dim Ching, Dim Hsuen, and Dim Mak, with its Nine Fatal Blows, as well as the Tenth and Eleventh, which are never spoken of. She learned how to give people heart attacks without even touching them, how to get them to fall from high places, and how through the Clouds of Guilt technique to make them commit *seppuku* and think it was their idea . . .

A curious amalgam, but it works. The reader is anchored in the known world through Pynchon's exquisite depictions of the late-modern (or postmodern) surface—the malls, the motels, the high-tech emporiums—and then pulled away into deep-sea dives into the incredible, which is always rendered with just enough cool poise to give pause. The political double-dealing of his Brock Vond and Frenezi Gates are out at the limit of the credible, but on this side; his organization of death-loving Thanatoids, while not far away as the crow flies, is nonetheless on the other side of the border. The task of setting out the line belongs to the reader—it is an apprenticeship in cultural studies.

Stone and Mailer engage the hidden hierarchies of power more directly and via more straightforwardly realistic means. Both have a strong grip on the concrete particulars of bureaucratic process and a shrewd sense of how the individual functions psychologically when confused, compromised, or in some other way tested to the limit. Stone, I would say, is more intent upon revealing the evil insidiousness of power systems, and in showing just how the hapless are victimized. Mailer, though known as an outspoken critic of government policies, is nonetheless more ambivalent. He finds in the complex deceptions and infiltrations of the CIA a subject worthy of his favored "existential" themes, but time and again his fascination bleeds over into something akin to hero-worship. Nevertheless, like Stone, and unlike DeLillo and Pynchon, Mailer would appear to believe that some sort of ultimate sense can be derived from the whole business. As *Harlot's Ghost* ends with the words "TO BE CONTINUED," however, this assessment must remain provisional.

Two other novelists who should be mentioned in or alongside this cluster are Native American novelist Leslie Marmon Silko and black writer John Edgar Wideman. Both are alert to the idea of ulterior power networks, and both interpret it in their work in strongly racial terms. Silko's enormously ambitious novel, *The Almanac of the Dead,* tracks the links between a vast array of characters—from Indian drug smugglers to white power brokers—in the present-day Southwest and Mexico. The sections unfold to depict both the systematic disenfranchisement of the Indian peoples and their large-scale retaliation. Amidst the chaos disclosed by her multifaceted narrative, we glimpse the telltale features of our age. We see how the signals and codes go flickering through the electronic meshes; we get close-up views of the eroded urban fabric and the desperate vices of so many raddled souls.

Wideman, who has for years been writing a more traditional sort of urban portraiture, breaks with precedent in his most recent novel, *Philadelphia Fire*. His protagonist, Cudjoe, wanders the ravages of the Philadelphia ghettos, looking for a child who may have escaped the 1985 MOVE bombings, but also searching through a tangle of broken connections—to old friends and lovers, as well as to the racial solidarity that had promised so much just a few years before. The novel is fragmented, with harsh, expressionistic panels stacked one hard upon the next, but beating in back of the prose is the unforgettable din of helicopters. White man's helicopters dropping ordnance on black people. Cudjoe cannot unravel the systems of power and repression that have brought things to such a pass, but he knows they exist and bears unblinking witness to their consequences.

These same systems, variously interpreted, bind together the often scattered scenarios of the paranoids. While not identified too explicitly—their complexity and reach prohibit it—they nonetheless form the backdrop against which all subsidiary actions take on relief. Whether the paranoia is justified or not—I, for one, believe it is—it fulfills an essential artistic function. It sponsors a literature that, if read seriously, cuts against our growing sense of social and political inconsequence.

.   .   .   .

*   *   *

The other promising trend—if it *is* a trend and not just a collocation of separate works by idiosyncratic talents—is composed of those writers who do not so much seek to provide a picture of the present as to refract an understanding of it through the crystal of the intellect. They are our intellectuals, our novelists of ideas, and what is remarkable is not that they should exist but that there should be so few of them in an age given over to abstract pursuits. The sad fact is that America, unlike Europe, has had a deep and abiding hostility to intellectuality, and that our serious arts reflect it no less than does our mass culture.

Our aesthetic climate notwithstanding, we can point to a hardy group of novelists with a bent toward ideas; many of them, moreover, are fairly young. But where the so-called paranoids manifested certain commonalities, these writers are as diverse as can be in their interests as well as their narrative strategies.

I need to make one other distinction, and that is that the novel of ideas can engage the present without necessarily having *ideas* about it. Our thinking writers are thinking differently than, say, novelists like Saul Bellow and Walker Percy, who both orchestrated their best works around conceptual, even philosophical, investigations of how it is with us in America today. I see no writer who takes on the full contemporary agenda in quite the same way. What we find instead are a number of approaches, all of which are less frontal, less totalizing, but which nonetheless carry a high intellectual charge. The novels may not attempt a full-spectrum panorama of the age, as did, perhaps, novels by Mann, Sartre, Broch, or Beauvoir, but they have several other vital uses. For one thing, they keep the intellectual option alive, and show how complex ideas and mental processes can still find a place in the novel. For another—and this is linked—they give proof that the novel can escape the straitjacket of conventional plotting and take stock of diverse planes of reality, including the inward. They keep the genre open to the currents of serious discourse. The separate endeavors, while not all uniformly successful, may yet pave the way for the great synthesizing works of the future.

The oldest and most anomalous of these novelists is Paul West, a maximalist modernist of great energy and verbal resource. West's intellectuality is not so much deployed in the creation of complex plots or cerebral protagonists, as is the case with some of the others. Rather, it has been put in the service of his novelistic imagination as a whole—it is the very context of his imaginings, the historical peregrinations that carry him from Nazi Germany in *The Very Rich Hours of Count Von Stauffenberg,* to postwar Paris in *Rat Man of Paris,* to Victorian London in *Jack the Ripper and the Women of White-chapel.* His settings are not lightly garnished, but are grasped and held from within. Further, West's prose narratives continually reflect his knowledge of the various practical as well as artistic disciplines. But his real intelligence is stylistic. West is one of a very few novelists committed to the project of translating the densities of consciousness into prose, and he is as convincing in his renditions of low-life characters as in his presentations of the educated and cultured. Here, from the *Jack the Ripper* novel, is West writing about the painter Walter Sickert, whose ambitions for artistic success are somewhat at odds with his appetite for prostitutes:

> For several years now, fired into emulation by hearing an Argentine guitarist speak to women after a performance, he had been polishing and practicing his skills at the *piropo*—the spontaneous and hyperbolical compliment men paid to women, perhaps uttered with some pragmatically lustful intent, but most often floated into the air to cause a surprised smile, a slight change in a woman's gait. His first one had been in a theater lobby, said more for practice than for anything else, although, being Sickert, he always expected the unexpected and was ready to profit by it.

And on and on he goes, not so much making thoughts as discriminations of behavior and intention, creating mental atmospheres, weather systems of language. West's verbal range, and the demands placed on our attention by syntax, as well as the sheer cumulative pressure of sustained interiority, qualify him, if somewhat loosely, for this category.

Norman Rush is far more intellectually referential on the page, and his courtship comedy, *Mating,* features an unnamed narrator with impressive strategies for bringing her wit and learning to bear on her account. Cohabiting with her lover, Denoon, in an experimental village in Botswana, she is apt to tender her observations thus:

.   .   .

There was also the delicate matter of our both being pretty much on the sendero leguminoso, dietarily, as he put it, so that there was some flatulence to deal with, simple flatulence. . . . We developed a fairly decent modus, I thought. He might say, when I was the author, Also sprach Zarathustra, or Ah, a report from the interior, as though he were an ambassador or proconsul.

Mating is a grand and roomy novel. Though its setting is Africa and its intellectual debates—about Marxism and utopian collectivism—are not central to our situation in nineties America, the idiom itself is a revelation. It shows fully and deeply just how our latter-day intellectual movements have imprinted sensibility. The narrator filters the world through a scrim of post-Freudian, post-Marxist, and post-feminist categories, and wears her ironic consciousness like a prophylactic.

A not dissimilar focus upon love among the brainy animates the early novels of Rebecca Goldstein—*The Mind-Body Problem* and *The Late Summer Passion of a Woman of Mind.* Goldstein is a philosopher by training and vocation and her female protagonists follow her lead. Long passages of these works are larded with discussions of language philosophy or Spinoza scholarship. But Goldstein has a way of linking her more scholarly debates with the unfolding crises of feeling in the lives of her characters, and we find ourselves engaged on a number of levels. Her most recent novel, *The Dark Sister,* marks a departure of sorts. Here Goldstein attempts a binary narrative—part historic, part contemporary—where the fates of two pairs of sisters are conceptually intertwined. The novel is undermined by its own hall-of-mirrors cleverness, but it raises important questions about the dilemmas that shape the fate of all free-thinking women.

Likewise philosophical, but with a very different orientation, is Bruce Duffy's *The World As I Found It,* a remarkable novel based on the life and ideas of Ludwig Wittgenstein. It might not seem, at first glance, that an engrossing narrative could be woven from the thoughts and doings of so hermetic an individual. But Duffy pulls it off, not only drawing his reader into the milieux of Vienna and Cambridge, but also uncovering the personal dramas that were the accompaniment to the philosophical revolution Wittgenstein carried out. The tensions are at once interpersonal—Duffy brings Bertrand

Russell, G. E. Moore, and the assorted eminences of Bloomsbury forward as dimensional figures—and cerebral. The author's greatest achievement is to have written a novel that is grounded in philosophy—difficult philosophy—but that reads in a way that the interested nonspecialist can attend.

The World As I Found It is, in a sense, a historical novel. If I include Duffy in my roster of intellectuals, it is because his focus on Wittgenstein short-circuits the merely retrospective tendency of the mode. Indeed, Duffy achieves a peculiarly late-modern resonance by taking a straight-on view of a man who gradually—and mainly posthumously—revolutionized the way we do our intellectual business. We almost feel as though we are watching a film running in reverse as the vast tentacle system of language philosophy draws back to its origins in the thinker and his milieu. Though it could easily be reductive, the result is clarifying—an understanding of the roots of Wittgenstein's philosophy sheds light on the ramified state of contemporary thought.

> Sir, said Wittgenstein, with yet a glimmer of admiration. [He is addressing Moore in a public forum] Your point is certainly *interesting*. But tell me, please, what *material* difference it makes? Whether I am material or immaterial—why should this affect the truth of what I say? If something is true, then it is true. We do not judge its truth by asking by what *medium* does it come to us. Do I say I will not consider your argument because you use *spoken* words only? I might say I believe only in the written word.

A more demanding integration of scholarship and narrative is found in Richard Powers's novel *The Gold Bug Variations,* where the author not only gives the reader a crash course in genetics and microbiology but makes a dense metaphoric braid from his many materials. And while *Variations* is part mystery, part love story, it is centrally and essentially a reconnaissance mission flown over the moving fringe of experimental science, a heroic effort to locate the terms of its larger general relevance, its place in the psyche's scheme of reference. For all of Powers's brio, however, and for all his inventive ways of making his data reader-friendly, passage after passage is bound to stump the noninitiate. The narrator's musing might typically run as follows (though at far greater length): "Might certain codons chemically *fit* their amino acid assignments? How literally should I take the tape analogy? Which half of the double helix is transcribed for reading? Can the tape play in both directions?" When she adds, in the next breath, "I am a rookie, a greenhorn, a tenderfoot in this new country," we know how she feels—and then some.

The reader may have difficulties with the layers of scientific speculation, and with the mental reflexes of the characters. They think differently, and more strenuously, than most other characters we are apt to have encountered. This reveals, as starkly as any other exposure, how poorly our basic liberal humanism serves us when we come up against the concept-world of the sciences. *Variations* thus raises once again the question that was at the heart of the C. P. Snow–F. R. Leavis debate some decades ago: Namely, is there now an unbridgeable abyss between the learning of the humanities and that of the sciences? Are there any possibilities for a common language? Powers would appear to find a meeting ground in the idea of structure itself, and the novel abounds in metaphorical suggestions that sciences and arts, no less than intellections and affections, all ultimately derive from the wizardry within the pattern-making cells. And from the right perspective the breakthroughs in gene mapping are as much art as science, while Glenn Gould playing the "Goldberg Variations" is as much science as art.

Though there are doubtless serious lacunae in this survey, I would end it with a nod to Paul Auster. Like West, Auster does not tend to treat of heady matters directly. Rather, he filters his narratives through a fundamentally interrogative, philosophically existential temperament. The novels of his *New York Trilogy,* for instance, take the form of cerebral detective stories, but with a twist. The twist is that Auster is far less interested in discovering who did what to whom, and far more keen to subject the whole business of perceiving and knowing to inspection. Similarly, his latest novel, *The Music of Chance,* tests the distinctions between events interpreted as chance and those that seem patterned to fate, or destiny. As he writes in the opening passage: "Three days into the thirteenth month, he met up with a kid who called himself Jackpot. It was one of those random, accidental encounters that seem to materialize out of thin air—a twig that breaks off in the wind and suddenly lands at your feet. Had it occurred at any other moment, it is doubtful that Nashe would have opened his mouth." The concerns, as well as the temperature of the prose, align Auster more with modern European writers like Max Frisch, Marguerite Duras, and Lars Gustafsson than with his compatriots.

"Paranoids" and "Intellectuals"—the pie is crudely cut. The categories are obviously provisional, and my selections—and descriptions—are certain to irritate some portion of the public of independent-minded readers. I am not even sure that the game of labels and trends has any uses, except to provoke or incite. But maybe it does. Maybe an effort to map the game can in some way affect the game itself, redirecting certain readers, offering a slight encouragement to some isolated writer. I would like to think that could happen. For I'm convinced that we are, as a culture, what we believe ourselves to be. And our beliefs are in crucial ways shaped by images and representations. So long as these are mainly domestic or backward-looking, we risk a flawed connection to the life of our times. The reader may sometimes feel—I often do—that our present is not adequately plumbed by either the Paranoids or Intellectuals. But they do make a beginning. It is vital that we have these markers planted in different parts of the field. In time, we can hope, other writers will venture to set down this or that part of the picture, and the space between will slowly be colonized. Perhaps one day we will be able to look to the novel again in order to see ourselves.

. . . .

Paranoids and Intellectuals: Keepers of the Flame

Fiction
in a Media Age

Somewhere in one of his later novels, Saul Bellow brings up the analogy of the life cycle of the beaver. I can't remember what it's an analogy *for,* but no matter—it has a nice general applicability.

A family of beavers has made its home in a certain stream. There the animals carry on their business: feeding, mating, rearing young, gnawing down trees to build their dams and distinctive rounded houses. As it happens, though, this stream flows through the midst of a large nature preserve. On a nearby hillside, the rangers have set up illustrated placards that trace and explain every creaturely move. Tourists gather as if for a performance, gawking while the beavers obliviously obey their instincts. The scene is as sad as it is comic.

Bellow's beavers keep coming to mind as I try to think through the subject given in my title. The connection is slightly obscure, but perhaps I can pin it down.

First, imagine another kind of scenario. Instead of tourists assembled on a hillside, think of a group of students in a classroom a century from now. Their seminar is in history. The subject for the day: literature in the age of print. As they make themselves comfortable in their seats, the audiovisual dome darkens. Soon they are immersed in what the educators like to call the "learning environment." Pictures flash, appropriate bursts of period music are cut into the voice-track. They look up to see faces of authors, images of books, and pages of text, single words that inflate and dissolve on the screen.

"In the golden age of print . . ." the voice begins. The students listen to the half-familiar names, recognizing a few in the way that one recognizes the names of lesser mythological figures. Hawthorne, Melville, Twain, James, Wharton . . .

"With the upheavals wrought by industrial expansion and global conflict," the track continues, "the great processional diminished—the end was drawing near." Images on the dome now of Woolf, Hemingway, Lawrence, Joyce. "But there were still flashes of greatness."

". . . but with the coming of the electro-media systems at the end of the last century, literature was forced to make its last—and, of course, futile—stand." Norman Mailer, Philip Roth, Saul Bellow, Walker Percy, then a series of photos of unidentified younger writers.

"The habits of the printed word, developed since the fifteenth century, were not extinguished all that easily." Pause. Shots of library facades, bookstore interiors. "At the time of the millennium there were still a handful of publishing houses and an estimated 10 million readers." Titters from the students. The lights go on.

A fantasy perspective, to be sure. But I confess to trying it out more and more often. And when I do, I can't help but see our contemporary writers, even the best of them, as so many oblivious beavers. They go about plying their craft—writing, rewriting, polishing, publishing—all the while unaware that their endeavor is part of the death-twitch phase of print culture. Doomed men and women—they cannot understand why their efforts have so little impact, why they cannot touch greatness. Naturally they blame the publishers, the philistine public, the corruptions of the marketplace. What they cannot see—because they, too, are creatures of instinct—is that the elusive angel of history has detached itself from the printed word and has taken up residence in the circuitry of electronic systems.

Silly? I invite you into a class—any class—of high school or college students. You have only to initiate a discussion about reading (not required reading, but *reading* reading) to locate the source of my apocalyptic forebodings.

I make it a point to have one such discussion every term with my freshmen. Out of thirty students, maybe five or six say that they read for pleasure. That is, that they read anything more taxing or enduring than Stephen King or Sidney Sheldon. The vast majority are just not at ease with the printed word. A strange irritability settles over them when they have to look at a text for more than a few minutes. They are not dull or inarticulate—quite the contrary. But their inner world is constituted from images, sounds, and spoken words. When they use the terms of that world, they are quick and confident. But bring them face-to-face with the demands of cultivated literacy, and they gasp like stranded fish.

I start with this because I want to establish a wide and nondisciplinary context for my remarks. Amplitude is essential, for I know that everything I venture will admit to a thousand exceptions. I'm glad of the fact, for every exception increases the possibility that my fears are unwarranted. But when the black cloud is over me, I know that I'm grasping at straws. Beneath and behind the exceptions runs a directional momentum that will not be stayed.

The great age of fiction is over. Kaput. The art that achieved its fullest fruition in the nineteenth century—because it entertained, because it presented for apprehension a sensible picture of the social order, because it marked the apotheosis of individuation within that order—has lost its principal justifications. Entertainment is now got more easily elsewhere; the social sphere is so fragmented that no picture but that of chaos is possible; the ideals of individuality are steadily giving way before the forces of mass culture. The needs that the classical novel evolved to meet are part of the dream of the past.

Indeed, those needs had already vanished, had given way to others, by the beginning of our century. Industrialism and global political pressures shattered the old hierarchies. The patient creation of encompassing social worlds became next to impossible (Forster's *Howards End* and Ford Madox Ford's *Parade's End* tetralogy capture this sense of cultural transition most poignantly). For a time, however, the breakup of traditional structures brought artistic liberation.

. . . .

SVEN BIRKERTS

Writers were suddenly freed to explore the cognitive possibilities of their art. The gates to the inner world were thrown wide open. The stage where society had stood was now occupied by the complex psyche of the individual.

But the innovatory options were not infinite, and in the hands of writers like Joyce, Woolf, Lawrence, Broch, and others, they were all eventually tested. This left their followers and heirs in a difficult position. The traditional approach was no longer viable, and the modernists had used up most everything else. What was left? One could either work a defunct *métier,* or else set up to try to outdo the giants, or—

In the sixties and seventies, several new moves were discovered. Novelists and story writers began to subvert the age-old reader/writer contract: they put together narratives that neatly unmasked their own illusory status. Metafiction. Others began to blur the boundary between the "real" and the "fictional" by using the self as a character (Mailer's *Armies of the Night*) or by applying fictional techniques to real-life situations (Capote's *In Cold Blood*). Finally, some writers saw that they could infuse "pop" genres like the western or science fiction with literary seriousness. Result: the myriad ironic artifacts of postmodernism.

Seen from close up, each of these developments looked bright with promise. But one after the other they dissolved into the cultural bloodstream, and in retrospect they seem more like novelty turns and distractions than genuine contributions to the form. The fact that the potential revolutionary force of each move was quickly dissipated tells us a great deal about the condition of our fiction. For revolutions presuppose the entrenchment of a norm, a stable order. They release blasts of energy through a process of fission, decimating the atomic bonds of the existing structure. But these innovations were all launched in a void. Fiction had already ceded authority to the bourgeoning video culture.

My use of the past tense is for dramatic effect, and therefore slightly misleading. Obviously there is still activity: books get written, published, sold, and read. But what about those books? Most of the work I see is circumscribed in scope, avoiding intellectual, social, or political challenges; it is certainly not artistically innovative. And my sense is that readers have long since given up on awaiting the extraordinary—they make do with the minor pleasures and recognitions that come their way.

This was to be about fiction in a media age—I have not forgotten. The media impact upon fiction (all print culture, really) must be contemplated through at least two different frames. Thus far I have been skirting the periphery of the larger of these: that of the epochal shift. The order of print has, in our era, yielded to the order of electronic communication. McLuhan regarded the changeover as no less transformative than the earlier shift, some five centuries ago, from oral modes to print. The potential consequences are vertigo-inducing. If we argue, for example, that print encouraged the historical growth of the individual subject—by diminishing the social link, by enforcing sequestration and interiority, by supplanting the need for collective memory, etc.—then the new shift might well submerge the individual subject back into the mass. For the character of electronic/media communication is that it is a circuit process; the person is hooked in at ever-more-ramified levels to the pulsations moving through the whole system. The residual contours of the self are worn down by the steady flow of an impersonally generated effluvium: everyone sees the same shows, gets the same bits of news pitched at them all day long. The preserves of privacy have been invaded. The inescapable message is that there is a larger Now that we are all sharing in.

If the larger frame has to do with the underlying historical change, the smaller involves the specific impact of this change on the writers themselves. To grasp how great that impact can be, we have only to consider the aesthetic (stylistic) gulf between two generations of practitioners. On one extreme are those living writers who reached artistic maturity before the large-scale incursion—if not invention—of television. (When I speak of television, I have in mind the whole spectrum of new communications and information-processing technology.) A list might include Saul Bellow, Eudora Welty, Robert Penn Warren, Peter Taylor, even John Updike. On the other, we find the generation that is just coming into its own—all of the children of the media culture. I'm thinking now of Jay McInerney, Tama Janowitz, David Leavitt, Amy Hempel, Mary Robison, Deborah

Eisenberg, Bret Easton Ellis, Ann Beattie, Bobbie Ann Mason . . . the bright lights of the big city of the future.

Even the most general—and generic—comparison is instructive. If we look at the work of the elder writers, we can abstract from it certain attributes: 1) linguistic and syntactic complexity, 2) a governing sense of causality and consequence (actions have effects), 3) an implicit moral accountability (actions and effects can—*must*—be judged), 4) historical depth and continuity, 5) psychological complication, roundedness of characters, 6) social dimensionality (interconnectedness of characters), and 7) a movement of situations toward resolution.

If we turn to the writing of the rising young, the contrast is startling. Their fiction tends to be: 1) verbally and syntactically impoverished, 2) acausal (fragmented, associative), 3) morally neutral (tonally cool), 4) ahistorical (everything happens in the present), 5) psychologically flat (we are to infer personalities, depths of character), 6) without social dimension, and 7) without significant resolution. The inversion is, in terms of symmetry, gratifying.

Let me underscore my point with a set of quotations. First, the opening paragraph of Peter Taylor's story "Miss Leonora When Last Seen":

Here in Thomasville we are all concerned over the whereabouts of Miss Leonora Logan. She has been missing for two weeks, and though half a dozen postcards have been received from her, stating that she is in good health and that no anxiety should be felt for her safety, still the whole town can talk of nothing else. She was last seen in Thomasville heading south on Logan Lane, which is the narrow little street that runs alongside her family property. At four-thirty on Wednesday afternoon—Wednesday before last, that is to say—she turned out of the dirt driveway that comes down from her house and drove south on the lane toward its intersection with the by-pass of the Memphis-Chattanooga highway. She has not been seen since. Officially, she is away from home on a little trip. Unofficially, in the minds of the townspeople, she is a missing person, and because of the events leading up to her departure none of us will rest easy until we know the old lady is safe at home again.

Now, here is a bit from McInerney's *Bright Lights, Big City:*

> At one o'clock you go out for a sandwich. Megan asks you to bring her a Tab. Downstairs, you semirevolve through the doors and think about how nice it would be not to have to return at all, ever. You also think about how nice it would be to hole up in the nearest bar. The glare from the sidewalk stuns you; you fumble in your jacket pocket for your shades. Sensitive eyes, you tell people.

My purpose here is not to extol one stylist over the other (not at the moment, anyway), but to remark the difference in modes and to question the reasons for that difference. And the obviousness of the answer floors me. Taylor's prose belongs to the old order of print. McInerney's—though it, too, is words on the page—is a verbal incarnation of the modes of electronic media. Its pulsation is present tense; the narrative slides forward in associative clips; the voice triumphantly asserts detachment from the larger social realm. I cite McInerney, but I could have found an equally suitable passage in any one of a hundred recent releases.

The simple fact is that writers born after 1950 were subjected—consciously and unconsciously—to an array of forces, or influences, that did not exist in the culture before. Subtle and deeply pervasive video emanations were taken in by the susceptible psyche—they shaped the viewers no less decisively than books and bedtime stories shaped the readers and listeners of earlier generations. But what a difference! Exposed to the latter, the child will internalize both the form of the tale and its content. With television, which purveys only the most ephemeral of contents, it was the form that exerted the crucial pressure.

Cecilia Tichi has touched on some of the effects of this pressure in her recent essay "Video Novels" (*Boston Review,* June 1987). In discussing the fiction of "the first generation of writers to grow up with the technology of television," Tichi identifies some of the more salient video-derived characteristics of their prose. All of them, she writes,

> present a reality that is on-going and in-the-moment, the moment itself endlessly protracted. That flow is enacted in Ann Beattie's

Distortions, in Bret Easton Ellis's *Less Than Zero,* in Peter Cam-
eron's *One Way or Another,* in Tama Janowitz's *Slaves of New
York,* in all of which the narrative consciousness is that of the
ongoing present.

Further, these writers "are in full revolt against the traditional structures of beginning-middle-end because it is false to their perceptual
experience." And: "the conventional chapter dissolves into a patch-
work of loosely related scenes without causal sequence—parts of a
perceptual environment."

Tichi's essential point, in other words, is that writers reared in a
media culture will evolve a perceptual organization, or sensibility,
different from that of their predecessors; they will manifest a different
picture of the world in their work. I couldn't agree more. Indeed,
the new fiction appears to be all the evidence that's needed. But the
conclusion that Tichi then draws is entirely off the mark.

After she has established a strong link between the media environment and the procedures of contemporary fiction, Tichi asserts:

> This should not be cause for alarm; quite the contrary. The last
> time technology brought radical change to the written word in
> this century, American literature was enriched by the work of
> Ernest Hemingway, John Dos Passos, and William Carlos Wil-
> liams, who were the first to live in an environment of machines
> and structures, of railroad locomotives and steel high-rise build-
> ings. What gears and girders did for prose and poetry of the
> 1920s, communications technology is accomplishing in the liter-
> ature of the '80's.

What Tichi does not seem to recognize is that the first change,
striking as it may have been, was one of degree; the second is one of
kind. Hemingway, Dos Passos, and Williams performed their stripping operations upon a shared literary tradition; their innovations
reverberated against a sounding wall of trained expectations. Bret
Easton Ellis et al., on the other hand, make their noises in what turns
out to be a soundproof booth. The recognitions that hold up their
prose have nothing to do with a tradition—they are drawn exclu-
sively from the indeterminate Now that encloses all of us. Insofar as
that Now is a chimera, a media construct, the work is chimeric as

well. Its ultimate—and antiliterary—effect is to link the reader more deeply into the circuitry of mass consciousness.

It's true, I'm pessimistic. If I haven't given in to total despair, it's because forces have a way of eliciting other, countervailing forces. Indeed, I do see one heartening indication of hope. For if we are living in the age of electronic communication, we are also, I observe, living in the age of psychotherapy. People are flocking as never before to the offices of therapists and counselors. Hour after hour, week after week, they seek to lay bare the complex tangle of their personal histories. They do what they can to penetrate the slick, distracting surface of the present and enter the realm of anger and pain. ("Only connect—" wrote Forster.) In those offices, they assay causes, search out the motivations for their actions; they expose the root system of their social relations. The process is implicitly historical, and as such it cuts sharply against the momentum of media erosion.

Therapy can be seen as the individual's outcry, his protest against the uncentered and fragmented quality of daily experience. In the world of the quick fix, only therapy seems to take forever. Through it, the individual struggles to recover—or discover—the boundaries of self. Clearly something in the psyche resists integration into the mass.

This *something* is the cause for which fiction—all art—must do battle. The writer cannot merely mirror the chaos and discontinuity of our surroundings. He has to answer to the buried needs of everyone who faces that chaos. The fate of our individuality is very much at risk; the self will not be secured without a genuine sense of context. The writer must find a way to navigate back and forth across the fault line: to comprehend the old order in terms of the new, and the new in terms of the old. The new conditions, and the crisis of the individual in the face of the new conditions—this may be the great modern subject. The literary imagination, which comprehends cause and connection, which masters the manifold perspectives of time, must engage it. Otherwise, we may find ourselves not reading, but living inside, some Jay McInerney novel.

SVEN BIRKERTS

The School
of Lish

When I had my interview with Arnold Gingrich at Esquire
*and he asked me what kind of fiction I was going to be
publishing, I said, "The new fiction." He said, "What's that?"
I said, "I'll get out there and find it, Mr. Gingrich."*

—Gordon Lish

Longtime readers of American fiction will probably have noticed
certain changes in the product during the last few decades. A
good deal of the gravity, scope, and narrative energy seems to have
gone out of our prose. Formerly there were lives, fates. Now, increasingly, we greet disembodied characters who move about in a generic
sort of present. Events on the page are dictated less by complex
causes than by authorial fiat. While adherents of the poststructuralist
disciplines may find this exalting and confirming, the "dear Reader"
tacitly addressed by a more traditional fiction registers a growing
despair.

The first signs of disturbance came during the late sixties, when
writers like Donald Barthelme, Kurt Vonnegut, Robert Coover, John
Barth, and E. L. Doctorow began to assault the narrative norms.
Different as their subversions were—they included surreal disjunctions, the mixing of high and low genres, and the use of self-reflexive
"metafictional" techniques—the end was the same: the sustaining pre-
tenses of fiction were powerfully undermined. The influence of this

attack was felt in every quarter; even professedly rearguard stylists found it ever more difficult to generate the necessary authority.

The spirit of playful subterfuge and interrogation vanished, however, along with the counterculture. In its place there appeared a deep unease. Fiction writers neither resumed the old ways nor went with the dare of the new. In a climate of social instability, both the novel and the story drew in their wings. Raymond Carver, Ann Beattie, Frederick Barthelme, and others tried to forge a prose out of whatever had not been decimated by their predecessors. Rooting their work in an indefinite present, they refused to essay the creation of coherent fictional worlds. Their example caught on. Styles everywhere became numbly diaristic. Structures were collage-derived. The episode, the paragraph, the sentence, the phrase, were the new units of composition. The literary glamour of the seventies attached to the fragmented writings of Renata Adler and Joan Didion, and an army of epigones rose up to follow.

If fiction was once an empire on which the sun never set, it is no longer. Nowadays we rarely meet with a work that tries to bring a larger social context to life, or that explores with any conviction what it means to live in an era of broken connections. In this media culture, fiction seems no longer charged with the mirroring of reality. And yet words keep coming. A whole new generation of prose stylists advances behind the Barthelmes, Carvers, Adlers, and Beatties, a generation that studies the moves and devices of these "masters" as avidly as midcentury writers studied Hemingway, Faulkner, and Joyce.

In casting about for some way to give the newest tendencies a habitation and a name, we might do worse than fix upon a particular office at the firm of Alfred A. Knopf, in which sits an energetic and outspoken editor named Gordon Lish. Lish is right now very much at the epicenter of American literary publishing. For one thing, he edits a fair number of "hot" young novelists and story writers. But there are his other activities as well. Lish has for years conducted highly selective fiction workshops in New York and elsewhere—not infrequently assisting his stars into print and into publishing careers. He is also presently neck-deep in preparations to launch a magazine, *The Quarterly*, which will be subsidized and distributed through the Random House network. (The first issue is scheduled for the spring

of next year.) On top of all this, Lish is himself a determined prac-
titioner of post-Carver fiction, with a story collection and two novels
to his credit.

Lish's diversified enterprise, and his literary and practical influence, have drawn extremes of response. Nothing could have been
more worshipful, for instance, than Amy Hempel's article in *Vanity
Fair* a few years ago ("Captain Fiction," it was called), which opened
with this bold-faced blurb: "Gordon Lish is the Lee Strasberg of
American fiction." Writing as a student and a published discovery of
Lish's, Hempel fizzed exuberantly about his qualities as a teacher,
dwelling upon his idiosyncrasy, his assertive candor, his engagement
("For thirteen weeks it is a class in which first Lish and then his
students get the spirit and testify"), and not least, his willingness to
perform extramural services for the deserving.

A more astringent view of this activity of discovery and promotion is to be found in Joe David Bellamy's essay "A Downpour of
Literary Republicanism" in a recent issue of the *Mississippi Review*.
Bellamy suggests that Lish is an institution in some ways as important
as the *New Yorker*. Calling him a "cultural commissar" and identifying
his aesthetic with Republican conservatism (for its interest in outer,
documentary narrative, as opposed to inner, subjective experimentation), Bellamy concludes by goggling at the power that Lish commands: "possibly enough to make it rain if he wants it to rain."

Hempel has evidently passed too many mesmerized hours staring
at her book contract, Bellamy too many brooding over his Saul
Steinberg poster of New York; but surely some truth can be shaken
out of both. Lish does command power. He has gone on from his
earlier days of publishing and proselytizing for writers like Carver
in *Esquire,* where he was fiction editor for eight years, to put together
a distinctive, if not universally appealing, roster of talents for Knopf.
His list includes Anderson Ferrell, Barry Hannah, Hempel, Bette
Howland, Janet Kauffman, Raymond Kennedy, Nancy Lemann, Michael Martone, Bette Pesetsky, Mary Robison, Leon Rooke. And he
has abetted a career or two; a few years back, for instance, Lish
secured a contract for his student Anderson Ferrell on the strength
of a few paragraphs of prose.

Still, it's obviously foolish to think of the man as omnipotent.
While he will extol the trust placed in him by Knopf's president,

Robert Gottlieb—"No question," says Lish, "I am able to indulge my fantasies at the expense of a powerful organization"—he does have a tether. He has tried for years to put across one of his favorite stylists, Stanley G. Crawford, author of the novella *Log of the S.S. The Mrs. Unguentine,* without success. Nor could Lish be called capricious. Ferrell's short novel, *Where She Was,* is a sharply realized work of prose; it amply deserves to have been published. The issue, perhaps, is not so much that Lish can indulge his fantasies, but that so few other editors manage to do the same.

What finally makes Lish exceptional among editors is his devotion to the young. A photocopied announcement for *The Quarterly* advises that the magazine "is open to all comers, but will doubtless prove to be particularly hospitable to the work of the young and unsung." Lish is frank about his predilections and his agenda. "If I were given the option of publishing the fourth great work by author A," he states, "and the OK first book by author B, I would be inclined to go with the OK first book."

But he also admits to an ambition greater than just discovering the publishable young. Lish wants to find and train the next title-holder, the future Great American Novelist. He uses the analogy of a boxing coach: "I can tell you how to take the guy, though I can't do it myself." And the guy, the writer that Lish admires above all others and hence is determined to unseat, is . . . Harold Brodkey.

Harold Brodkey? Yes, emphatically. Lish admits no reservations to his adoration. Brodkey-love swamps every other subject of conversation, though Lish will, to be fair, also sing arias of praise for Cynthia Ozick and Don DeLillo. He is convinced, in part on the strength of published work, but especially on what he has read of the legendary (some would say too legendary) work in progress, *A Party of Animals,* that Brodkey is the prose master of our century. He acknowledges, of course, the credibility problem that comes with declaring the preeminence of a novelist whose major work is still under wraps, but as he puts it, "The evidence is before me . . . and there it is."

Lish cites as the cardinal virtues of Brodkey's prose its intelligence, its moral seriousness, its relentlessness. He particularly admires what he sees as the author's willingness always to remake himself. "I don't think there's anyone who is coming onto the page

. . . .

SVEN BIRKERTS

so ferociously," he says. "I read Brodkey and I can't catch my breath."
Brodkey presents, for Lish, in every way the opposite of the writing
represented by Saul Bellow, whose fiction he derides as pretentious
and predictable. Asked if anyone can challenge this Goliath, he
smiles. "Somewhere out there is a young writer who has what it
takes."

It's hard to get things square. Here we have Lish's testimony on
behalf of Brodkey, a writer well along in his career, who is working
with a perfectionist's resolve on a grand novel, refusing to publish
before he's ready. There we have the example of Lish himself, editor
and evangelist of the unsung, doing everything he can to get their
young prose in front of an audience, hoping that one of them will
be the next Brodkey. But there is still a greater contradiction. Where
Brodkey's prose aims at grandeur, at a dynamic totality that can
embrace ideas, psychological motivations, moral and spiritual questioning, Lish's progeny come across almost without exception as
purveyors of the slight and the fragmented. They are sculptors of
sentences rather than of worlds. Their hunt for essences bypasses
existence. Ferocity is nowhere in evidence.

Of course, Lish's authors are not all of a single stripe. Though
they tend to youthfulness, and their productions to slimness—each
one can be read in an evening—there seems to be little similarity
between a book like Leon Rooke's *Shakespeare's Dog,* which looks at
the Bard through the eyes of his randy and highly verbal dog, Mr.
Hooker, and the pruned contemporaneity of a story collection by
Mary Robison or Amy Hempel. And between these two poles we
get the denser domestic portraits of Janet Kauffman and the airy
biographical fantasies of Michael Martone. But underneath the variegated surface, behind the sentence-by-sentence expertise, are indica-
tions of what is either a new aesthetic or else a crisis in the art.
Whichever it is, it has very little to do with Brodkey, Ozick, or
DeLillo.

Joe David Bellamy's charge of "literary Republicanism" is misleading when applied to this group of writers. Doubtless Bellamy had
Carver's fiction in mind when he coined the epithet. And while
Carver's fidelity to grim, middle- , and lower-class exteriors, and to
a tactic of unstated motivation, has been influential, things have

changed since his heyday in the early seventies. Lish's writers take a much freer hand with subject matter, voice, and narrative exposition. And what has passed into their fiction, whether from Carver, Beattie, or the spirit of the time, is a total refusal of any vision of larger social connection. Indeed, in this respect Lish's authors are only a case in point. Most of contemporary fiction is similarly skewed. Characters are shown as moving in contained worlds, alone, or with family, friends, and lovers. Everything beyond the local is alien chaos. The social fabric, once the complex and comprehensive subject of fiction, can no longer be found. Nor is there any attempt, as in the novels of Don DeLillo, to make a subject out of this very absence of social bonds. Among these writers a centripetal isolation prevails; the world never extends illusionistically beyond the cast assembled on the stage. This might explain why so many of these books are slight. The writers have shorn themselves, or they have been shorn of, a central resource.

Lish's own work is relevant here, for he preaches what he practices. The stories in his 1977 collection, *What I Know So Far,* progress by way of an anxious staccato, building their episodic structures along the fault lines of discontinuous speech patterns. The sentences capture the reader with their erratic and colloquial beat:

> Alan Silver moved in. He moved in when there were seven houses and four still going up. He was twelve. Maybe I was nine by then. So that's the boys from two houses. The other five had boys in them too.

They deny him, however, any kind of stable fictional order. Lish's novel *Dear Mr. Capote* (1983) worked similarly, though the subject matter was horrific: the colloquial jumps came out of the mouth of a demented serial killer. But *Peru,* his novel published this year, achieves an eerie profundity absent from the other work. For Lish has finally matched this talky, nipped-off style to its ideal subject— the gradual recovery of a repressed childhood memory. The flat word-sounds and incessant repetitions eventually reveal the violent psyche of a lonely child. Needless to say, nothing exists beyond the recursive monody of the narrator's voice and the handful of images that it summons up. Lish, then, is the paradigmatic Lish author.

. . . .

SVEN BIRKERTS

The others can be parceled into several roughly bounded camps. Mary Robison, Bette Pesetsky, and Amy Hempel would definitely fit together into one of these. They might be described as the main legatees of the Carver influence. Their collective muse owes a great deal to his opaque technique and his close-focus scene building. In their stories (though Robison and Pesetsky have written novels, their talents favor brevity), we encounter sudden, brightly lit tableaux animated by characters who have either been damaged into eccentricity or else scorched to blankness by the inchoate forces of modernity. Strange behavior and terrifying revelations are set before us in neutral, nonjudgmental tones. Scenes are generally given in the present tense, and all background has been carefully cut away. The reader's job, it appears, is to supply the excised humanity, to be shocked and stricken on behalf of the affectless.

In Mary Robison's "Weekday," from *Days* (1979), a divorced couple has a short reunion that is at once intimate and edged with hostility. As Christine, the ex-wife, cuts Guidry's hair—both have been swilling vodka all morning—we hear the following exchange:

> "I think you hang around with faggots," Guidry said.
> "Don't forget I'm cutting your hair. You could come out of this looking pretty funny."
> Guidry said, "I don't think you're taking your life seriously."
> "Probably not."
> "Not," Guidry said. "Just not. Your father died last year. Your daughter had her first period, which you don't even know about."
> "Michelle?" Christine said.
> "That's the one," Guidry said. "I had to send her up to Mom's. I know a little about it, but."
> "When?" Christine said.
> "A month ago."
> "She's only ten."
> "She's eleven."

The title piece of Bette Pesetsky's *Stories Up to a Point* (1981), meanwhile, presents this give-and-take between husband and wife on the subject of their estranged daughter:

My husband sits down at the breakfast table and slams the *Times* across the toaster. "If she ever calls," he declares, "if she ever calls, you are to hang up at once, do you hear?" "I will," I reply. "No, wait," he says. "Don't do that. Talk to her first. But coldly. Let her ask to come home or for money. Then tell her about her room. Tell her how I sold everything—her furniture, her pictures. Be sure and tell her how I burned her papers, her books, her clothes, and her record collection. Tell her that her room is now an upstairs den. Mention the console television in the corner. She'll hate that." "I'll do just that," I say. "Swear it to me." "I swear," I say. "How do you want your toast?"

Finally, Amy Hempel's story, "In the Cemetery Where Al Jolson Is Buried," moves from scene to scene by tracking the tough wise-cracking between two friends, one of whom is dying in the hospital:

> She is flirting with the Good Doctor, who has just appeared. Unlike the Bad Doctor, who checks the IV drip before saying good morning, the Good Doctor says things like "God didn't give epileptics a fair shake." The Good Doctor awards himself points for the cripples he could have hit in the parking lot. Because the Good Doctor is a little in love with her, he says maybe a year. He pulls a chair up to her bed and suggests I might like to spend an hour on the beach.
> "Bring me something back," she says. "Anything from the beach. Or the gift shop. Taste is no object."
> He draws the curtains around her bed.
> "Wait!" she cries.
> I look in at her.
> "Anything," she says, "except a magazine subscription."
> The doctor turns away.
> I watch her mouth laugh.

Here we have a finger on one of the central pulses of contemporary fiction. This stuff is state-of-the-art. The same tonality can be heard in thousands of stories coming out of workshops and writing programs. It is choking the pages of literary magazines as well as glossies. This manner is what results when talent and inexperience go out looking for subject matter. The cuttings show three orders of tragedy—a lost marriage, a lost daughter, the imminent loss of life—and a single mode of response. In each case there is a displacement of crisis by repartee, an avoidance of human depths that a different sort of author would choose to plumb and to illuminate.

In the understated scenarios of Carver, who learned much from Hemingway, the unspoken or avoided material has a chance of reaching the reader. The opaque surfaces are designed to transmit suffering. Carver's characters do not reveal emotion, either because it overwhelms them, or because muteness is seen as a talisman of resistance; but the reader does believe that somewhere, perhaps only in the author's heart, the real emotion existed, was felt. No chance of that here. The diction of Robison, Pesetsky, and Hempel ensures that we will remain unaffected. Everything genuine has been transposed into the key of the one-liner. We are to remark, rather, the disjunction between the presentation and what it buries, and so we do. But we can do nothing about it. We know that there is no payoff.

This prose has been styled to look "real." It vigorously mimes the banalities and the discontinuities of ordinary speech. And yet, reading these stories, I am struck by nothing so much as their falsification of the grain of experience. These writers may owe some of their tricks to Carver, but their real antecedents are not literary at all. They're televised. The pace and pitch, the timing—everything has been deftly lifted from the screen, even from the prime-time sitcom. Not intentionally, I imagine. Still, listen in as you read. Do you hear human voices, or something closer to TV gabble? In certain passages I almost expect to hear the laugh track start up.

Fortunately not all of the fiction, not even by younger writers, has been bent by these pressures. Within this same Knopf corral, a very different, and in some ways more salutary, approach has been taken by linguistically attuned stylists such as Barry Hannah and Leon Rooke. In their work, we at least get the freshening pleasures of language and a feeling of anarchic sport. Their fiction does not derive from the imperatives of plot or character; it has its source in the rhythms and sound-play options of the sentence. Hannah, whom Lish credits with "more of an impact on how sentences get written all round than Raymond Carver," takes obvious delight in his ability to jump through hoops with a flourish. Opening his novel *Ray* (1980)

. . . .

The School of Lish

quite at random, I find his amoral but tenderhearted doctor reminiscing as follows:

> One night, when I was in Saigon, a chicken colonel's wife walked past my Yamaha motorbike on the street. My eyes got wide and my heart was molasses. She walked by me, clicking her heels, tanned legs so lean, a fine joyful sense of her sex uplifted at the juncture of her thighs.

We see the craft and care of making, but only later, after we have siphoned up the pleasure.

And here is Rooke's Mr. Hooker, dilating on the charms of his beloved bitch, Marr:

> I have always liked her feet: the hobgoblin tufts of brightness growing up between the black pads like weeds through stone; the smooth nails that curve as little moons to reach points sharper than my own. Her deft ankles too. The beauteous knees. She shook herself, then licked her upper thigh.

Hannah and Rooke are word-men. Sprinters. Sentence acrobats. They can peg to a millimeter a physical sensation. They can start a rumble between clauses, if they've a mind to. This is what we turn to them for. And this is their limit. No use looking for excavated depths of character or immersions in plot. As in the stories of Robison and company, lives are caught in midflight. The past is alluded to randomly, in fragments, if at all. What keeps us going in Robison's work are the promises of incongruous surprise and the blandishments of paradox. (Meager fare, I'd say.) With Hannah and Rooke, it's the velocity of the prose, and the flash that comes when word-sounds touch and ignite in the ear.

Two novellas of the Lish school, Ferrell's *Where She Was* (1985) and Kauffman's *Collaborators* (1986), come slightly closer to rewarding conventional expectations. Each undertakes, in its way, to develop a character portrait through a succession of carefully placed vignettes. Again, there is nothing so overt as plot. *Collaborators,* the more successful of the two, reveals to us the complex, yet distinct, stages of a mother-daughter relationship. A tragic event is at the root—

the mother has a disabling stroke midway through the book—and
Kauffman meets the emotional demands squarely. The mother's efforts to recover speech and motor skills press sharply on the daughter's maturing sensibility:

> She pointed at the ground, saying, Dare, dare, or There, there.
>> What is it?
>> There! she said.
>> In the ditch at the edge of the field was a groundhog hole.
> That's all I could see.
>> That? You mean that groundhog hole?
>> Yes! Her face was red with the explosive sounds of the word.

Kauffman's novel is set, for the most part, on a tobacco farm in
Pennsylvania. Ferrell's *Where She Was* is also located, interestingly
enough, in tobacco country. The focus, however, is much less on
relationships. Ferrell is after a more solemnly mythic, a more truly
existential, portrayal. His Cleo Lewis, a hardworking mother and
wife, is full of inarticulate longings. In the face of these, the husband
and children appear peripheral. But she does not know what she
longs for. When local churches and preachers fail her, she succumbs
to the call of a mysterious drifter.

Though Ferrell tends to overwrite in places, to layer atmospheric
effects with a loaded brush, he does at times achieve a genuine force.
Building periodic rhythms account for much of the effect:

> They walked through the forest. The trees began to be farther
> apart and taller. Cleo smelled creek water. It was as if the smell
> came from his hair and blew around her, a cool smell, a smell
> so strong Cleo could feel it against the back of her throat, a
> damp, rich smell as rank as the dirt—a smell that would grow
> things.

How different from this is Nancy Lemann's light-handed conjuring of New Orleans in *Lives of the Saints* (1985). Where Ferrell is
dense and portentous, Lemann is nimble and casual-seeming. The
ghost of a story—no more—emerges from the vignettes she con-
vokes. A young woman, Louise, is in love with a gallant and eccentric
ne'er-do-well named Claude. He moves in and out of her sights,

mostly against an impressionistically dabbed backdrop of New Orleans. Louise's voice trips erratically through the vast registers of love, coaxing, denying, breaking down in admission:

> Yankee girls probably sat around having philosophically inquiring conversations about the meaning of art. But Claude would never talk about serious things. He was always too busy making lame-brained jokes or talking about the small things. He would probably tell them that the dress they were wearing reminded him of some huge thing—all he wanted to do was plummet to the depths of factuality about what you were doing at that exact moment, and what you were really like. He was just a simple dark-haired Tareyton smoker, completely wry.
> My heart was not trained to love anyone but him.

This, then, is Lish's squadron, most of it. The writers are, as I say, outwardly various enough. But from a certain angle, taking a tight noon-hour squint, one can discern a common style. It is all very modern, or postmodern. The byte-sized perceptions, set in an eternal present, are the natural effluence of an electronically connected, stimulus-saturated culture. In a sense, they are what we have earned for ourselves: these writers may satisfy themselves that they have, intentionally or not, mirrored our world to us, mimicked the sensations of contemporary experience. Still, in another sense, their work represents an abrogation of literary responsibility. If fiction is to survive as something more than a coterie sport, it must venture something greater than a passive reflection of fragmentation and unease. Indeed, it must manifest some of the very qualities that Lish has attributed to the work of Harold Brodkey: intelligence, moral seriousness, and relentlessness. And, I would add, comprehensiveness and scope.

I am not calling for a curmudgeonly return to the tradition of the nineteenth-century narrative. Far from it. The modernist revolution in the early part of the century left the writer with an arsenal of new devices and modes—interior monologue, shifting narrators, collage, and temporal modulation, to name but a few—as well as a high injunction: to dare a prose that can face chaos and master it with vision. Woolf, Joyce, Lawrence, Faulkner, Musil, Broch,

·

Kafka—these artists did not finish off fiction; they opened new sluices for it. And in our own time American novelists like Pynchon, Bellow, and Percy have carried on the hard task of probing our place in the turbulent cultural present. All three have managed to keep their focus wide and their grasp on the particular steady. Not one of them has fallen back upon convention for its own sake.

Of course, these are all masters in late career. Theirs will not be the shaping voices of the coming decades. It will fall to the younger authors, Lish's among them, to bring the world over into words. But this will not be possible without more exertion and more willingness to risk than many young writers have shown. The careful construction of sentences and paragraphs is a first step, not a final goal. The world of the future is bound to be more dispersed and more synthetic than it is now. There is a real danger, then, that reality will outstrip the writer's ability—if expression fails, understanding fails too. It is necessary to believe, with Gordon Lish, that there is undiscovered greatness in the young. But it is hard to rest easy with the growing cult of small-stage pyrotechnics. The impending challenges are of a different magnitude.

Writing
Black

The basic premise of Gayl Jones's *Liberating Voices: Oral Tradition in African American Literature* is as follows: that modern African-American writers did not begin to realize their true literary identity until they either rejected the dominant modes of the European American tradition, adopting instead the forms and approaches suggested by their own oral and musical traditions, or else found ways to transform the received patterns through the deep incorporation of indigenous elements. Jones is highly discriminating in tracing the evolution of the various strategies of adoption and incorporation—of dialect speech, say, or the structures and idioms of blues, spirituals, and jazz—in the poetry, short fiction, and novels of isolated practitioners. Her discussions hew close to her chosen texts. She shows, for instance, the gradual liberation of dialect usage from Langston Hughes to Paul Laurence Dunbar to Sterling Brown to Sherley A. Williams, and the increasingly sophisticated implementation of musical modes from Jean Toomer to Ann Petry to Amiri Baraka. But her procedure of working with isolated texts, and of assuming a high degree of familiarity on the reader's part (with

Toomer's story "Karintha," Baraka's "The Screamers," etc.), is likely
to keep her study out of the hands of the interested lay reader. This
is a book for the library stacks.

And this is a shame. Jones has targeted a topic rich in issues and
implications, but she has taken it on with the scholar's narrow range
of focus. For all its local acumen—and Jones is a skillful close reader
with a sure sense for the symptomatic textual turn—*Liberating Voices*
is neither particularly liberating nor revelatory. Certainly not the way
it might have been if Jones had addressed certain core questions,
most pressingly that of authority.

To get to this authority question, I must first take up what I see
as the central problem of Jones's study. And this is, simply, that to
set up her thesis, she also decides to set up a straw-man figure called
the "European and European American traditions," and, alterna-
tively, "Western literary forms." This shorthand seems tenable
enough at first glance—we have a reflex sense of what she means—
but on closer inspection it crumbles away. In that crumbling, certain
deeper and more vexing issues are disclosed.

When I hear the words "European and European American traditions," I do not, like Göring, reach for my revolver. But I do reach
into the banks of my literary memory and try to figure out exactly
what this means. Given the context, African-American literature, and
the title's telltale "liberating," I cannot but pick up certain trace
elements of the pejorative. And though Jones never spells out her
conception of these traditions—which she absolutely should—I
sense throughout that she has them construed as essentially upright
(or uptight), formal, prescriptive, exclusionary, and canonically oriented in their references, and altogether unsuited to the expressive
needs of the African-American culture—indeed, of any Third World
culture.

This is important. What *is* Jones talking about when she conjures
up this monolithic entity? What underlies the conjuring? Is she
suggesting that there is some general way in which these traditions
prescribe what literature ought to be and proscribe everything else,
or is she referring only to specific forms and conventions? If the
latter, then which ones does she have in mind: naturalism, rhyme
and meter, symmetrical construction of narrative, standard orthogra-
phy in the transcription of dialogue, certain norms of "Standard"

English—what? Jones never makes this clear, and by not doing so she leaves the impression that they, whatever *they* were, remained closed to the kinds of expression that African-American writers found imperative.

Leaving such an impression, which is bound to have its truths, Jones effectively preempts any discussion of European and American modernism, which was not only contemporaneous with the careers of most of the writers under discussion, but which was also entirely given over to cutting ancient boundary wires and opening up aesthetic options of every sort. *Liberating Voices* gives almost no inkling that this was a revolutionary era within the white European tradition. It makes little sense to posit the restrictiveness of white forms—Jones never calls them that, but she might as well—when writers like James Joyce, William Carlos Williams, Gertrude Stein, Ezra Pound, Virginia Woolf, Guillaume Apollinaire, Hermann Broch, and a phalanx of others were turning them into Plasticene pretzels. Jones does, to be fair, mention Dada and Surrealism, but she does not linger to assess their artistic implications.

My question, then, is not why the African-American writer should look to the oral and musical heritage of his culture for inspiration—there were certainly good reasons for this—but rather why Jones should present this as a choice made necessary by the limitations of the available forms. That is, the available *white* forms. The obvious implication is that these forms were in some way analogous to, or even a continuation of, the societal institutions and ideologies that have wreaked such injury upon the African-American people. It is tempting to draw the link, but it is also inaccurate.

There are two questions that must be asked. First, whether it is true that the available models did not allow the necessary expressive options? And second, whether there is some way in which forms or modes (naturalism, formal meter, etc.) are *intrinsically* value-laden? The answer to both is no. The entire aesthetic spectrum was open to the informed modern artist. James Joyce himself exploited many of its possibilities, including the unmediated incorporation of dialect and the experimentation with musical structures. As for the values that might be felt to inhere in any given form—these are clearly the result of accumulated historical associations. One is not a monarchist because one writes in regular meters.

· ·   · ·

SVEN BIRKERTS

I would argue that the African-American writer's turn to the oral and musical traditions was not due to the insufficiency of existing forms, but that it was, rather, an essential founding gesture that was vitally bound up with authority. Literature, like any art, requires above all else a secure cultural grounding. Without such a grounding it is a peacock's fan of aesthetic gestures, nothing more. Adjacent terms for this authority are *history* and *tradition*. Indeed, what is a tradition but cultural identity as it is established in and through historical circumstance, and what is authority but tradition revealing itself in a work? This is why the academic debate over the canon is creating such divisions and animosities. Opponents of the multicultural agenda fear more than anything else the leaching out of the substrata of tradition and the inevitable divestiture of authority that would follow. A tradition is, after all, a kind of deed establishing the history of ideological ownership. And in terms of the artistic culture it ends up being a record of prior use.

The point is that while the African-American writer might very well have developed a wide and useful expressive idiom from available models, the expression itself would necessarily carry the taint of prior use. A work could manifest every artistic excellence and still lack the authority conferred by a sustaining cultural connection. It makes perfect sense that the African-American writers should have sought to anchor their production in what are widely felt to be the wellsprings of African-American culture—oral narrative and music.

This turn, toward music in particular, raises certain questions, and Jones could have added some speculative weight to her book by taking them up. For instance, what does it *mean* to appropriate elements from the blues or jazz tradition for a literary work? Is it merely a way of expanding the stylistic reach? It strikes me that there is also a sense in which such a move signals an insufficiency of the usual linguistic tools; and signals, too, that the affective core of the subject or experience is more readily accessible through musical reference. The function of the musical incorporation, in other words, may be to root the credibility of the enterprise in a genre that is closer to the authentic stuff of African-American culture. The paradoxical result—this is at least open to serious questioning—is that while such a strategy can enhance the work with diverse textures, rhythms, and structural possibilities, it may in some subtle way also depreciate the original literary genre. This is, of course, one of the key questions in the debate over postmodernism: whether the cross-pollination of genres and breakdown of distinctions between "high" art and "popular" art does not ultimately take away from the expressive power of the art. This is not an issue, as some believe, of snobbism versus egalitarianism; it has more to with the origins and evolutionary necessity of distinct genres. At what point do borrowings stop counting as artistic enrichment and begin to indicate a crisis in the genre?

But this is not a debate I want to engage in here. Let me resume my contention: that it was not an unsuitability of available forms that directed the African-American artist to oral and musical traditions, but that it was a desire to acquire some of the authority embodied by these traditions. The decision had political, even legalistic, overtones. For the problem with those "European and European American" forms did not have to do with ownership but with prior use. Ownership is a synchronic phenomenon—one either owns something or not, and that thing can be taken away. Prior use, seemingly less binding, in fact is far more of a threat. It is diachronic, and thick with psychological implication. It means that no matter what the latecomer does, it will always be *after*. To be after is to be deprived of the historical claim—that one was there as witness, maker, or participant. All the good will in the world, and all the excellence of subsequent accomplishment, cannot undo it. Symbolic parricide is not the answer. The better way is to change the game, or find a new game—and in the process establish a new authority base.

We can think of the issue by way of analogy, taking the case of white singers and musicians setting themselves up as performers of the blues. There has always been a sense, on the part of whites and blacks alike, that this represents a trespass of sorts. And many white blues artists, recognizing this, have sought the sanction of some mentor from the "real" blues tradition—witness Bonnie Raitt hooking up with Sippie Wallace and Canned Heat cutting records with John Lee Hooker. Many people believe that the form itself, its basic patterns and variations, belongs to the African-American. Does it? That is, does it any more than the sonnet *belongs* to the white European? Or is it just that the African-American artists have stamped it so tellingly through prior use that any white adoption cannot but seem imitative and lacking authority? Where does the authority originate—in having shaped and refined the form, in the tradition of powerful expressions registered using the form, or in having experienced the suffering that is the content? Interestingly, nearly all white blues musicians have paid some lip service to initiation through suffering or social disenfranchisement that runs parallel to what the African-American has known—perverse irony intended—as a birthright. "You've got to pay your dues—you've got to suffer if you want to sing the blues."

At issue, with blues as with literary forms, is the authority of the artist. You can mimic the outer forms—anyone can—but they mean little without the sanction of tradition. You have to have *had* the blues in order to sing them right—the listener will know if you have not. But wait—if you are white, even if you have paid your dues, you still cannot sing the blues. Not *really*. You may have the private authority—earned through hard living—but you will never have the cultural authority. If you are white, you are a latecomer to the blues, and you will always be a latecomer. It cannot be undone.

We might now consider the same notion, authority of prior use, as applied to traditional (European etc.) forms, and ask whether the same principle—the "blues principle"—applies. That is, whether in order to use one of these forms a writer must in some way *be* a vested member of the cultural tradition? If the writer is *not* a member, will the use, no matter how accomplished, be classed as an imitation? If so—and I will leave these questions dangling—wouldn't we have to say that there is an ineradicable color line running through literature no less than music, and that the African-American writer has had to found a literature by reaching to one side and the other but without stepping over the line? The liberation of voice, then, would have to be seen as a reaching inward, and the successes of the literature as a vindication of a larger sort. Gayl Jones's study raises many of these questions implicitly. I wish that she would have taken some of them on.

Liberating Voices: Oral Tradition in African American Literature. Gayl Jones. 228 pp. Harvard University Press. 1991. $27.95

. . .

Destinies of
Character: A Reading

A few months ago, and purely for pleasure, I read Anne Tyler's latest novel, *Breathing Lessons*. It is as good an example as I can think of just now of a serious, naturalistic, mainstream novel. The two main characters, Ira and Maggie Moran, a middle-aged married couple, are the solid supports for—and makers of—the book's simple plot. The novel begins as they are about to set forth by car to the funeral of the husband of one of Maggie's oldest friends. Their long day will be filled with incidents and encounters. First they will meet up with a number of old friends at the funeral. Later, as they are driving back, Maggie will insist that they visit their former daughter-in-law—she has a scheme, which ultimately fails, for re-uniting her son's family. The novel will end with Maggie and Ira back in their bedroom, preparing for sleep.

Outwardly it is not an enticing story line—certainly not as I have summarized it here. But every reader knows how irrelevant such summaries are. They characterize a novel about as usefully as an occupation defines a person. The presentation is everything, the registration of sensation and the weaving of a credible texture of psychic life. And, no less important, the creation around each principal character of a receptive space. This is hard to define. I'm thinking in terms of an opening or access, a means of getting close up to the life, but an access with certain set limits. For there must be an opacity as well, a degree of otherness that keeps the characters at a slight remove; we accompany them without *becoming* them. Some romances or thrillers may ask for a maximum investment of our fantasies. The more "serious" novel, however, has less to do with what we wish than with what we are; identifications are always partial.

Breathing Lessons opens as follows:

> Maggie and Ira Moran had to go to a funeral in Deer Lick, Pennsylvania. Maggie's girlhood friend had lost her husband. Deer Lick lay on a narrow country road some ninety miles north of Baltimore, and the funeral was scheduled for ten-thirty Saturday morning; so Ira figured they should start around eight. This made him grumpy.

At first, we do not so much suspend disbelief as give consent; we decide to let the natural momentum of our imaginings give life to the figments assembled on the page. When I first encounter a character, my response may be likened to the throwing of a switch. I confer not only potential identity, setting up a contour that I believe will soon start to be filled in, but I also establish an axis of past, present, and future along which the life, or lives, will flourish. Maggie and Ira, whom I assume out of convention to be married, are equipped with a generic marital history (which will be modified as needed) and a future that may or may not find them still together. I read on, starting in now on the second paragraph:

> They planned to wake up at seven, but Maggie must have set the alarm wrong and so they overslept. They had to dress in a hurry and rush through breakfast, making do with faucet coffee and cold cereal. Then Ira headed off for the store on foot to leave a note for his customers, and Maggie walked to the body shop. She was wearing her best dress—blue and white sprigged, with cape sleeves—and crisp black pumps, on account of the funeral.

I am enlisted. I don't yet see Maggie, I'm not sure what sprigging is or what cape sleeves look like, but a person is stirring to life—

and the obstacles of page and print begin to recede. Though at first I know little more than that Maggie drinks coffee and is old enough to have a friend who has lost a husband, I feel myself being taken up into the momentum of her day. That day is already tinctured by her character. Faucet coffee and cold cereal. I see a habitually late person, a bumbler, but one who also possesses an inelegant, improvisational readiness. I am inclined to like her—certainly I'm not threatened or warned away. And when I learn that she is wearing her *best* dress, that she is the kind of person who keeps a best dress, I feel touched. It's already clear to me that while untold mischief may erupt from this woman, she bears no evil. I adjust my reading sights accordingly.

But even less than two paragraphs into the novel, I am doing a good deal more than concretizing a pair of personalities out of a set of given signals. I am also already engaged in laying slight translucent strands—webs of association and memory—athwart the narrative. "Faucet coffee" conjures a flash of myself in a room I once rented, fixing a cup of Maxim from the tap (a ghost of a taste, a split-second snapshot of the blue metal cup I used to drink from); simultaneously, or nearly so, I get an equally fleeting image of Glenda Jackson in the movie *Sunday, Bloody Sunday:* her character at one point also makes coffee at the sink.

I mention these instances because similar perceptual flickerings accompany my reading with varying intensity from the first page to the last. They do not merely happen alongside my reading—in some important sense they *are* my reading. Or, to tilt the emphasis slightly, they are *my* reading. Granted, I cited relatively trivial associations. At other times, though, perhaps when I am more caught up in the emotional rush of a given scene, I may experience a more extended wash of memory. No matter the scale, it is always my life coming toward me—but obliquely, held inside a frame of fictive reality. And snatching myself from an unexpected angle gives me a vitalizing shock, the emotional equivalent of a double take before a surprise mirror.

Precise physical visualization of characters is not all that important to me when I read. A book is not a movie. I don't need to know what

Maggie's nose looks like, or how she styles her hair—unless, of course, her hairstyle tells me something about how she views herself, in which case it is information I'm avid for. Indeed, my outward picture of Maggie and Ira remains quite blurry throughout. I see pleasant general faces, bodies with a normal stock of gestures and tics. I notice, too, that Tyler has gone to no great lengths to incise highly specific images in my mind. No, she has given me just enough to support the illusion of their in-the-world existence. The rest is for me to fill in, should I choose to. (I do not.) This is not, on Tyler's part, an abnegation of authorial responsibility. To the contrary, she has allowed me to know Ira and Maggie better than I know most "real" people, precisely because the distracting and limiting details of outwardness have been cut away. I get direct access to the voices of the inner life.

The opening sections always make for the hardest work. The reader has to exert considerable energy to get the world into place and to make out the basic character relationships. We do construct— the novel's world does not spring to life of its own accord. But soon enough this changes. Situations and settings have been pegged out; the characters are convincingly in motion. What's more, they have very quickly acquired their own store of time. Within pages we feel them to possess a past, even if it is only the past of those pages. And as the novel gathers momentum, this illusion deepens, adding ever-greater verisimilitude.

The characters' emergence into time works to activate our own time-sense. We are suddenly aware of ourselves less as entities in a constantly shifting present, more as cumulative beings: we open up to our own histories. And this, in turn, makes us all the more susceptible to the kind of associative play that turns reading into self-exploration.

A third of the way into Breathing Lessons, Maggie, Ira, and the others who have come for the service return to the widow's house. She has a surprise planned. When everyone is assembled in her living room, she brings out a projector and shows an old home movie that was made at her wedding. The guests are taken aback. All at once they are staring at the light-scarred images of their former selves:

Then the camera swooped and there was Sissy playing the piano, with one damp curl plastered to her forehead. Maggie and Ira, side by side, stood watching Sissy gravely. (Ira was a boy, a mere child.) They drew a breath. They started singing . . .

By the time we reach this section, we are reasonably well acquainted with Maggie and Ira—Maggie especially. We have seen their way with each other in the present (tolerant, alternately affectionate and irritated), we know something of their past (though the full story of their courtship has yet to be told), and we have a very strong sense about Maggie's inner life. We know what her concerns are, how her thoughts move, what kinds of connections she makes. Following along through the scene, we are not in her mind, but we are beside her. Our vantage allows us an exalting sense of intensification. The time-line that we have been tracing, comprised mainly of incidents in the narrative present, is suddenly ruptured. Drawing analogies to our own confrontations with the past—as we inevitably do—we encompass the depth of Maggie's time. Her presence is immediately augmented.

Of course, we all know these intrusions of past, the irrefutable proofs that we really were once different. We are doubly stricken: we not only feel the gap from now to then, but we also grasp that there was once a then that had no inkling of its future. We glimpse ourselves "objectively," deprived of the blendings and distortions that usually soften the memory process. We are face-to-face with the truth about the passing of time, our aging; the day will come, we realize, from which our now will seem as quaint and diminished as that arrested moment of the past.

These thoughts arise in me as I read this scene, but more as sensations and intimations than as formulated ideas. I participate in Maggie's looking at the past, but it is at the same time very much my own looking. I am not merging, or losing myself, but I am identifying. The distinction is important. The contact I make with myself is not vicarious; it is direct. Maggie becomes an agent, a *medium,* for my own responses to my life. The picture is complicated when I realize that Maggie is also, in a way, a medium for conveying Tyler's own sensations about *her* past—that it is her life I am indirectly in contact with.

. . . .

SVEN BIRKERTS

My experience of Tyler's characters, then, is neither the result of pure suspension of self, nor the simple product of mental construction. It is something in between. While reading, I surrender parts of my customary self-awareness in order to participate in the lives created. But while I may forget that I am in a chair, I do not forget that I exist. Rather, my inner self, that chaotic bundle of emotions, longings, and memories, comes loose from its moorings. These previously latent elements circulate freely about the characters and settings. I cannot always say clearly where I stop and the fictional life begins. My thoughts swarm over the phantom selves of Maggie and Ira, occupying them in part; *their* thoughts and experiences—in the form of the language that creates them—fill me and seem mine. The interchange brings about a kind of amalgamation.

I am living under a spell while I am reading: I am dreaming with my eyes open. In night dreams, I often feel the same familiar sense of flowing over boundaries. One person is readily combined with another, or else I feel perfectly intimate with someone I scarcely know—yet everything seems right and profound. The same familiarity and rightness move through me as I read certain novels. I keep reading because I long to perpetuate the feeling.

But this wakeful dreaming has direction and shape. The author controls me, moving the characters—and me with them—toward some determined resolution. So long as I am within the force field of the book, I am the subject of a powerful shadow reality. The phone may ring, or I may jump up to get to the store before it closes, but when I pick up the book again, I have only to wind my way back a sentence or two. Right away I locate my place in this other place; I return, and it is as if I had never left.

But novels end. The characters and the life they sustain become colored with the futurity of their imminent parting. How soon Ira and Maggie are back in their bedroom—only a few pages remain. I am going to have to finish with them just when I've come to know them most intimately. It's hard not to feel some of the twinges we reserve for real-life partings. Ira, now become so familiar, is laying out his solitaire; Maggie is looking on:

He had arrived at the interesting part of the game by now, she saw. He had passed that early, superficial stage where any number of moves seemed possible and he had to show real skill and judgment. She felt a little stir of something that came over her like a flush, a sort of inner buoyancy, and she lifted her face to kiss the warm blade of his cheekbone. Then she slipped free and moved to her side of the bed, because tomorrow they had a long car trip to make and she knew she would need a good night's sleep before they started.

A complex, triumphant finish. Maggie, we know from that "little stir of something," has registered a metaphoric understanding of their situation: their place in life, in time, is momentarily connected to Ira's place in the game. Options have narrowed, "skill and judgment" will now be required. But the implication is that the game can be completed successfully, with nothing left over or gone to waste. As readers, we share Maggie's insight, but we also gain an added perception. We get the analogy to the fiction itself: this moment is, in effect, the last right placing of the final card. With one stroke, Tyler has flashed forth the depth of Maggie and Ira's married love and has surrounded it with the promise of a future. It is an illusionistic future—it waits off the page—but we take leave of the novel by walking a short distance into it.

The sensations we feel as we finish a novel like this are strange ones. Even as we close the covers, the mirage begins to fade; the chair, the room, everything we were insensible of, comes crowding back. It is, truly, as if we were waking from a particularly vivid dream. That feeling of fusion, of blurred boundaries, is gone. What are we left with? A set of memory traces, a lingering responsiveness to an undefined otherness of person and place, a temporary sense of completeness. We have been somewhere, and now we are back. The world has the color of our traveling.

.   .   .

SVEN BIRKERTS

AMERICAN
WRITERS

Henry
Miller

In his recent film *Henry & June*, director Philip Kaufman introduces his male hero with the kind of lingering vertical pan usually reserved for femmes fatales or tall gunmen of the Clint Eastwood stripe. The trick is obvious, but it works. The eye is drawn up button by button along the lines of a rough though well-made suit. Suddenly, under the lowered brim of a gangster hat, the face—the *mug*. We do a double take at the squint-clenched cigarette, the cocksure leer. The camera plays to audience expectations. Here he is, folks: Henry Miller. Tough guy, bohemian, sexual threat, literary hero.

Kaufman is, of course, activating only one of the collective stereotypes of Henry Miller. In others Miller is the pornographer, the crusading liberator, the sham mystic, or, in the worn jargon of feminism's more militant period, the sexist pig. And in this, the centennial of Miller's birth, it is likely that all these stereotypes, and others besides, will be toted up. Two major biographies are being published, one by Robert Ferguson, the other by Mary Dearborn, while a third book on Miller, by Erica Jong, is in the works. Once the trajectory of the life and career has been set out, the commentary and criticism will surely follow.

Consensus, however, is not likely, no more now than in the past. Indeed, probably no major American writer has had so mixed a reception or had his literary status so fiercely contested as has Miller. Even the question of his being "major" is open. When Miller first published *Tropic of Cancer* in 1934, writers as diverse as T. S. Eliot, Ezra Pound, George Orwell, and Aldous Huxley stepped forth to praise him. But Miller went on writing for nearly fifty years, and much of the later work was second-rate. For this reason, or perhaps because he is just not likely dissertation fodder, he has been all but ignored by the critical establishment. Then there is the matter of his fictional treatment of women. Kate Millett's take-no-prisoners attack in *Sexual Politics* (1969) decimated Miller's macho ethos. When Norman Mailer, as if in rebuttal, offered up *Genius and Lust* (1976), an anthology with commentary, the book fell flat. And yet the myth persists. The image of the iconoclast and free spirit exerts ongoing appeal. Historical shifts of sensibility both made and unmade Miller. It remains to be seen whether they can make him again.

Born in Manhattan, Miller grew up in the Williamsburg section of Brooklyn. He wrote about his early years in *Tropic of Capricorn* and elsewhere—about his kind but emasculated father, his cold and carping mother, about his street adventures with neighborhood gangs, about the early collision of aspiration with obstacle. Miller was never able to do the expected thing. He dropped out of City College after two months and began his decades-long drift from one hated job to another. He married for the first time in 1917 (there would be four other marriages) but soon grew bored and took up with other women. Then, in the early 1920s, Miller finally tried his hand at writing. He wrote his first novel, *Clipped Wings* (which remains unpublished), during a three-week vacation from the Western Union Telegraph Company, where he worked as employment manager. The title suggests a great deal about his self-concept at the time.

In 1923 Miller fell in love with June Smith, a Broadway taxi dancer; he married her the next year. To his workaday frustrations and his apprenticeship struggles with writing were added the torments of a mad relationship. June was, by all accounts, a sorceress.

. . . .

SVEN BIRKERTS

She was beautiful and passionate, but she was also a compulsive liar
and a cocaine user. She made money for both of them by taking up
with rich men. Miller was half-insane with jealousy, but he needed
her. And it was June, in a sense, who helped make him a writer. She
backed his efforts. She raised the cash to send him to Paris, where
his vision would first take shape. And she fired his rage—and writing
will—to incandescence.

The story of Miller's Paris decade is well known. It was *la vie
bohème,* only not the airbrushed sort with picturesque garrets and
merry artists' balls. Miller lived most of the 1930s in excruciating
poverty, moving from one bug-infested nest to the next. He took
handouts wherever he could find them (Anaïs Nin, his friend and
sometime lover, was one of his more reliable patrons). And he wrote.
Paris freed Miller as a writer. He saw, at last, that his true subject
was himself and that his voice should not be literary but that of a
man speaking the intimate, and at times shocking, truth of his life.

In just a few years, Miller produced the three books that are the
foundation stones of his reputation: *Tropic of Cancer, Black Spring,*
and *Tropic of Capricorn.* Out of the poverty, failure, and heartache
of his circumstance he blew a chorus of triumphant self-assertion. It
was a most peculiar thing. Here was a world in depression, verging
toward war, and here was an American not only accepting but *rel-
ishing* the chaos all around him. A passage from the opening of *Tropic
of Cancer* gives the idea: "I have no money, no resources, no hopes.
I am the happiest man alive. A year ago, six months ago, I thought
that I was an artist. I no longer think about it, I *am.* Everything that
was literature has fallen from me. There are no more books to be
written, thank God."

Miller would go on to write a long shelf of books, but never
mind. In the face of such evident gusto, one forgives a good deal.
And for many readers of the early Miller there was a good deal that
needed forgiving.

In the pages of *Tropic of Cancer,* he brought the seamiest side of
Parisian lowlife into vivid focus. Like a kid crying "Watch me!," he
went swaggering through what others might deem the most depressing of circumstances. His was a world of hunger and physical
privation but also of sexual piracy. Miller's "I"—not just in the
Tropics but throughout the oeuvre—navigates without compunction

. . . .

Henry Miller

among prostitutes and women of easy virtue and voracious sexual appetites (nearly all of his fictional women fit in one or the other category); he takes what he wants and moves on. The structural logic of the books follows a simple serial pattern: the desire (or need), the hunt, the gratification, the desire renewed . . .

But the writing itself, at least in these early books, is fresh and vigorous. Miller had the raconteur's knack for setting a scene and enough literary control to keep his prose rhythmic and strongly sensory. We can almost feel his joy in finding a way to release his experience into language:

> Boris is rubbing his hands again. Mr. Wren is still stuttering and spluttering. I have a bottle between my legs and I'm shoving the corkscrew in. Mrs. Wren has her mouth parted expectantly. The wine is splashing between my legs, the sun is splashing through the bay window, and inside my veins there is a bubble and splash of a thousand crazy things that commence to gush out of me now pell-mell. I'm telling them everything that comes to mind, everything that was bottled up inside me and which Mrs. Wren's loose laugh has somehow released.
>
> —*Tropic of Cancer*

Indeed, one could say as much of Miller's entire early output, that it was a pell-mell scattering of goods. We find pipe dreams wrapped around actual street-corner adventures, pornographic interludes abutting high-minded meditations on human destiny—all of it somehow contained and controlled by this speaking voice. In his time, Miller was regarded as a revolutionist of the literary.

In 1940, fleeing the war, he returned to America, living for many years in a shack at Big Sur. Though he wrote voluminously, completing his immense trilogy, *The Rosy Crucifixion* (comprised of *Sexus, Plexus,* and *Nexus*), as well as dozens of essays, pamphlets, and chunks of memoir, the writing itself did not measure up. Some mainspring of tension seemed to have broken. Miller slackened his rhythms and began to repeat himself; worse, he became a crank, airing his often less-than-savory views on money, Jews, spiritualism, white bread, you name it. With every new work he undermined the authority of his earlier attainments.

What happened? One sort of explanation comes from George

Orwell, who, in his 1940 essay "Inside the Whale," gave Miller high marks for style but also predicted that he would not go on to write further work of substance. Miller, he believed, had walled himself off from the world; he was a Jonah in the whale's belly, which is "simply a womb big enough for an adult."

What Orwell had identified was Miller's narcissism. The writings and biographical data put it beyond dispute: the whale that imprisoned Henry Miller was named Henry Miller. The core drama of the world was *his* drama; its pleasures and pains had all been devised with him in mind. And no matter where we look in the oeuvre, we find a man striking poses in a mirror, playing to his own inflated self-regard. He is always the happiest, healthiest, or most miserable, most abject, of men—he is never just a normal, fallible human being. The Paris books refracted that narcissism through an immense accumulated fury and did so with considerable artistic power. But after that deluge, there was only "me."

The American reception of Miller was the echo that chased the explosion. This is one of the central ironies of his career: Miller was well into his meandering years when Grove Press finally issued his *Tropics*. It was the beginning of the 1960s. The old outlaw and icon-breaker—he was about to turn seventy—was suddenly everywhere in the news, shocking readers, raising censorship issues, and exerting influence on a new generation of young writers. Henry Miller, the curmudgeon of Big Sur, was the most exciting and artistic dirty-book writer around. Pilgrims came to his door in droves and would continue to, despite his protests, until he died in 1980, wheelchair-bound and nearly blind.

Miller's writings, his public image—the press made him out to be an apostle of free love—the cocksure anarchism of his philosophy, all heralded the great social liberation of the late sixties. Miller, if anyone, was seen to stand for free speech and the destruction of puritanical taboos. But the revolution that he helped to sponsor was also, in a sense, his undoing. For the widespread clamor for social and political freedoms also brought about the mighty rise of the women's movement. What was given with one hand was taken away with the other. The shock value of Miller's work brought notoriety. He was seen as an avant-gardist, a crusader. He broke barriers, opening our literature, much as Whitman had done a century before, to the voice of the man (or woman) in the street—the direct, confessional voice. He was the writer who helped to make Norman Mailer, Erica Jong, Philip Roth, and a host of others possible.

But shock value, as we know, is ephemeral. And once the "how" of the saying lost its dazzle, it was easier to see the "what." To the newly emancipated post-sixties sensibility, that "what" looked cruel and degrading. No longer is it possible to talk about Miller without talking about his attitude toward women. Wounded by his mother, by June, perhaps by others, Miller sought to avenge himself upon the whole gender. His was not just the habitual sexism of the times. It was deeper, more virulent, and it cannot finally be separated out from the work as an unfortunate component. For the work is saturated with it.

I open *Tropic of Capricorn* and find: "He took pleasure in degrading her. I could scarcely blame him for it, she was such a prim, priggish bitch in her street clothes." Or in *Tropic of Cancer:* "When you look at them with their clothes on you imagine all sorts of things: you give them an individuality . . . which they haven't got, of course." And on and on—the most revelatory passages, of course, cannot be printed here. Kate Millett put it most tactfully, but also most devastatingly, in her *Sexual Politics.* "Miller's sexism," she wrote, "is beyond question an honest contribution to social and psychological understanding which we can hardly afford to ignore. . . . To confuse this hostility . . . with freedom were vicious, were it not so very sad."

Yet for all this, there is, and will continue to be, a Miller legacy. Readers, especially young readers, are bound to repeat for themselves the larger cultural process I have sketched. They will find in the best of Miller's books a curious mixture of beauty and brutality, not to mention a sense of the gritty real that is not readily available elsewhere. They will also find what Anaïs Nin called, in her preface to *Tropic of Cancer,* "a wild extravagance, a mad gaiety, a verve, a gusto, at times almost a delirium." Nor should we forget that such self-celebration—against all odds, defiant before crushing forces of conformism—is a heady elixir to anyone engaged in the staking out of an identity. Later, of course, the mixture loses some of its fizz.

·   ·   ·

SVEN BIRKERTS

Walker
Percy

O dds are that when John Updike wrote *Rabbit, Run,* he did not
have sketches for *Redux* and *Rich* on the drafting table. Similarly, the perpetual return of Nathan Zuckerman is more likely the
result of Philip Roth's ongoing self-examination than of any long-
term literary calculation. But both novelists are occupied with character and change, so the idea of going back to a past creation is perfectly
natural. In some ways it's even heartening, since it suggests that
figments can acquire a certain independence, that they may have the
power to direct their author's hand.

Walker Percy also seems to be making the reincarnation of characters a feature of his literary practice. First he brought back Will
Barrett, the youthful protagonist of *The Last Gentleman,* to play the
middle-aged lead in *The Second Coming;* but that title was little more
than a sly wink, since the passing of decades, as well as Percy's
determined focus on the events of the present, dissolved any sense
that a single Barrett was persisting in time. Now *The Thanatos Syndrome* picks up another Percy familiar. When we last saw Dr. Tom
More, at the end of *Love in the Ruins,* he was settling in to spend his

golden years with his lovely new wife, Ellen. But the calm, like the calm that descends every so often upon the great houses of Carrington and Colby, was apparently not destined to last. "For some time now," says Dr. More at the outset of the new novel, "I have noticed that something strange is occurring in our region." The old knight is already getting his armor out of storage.

To be fair, Percy does oblige his reader with a few connecting strands. More alludes once or twice to his former travails. ("At one time I thought the world was going mad and that it was up to me to diagnose the madness and treat it. I became grandiose, even Faustian.") His wife is still Ellen, and he has kept his psychiatric practice in Feliciana Parish, Louisiana. But Percy could have named his hero Binx Bolling, Lance Lamarr, or anything else, for all that it ultimately matters. For unlike, say, Updike, he has no compulsion to probe the mysteries of character change. Percy uses More merely because it's convenient to do so. He's already been created; he has a past and a profession. And his genial, bourbon-cured cynicism has proved to be a most effective filter for the kinds of in extremis scenarios that Percy favors.

But all those traits, too, are finally vehicles. Percy is a novelist of ideas who just happens to have a knack for creating distinctive (if somewhat flat) characters and riveting (if somewhat improbable) plots. His interests and methods have changed considerably over the years. His first novel, *The Moviegoer,* was a Kierkegaardian meditation on the attainment of authentic selfhood. Its thrust was philosophical, not psychological; Binx Bolling's intriguing reflections all but buried the plot. Since then, however, Percy has become ever more venturesome about devising situations and complications that can embody contending concepts. He has decided that it is the reader, not the characters, who should do most of the thinking. And his scope has widened accordingly. The later novels turn from the malaise of individual consciousness to the larger infections of the social organism.

More's serenity at the close of *Love in the Ruins* was, it seems, an illusory triumph. At the beginning of Percy's new novel, we learn that he has just returned from a two-year stint in a minimum-security prison for supplying amphetamines to truck drivers. Now under the probationary care of Drs. Max Gottlieb and Bob Comeaux, he resumes his private practice. Still, as indicated, something is amiss. His old patients are showing the most curious behavioral symptoms: an absence of former (indeed any) anxieties, verbal simplification, uncanny factual recall, and, among some of the females, a tendency to "present rearward." Nor is this monkey business confined to the consulting room. Ellen has quite suddenly—under the tutelage of doctor, educator, and bridge wizard John Van Dorn—revealed an almost superhuman ability to compute bridge combinations. She has also lost her former pudency; More finds her striking an inviting quadruped pose in the bedroom.

Though More retails his observations with a characteristically bemused detachment, the graver implications do nag at him. As he says right at the start: "A great scientist once said that genius consists not in making great discoveries but in seeing the connection between small discoveries." More will try to be that genius. Before we've even creased the binding, we have been drawn into his obsessive search for explanatory links. It would be robbing the reader of much good sport if I disclosed the process in too much detail. But some revelation is necessary.

More quickly teams up with his cousin Lucy, one of Percy's many can-do southern women. As luck would have it, Lucy is both an epidemiologist and a crackerjack computer hacker. Together they map out the geographical distribution pattern of the cases. They discover in progress a high-level (and highly illegal) experiment in social control. A group of scientists, including Gottlieb, Comeaux, and Van Dorn, has been diverting sodium waste from the Grand Mer reactor into the regional water supply. It is, as More later describes it, an "aberrant local initiative . . . people using discretionary funding to run a pilot which might otherwise not be funded and then present[ing] them [the government] with a fait accompli which they can't turn down." The daily news almost makes the author look like a haruspex.

The doctors are armed with some stunning statistics: the suppression of isolated cortical functions by sodium ions has brought about dramatic reductions in crime, homosexual activity, reports of AIDS. Street kids are volunteering for community service. The football team is unbeatable. When More eventually raises the tricky question of ethics, the doctors have a ready answer: they compare their project to the initially covert, and finally beneficial, fluoridation of water. What is involved here, however, is something more like a fluoridation of the psyche—a riskier venture. The doctors naturally want More on their side. They offer him a high-paying research post with perks. But More, old-style soul doctor that he is, cannot be persuaded. He mistrusts any kind of spiritual quick fix. Where there is no suffering, there can be no soul, no grace; God disappears. More, another of Percy's lapsed-Catholic narrators, never says this directly; but anyone who knows Percy's work can fill in the blanks.

Percy takes obvious pleasure in playing More's curmudgeonly skepticism off the slick cajolery of his colleagues. Over the years he has perfected his rendering of the subtle signals of southern male bonhomie. The procedure is set, but it works. More refuses the moralistic pose; his opponents hoist themselves with their own petard. Here Comeaux has taken the doctor out for a drive and a "chat":

> We're sailing through the sunlit pines, "The Beautiful Blue Danube" all around us. Bob is enjoying himself. He puts a soft fist on my knee.
>
> "Tom, we need you. We want you on the team. We need your old sour, sardonic savvy to keep us honest. You understand, don't you?"
>
> "Yes."
>
> "Okay, one thing. Tell me honestly. Don't pull punches. Has anything you've heard in the last few minutes about the behavioral effects of the sodium additive struck you as undesirable?"
>
> "Not offhand, though it's hard to say. I'll have to think it over."
>
> "There you go!" Again the soft congratulatory fist on my knee. "That's the answer we're looking for. Be hard on us! Be our Dutch uncle!"
>
> "But what about the cases of gratuitous violence—Mickey LaFaye shooting all her horses—the rogue violence of that postal worker in St. Francisville who shot everybody in the post office?"
>
> Now he socks himself. "You've already put a finger on it!" he cries aloud. "That's why we need you."

·   ·   ·

SVEN BIRKERTS

The complexity of human exchange has always fascinated Percy (as his two essay collections, *The Message in the Bottle* and *Lost in the Cosmos,* demonstrate). He wishes to understand how two people can be speaking on one level while understanding each other on another. Once we catch on to More's strategically (and psychiatrically) neutral style, we realize that the whole novel turns on these semantically overdetermined interchanges. Their cumulative resonance grows by the chapter, turning what could be a conspiracy plot by Crichton or Cook into a statement of genuine minatory power.

More quite rightly suspects a catch. Too many people are trying too hard to win him over. He keeps connecting discoveries, following hunches. The indicating arrows start pointing to Belle Ame, the elite school run by Van Dorn. There is evidence of sexual abuse. When he finds out that Ellen has left their own children in Van Dorn's care, More decides to visit the school himself. The ominously hilarious climax finds him quite literally giving the whole Belle Ame staff a dose of their own medicine.

Though *The Thanatos Syndrome* reads like a good thriller, it plays for bigger stakes. And in one respect it plays too hard. Perhaps out of fear that a one-track narrative might prevent his message from shining forth, Percy has outfitted the novel with a most perplexing subplot. Father Simon Smith (he made a cameo appearance in *Love in the Ruins*) has shut himself up in a fire-watcher's tower and refuses to come down. Comeaux prevails upon More to exercise his therapeutic gifts. But the old priest ("he still looks like an old Ricardo Montalban with a handsome seamed face as tanned as cordovan leather, hair like Brillo, and the same hairy *futbol* wrists") won't budge. He is suffering from some peculiar sickness of the soul. During More's first visit, he moves in and out of catatonia, ranting during his "lucid" moments about Jews and the evacuation of all meaning from our word-signs. "Tenderness," he says, fixing on his interlocutor, "leads to the gas chamber."

It turns out that as a young man Smith had traveled to Germany with his father, where they visited with a Dr. Jäger, an eminent psychiatrist, and his two sons. He formed a close friendship with Helmut, the younger son, who was about to join an SS officer school.

At their parting, Helmut presented Smith with a dagger etched with the words *Blut und Ehre*. Grabbing More's arm now, the priest confesses: "If I had been German, not American, I would have joined him."

As we know very little of Father Smith, except for his dementia, it's hard to know what to make of this information. But the rest of his tale is perfectly clear. Returning to Germany in 1945 as a soldier with the Seventh Army, Smith participated in the liberation of the very hospital at which Dr. Jäger had worked. The doctor himself had fled, but one of the nurses showed him the *Kinderhaus,* where lethal experiments were carried out upon children. Jäger—musician, scholar, the same man who had expressed his outrage at the brown-shirt thugs—had been the chief researcher. "I'm not sure I understand what you're trying to tell me—about your memory of—about Germany," says More. To this the priest replies: "What is there to understand?"

We are in the century of mass death, the age of Thanatos. Percy wants to ensure that we make no mistake about the moral and historical connection: the logic of the sodium project is, slightly extended, the logic of the Nazi exterminators. *Any* action undertaken in the name of a principle or an abstraction is dangerous. The ethical conclusion is to treat all human beings with reference to their individuality, not their similarity. Percy said as much in an essay on "The Diagnostic Novel" in *Harper's* last June. Remarking on our idolatry of science, he wrote: "As a person educated in science . . . it dawned on me that no science or scientist, not even Freud, could address a single word to me as an individual." The novelist's role is implicitly moral—to make up the deficit, to say what it is like "to be an individual living in the United States in the 20th century."

The Thanatos Syndrome manifests this calling with great vigor, even without the counternarrative. If Percy's intent was to intrude the Father Smith chapters as an irritant, as a way of forcing the reader to look past the seductive surface of his novel's plot, he has succeeded. But I can't help feeling that these more loaded episodes could have been worked in with greater elegance. "Tenderness leads to the gas chamber" certainly strikes one as, shall we say, a contradiction;

· · · ·

SVEN BIRKERTS

but it does not shock, and it isn't placed in a way that would make it a "lever of transcendence" (the phrase is Simone Weil's).

This problem by no means hobbles the novel. Percy controls his main narrative with great sureness; it is suspenseful, it is provocative, it is witty. Nobody presently writing has so keen an eye for the surreal quality of our cultural topography. Percy is especially good at catching the way that media figures and media usages infiltrate every corner of daily life. Afternoon soaps, Dr. Ruth, Robin Leach, M*A*S*H reruns: little escapes Percy's whirring darts. And though his quips are never didactic, we can sense a more serious concern in the background. There's a hint, nothing more, that the happy vacuousness streaming from the screens of several hundred million televisions somehow makes his fantasy scenario less and less impossible.

The Thanatos Syndrome ends . . . well, happily. In the last chapter, More is back in his office, listening to what suddenly sounds like beautiful music: a patient's litany of anxiety and despair. It's a masterful final stroke. For only by this contrast do we register the true horror of the sodium cure: that the end of suffering and dread is for us, paradoxical creatures, the end of the path to awareness. Indeed, as we leave Tom More, old Kierkegaardian soul doctor, back in his element, we feel decidedly better about our own unmedicated condition.

The Thanatos Syndrome. Walker Percy. 372 pp. Farrar, Straus & Giroux. 1987. $17.95

Jack
Kerouac

I first read Jack Kerouac's *On the Road* when I was a junior in high school—a little more than twenty-one years ago. Someone had given my mother a copy of the book; I immediately "borrowed" it, consumed it, and started it circulating among my friends. Soon we were all obsessed—hitchhiking everywhere we could, trying to be like the characters in the novel.

Our every late-adolescent desire for movement, escape, *action,* was brought to a blaze. Not that much fanning of sparks was needed. After all, it was 1968. If it hadn't been Kerouac, it would soon have been someone else.

Though Kerouac had begun writing *On the Road* in 1948, and it had first been published in 1957, the book could not have felt more present tense. Kerouac had caught hold of a spirit we understood; he raised a call to arms. What for me had been just inchoate turmoil and longing had now been set down in words. I grew restless and excited when the book's narrator, Sal Paradise, announced:

... the only people for me are the mad ones, the ones who are mad to live, mad to talk, mad to be saved, desirous of everything at the same time, the ones who never yawn or say a commonplace thing, but burn, burn, burn like fabulous yellow roman candles exploding like spiders across the stars and in the middle you see the blue centerlight pop and everybody goes "Awww!"

That was it right there: madness, excess, something nonstop and feverish to hold against the blandness of our suburban childhoods.

When I went off to college, I found that we had not been unique: everyone, it seemed, had been reading Kerouac. And Ginsberg and Corso and Burroughs and Kesey (and Wolfe *on* Kesey). This was our noncurricular education. These were the spirits who conferred their benediction upon us, upon our efforts to live differently—more intensely—than our parents had.

What a shock it was to hear, late one fall afternoon in 1969, that Kerouac had died. At forty-seven. Of an abdominal hemorrhage. Our perennially young and vital adventure guide—aka Sal Paradise—was gone. The friend who called with the news said that we had to go to the funeral. I agreed. We packed our knapsacks and left immediately, determined to hitch from Ann Arbor to Lowell, Massachusetts—wherever *that* was. We got as far as Boston; by then the funeral was over, and we were cold and jittery from lack of sleep. We told each other that it was the going, not the getting there, that mattered.

Other shocks followed. Obituaries reported that Kerouac had lived out his last years in an alcoholic stupor. The photos confirmed it—his once beautifully chiseled American face looked bloated and sad. We hadn't known. And then came the most distressing story of all. Our hero had told reporters some time before his death that he felt alienated from the "counterculture." He'd tagged himself—I remember wincing at this—"a bippie in the middle."

Later I learned of other myths, not only about Kerouac the man—his politics and attitudes—but also about the writer. The myth about the way he wrote *On the Road* is a case in point. The story—which the author did nothing to discourage—was that he had written the

·   ·   ·

Jack Kerouac

book in a record-breaking three-week burst; that he had lit himself up with Benzedrine and had typed his inspired recollections directly onto one continuous roll of teletype paper. Now, this is not pure invention. The final version *was* written quickly, with the help of pills, onto just such a roll (Kerouac dumped it proudly in front of his editor, Robert Giroux). But Kerouac was not taking dictation from the angels. He had been working on the book for close to eight years, wrestling it through innumerable drafts. Kerouac adopted his final compositional stratagem because he was after a quality of improvisatory immediacy. He wanted to break with the stolid straightforwardness of his first novel, *The Town and the City* (1950). He had picked up cues from the simplified notational prose of William Burroughs's *Junky* as well as from the breathless letter-writing style of his friend Neal Cassady. He announced his new prose in *On the Road's* first lines:

> I first met Dean not long after my wife and I split up. I had just gotten over a serious illness that I won't bother to talk about, except that it had something to do with the miserably weary split-up and my feeling that everything was dead. With the coming of Dean Moriarty began the part of my life you could call my life on the road.

Kerouac's opening may owe a debt to the "Factualist" aesthetic that Burroughs was then advocating. But its beguiling promise of escape and renewal connects it with two great classics of American individualism. Listen first to the voice of Melville's Ishmael:

> Whenever I find myself growing grim about the mouth; whenever it is a damp, drizzly November in my soul; whenever I find myself involuntarily pausing before coffin warehouses, and bringing up the rear of every funeral I meet . . . then, I account it high time to get to sea as soon as I can.

Now listen to the voice of Mark Twain's Huck, as he shakes free from the oppressive confinements of the Widow Douglas:

> Says I, "*me-yow! me-yow!*" as soft as I could, and then I put out the light and scrambled out of the window onto the shed. Then I slipped down to the ground and crawled in amongst the trees, and sure enough there was Tom Sawyer waiting for me.

. . . .

SVEN BIRKERTS

But unlike *Moby-Dick* and *Huckleberry Finn, On the Road* is not mostly a work of imagination. Rather, it details, adhering quite strictly to circumstance and chronology, Kerouac's adventures during four separate cross-country jaunts undertaken between 1946 and 1950. He changed the names, of course, and highlighted or downplayed certain episodes, but the result—to judge by the biographies—is remarkably true to his own experience. Kerouac is Sal Paradise, the narrator; Neal Cassady (later the star of Tom Wolfe's nonfictional *The Electric Kool-Aid Acid Test*) is Dean Moriarty; Allen Ginsberg is Carlo Marx; William Burroughs is Old Bull Lee; and so on. (Part of the enduring cachet of *On the Road* has to do with the fact that so many of its main players became notorious counterculture icons.)

I decided that I would commemorate the passing of two decades by rereading *On the Road*. I knew, of course, that everything would be different. How could it not? In 1968 it had been a book whose title promised *discovery*. Now the cover blurb announced that I was about to read "the book that turned on a generation." Braced as I was, however, I still got a terrible jolt. There is simply no adequate protection against the ways we grow and change.

The novel, *qua* novel, is not really much at all. Kerouac's alternately matter-of-fact and ebullient prose tracks Sal Paradise through his far-flung travels. The pattern is simple: About once a year, Sal gets restless in his secure lodgings with his aunt (the *mémère* to whom Kerouac remained neurotically attached all his life) and launches forth from New Jersey to the beckoning West. Each time, he hooks up with Dean Moriarty, his "mad" mentor, the aging juvenile delinquent who represents (to him) velocity, kicks, and enlightenment. Others join up and disperse, moving about like molecules of a boiling liquid. The American highway system is the spice route of their dreams. "Somewhere along the line," says Sal as he first sets out, "I knew there'd be girls, visions, everything; somewhere along the line the pearl would be handed to me."

Kerouac is sequential, at times almost diaristic. On the first trip West—perhaps because it *is* the first—every movement is tabulated. We follow Sal from the bus rides that get him started, to the long, "careening" (a favorite Kerouac word) rides that come once he gets west of Chicago and puts out his thumb. But Sal's enthusiasm allows for a heady narrative pace:

> The greatest ride in my life was about to come up, a truck, with a flatboard at the back, with about six or seven boys sprawled out on it, and the drivers, two young blond farmers from Minnesota, were picking up every single soul they found on that road . . .
>
> I wasn't on the flatboard before the truck roared off; I lurched, a rider grabbed me, and I sat down. Somebody passed a bottle of rotgut, the bottom of it. I took a big swig in the wild, lyrical, drizzling air of Nebraska. "Whooee, here we go!" yelled a kid in a baseball cap, and they gunned up the truck to seventy and passed everybody on the road.

Wild and *lyrical* are two more favorite Kerouac words—they crop up in most of his more energized riffs, especially through the first half of the book. It's as if Sal can't kick the language up quite as high as he wants it—he makes these loosely deployed adjectives carry so much of the freight of the inexpressible. But once—for me at least—they did carry it. When I first read *On the Road,* no one needed to tell me how a night, or a town, or a train, or a bum, could be "lyrical"—they just were. Kerouac's scattershot words and phrases accorded perfectly with my jumbled-up feelings about life. Now, for whatever reason, I seem to crave more precision—a passage like that no longer delivers.

On Sal's first trip West, he wants to "dig" everything. And everything is there to be dug. When he gets to Denver, his first real layover, a gang of friends and friends of friends is waiting. There follow rampaging nights with the hard-partying Bettencourt sisters and the Rawlins clan: "We started off with a few extra-size beers. There was a player piano. Beyond the back door was a view of mountainsides in the moonlight. I let out a yahoo. The night was on."

New sights and the promise of good times are, of course, part of what lures Sal away from home again and again; but the real draw is Dean—the outlaw, the limit-breaker. Sal wants to be near him as much as possible. Dean steals cars, he tears between the coasts in nonstop driving binges, he loves every "gal" in every diner along the way. He is Sal's "yellow roman candle," his life force; he is the catalyst that helps Sal break through his essential passivity.

Sal and Dean have one of those eternally boyish American friendships. Though women are desired, discussed, and dallied with, they are also always in the way—nagging, getting pregnant, threatening to stop the fun. Leslie Fiedler long ago identified the homoerotic nature of the bond (yes, Ishmael and Queequeg, Huck and Jim . . .) in *Love and Death in the American Novel*. And biographers of Kerouac now bear out that his friendship with Cassady did extend to some hesitant, experimental sex.

In any event, what weaves together the separate travel episodes is the unfolding history of a friendship—a history that begins with Sal's enchantment with the charismatically amoral Dean Moriarty and that ends with his pained disillusionment. In an early, blinded description, Sal writes: "And a kind of holy lightning I saw flashing from his excitement and his visions, which he described so torrentially that people in buses looked around to see the 'overexcited nut.' " But after he has been deserted and betrayed enough times, Sal finds his perceptions shifting. Dean's mad avidity is not so much heroic as desperate. He is fleeing his own inner void—the legacy of his rummy father, who abandoned him among the bars and poolhalls of Denver when he was a young boy.

By the end of the book, Sal's "thin-hipped" hero has become a figure of profound sadness. In the very last scene, when Sal is on his way to a concert, riding in the back of a hired Cadillac, he looks out at his friend: "Dean, ragged in a motheaten overcoat he brought specially for the freezing temperatures of the East, walked off alone . . ." He then adds this valedictory cadenza: ". . . nobody knows what's going to happen to anybody besides the forlorn rags of growing old, I think of Dean Moriarty, I even think of Old Dean Moriarty the father we never found, I think of Dean Moriarty."

It is probably a mistake to go back to the decisive books of one's youth. They are causes; the reader has long since become, in part, their effect. Clear vision is just not possible. I feel myself in a position somewhat like Sal's. It was not so much that Dean had changed from what he was—more that Sal had watched the vivid mantle of desires and dreams that he had created around Dean slowly dissipate. So, too, has the magic of *On the Road* dissipated for me.

Reading this book at sixteen, my friends and I wanted nothing so much as to be like Dean and Sal—close to the ground, connected, in motion, "paying our dues." We aspired to the "beat" ideal, with its double connotation of "worn-out" and "beatific." And when it led, as it inexorably did, to the hippie ethos of turning on, tuning in, and dropping out (how quaint it sounds!), many of us followed. But that next step was also a kind of last step—the premises of hippiedom were quickly consumed on the pyre of its excesses. Thus, once again, effects had come around to swallow their causes; henceforth, "beat" would also mean something like "protohippie."

All of this went through my mind as I reread *On the Road*. Indeed, at some point I realized that I was not so much reading a book as taking stock—of those times, of these times, of myself in both. For me, the hardest thing was to see past the jadedness and cynicism of the eighties—to remember even a little of what life felt like back then. I don't know that I was able to, finally. The notes were as scored, sure, and the sounds were the same. But I kept feeling as if I were listening to a party record the morning after the party. It sounded sad, nothing like the way it had sounded while I was dancing to it.

·   ·   ·   ·

SVEN BIRKERTS

William
Styron

O f the many formidable novelists of the first postwar generation—the generation of Mailer, Heller, Roth, Updike, and
Bellow—William Styron has been the hardest to fix a frame around.
Gifted with a lyric sensibility that has always been one of the hall-
marks of the "literary," he has also, in novels like *The Confessions of
Nat Turner* and *Sophie's Choice,* manifested considerable crossover
appeal, a quality often fatal to a serious literary reputation. Indeed,
more than any of his contemporaries—except probably James
Jones—Styron has been made to wear the middlebrow mantle.

But "made to wear" is too simplistic, suggesting some imperial
board of artistic overseers and a scenario of writer as victim. In truth,
novelists who get tagged "middlebrow" often *do* expend some of their
best energies courting the middle. They find ways to heat up their
plots with sex, violence, and fantastic coincidences while at the same
time lowering the coefficient of difficulty of their prose. Of course,
there is a price to pay. These writers seldom escape getting nipped,
in public and private, by their watchful colleagues.

It is interesting, in this regard, to hear what the young Norman

Mailer had to say about the career possibilities of the young William Styron. The passage is from *Advertisements for Myself* (1959), and can now, given three decades of hindsight, be filed in the "pot calling the kettle black" department:

> He has been working hard over the years on a second novel, *Set This House on Fire,* and I hear it is done. If it is at all good, and I expect it is, the reception will be a study in the art of literary advancement. For Styron has spent years oiling every literary lever and power which could help him on his way, and there are medals waiting for him in the mass-media. . . . But if Styron has compromised his talent, and written what turns out to be the most suitable big book of the last ten years, a literary work which will deal with second hand experience and all-but-deep proliferation on the smoke of passion and the kiss of death . . . then Styron will receive a ravingly good reception, for the mass-media is aching for such a novel like a tout for his horse.

Mailer's estimate has, one must admit, a certain blustery prescience. If he missed the mark with respect to *Set This House on Fire,* he pinned the tail on *The Confessions of Nat Turner* and *Sophie's Choice.* Both were powerfully orchestrated, historically situated, and sensation-laden "big" books. Both rode comfortably on the bestseller lists, and the latter was made into a hit movie. Neither is often brought forward when the conversation turns to serious literature of the postwar period. After *Sophie's Choice* (1979), a long silence followed. Except for the publication of a miscellany of his essays and reviews, *This Quiet Dust and Other Writings* (1982), there has been nothing from Styron. For a time rumors were heard that a big novel based upon his war experiences was imminent. Other rumors followed—that he was stuck, blocked, written out; that the book had been jettisoned. And then more circumspect bulletins came from sources closer to the author: he was having a breakdown, he was suicidal, he was getting treatment. . . .

In December of 1989, Styron broke the silence. He published a lengthy piece in *Vanity Fair* in which he detailed his battle with depressive illness. That essay, with several sections of introductory material, has now been issued as *Darkness Visible: A Memoir of Madness.* Alas, long articles make slim books. Styron's brief account is not commensurate with the gravity and complexity of his subject—it will likely suffer from comparison with Kate Millett's more exhaustive recent memoir, *The Loony Bin Trip*.

"In Paris on a chilly evening late in October of 1985," begins Styron, "I first became fully aware that the struggle with disorder in my mind—a struggle which had engaged me for several months—might have a fatal outcome." What follows is the narrative of how this first realization led the author, through a series of ever-intensifying stages, to the very brink of suicide, whereupon crisis precipitated a successful drive for recovery. Styron invokes Dante's *Inferno* near the end as a sort of analogy text. But he does not mention the key difference: that Dante's protagonist ventures down through the circles of hell by choice and with a guide, while our author goes forward in terror, unattended.

The story begins not in a dark wood but in Paris, where Styron has come to receive the Prix Mondial Cino del Duca. It ought to be a happy occasion, but Styron suddenly finds himself overwhelmed by a paralyzing and incommunicable despair; he cannot eat, sleep, or take the slightest pleasure in conviviality. "While I was able to rise and function almost normally during the earlier part of the day," he reports, "I began to sense the onset of the symptoms at mid-afternoon or a little later—gloom crowding in on me, a sense of dread and alienation and, above all, stifling anxiety."

Despite his proven descriptive and dramaturgical abilities, Styron has a hard time giving a convincing account of what he soon comes to understand is a depressive disorder. Part of the problem, literarily speaking, may have to do with precedent: the literature of despair is, sad to say, a rich one, so rich that a writer stands little chance of breaking new ground or startling the reader. Alongside Augustine, Kierkegaard, Pascal, Kafka, Schopenhauer, Pavese, Woolf, Beckett, Sartre, and Bernhardt (to name a few), Styron's evocations sound a bit flat. This is not, I realize, a literary competition, and Styron's is a sincere record undertaken in good faith—but readers are demanding creatures, and good faith is not always enough.

Here is the bind. A major American writer publishes a record of his descent into depression, lays himself bare (though not, we shall see, entirely) about an experience that has brought tremendous pain to himself and those around him. How is a reviewer to step forward

.   .   .

William Styron

and profess disappointment? And on what grounds? For Styron has moved to preempt criticism. Insisting upon the indescribable nature of the malady, he has set up a kind of aesthetic catch-22:

> It has to be emphasized that if the pain were readily describable most of the countless sufferers from this ancient affliction would have been able to confidently depict for their friends and loved ones (even their physicians) some of the actual dimensions of their torment, and perhaps elicit a comprehension that has been generally lacking; such incomprehension has usually been due not to a failure of sympathy but to the basic inability of healthy people to imagine a form of distress so alien to everyday experience.

I see no choice but to be harsh. The "you would have had to have been there" gambit cannot work here; it is a signal of artistic failure. Indeed, if literature has a reason for being, it is to open passages into privacies and alien experiences. What healthy—that is to say "innocent"—person could understand anything of combat, or torture, or adulterous passion, or religious yearning? The beauty of our natures is that we can be brought out of our ignorance by words, sounds, and images. The sufferer, Styron, must put more trust in the empathic intuitions of others and the adequacy of language. The depression he describes is profoundly narcissistic: the victim cannot—and will not—try to imagine the concern and bafflement of the unafflicted.

Once Styron has identified his illness, given it a name and a historical pedigree, he tries to grasp the why of it. He makes a preliminary link between the onset of depressive symptoms and the fact that he had recently stopped drinking—after what he admits was forty years of "abuse." The day came when the body would no longer accept alcohol in any dose. "Suddenly vanished," he laments, "the great ally which for so long had kept my demons at bay was no longer there to prevent those demons from beginning to swarm through the subconscious, and I was emotionally naked, vulnerable as I had never been before."

At doctor's orders, Styron tries various drugs, experiencing different degrees of success. None can provide the surcease he needs. He tries therapy, too, but finds that its efficiency in his "advanced stage" of illness is "virtually nil." The inward sense of gloom and terror mounts, leading him to an ever more serious consideration of suicide. He admits as much to his psychiatrist, but he does not particularize for him the detailed fantasies that have started to grip him—of rafters, knives, and self-induced pneumonia. Styron writes of these thoughts, "They are doubtless especially repugnant to healthy Americans, with their faith in self-improvement. Yet in truth such hideous fantasies, which cause well people to shudder, are to the deeply distressed mind what lascivious daydreams are to persons of robust sexuality."

The problem with the long middle portion of Styron's chronicle is that much of it reads just like any person's account of the ups and downs of illness. We hear about various drug dosages, sleep and bladder discomforts, and so on. Which is not to say that these are not genuine concerns, or that any sufferer can avoid the exhaustive logging of bodily vicissitudes, but the reader does wonder whether there might not be another, shadow tale that needs telling. Where is William Styron in all this? It cannot be that depression is a feeling that floats free of all content. What about the movement of thoughts, fears, and memories? It is only when Styron moves toward his finale that a hint of the shadow tale—the untold story—emerges.

There is a perceptible gathering of momentum as the suicidal thoughts intensify. Then Styron brings on the crisis. He tells how one night he suddenly gets up from a dinner party at his home and retrieves his private notebook; how he wraps and tapes it with great care and sneaks it out to the garbage. This is, he knows, the signal: the time has come to end his despair. Though he does not yet know how he will take his life, he is now certain that he will.

What follows is the most poignant passage of this memoir. Late one winter's night, after his wife has gone to bed, Styron tries to watch a film on the VCR. He does not tell us the name, or even much of what happens, except that in one scene a contralto voice is heard singing a passage from Brahms's Alto Rhapsody. This sound, he writes, "pierced my heart like a dagger, and in a flood of swift recollection I thought of all the joys the house had known: the children who had rushed through its rooms, the festivals, the love and work. . . ." He decides at that moment to save himself. The very next day he is admitted to a hospital for treatment.

. . . .

William Styron

The dark night is over, and equilibrium will soon arrive. At first Styron experiences a numb tranquility; then, as his medication is changed, the thoughts of suicide evaporate. "For me," he states, "the real healers were seclusion and time." And it is, presumably, seclusion and time that at last allow him to turn his thoughts to what might be considered the deeper causes of the malady. But what could be, and ought to be, the most important and revealing part of the narrative is sharply truncated. Styron writes, for instance, "Until the onslaught of my own illness and its denouement, I never gave much thought to my work in terms of its connection with the subconscious—an area of investigation belonging to literary detectives." I find this an astonishing admission. That a writer of fiction in our age, a writer, moreover, who plays out themes of private apocalypse in his work, should confess such self-ignorance is scarcely to be believed. It suggests, I think, the extent of Styron's repressions.

Our author then makes a series of monumental observations, tossing them off as so many incidental asides. He mentions, for instance, that his father had "battled the Gorgon" of depression for much of his lifetime (and had even been hospitalized for it). Next we learn that his mother died when he was thirteen, and that this may have some connection with his state, the more so as he admits that he may not have mourned her death completely. And then, in the briefest flickering aside: "I do know that in those last hours before I rescued myself, when I listened to the passage from the Alto Rhapsody—which I'd heard her sing—she had been very much on my mind."

The merest phrase—"which I'd heard her sing." There is more of a story in those five words than in the pages and pages of explanation that surround them. Imagine them alone on the page, like some fragment recovered from a worn papyrus.

Styron has written a short, frustratingly incomplete book. Given the state he has described, even this much can be viewed as a significant act of self-conquest. For the author the book was, I'm sure, necessary. But for the reader it is not enough. The extent of the failing comes clear in the last few pages, for only then does the thread of truth slip free from the weave of the prose. I wish Styron well in his recovery and wait to see what he will do next. I'd like to think

. . . .

that it has been the purpose of this book to bring him to the place where the path starts. The way to the deepest Dantean places still lies before him.

Darkness Visible. William Styron. 84 pp. Random House. 1990. $15.95

. . . .

William Styron

James
Salter

For the past few years, North Point Press in San Francisco has been waging a vigorous campaign to prove that quality publishing is still possible in this country. Not only are its products well made (sewn-in signatures on acid-free paper) but some of the freshest writing of our time appears under its imprint—works by Evan S. Connell, Guy Davenport, Wendell Berry, and Gilbert Sorrentino, to name a few. Now, with the republication of James Salter's novel *Light Years* (originally published by Random House in 1967), another hectare of talent has been annexed.

Light Years features a reproduction of Pierre Bonnard's "The Breakfast Room" on the front cover. Its textures, tones, and silences are so consonant with those of the novel that the reader cannot help seeing its afterimage throughout, first as an emblem of the calm and abundance of family life, later as a reminder of how much has been undone. For this novel—explicitly moody, tender, elegiac—details the disintegration of a love and the unraveling of a well-knit life by the hearth. It is no matter that the terrain—affluent America in the

1950s and 1960s—has been trodden and retrodden by Cheever and Updike: Salter demonstrates the inexhaustibility of private destinies. As Tolstoy wrote, "every unhappy family is unhappy in its own way." Salter's lush yet quick style, his mastery of domestic resonances and, finally, his creation in Nedra and Viri of two urgent, susceptible natures assure that his treatment will be singular.

Nedra, the woman, is the active core of the book. Her discovered needs—for more meaning, more *self*—supply the centrifugal energies that will, to a large extent, determine the fate of the family. Described in the opening pages, at twenty-eight, the mother of two daughters, Nedra is

> slim as a pike. . . . She has a wide mouth, the mouth of an actress, thrilling, bright. Dark smudges in her armpits, mint on her breath. Her nature is extravagant. She buys on impulse, she visits Bendel's as she would a friend's, gathering up five or six dresses and entering a booth, not bothering to draw the curtain fully, a glimpse of her undressing, lean arms, lean trunk, bikini underpants. . . . Her dreams still cling to her, adorn her; she is confident, composed, she is related to long-necked creatures, ruminants, abandoned saints. She is careful, hard to approach. Her life is concealed. It is through the smoke and conversation of many dinners that one sees her: country dinners, dinners at the Russian Tea Room. . . .

I quote at length, in part to show Salter's style but also because he has given us, with a few quick strokes, a feel for a milieu and its rites. Much of the book unfolds in the course of these dinners, at these places, among people for whom sprees at Bendel's are a matter of course.

And Viri?

> He was a Jew, the most elegant Jew, the most romantic, a hint of weariness in his features, the intelligent features everyone envied, his hair dry, his clothes oddly threadbare—that is to say, not overly cared for, a button missing, the edge of a cuff stained, his breath faintly bad like the breath of an uncle who is no longer well.

The tragedy of Nedra and Viri is already implicit in these two descriptions: character is fate. In spite of the love and companionship they share, their energies are fundamentally alien. Nedra, like a flower will turn her soul to the strongest light; Viri will brood perversely near the glow of failure. As tender as he is to wounds and yearnings, Salter has a tragedian's grasp of implacability. What God has put together, man must sunder. The children grow up; Nedra and Viri—only then—divorce. In the end, Nedra achieves a hard-won, solitary fulfillment and dies of a mysterious illness; Viri flees into a disastrous second marriage.

Light Years is about the breaking of invisible human threads—it is in no sense a happy book. The process is slow, painful, and reluctantly undergone. Each broken filament is a consequence of forces and needs that are felt but in no way understood. Impulse, longing, change—these are mysterious and irreducible. And in this respect one does not feel that Viri and Nedra have betrayed each other. If anything has betrayed them, it is time itself, time rearing up against the heedless optimism of a present that cannot believe that things will change. This is Salter's pivot. He moves the plot forward not on its own dynamic force but by way of elision. We are given one richly detailed cross section after another. The further we get into the novel, the greater and more eloquent are the intervals. Events and the changes they have wrought are given *en passant*—it is for us to register the recoil. What finally emerges is a narrative that corresponds to life as it is felt and remembered; the elisions are the same kind that we practice on our own experience.

But there is something about this novel that is more thrilling than its cadences, its descriptive felicities, or its evocations of character. It is the sense we get, in places almost overpowering, that the book is not about Nedra and Viri at all, that its real protagonist is time. Time is the element featuring itself through the lives of these people, sweeping them up, fingering them like the stops on an instrument, revealing only gradually its force and immensity. The characters, lacking the purchase conferred by genuine suffering or privation, cross its expanse like so many water-striders. They do not penetrate the mystery. It penetrates them, exhausts them, wears away the last vestiges of pride, vanity, and self-love. Living wisely means recog-

. . . .

SVEN BIRKERTS

nizing this and submitting to it. Conveying this is Salter's useful, durable gift; his book is a *memento mori* that quickens us in the here and now.

> *Light Years*. James Salter. 308 pp. North Point Press. 1982. $8.50

·   ·   ·   ·

James Salter

Richard
Stern

*N*oble Rot, the title of Richard Stern's collection, is a translation
of the title of one of the stories, "*La Pourriture Noble,*" and
refers to the grape residues used in the distillation of fine dessert
wines. A peculiar, almost deprecatory choice, but one that was surely
deliberated. I fancy Stern was attracted by the oxymoronic word
collision, the high and low connotations. But it could be that he was
also after a certain larger resonance, a suggestion that in an active
career as a novelist (and essayist) he has tended to view his shorter
fictions as a proving ground, or (to stay with the analogy) as a kind
of compost for his more cherished growths. It is not likely that Stern's
readers will back such a discrimination of relative worths. These
stories are some of the liveliest and freshest around; they need not
bow low before the novels.

Stern has been writing for more than three decades; he has
produced, to date, some fifteen books. Many—most—of them have
been greeted with great critical enthusiasm. Reviewers, some of our
most esteemed writers among them, have exclaimed over his inventiveness, over his psychological acumen, over the sheer sentence-by-

sentence *sprezzatura* of his style. Yet for all this Stern is hardly a household name. In an era when writers barely old enough to drive are garnering enormous advances and, worse, enormous reputations, how is it that a writer of Stern's caliber still waits for recognition?

My own theory is that Stern has become identified in the public mind—in that part of the public mind that cares about these things— with his friend Saul Bellow. Not only do both live in Chicago and share an affiliation with the University of Chicago (Stern has taught there for over thirty years), but certain of their subjects and approaches could be said to overlap. Both tend to feature educated and culturally sophisticated male protagonists in their novels. Thinkers and talkers. And these Herzogs and Citrines, Wursups (*Natural Shocks*) and Riemers (*A Father's Words*), are, as often as not, in various stages of romantic disrepair. They get divorced, chase skirts, and suffer in the amatory arena. They also take time out to brood over the larger state of things. Bellow, the senior, gets the Nobel Prize; Stern, in many ways as talented, gets seen as the shadow-man.

Such superficial perceptions can play havoc with a worthy writer's reputation, and need to be countered. For Stern is no more derivative of Bellow than, say, Raymond Carver was of Hemingway. The resemblances are nothing beside the differences of style, temperature, and vision. Bellow is a seeker, a metaphysical dramaturge; his focus is on the soul-condition of late-twentieth-century man. Stern is a crisper and quicker talent. He is a realist looking at the here and now. He is Chekhov to the other's Tolstoy, and to choose between them is a mistake.

In *Noble Rot,* Stern includes stories from three previous collections (the earliest from *Teeth, Dying and Other Matters,* 1964), as well as a generous assortment of fugitive pieces. He has made no attempt to render his development chronologically. Stories from different epochs sit side by side like guests at a banquet. A prefatory note explains: "The arranger thinks of the reader as a story lover looking forward to his nightly story fix." Enough said; the sequences have been arranged with an eye to the pleasures of diversity. And this they supply in abundance.

The reader not familiar with Stern's other work will marvel first at what a variegated surface the characters, situations, and styles compose. Stern is by turns fast and talky, drolly lugubrious, whimsi-

.　.　.　.

Richard Stern

cal, ironic, and straight-on matter-of-fact. Prodigally inventive, he is as gifted with burlesques as with more serious modes. The sharp sense of discontinuity that we register between one story and the next all but forces us to savor the works in isolation—in nightly fixes. Which is also the best way, for they are written with an ear and a sensibility (the former serving the latter) as delicate as any in the business. Which brings up the second striking attribute of this prose: that it is quite dramatically different from the prose of the novels. Noble rot? Why not just say it's a different vintage?

Listen first to the opening passage of the novel *Natural Shocks,* which appeared in 1978:

> Three years after Frederick Wursup moved across Lexington Avenue and turned his office into his home as well, he discovered that he could see his old apartment—where his ex-wife, Susannah, still lived with their two sons—from the roof. He'd never paid any attention to the cross-planked square on the ceiling of his back bathroom, but it was through this that Mr. Spinkel, the janitor, admitted the roofers one September afternoon. They climbed through and Wursup followed, hoisting himself up from the lidded toilet seat. While they checked for clogged spouts and worn asphalt, Wursup surveyed the avenue.

The setup is traditional. The principal characters and their governing context have been deftly sketched in. The reader is taken by the hand and led, one step after another, into the world of the novel.

Now consider (these excerpts are representative) the openings to two of the stories. "Idylls of Dugan and Strunk" begins:

> On a hunch, Strunk took the check over to Dugan in the hospital. "Is this your baby?"
> Dugan's head is mummified, chin to scalp; the coca-colored eyes peer over the damaged cheeks. "Lire. The rat." He passes the check to Prudence, sitting in the armchair.

"In the Dock," meanwhile, starts out with these sharp assertions:

> I've cut lots of corners. Dochel's Nail of the Month claims I do little else. Her delicate point is that I've wasted my talent.

· · · ·

The gulf between the modes is enormous. The novel invites, seduces with narration. The stories, on the other hand, almost always plunge us *in medias res* and set our reading antennae to bristling. We have to work to sort out the references, chronologies, and twists; half the time the key to a given story is buried in some casual remark or snatch of off-kilter dialogue. While the exertion is initially great, often slowing our involvement, the payoff is worth it. Collaboration brings the contours more firmly into place; the receptors, tensed up by the effort, register the word music and the sentence rhythms more acutely. Stern, more than most contemporary stylists, writes to be *heard.*

I can do little more than suggest the range of character and situation in these thirty-two stories. Stern has challenged himself to penetrate the confined but emotionally intricate lives of a great gallery of so-called "ordinary" people. The pages teem with grumbling husbands and wives, depressed grad students, small-time operators, lovelorn spinsters, struggling retirees—but there is room as well for professors, thinkers, and leisured travelers. All have been rendered with a fascination for circumstance and setting—for the why and how of their dailiness—and with an eye for their psychological particularity.

In "Teeth," for instance, a less-than-gainly Miss Wilmot endures an epic of dental woes, dreaming of romantic redemption at the hands of her dentist, Dr. Hobbie. Stern's sharp-eyed but loving staccato captures the feel of her solitude:

> . . . Miss Wilmot had a bad night. The heat was low, her bed was cold. She got up, put on her sweater and the furry bathrobe her father'd sent her for her birthday. Feb. 2. Thirty-one. She turned on WFMT. Buzz. It was three o'clock. Dr. Hobbie'd be coming home from the Tall Girls. She sat back in the terrible green armchair she'd gotten at Carmen the Movers for eight dollars. A troglodyte. The only arms that ever held her.

But in fact the night is young. Miss Wilmot ends up in Dr. Hobbie's office for what has to be one of the most extraordinary sessions of emergency dentistry ever recorded. The outcome, so to speak, must be left for the curious reader.

. . . .

Richard Stern

"Zhoof," retrospectively one of the more memorable tales in the book, grows out of what at first might seem the slightest of episodes. Powdermaker is a distinguished-looking Jew—in fact, a professional distinguished-looking Jew (he makes his living posing for glossy advertisements). He is traveling by train in Europe when he encounters, and gets snubbed by, a middle-aged German couple. He sits down near them in the dining car; they get up and change seats. Powdermaker hears the man mutter "Zhoof," which he realizes just a second later is his mishearing of "*Juif*":

> Sitting with his cold white wine by the beautiful lake, Powdermaker felt as if his head had been sliced like a grapefruit and put on a plate. Everything cold in the universe poured into his decapitated trunk. His heart thumped, his hands shook the wineglass, perspiration rolled from forehead and cheeks to the white tablecloth.

A part of Stern's artistry is reflected in his use of the double take, the tiny lag between the hearing and the grasping. How better to suggest the caesura between our animal selves and the elaborate structures of civility? No less original, though, is his way of building upon the horrific moment. First, Powdermaker finds that the man's hatred has invaded him. He broods over fantasies of vengeance. But Stern denies him any direct gratification. Powdermaker must experience, instead, what amounts to a New Testament kind of forgiveness. He must turn the other cheek:

> As the train pulled into Brussels' Gare du Nord, the couple stood behind Powdermaker. When he got off, he looked behind. The woman looked at him, flushed, almost pleading. He gave her a small nod, a sympathetic, a human nod. She understood.

For all the variety among these stories, there is nonetheless one situational archetype, one motif, which recurs often enough to set a mood swirling about the whole. This is the bittersweet legend of failed love that is reprised in various guises, though nearly always from the vantage of the man. In "The Sorrows of Captain Schreiber," an officer stationed in a small French town falls in love with a certain Mlle. Verité. After a dutiful courtship—a courtship during which we are drawn into the vicissitudes of town life—Schreiber succeeds in winning her affections, only to find that he has been transferred to another post. He promises to return, of course; and he does. But what he learns is that his Verité has gone off with his black corporal, Tiberius. The triangle is as old as Adam, Eve, and the snake, but Stern reanimates it with incisive pacing and phrasing:

> He started to say, "What's wrong?" but he couldn't summon the French for it.
>
> Old Cassat said, "Mlle. Verité is gone, Captain, gone off."
>
> "With the black one," said his wife. "No one knows where. Nearly two months."
>
> Schreiber looked at them all and turned away. At the gate he said in English, "A taxi is waiting for me."
>
> He walked down the side path to the river. He didn't dare look at the bridge.
>
> The taxi should be coming soon, he thought. He wondered if he should wait for it in the bushes and then slip under the tires. "I'm thinking of suicide," he thought. "Over love." In his pain, he was almost proud. He said, "*Un peu ridicule.*"

The story continues for a few more paragraphs, just long enough to take the weight of portentousness off this beautifully managed inner exchange: an unobtrusive discrimination of tones and tongues has recapitulated all the folly of his involvement with the faithless Verité.

Other voices tell of other pains. In "Orvieto Dominos, Bolsena Eels," Edward, the would-be seducer, is deserted by his quarry, Vicky, in the Italian hill town of Orvieto. None of the fabled pleasures of the region can assuage his sense of defeat. After a restless night in a local hotel, he finds his way, via Baedeker, to Lago Bolsena, famous for its eels. But Edward has no appetite for eels; he has already stopped at a roadside trattoria and gorged himself on rolls with jam and butter. Ignoring the signs about not swimming "*dopo pasta,*" Edward heads far out into the water. But then "he felt a fire shoot through his stomach . . . Cramps." No, Edward does not drown. Nothing so dramatic. He vomits into the lake and then gasps his way back to shore. Finis.

Stern, like his Russian counterpart, favors the diminuendo ending, especially for these narratives of ill-sorted love. The narratives themselves are apt figures for the greater part of earthly experience,

· · ·

Richard Stern

which is probably why Stern is so drawn to them. Over and over he plays the spume of fantasy and expectation against the limiting wall of circumstance and human nature. Juggle the terms, and you get something like "nobility" versus "rot." In the realist's vision, life is always a diminishment of the desired, seldom an abject failure but always a disappointment. A compassionate art makes the truth bearable, even tonic.

Noble Rot: Stories 1949–1988. Richard Stern. 367 pp. Grove Press. 1989. $22.95

SVEN BIRKERTS

William
Kennedy

The city of Albany, New York, has in William Kennedy, its much-lauded citizen—winner of Pulitzer, National Book Critics Circle, and MacArthur Foundation awards—found its Homer. In his trilogy, *Legs, Billy Phelan's Greatest Game,* and *Ironweed,* Kennedy put together a portrait from street level, showing the city through the eyes of its mobsters, newspapermen, hustlers, and hard-luck Irish. *O Albany!,* by contrast, served up the histories and legends of the place from the more detached altitude of the chronicler-raconteur. Now, with *Quinn's Book,* Kennedy has attempted a novelistic fusion of history and fancy. Alas, even Homer nods.

To begin with, not only is Kennedy mesmerized by the possibilities of his chosen setting, he is also showing signs of the Balzacian itch: he seems to want his novels to link up through character-crossover until a whole imaginary world has been populated. Billy Phelan, for example, is the son of Francis Phelan, the protagonist of *Ironweed.* In the new novel, a deeper ancestral link is forged. Daniel Quinn, the hero, is grandfather to his namesake Danny Quinn, also of *Ironweed*. As Kennedy affirmed in an interview in a recent *New York Times Book Review:* "They're all interconnected. I've worked out the genealogies. New lines are established that I hope will be part of future books. It's inexhaustible. . . ."

The link between the earlier works and the new novel seems merely expeditious, however. For while the trilogy is sharply natural-istic, *Quinn's Book* may be viewed as Kennedy's flirtation with genre fiction—specifically, with the sort of parodic extravaganza attempted by John Barth in *The Sot-Weed Factor* and by Erica Jong in *Fanny*. Historical circumstance is the springboard, the source of situations and stylistic inventions. The general idea is to filter period material through an authorial presence rendered ironic by much historical hindsight. The result, at least in this case, is an awful conspiratorial winking in the tone, a prose incessantly parading around in some silly costume. Here is Kennedy's opening:

> I, Daniel Quinn, neither the first nor the last of a line of such Quinns, set eyes on Maud the wondrous on a late December day in 1849 on the banks of the river of aristocrats and paupers, just as the great courtesan, Magdalena Colón, also known as La Última, a woman whose presence turned men into spittling, masturbating pigs, boarded a skiff to carry her across the river's icy water from Albany to Greenbush, her first stop en route to the city of Troy, a community of iron, where later that evening she was scheduled to enact, yet again, her role as the lascivious Lais, that fabled prostitute who spurned Demosthenes' gold and yielded without fee to Diogenes, the virtuous, impecunious tub-dweller.

These first words, I have already read in reputable places, herald a narrative that is Dickensian in amplitude and García Márquesian in its magical animation. Certainly we are to applaud the ambitious blending of the ribald and picaresque with the matter-of-fact. But there is nothing original here. The passage is pure pastiche, a rip-off of the Colombian master that is not made clever or excusable by the play with a Latino name. In García Márquez, the complex manipula-tion of tenses and the shuffling together of image-laden clauses is done in the service of an awestruck narrating sensibility—a sensibil-ity invaded and transformed by the visions it would relate. There is nothing of the kind in Kennedy's book. The grown-up Quinn who is looking back to tell his story is supposed to be a journalist and war correspondent of some repute. But he is posing when we first shake hands, and, as a result, we never trust him again.

The García Márquez lead also proves to be a red herring, for after a few trial shots at magic realism—a prophetic vision descried in the open eye of a corpse, an ice jam that grows into a mountain—Kennedy jettisons the mode. It's almost as if he decided in midchapter that a more native prototype would be better suited to his needs. Would that he had gone back and erased his footprints.

The other big name invoked is, as I said, Dickens. But that's not quite accurate, either. Kennedy's prose has nothing of the richness of detail or comedy; nor can he even approximate the flash and sparkle that Dickens elicits from his collisions of characters. No, in its thin superficiality and deus ex machina improbabilities, *Quinn's Book* is better compared to those quickly concocted dime novels that eviscerated Dickens for devices and played to the public's enormous appetite for sensation and melodrama. Just listen to the basic plot line.

The whole show starts on that dark, disaster-filled December day—a day of flood and fire and mounting calamity that surely blazed with apocalyptic suggestion in the memories of the denizens of Albany. Young Daniel Quinn, fourteen-year-old orphan, errand boy for "John the Brawn," local strongman and river rat, witnesses the capsizing of the aforesaid skiff. Quinn and his boss hasten to the rescue. But they are—it seems—too late. La Última is frozen stiff, a clear goner. Quinn, however, managed to catch the hand of her pretty twelve-year-old niece, Maud, who is very much alive. The two fall promptly and irrevocably in love.

Back on shore, Quinn and Brawn hie the body and the girl to the mansion of one Hillegond Staats, a wealthy and eccentric widow devoted to good deeds. (Her estate is also a station stop for runaway slaves.) No sooner has La Última been laid out in the special "dood-kamer," or death chamber, of the house, than Brawn conceives a necrophiliac lust for her. And lo! A little tickle to those experienced old loins and the lady sits up with a smile. Soon the lusty rogue has his paddle in the good widow's waters as well (the genre is, briefly, pure Frank Harris), while the hand-holding innocents, Quinn and

· · · ·

William Kennedy

·

Maud, look on. The two then seal their private vows with a soul kiss, and Maud makes Quinn swear that he will come to rescue her—she doesn't specify from what or whom—whenever she gives the signal. He agrees.

Hereupon the narrative becomes too episodically fractured for close tracking. New characters are introduced by the page, many of them disappear just as quickly. The foursome sets out via canal-boat toward Buffalo. But on the morning after departure, Quinn wakes up by the side of the canal—dastardly John the Brawn has betrayed him. Alone, disconsolate, pining for his Maud, our hero makes his way back to Albany.

There, in a trice, he is up to his neck in adventure and intrigue, getting the ingenu's obligatory education in hard knocks. Quinn gets caught up in the smuggling activities of the underground railroad; he tags along during a riot by factions of the Irish underclass; he finds out about a hush-hush cabal of bosses and thugs known as The Society. In short, he functions as the sugarcoating on the pill of a history lesson. Oddly, none of his experiences change or enlarge him—he remains the same eager, upright, and dim stick figure throughout. The only changes that Quinn undergoes are external. He comes under the protectorship of Will Canaday, idealistic editor of the *Albany Chronicle,* learns the arts of reporting, begins a career as a journalist. The mirage of Maud, of course, never stops wavering in his soul.

A few years pass. Quinn is made to meet up with Maud for one ill-timed moment—just long enough to show us that Maud is going the route of her aunt and becoming a stage performer—then they are again parted. The next section opens in 1865. Quinn is now a celebrated correspondent from the front lines of the Civil War. Maud, having predictably become a star (the aging La Última has retired), is engaged to a Gordon Fitzgibbon, who happens to be the new owner of the Staats manse. Kennedy then quickly ties all loose threads together into one big efficacious lovers' knot: the four who so gallantly breasted fate together many years ago are reunited. La Última, who throws a soiree because she believes she is dying, ends up in the arms of John the Brawn, now a prosperous retired boxer. Maud and Quinn are last seen in the clinch of true passion. Finis.

. . .

SVEN BIRKERTS

* * *

Kennedy is evidently enraptured by the legends of Albany—its rough river-men, its power politics, its formative ethnic clashes. And, truly, the materials for a major historical novel are all there. But *Quinn's Book* is not that novel, not by a long shot. Kennedy has rashly assumed that a set of typecast dime novel characters are sufficient pretext, and that the swirl of history around them will provide color and content in abundance. But the flatness of these cartoon figures— Quinn as do-gooder and blank slate, La Última as gold-hearted old bawd, Brawn as lovable scoundrel, and Maud as the ultimately virtuous prize—ensures that the events will be registered with equivalent flatness. The history cannot live apart from the consciousness that perceives it. All of the brawls and catastrophes and glimpses into the dark cog-works of power politics read like scene sketches from a novelist's notebook.

Here, quite randomly excerpted, is Quinn's recounting of how he came upon Dirck, the kidnapped son of Hillegond Staats:

> I found Dirck in the farthermost stall, face down in soiled hay, wearing the same ill-fitting clothes he'd been wearing when abducted. On close look it was not animal droppings but his own blood that had soiled the hay. I rolled him over to see his face and found it a total wound, a horrifying smear of blood, gash, and swelling. His eyes told me that he was still alive, but not for long, I judged. I did not know how to help him, but my instinct was to clean his face, find his bleeding and stop it, just as I had aided John the Brawn in conserving what remained of his blood after a street fight.

Nothing wrong with this, you might say. Not technically, no. The sentences follow in order, provide the basic clues for a reader to visualize. But that's all—basic clues. There is no precision, no conveying of shock or fear, no fastening on the quick, living details. The passage is representative. Kennedy rarely gets any better, or worse, than this. The story slogs on in just such undistinguished, tired sentences. Open to any passage in, say, *Ironweed* and you will see how far the stylist has fallen.

And the reason? Hard to say. It may be that the historical distance

·   ·   ·   ·
William Kennedy

was just too much for the author to bridge in imagination. But the problem may also have to do with Kennedy's recent exposure to screenwriting and its less arduous demands. I suspect that the writing of *Quinn's Book* coincided, at least in part, with Kennedy's work on the screenplay of *Ironweed*. The pace and exteriority of the new novel are patently celluloid. Indeed, the screen, rather than the page, might be the destined home for these slight lives. For the camera inevitably enriches stereotypes, and it catches the grain of concrete details that prose cannot always reach. Kennedy would not have to change much—just the second word of the title. That job done, he could get back to what he ordinarily does so beautifully: real writing.

Quinn's Book. William Kennedy. 289 pp. Viking. 1988. $18.95

SVEN BIRKERTS

Paule
Marshall

E very now and then it happens. The critic—this critic—finds himself split down the middle over a book. Schizophrenic. Compelled to write a review that will give with one hand and take away with the other. As the old joke has it: I've got good news and bad news. The good news is that Paule Marshall has written a powerful novel about family bonds and the wages of power, political and other. The bad news is that she has impaled the black man in the process. The good news first.

Since the publication in 1959 of her first novel, *Brown Girl, Brownstones,* Paule Marshall has made her place as one of our leading black novelists. Drawing on her background as the daughter of West Indian immigrants, she has—like the younger Jamaica Kincaid—schooled her reader in the uneasy overlapping of culture and race. But where Kincaid favors impressionism and epiphany, Marshall lays a more traditional brick. Her two other novels, *The Chosen Place, The Timeless People* (1969) and *Praisesong for the Widow* (1983), are strongly built around situation and setting. She plants her characters as credibly in urban America as in the towns and villages of the Caribbean.

Daughters, her newest book, plies between the New York City life of Ursa Mackenzie, a free-lance researcher, and the saga of Ursa's family on the fictional island of Triunion. While it is the figure of Ursa who frames the action, Marshall is so nimble at slipping into the skins of her other characters that we come to care about both worlds equally.

The novel begins with Ursa on the brink. She has just had an abortion, and she sits in her tiny apartment, hugging her coat around herself. Her love life is a botch. Her lover, Lowell Carruthers, knows neither that she has conceived nor aborted. Ursa believes that he is too wrapped up in his career problems to care. Her own job situation is up in the air—she is waiting for a grant that refuses to come. Then in the mail she finds a letter from Primus, her father. Blue envelope, government seal. She puts it aside, unopened. The man she idolized as a young girl is now a compromised politician who threatens to destroy his home district with development schemes; she cannot bear to think about him.

Marshall lays out her weaving materials a bit too schematically, but once the shuttles start to move, the novel comes brightly to life. Ursa's story is played off against that of her father, the charismatic Primus, or PM as he is called. In their early days together, when PM stumped for votes and his wife, Estelle, stood by his side, he seemed a god: "Primus Mackenzie paused, and everyone and everything within the sound of his voice also paused . . . The insects in their giddy orbit around the lamp came to a stop . . ." Writing home to her family, Estelle boasts proudly: "He's gon put fire to the tail of those thieves running the government." Soon enough that fire starts to consume Primus. Through Estelle; his lifelong servant, Celestine; and his feisty mistress, Astral Forde, we witness the corruption by power of an ambitious but ultimately weak man.

Marshall does her voices superbly. She is as deft with interior monologue as she is with dialogue, and she ranges freely between urban homegirl, standard English, and the peppery patois of the islanders. Ursa's friend Viney is absolutely convincing in her dissing of black men. She carries on about "the little white girls out there eyeing what we eyeing, and the brothers who only have eyes for them. And not to mention, not to mention *pu'leeze* those among the brothers who have eyes only for each other, or for themselves—you know, the me-me-mes; or the ones who believe, really and truly believe, that things go better with coke. . . ."

Set this voice beside Astral Forde's, before she becomes PM's mistress. She spots a girl who reminds her of her younger self. "Country!" she exclaims. "Bare country from her head down to the old pair of shoes on her foot. The dress looking like she run it up on somebody's Singer this morning before she took the bus to town. Hot needle and burn thread. And the hat on her head like it say 'heap-me-on.' Bare bare country." Only a few sentences, but already Astral Forde is flush with cantankerous life.

It is for Ursa to mark the convergences between the two worlds. When she goes to meet Sandy Lawson, an old politico friend in New Jersey, she is stunned to see that he has sold himself out to white power brokers. But she is more shaken still when she draws the parallels between Lawson and the PM of recent years. It is as if she is seeing double.

Marshall creates these concentric rings, but subtly. It is only when Ursa finally returns to Triunion at election time that the scattered suggestions are drawn together. The resolution must be left for the reader to discover. Suffice it to say that Marshall's strategy works beautifully.

But now the bad news—at least, this white male critic *thinks* it's bad. And that is, for all its novelistic excellence, *Daughters* seems to have an ideological ax to grind. The three key male figures are all shown to have been divided from their true selves or broken by the machinations of power—white power. Lowell, who once dreamed of doing outreach in the ghetto, is enslaved by the corporate gamesmanship of his white boss. Lawson, the politico, has quit his fight for reform and is now the white man's lackey. And Primus has disgraced himself in his zeal to serve outside (American) interests.

The reviewer walks a minefield. He needs to ask first whether Marshall is simply telling the hard truth about how it is out there and, second, whether considerations about ideology ought to impinge upon a writer's free expression of her vision. Fundamental questions about the relation between art and society are raised.

Still it nags: is some vital part of the truth spectrum missing? It

·   ·   ·

Paule Marshall

is easy to argue, as many do, that Hemingway's work is diminished by his substantially negative treatment of women. Is it any different when a black woman writes about black men? Writing in a review of *Praisesong for the Widow,* black critic Darryl Pinckney noted: "This seems to be a favorite notion of Marshall's: the price of pulling up one's bootstraps is the soul, and men are more likely than women to sell theirs."

Marshall is one singer in a sizable chorus. Black women writers appear to have declared open season on black men. In best-selling novels by Alice Walker, Toni Morrison, Gloria Naylor and others, I hunt in vain to find males as strong, as honorable or as emotionally mature as their female counterparts. They are more often depicted as irresponsible, brutal, dissolute or, in a novel like Terry McMillan's *Disappearing Acts,* crushed and humiliated in the workplace.

Again, tricky business. Maybe it's true. Maybe black women *are* stronger and more emotionally resourceful. On the other hand, they may have had it easier in some ways; it could be that the brunt of racial hatred has fallen on the male. As a critic, I can see that the call for more compassionate treatment may almost sound like a call for affirmative action in the novel—or a denial of the reality that a great many black women obviously feel negatively about black men. I don't mean that. But reading *Daughters* and these other novels as well, I can't shake the sense that something is skewed. A person trying to understand black culture solely on the basis of these books would have to conclude that the black male has few if any redeeming attributes.

But, of course, art is not a balm to be poured on a wound. It is under no obligation to show compassion, to probe for deeper social or historical causes, or to consider whether there might be other versions. What I find wrong with these novels is more likely something wrong in the world. I have to learn to tell the difference—and it's hard.

Daughters. Paule Marshall. 408 pp. Atheneum. 1991. $19.95

·   ·   ·

SVEN BIRKERTS

Harold
Brodkey

There are two Harold Brodkeys parading past us in this gargan-
tuan collection of prose. One is a writer of fairly conventional
storytelling ambitions and considerable ability, and his contribution—essentially the first five stories, all of them written before
1969—can be praised and questioned in conventional terms. They
are serious and well crafted, placing characters in morally and psychologically complex situations. In "The Abundant Dreamer," to take
the most challenging example, filmmaker Marcus Weill, on location
in Rome, receives word that his grandmother has died. The news
jolts him, and the rest of the narrative, which tracks Weill's every
moment and thought during the day's preparation and shooting, sets
up an intricate weave of recollected moments. The free thread, which
dangles tantalizingly before us by the end of the tale, and which
could, if yanked, unravel the whole of Weill's disciplined inner life,
has to do with the young man's first love, a pregnancy, and a coolly
willful abrogation of responsibility. The filmmaker's grandiose self-
image has a questionable foundation; he has bought his art at a price.
But whatever the reader feels about the man—and this reaction has

231

to contribute to the effect—he is not likely to dispute the controlled power of the telling.

This holds true for the other opening stories as well. Craft and the subtly insightful turns of the prose counteract the often disagreeable impressions left by Brodkey's male protagonists, who tend to be morally righteous and more than a little self-involved. Take Avram, in "Bookkeeping," of whom he writes: "Avram darted down the steps of his brownstone with that quick boyishness of his which aroused the sarcasm of so many of the intellectuals who wrote for his magazine." Though the author looks to preempt criticism by incorporating it, the ploy fails; we side with the snipers and despise the character.

But never mind. It is the other Harold Brodkey who concerns us here. The writer who came to resist the death kiss of "promise" bestowed upon his earliest work (the stories collected in *First Love and Other Sorrows*) and began venturing a far more difficult and unlikely style and subject; who has been toiling for what must be decades at *Party of Animals,* the novel touted by the happy few who have seen it take shape as a work to rival Proust (critic Denis Donoghue); and who has gathered in the rest of this book substantial chunks of material in the voice of Wiley Silenowicz—the supposed narrator of the novel—for our inspection. This Brodkey is now soliciting response and readership for his distinctive and risky fictional project. Parts of the work have appeared in magazines, it's true, and the Jewish Publication Society did release a limited-edition selection several years ago, entitled *Women and Angels,* but seeing the material assembled in bulk and sequence produces a whole new impression. The presentation is not uncalculated: we must consider it a preview or a gauntlet, or both.

I referred to these prose pieces as "chunks" rather than stories because I feel that there may be some debate about their intrinsic genre. Many of them, certainly, read like sections from something larger; we sense that they might have been eased—not ripped—from the body of some encompassing urtext. The beginnings and endings have, at times, an arbitrary, *in medias res* feeling. But then, that appears to be the nature of the enterprise; the prose, too, conveys that feeling—deliberately. The writing does not so much tell a story or instigate a progress as deliver a dense mass of perceptions, feelings,

. . . .

SVEN BIRKERTS

and thoughts about some small but vital portion of Wiley's experience. In most of the pieces he is a child, and his child's sensorium is focused upon one or another of the people closest to him: mother, father, sister, nanny, and so on. Only in two, "Innocence" and "Angel," is he older (college age), but the procedure is not so different. The first, highly controversial when it was originally published in *American Review,* plunges him into the throes of carnality—he is trying to bring a young coed to orgasm. The other has him standing in place, witnessing the manifestation of a real angel in Harvard Yard.

Whether these are stories in the strict sense or not is ultimately irrelevant. The point is that this is an extraordinary (I use the word in its etymologically neutral sense) prose: relentless, demanding, overwrought, eternal-seeming, demented, crammed with flashes of light. It is good, bad, awful, brilliant and it is deeply, shudderingly, *effective.*

Brodkey provides something like an aesthetic announcement early on in "Innocence," when he has Wiley say:

> I distrust summaries, any kind of gliding through time, any too great a claim that one is in control of what one recounts; I think someone who claims to understand but who is obviously calm, someone who claims to write with emotion recollected in tranquility, is a fool and a liar. To understand is to tremble. To recollect is to reenter and be riven. An acrobat after spinning through the air in a mockery of flight stands erect on his perch and mockingly takes his bow as if what he is being applauded for was easy for him. . . . I am bored with that and with where it has brought us. I admire the authority of being on one's knees in front of the event.

On his knees he is, if not literally, then almost: Wiley the child experiences his world and the people in it within a radius not much greater than ten feet. On page after page we are inside his three- or five-or ten-year-old self—both body and soul—registering the incremental flux of his habitat. Voices, sighs, faces, bodies in space, furnishings, the ambience of certain corners and rooms—this primary data has probably never been put into language so densely or exhaustively:

. . .

Harold Brodkey

Sometimes when I wake, I am eleven years old; and the underside of the bedsprings, the rows of coils that face me, sag, squeak, clatter against the wooden bed frame, flabbily press air—a slow sound—when I grip the curved enamel wires of the coils with my hands and bare feet, and move horizontally, hand over hand, foot over foot.

And so on. Brodkey wants nothing so much as to reanimate childhood from within. The outer descriptions move out in widening circles, tallying sensation, annexing the subaqueous drift of emotion and thought, advancing with little or no culmination. We either enter that world or we reject the prose—there is no middle path.

The fundamental family diagram is laid out in the piece called "A Story in an Almost Classical Mode." Interestingly, this is the one time Brodkey uses his own last name as the family name. Joe and Doris Brodkey have adopted Harold—whom they call "Buddy"—at the age of two; his real mother died, and his real father, an incompetent drifter, "more or less sold me to the Brodkeys." The family lives in University City outside St. Louis. Later sections change the names (Joe and Doris become S.L. and Leila Cohn, later S.L. and Lila Silenowicz), and an older sister, Nonie, and a nursemaid, Anne-Marie, appear. But the structure of the family, what Freud called the "romance," stays more or less constant. Lila is intense, histrionic, an emotional bully with an urge to dominate that grows as her health starts to falter; S.L. is passive, doting, easy of manner and affectively detached; Nonie is sadistic and vengeful (in "The Pain Continuum" she does nothing but torture a very young Wiley); Anne-Marie is warm and nurturing, and her marriage and departure serve as one of the few crises of this chronicle. The variously titled segments render one phase or another of Wiley's growing up. What conflicts there are develop not from plot or situation but from the recursive close-up inspection of Wiley's psychic shifts. In a piece like "Play," for instance, he grapples with a despised younger playmate; hurtful urges and aggressions slowly melt and become something else—the first flashes of sexual awakening—as their game of "Tarzan" turns unexpectedly tender. Brodkey maps the gradations of change with care and accuracy. Here, as elsewhere, he allows

.　.　.　.

the moment to expand in slowed motion until every breath sounds deafening.

The paradigm instance of this is in the oft-cited "His Son, in His Arms, in Light, Aloft," which takes seventeen pages (it is one of the shorter pieces) to detail Wiley's experience of being lifted up into his father's arms and carried across the garden. "My God, I feel it up and down my spine, the thumping on the turf, the approach of his hands, his giant hands, the huge ramming increment of his breath as he draws near: a widening effort." But of course not even Harold Brodkey can stretch pure description over such a distance. The stages of Wiley's "enskyment" (Robinson Jeffers's coinage) are like sections of a shattered picture-plane, except that each contains some dilation or divagation that expands the picture. In places we get pure perception, in others a kind of matured retrospection on how it was between father and son: "Sometimes he becomes simply a set of limits, of walls, inside which there is the caroming and echoing of my astounding sensibility amplified by being his son and in his arms and aloft."

This switching of perspectives and modes can work beautifully at times. The prose rhythms catch us up until we suddenly feel that we have returned to the duration-state of childhood, the state in which time is known not in successive units but in unmarked rushes and sweeps. At other times, though, the sentences rage and clatter, chewing, as someone once remarked of Henry James, more than they have bitten off:

> The lip shapings S.L. does seem more like pantomimes of meaning than aspects of taming and guiding the noise of his voice. His throat-hurled noises and the palatal echoes and nasal shadings are special to him—that stuff can't be notated. He applies a male, pale lacquer of breath outside a syllable so that *are you smiling* has in the final breath of each syllable, in the paling and dwindling *r*. . . .

Suffice it to say that that last sentence is just getting warmed up. And when Brodkey gets on one of these runs, the profoundest duration spell dissolves into alphabet soup. But then, every break with convention has to carry its own hazards.

·   ·   ·

Harold Brodkey

"Innocence" and "Angel," our two exposures to an older Wiley, confirm Brodkey's interest in creating—or recovering—duration experience. Who knows but that its attainment is not the major impetus behind his art? Is it pure coincidence that the only two forays into postadolescent consciousness set out situations that break with event-as-chronology—that is, eros and mystical visitation? I doubt it. I would sooner argue that Brodkey has found what is for him a workable mode and is determined to push it as far as he can. Of the two, "Angel" is the more memorable. Wiley's sexual pyrotechnics quickly carry us from interest to irritation to stupefaction. In contrast, the appearance of a giant visage in the middle of Harvard Yard, and the fact that it resolutely refuses to *do* or *indicate* anything, becomes increasingly haunting. The piece makes an apt finale for this static but ecstatic collection of prose.

Writing recently in *Vanity Fair,* critic James Wolcott expressed doubt that Brodkey's big novel would ever see the light of day. Why else, he wondered, would the author be giving us these pieces of the Wiley saga, "unless he had given up hope of fusing them into a coherent novelistic whole?" A good question. Indeed, given the nature of this material, its narrative method, we have to consider if any sort of whole is even possible. Brodkey's bold independence—his decision to junk the artifice of telling and its implicit "gliding through time"—may well have landed him in an impossible corner. Is there any way in which such exploded moments can be forged into a viable larger entity? Could readers bear to know any more about Wiley's inwardness than they now know? How long can an author sustain such centripetal prose without introducing tensions of a grander dimension? It is not enough to point to Proust, asserting that he, too, lowered his diving bell into the past and reconstituted the inner scape of childhood. Proust achieved what he did only because he was also able to engineer a massive and sophisticated supporting structure. He contrived around Marcel a freestanding world of rounded individuals, societal hierarchies, and historical consistency. Brodkey has done nothing of the kind, at least not in the Wiley pieces gathered here. As readers, we are confined to a small stage lit by powerful but directed beams. The infinity of inwardness is not to be compared to the infinity of material reality—at least not as a subject for fiction. The relentless self-exploration of Wiley Sileno-

. . . .

SVEN BIRKERTS

wicz, rich and unique though it is, will have to be counterbalanced by something resembling a world. How Brodkey might accomplish this is one of the great literary mysteries of our time.

Stories in an Almost Classical Mode. Harold Brodkey. 596 pp. Knopf. 1988. $24.95

·　·　·　·

Harold Brodkey

Paul
West

In a recently published interview, Paul West spoke tellingly about the psychic process that underlies his writing. "All the time, whatever I'm doing," he said,

> I hear this noise in my head that really never goes away. . . . Like a squeaky conveyor belt. There's always something on it, and perhaps that something isn't useful all the time. When a novel begins, there's just more on the belt, just images and phrases, really quite obsessive things start coming along, and I ask, "What's this? Is this worth pursuing?"

Writers, like real people, can often be typed according to what the psychologist David Shapiro called "neurotic styles." West is clearly a compulsive, a writer who could not *not* write. Indeed, the British-born West is probably our leading graphomaniac (after Joyce Carol Oates), completing books in various genres faster than most of us are able to write a shopping list.

Counting his newest work, this writer who just last year turned sixty has brought out fourteen novels, including the acclaimed *Rat Man of Paris, The Very Rich Hours of Count von Stauffenberg,* and *Lord Byron's Doctor;* a clutch of criticism; several books of poetry; and various altogether sui generis nonfictions, among them *Words for a Deaf Daughter, Out of My Depths: A Swimmer in the Universe,* and, just last year, *Portable People,* a charming collection of invented monologues by historical figures. It would be one thing if West were simply productive, but he is productive across a wide range and at a high level of artistic attainment.

He is less like Oates, in fact, and more like Anthony Burgess. Both writers are maximalists, lovers not only of the word but of the sweeping long sentences and logjam paragraphs that characterize a certain kind of baroque English prose style. Both are broadly lettered, addicted to odd bits of lore as well as deviations, heresies, and unexpected byways of thought. Both have a special proclivity for inhabiting historical figures and recreating the world through their eyes. But Burgess is known and celebrated, while West awaits his apotheosis. His career to date has illustrated the forest-for-trees paradox: if you do too much of a good thing, you are as apt to be overlooked as if you had done nothing at all.

Jack the Ripper and the Women of Whitechapel may change that. It is superbly written and intricately choreographed, a work both sensational and serious. On one level it is a telling of the gruesome Jack the Ripper murders that horrified London in the late 1880s. But it is also a fabulous word-portrait of the Victorian lower depths, of the street life of women whose circumstances left them no recourse but prostitution. And it is also a searching meditation on the less savory machinations of social and political power, as well as on the ambivalence that is sometimes found at the root of the artistic temperament.

West acknowledges in a prefatory note that his account is novelistic, and that he will be taking certain liberties with the historical record. He also remarks, however, that the line between history and literature is not always clearly inscribed. "Years ago I found out, when researching the Nazis for my novel about Claus von Stauffenberg, that historians compulsively embroider and embellish; when I got to the facts, the fiction had already begun." The unsolved Jack the Ripper case along with the persistent but unprovable rumors about the involvement of the royal family have given West richly ambiguous terrain to mine.

Perhaps the greatest of the liberties he has taken is his casting of the painter Walter Sickert (1860–1942) in a central role—indeed, implicating him in the actual murders. I have found no basis for this in accounts of Sickert's life. West has taken the great risk of moving the dare-you line separating fiction and fact. It was one thing for Tolstoy to maneuver Napoleon for his own fictional ends, another for E. L. Doctorow to have Jung and Freud visiting Coney Island. But here is an author actually tampering with the reputation of a historical figure. Why not cast Stalin as a well-meaning but over-worked friend of the people?

Why Sickert would suit his purposes, though, is easy to see. His position allows him to have connections among the higher social echelons, even with the royal family, while his vocation and his temperament encourage him to consort with the women of Cleveland Street, where he keeps his studio. Moreover, as an artist bent on peering into the darkest pockets of human experience, and on explor-ing the taboo, he is the perfect medium for West's thematic concerns.

The basic plot is as follows. Through a friend with close ties to the royal family, Sickert is entrusted with the task of chaperoning Prince Eddy, Queen Victoria's grandson, during his frequent London escapades. Eddy is a problem case—illiterate, openhearted, utterly impulsive in his lusts. Though he prefers to spend much of his time in London in a male brothel, Sickert introduces him to Annie Crook, a young Scotswoman turned prostitute. The two fall in love, and soon Annie is with child. The royal family intervenes, arranging for the lovers to be separately abducted; Eddy is taken into protective custody, while Annie is hied away to Guy's Hospital, where Sir William Gull, physician to the queen, expertly lobotomizes her. Annie lives out most of the rest of her life in a dingy hospital, drooling and insensate. Her child, Alice Margaret, is passed along to the royal nannies, and much later ends up as Sickert's ward.

More ghoulish complications ensue when Mary Kelly, a prostitute friend of Annie's and sometime model for Sickert, writes a blackmail letter to the queen and, thinking to add weight to her appeal, gets a number of her cronies to add their signatures. These women, who all live from one glass of gin to the next, and who worry mainly about finding the next customer and a doss for the night, have no notion of what a terrible process they have set into motion. But in the remote precincts of power the nod is given—the subtle, untraceable nod. As West puts it: "He [Sickert] knew how things got done, how one old boy lovely phrasing shaded his preference into the other's pragmatism, and something happened, although nobody quite remembered why, such was the onrush of events, the terrible Niagara of Empire."

That "something" takes explicit, bloodcurdling form in the person of Sir William Gull. Apart from being a distinguished man of science and a power in the Masonic brotherhood, Gull was also "the silencer, one of life's more questionable addicts, a lover of the half light and in-between states, an infernally wound-up doer of lofty commands." He sets about systematically to track down the signatories, luring them into a horse-drawn van called Crusader, where he plies them with doctored grapes. Then, clip-clopping through the London night, he slashes them with a zeal that will very likely make the reader gag. Each murder is more horripilating than the previous one. By the end Gull is carving Masonic symbols into his victims' flesh and performing prodigies of evisceration.

Beside him in the van, anguished and fascinated in spite of himself, sits Walter Sickert. Sickert has always been drawn to the dark side. At one point early in the novel, he fantasizes about watching convicts work at fetching up mutilated corpses from the Thames:

> He always wanted extremes, even if only to paint what was middling and middle-of-the-road. "Otherwise, gentlemen," he'd always say, "we have no north, no south. . . ." He doted on the prospect of green marrow-fat remnants—human sirloins—afloat on the river as toiling convicts dropped them. . . .

But as the old wisdom has it, one best be careful what one wishes for, because it may be granted. It is a sort of justice that Gull should tap him to attend his ghoulish rites, and that Sickert should find himself unable to refuse. "What had once been his natural morbidity, his love of the gutter as a subject and a theme," writes West, "had now become a trap, no longer optional."

West has set up the old devil's bargain: Sickert has had to trade his will, his moral compass, for his artist's ability to reckon true north. And though he thinks through countless ways to escape these midnight rides, and is ever at the point of tipping off the prospective victims, something stops him. He must concede that he finds these bodily desecrations strangely riveting. Staring at the gore, the shapes and the colors, there comes a moment when metaphysical curiosity overpowers the regard for the human. And this, certainly from the perspective of the novel, is the gravest danger, graver even than the psychopathology of a Gull. For *that* we can at least understand as insanity.

The perpetrators are eventually punished for their sins. Though Gull is never officially apprehended, his fellow Masons, after giving him a testimonial dinner, "first stuffing him with food then quietening him with grapes, took him away to the inferior purlieu of Islington and put him in a straitjacket in a private asylum there. . . ." He dies, insane, a few years later. Sickert, meanwhile, lives on for long years; he takes in Annie and Eddy's daughter, Alice Margaret, who eventually bears him a son. He becomes one of the self-condemned. "Weary of being a painter's painter, he slaved on, afflicted by sudden bouts of weeping, but trying to close the drawer full of blood that kept sliding open in his mind. . . ." He later works on a series of paintings called *The Camden Town Murder*. "This particular murder," we are informed, "had taken place in 1907, but he was really painting 1888." Sickert's punishment, we gather, is that he has to continue to be Sickert, with sanity a more fitting torment than any dementia.

West has worked a thread of fierce moral interrogation throughout the book. It brings tension and shape to what threatens, in places, to become an uninflected backdrop account of the lives and doings of the victims-to-be. His gift, as his own conveyor-belt analogy suggests, is for the sentence-by-sentence accumulation of impressions, not for structure. Left to itself, one senses, the prose would just build to a cataract and push all else before it. His subject, fortunately, requires certain architectonics, and West obliges, varying his voices and breaking up the slow-movement passages with well-timed shifts of perspective.

West is very adept at writing descriptions and catching the syncopations of conversation among familiars. He is sure, too, in his renderings of atmosphere, especially the disheveled rooms and gin mills where the women gather. The women themselves, while not deeply differentiated as characters, are convincing—plucky, foul-mouthed, sentimental but never sentimentalized. When they take the stage, as they often do, the language bubbles with cockney idioms. Here, for instance, we are made privy to Mary Kelly's night thoughts, in the hour when, as West puts it, "her vernacular came alive":

> Oh to drive through the Park in a pony phaeton, even if empty-bellied and scared to death you'll finish as a bag of bones under the floor to be dug up in 1900. My hands was so filthy you could have sown mustard-and-cress on them and had a good crop. It's a mortal shame. Praps not. I fought like a brick for my fried fish and bread-and-dipping even if it did nearly kill me slick off.

But what finally remains vivid, long after the novel has shrunk down to its afterimage in the mind, is the feverish abandon of Gull and the descriptions of his myriad mutilations. I have deliberately abstained from citing excerpts, not so much out of fear of giving offense (though they very well might), but more to allow the prospective reader the full frisson, which is very much part of the experience of the book. The passages are raw and uninhibited; they transmit perfectly Sickert's fascinated repulsion. The visual precision is a triumph of artistic detachment, even as it horrifies. *The Women of Whitechapel*, however, is no *American Psycho*. In Sickert, West has created the very thing that Bret Easton Ellis lacks: a ravaged conscience capable of examining the moral ramifications of the gratuitously perverse.

Still, a question arises. Is there something to this recent fascination with vile acts of mutilation in our arts? I'm thinking not just of West and Ellis, but also of Jonathan Demme's *The Silence of the Lambs*. Are we searching for the last taboo—the desecration of the radiant human form divine—or simply proving that there is no taboo

.   .   .

Paul West

left? Or is it that our instincts of response have so atrophied from the media's parade of carnage that the artist is urged to raise the stakes? West's vision is probing in this way, but he is finally searching for the psychology beyond the pathology.

Jack the Ripper and the Women of Whitechapel. Paul West. 420 pp. Random House. 1991. $22.

·   ·   ·   ·

John
Barth

J ohn Barth likes to recount the story of his literary education—
how, as an undergraduate at Johns Hopkins, to which he has by
a *commodius vicus* of recirculation returned as a professor, he had a
job filing books in the stacks of the classics department; how he
became intrigued by the volumes of ancient narrative that he carted
to and fro—Burton's *Book of the Thousand Nights and a Night,* Petro-
nius' *Satyricon,* Urquhart's *Rabelais,* the Sanskrit *Ocean of Story*—
and thereupon launched himself forth upon an epic reading quest.
"Tales within tales within tales," Barth writes in one of the essays in
his 1984 collection, *The Friday Book,* "told for the sake of their
mere marvelousness. . . . I was permanently impressed by the *size* of
literature and its wild variety."

Barth has long since moved from storing to storying; size and
wild variety are now attributes of certain volumes in his own ample
oeuvre. *The Sot-Weed Factor, Giles Goat Boy, LETTERS*—these are
veritable language banquets, grand outpourings reminiscent of the
days when novelists were paid by the word. And though Barth has
proved, with novels like *The Floating Opera* and *The End of the Road*

and fictions like *Lost in the Funhouse* and *Chimera*, that he doesn't have to write at length, the uncorseted prose of the big books, the obvious delight he takes in cantilevering long subordinate clauses and instigating complicated digressions, suggest that he prefers to. *The Tidewater Tales*, Barth's latest novel, only confirms the impression. The book muscles past every attention-span barrier to check in at 656 pages. You can read it, and you can stand on top of it to change a light bulb: pleasure and practicality are seldom so felicitously combined.

The Tidewater Tales, a shipboard divertissement, follows in the wake of Barth's *Sabbatical: A Romance* (1982), which likewise took place on the deck of a cruising sailboat. "My books," writes the author, "tend to come in pairs; my sentences in twin members." He relates the fact to his own biological circumstances, to his having been born an opposite-sex twin. Within the pairing, however, thematic opposition often prevails. Where the husband and wife in *Sabbatical* agonize over whether or not to bring children into this "powder-keg" world, and ultimately decide not to, Katherine and Peter Sagamore, the protagonists of the new novel, are in a very different situation. As the narrative begins, Katherine—or "K," or "Kate," or "Katydid"— is eight-and-a-half months pregnant with, you guessed it, twins.

"SET ME A TASK!" demands Peter Sagamore of his wife. The two are ensconced in the luxury guesthouse belonging to Katherine's parents, the more than moderately well-to-do Sherritts. There Katherine plans to await her full term, while Peter, a writer, hopes to come to terms with the increasingly diminishing returns of his minimalist aesthetic. Over the years he has pruned down his once-amplitudinous fiction until the merest bones remain. These, too, he has whittled. Of his latest work only the title still stands. When Peter finds himself deleting that as well, he knows that he has come to a crisis. His capitalized cry is one of artistic desperation.

Katherine is afflicted with her own uncertainties. She has fears about bringing children into the world. Her well-meaning parents are smothering her with their solicitude; she has to keep reminding them that she is almost forty. She therefore harkens to Peter's call, countering with a command of her own: that he take her sailing. Before long, they are aboard their own vessel, the *Story,* leaving the family cove for the open waters of the Chesapeake. Their plan is to sail, swim, rest, reconnoiter their lives, and indulge their mutual love of storytelling (Katherine happens to be the founder of the American Society for the Preservation of Storytelling). So great is their delight in the first day's sailing and telling, however, that they risk a change of plans. Trusting in their shortwave radio and the propinquity of the Sherritt family's sophisticated yacht, they decide to extend their jaunt for as long as they can, perhaps right up to the onset of labor.

Barth's opening chapters commence an engaging periplus. We are given lively and witty introductory sketches, not just of Peter and Katherine, but also of the patrician senior Sherritts and their two sons—the ne'er-do-well entrepreneur Willy and the winningly pubertal "Chip." In the course of their first day's sailing, we are also told just how Peter, the boat-builder's son from Dorchester, came to be the one-night lover and then, years later, husband of the beautiful and accomplished Katherine. Barth weaves these establishing accounts together with the sense-active descriptions of the *Story's* progress over the waters. As we read, we feel ourselves moving among the coves, rivers, and estuaries of the Chesapeake. In time, through the skillful counterpointing of anecdote and present-tense depiction of surroundings, these labyrinthine waterways become the topographic equivalent of the stories that keep emerging.

Tales within tales within tales. In several of the essays in *The Friday Book,* Barth rhapsodizes about the complexity of pattern in the ancient story cycles, remarking in particular the interplay between the frame narrative and the subsidiary tellings imbedded within it: "It was never Scheherazade's stories that seduced and beguiled me, but their teller and the extraordinary circumstances of their telling." If there is a central weakness in *The Tidewater Tales,* it's that Barth has nothing like the threat of a vizier's dagger to tense up his frame. The kicks and quivers of the forthcoming twins are nothing to the stroke of a blade. The hard work of seducing and beguiling therefore has to fall to the stories themselves.

Fortunately, Barth has command over the full narrative lexicon. Short, long, realistic, fantastic: he spins out legends of every description. In the course of the book we are treated to personal histories (the romance between Peter and Katherine, Katherine's first marriage to the boozy pervert "Poon" Baldwin, Peter's journey from the docks of Dorchester to literary and academic success); intrigue (an impossibly involuted account of CIA and KGB double-dealing with regard to the prospective sale of a certain Bayside property to the Soviet Embassy); farce (the Sagamores find floating canisters containing installments of a preposterous play for eggs and sperm); and, finally, epics. Or, to be precise, epical retellings of epics. These are the mainstay of the novel and require some comment.

At various intervals during the *Story*'s fourteen-day excursion, Peter and Katherine meet up with diverse navigating folk, strangers as well as friends. They even have a gam with Franklin and Leah Talbott, the sailing couple from *Sabbatical*. It is from these invariably convivial others that the truly astonishing tales are heard. When they start speaking, the otherwise naturalistic spacetime frame of the novel bends to accommodate the fantastic.

On the second day of their sail, as they pull into Madison Bay, the Sagamores espy a most unconventional-looking craft: "A weathered black hull with a bank of rowing ports, its transverse bow thrust forward at the waterline as if for ramming, its high stern curved and curling like an outsized Venetian gondola's, with no visible rudder." Later that day—we did not doubt it would happen—they meet and befriend the ship's owner. Theodoros (Ted) is: "Curly, burly, tan and gray, grizzled of hair and beard that once were auburn; middle-aged, robust, rather handsome, at once weathered and subtle-appearing—and dressed in a short white tunic loosely belted at the waist: a chiton!" His beautiful companion, Diana, has a gold fillet circling her hair.

The couples settle in for an evening of chat. Peter's interest in the peculiarities of boat design leads the conversation around to Homer. Soon Peter and Katherine are retelling their favorite episodes from *The Odyssey*; Ted and Diana, they note, are listening with great animation. Then, uncorking more retsina, their hosts launch into an account that will leave the Sagamores gaping.

Theirs is an after-*Odyssey*, a tale that starts where Homer's left off. Odysseus has returned from his travails, has vanquished the suitors, and once again shares the marriage bed with Penelope. But the hero discovers that he is restless; his heart keeps pining for the Nausicaa of distant memory. Penelope, for her part, starts longing for the caresses of Phemius, the singer who kept her company (and later, she confesses to Odysseus, made love to her) during the long years of waiting and weaving. The jealous Odysseus tracks down Phemius, blinds him, and sends him packing. But the marriage is finished.

Odysseus then sets off alone to search for Nausicaa. And, after all kinds of vexing delays, he finally locates her. She is living on a mountaintop with none other than the blinded Phemius. The singer is now something of a legend, captivating his audiences with his accounts of the homeward journey of Odysseus. Nausicaa has put up with his lecherous gropings for the sake of his song: she cannot hear enough about the man she still loves.

Odysseus finally claims his Nausicaa, and the two make a bold plan. They obtain and outfit the swiftest ship known to man; then they sail due west, chasing the sun through the Pillars of Hercules (here Barth takes his cue from Dante's version of Ulysses' last voyage). Odysseus has calculated that by matching the speed of their flight to that of the sun's decline, they can reach a timeless state— they need never age or die. "Whew," exclaims Katherine. "What happened after that?" Diana replies: "Nothing. They lived happily ever after." The Sagamores return to their own boat in a stupor, neither of them willing to voice the obvious surmise.

Barth later works in two other variations on the familiar, first when Peter and Katherine encounter a garrulous old mariner named Donald Quicksoat (his boat: the *Rocinante IV*), and then when they hook up with the Talbotts, who tell how the original enchantress, Scheherazade, magically appeared in their lives. We are given proof positive, should we need it, that the old tunes can still be made to dance. Still, it is a fine line that Barth elects to tread. For one thing, these airings of the incredible strain forcibly against the otherwise scrupulously rendered here and now. For another, the novel is severely hobbled by its lack of a governing structure. Barth's sly self-critique—he has Peter muse about writing a novel "in which next to nothing happens beyond an interminably pregnant couple's swapping stories"—cannot disarm the reader's own critical impulse. The book's success has nothing to do with its design: the whole lives only through the vitality of its parts.

On the surface, these parts have about as much in common as the objects in a scavenger's bag. A play for sperm and eggs? A CIA-KGB thriller? An apocryphal episode from the life of Don Quijote de la Mancha? But Barth's art is such that a subtle thematic tension emerges from beneath the surface jumble. We find an insistent to-and-fro starting up between the cyclic and the linear. Repetitive patterning yields to the eruptive breakthrough, then reasserts itself. On the one hand: tides, menses, the nightly appeasement of the vizier, Penelope's weaving and unraveling. On the other: the issue of twins, the sailing forth out of time by Odysseus and Nausicaa, the end of Scheherazade's inventions after the 1,001st night—I cite but a few of myriad instances. They function, much like the metaphors of telling and sailing, to hold the heteroclite pieces of Barth's collage together.

The contesting forces don't finally discharge themselves in any dramatic fashion. The babes (cleverly, then irritatingly, addressed with in utero monikers like "Tweedles Dum and Dee" and "Toil and Trouble") are born; the offstage villains (Willy and "Poon") reap their reward; and Peter passes through the needle's eye of his artistic crisis and starts to write. He closes the circle with his last-sentence decision to pen: "THE TIDEWATER TALES: A NOVEL." But for all its sprawl and diffuseness, the book is decidedly uplifting. The means so overwhelm the ends that we give up questioning necessity. We accept the gifts in the spirit in which they are offered.

The Tidewater Tales. John Barth. 656 pp. Putnam. 1987. $21.95

·   ·   ·

SVEN BIRKERTS

John
Updike

ohn Updike first set Harry "Rabbit" Angstrom loose upon the world in 1960. *Rabbit, Run* followed the basketball star of Brewer, Pennsylvania, through the ups and downs of marriage and work, and saw him through the defining tragedy of his young adulthood, the death by drowning of his infant daughter.

Since then, almost with the steadiness of a chronometer clicking off decades, Updike has given us *Rabbit Redux* (1971), *Rabbit Is Rich* (1981), and now, right on the dime, *Rabbit at Rest*. But this is the end of the saga, really. As the author himself wrote, in a reflection published in *The New York Times Book Review:* "We've all heard of tetralogies, but after that there's no word for it." Anything further, he remarked, if only for technical reasons, would become "very messy."

Possibly ghoulish, too. For as the final title intimates, Rabbit is quite literally "laid to rest" at the close of this fourth installment. His battered heart at last gives out, thus bringing to completion what has to be seen as one of the big fictional projects of our period. But by beginning with the end, I am getting slightly ahead of myself.

The Harry we meet in the first sentence of *Rabbit at Rest* is in his late fifties, and is in failing health. He carries around his waist the evidence of his tireless munching of salty foods, and in his memory cells the rich deposits of a man who has lived to capacity the life of his times. Readers of *Rabbit Redux* and *Rabbit Is Rich* will recall with what passionate confusion Harry navigated the Aquarian sixties and the belt-tightening rigors of the Jimmy Carter years. He took his knocks, and his pleasures—more than once jeopardizing his marriage. But if he was not always faithful, he did, in his way, stay true to his wife and first love, Janice.

She now stands at his side at the Southwest Florida Regional Airport, waiting to greet their son, Nelson, his wife, Pru, and their two children. Harry and Janice are now semiretired; they divide their time between their Florida condo and their house back in Brewer.

The possibilities for narrative excitement appear somewhat slim. True, we get flickers of the father-son animosity that flared so wildly in the earlier novels. Within minutes of their greeting, Harry and Nelson are flinging barbs just like in the worst of the old days—only now Harry must suffer for his satisfactions: "A cold arrow of pain suddenly heads down his left arm, through the armpit." Still, feuds and bodily tremors are hardly the frame to build a novel of such heft around. Or are they?

The reader of this longest of the Rabbit books is hereby asked to put any King- or Clancy-inspired expectations to the side. The actual plot structure of *Rabbit at Rest* could be diagrammed on a paper towel with a crayon. Nelson and family visit; Nelson is discovered to have a serious cocaine habit; Harry has a massive heart attack but bounces back; Harry and Janice return to Brewer, where Harry fills in at the family Toyota dealership while Nelson enters a rehab program. . . . There are a few more turns, but those are best left for the prospective reader.

Fortunately, we are sufficiently schooled in the lessons of modernism to appreciate that plot is not the sine qua non of the novelist's art. There are other ways to hold a reader. And one such way is through the sheer accuracy and intensity of delivery—this is Updike's way. A masterful, if often precious, stylist at the outset of his career, Updike has in late career learned to bring the whole gritty mass of inner and outer reality into the sentence. He is entirely persuasive. We walk along a wire made of words for five-hundred-plus pages and hardly ever look down to see that there is no net below.

Rabbit at Rest is far and away the most interior of the Rabbit books, for the very good reason that the substance of life itself becomes increasingly interior with the passing of years. Rabbit had to live hard in the earlier novels so that he could have memories in this last one. We grasp the full fascination of the fictional artifice time and again as we realize that this is a created character experiencing as memories events that were *created* for him decades ago: "Think of playing basketball, that little country gym, the backboards flush against the walls, before all the high schools merged into big colorless regionals and shopping malls began eating up the farmland. Think of sledding with Mim in her furry hood, in Mt. Judge behind the hat factory, on a winter's day so short the streetlights come on an hour before suppertime calls you home."

I do not mean to suggest that Rabbit lives only in the past, or that the other characters do not push forward to claim their meed of attention, or that the vast and complex public world is not sharply etched in all about. To the contrary, here as in the earlier books, the variegated hard walls of reality are everywhere to be knocked against. And Rabbit remains an inveterate sniffer and noticer—of places, atmospheres, things great and small ("The elevator has a different color inspection card in the slip-in frame, the peach-colored corridor smells of a different air freshener, with a faint lemony tang like lemonade."), and events. Like any good citizen, moreover, he is haunted to the point of distraction by news bits (the Bush campaign, the Lockerbie explosion, Jim and Tammy . . .).

But Rabbit is never so much aware of process and materiality as when he turns his attention—increasingly as the book proceeds—to his own flesh-and-blood interior:

> So the idea of a catheter being inserted at the top of his right leg, and being pushed along steered with a little flexible tip like some eyeless worm you find wriggling out of an apple where you just bit, is deeply repugnant to him, though not as much so as being frozen half to death and sawed open and your blood run through some complicated machine while they sew a slippery warm piece

of your leg vein to the surface of your trembling poor cowering heart.

Suffice it to say, *Rabbit at Rest* is not the cheeriest of books. Subject matter aside, the prose is suffused with a particularly autumnal longing. We come to sense, as Updike clearly does, what it means for a human life to run its course. In spite of this—*because* of this—the last pages carry a surge that is very nearly exalting. As Rabbit crashes deathward, the far-flung threads of memory and association are gathered in, and we come as close as we ever do in fiction to an intimation of what privacies of meaning another life holds concealed. We feel, at last, a brotherly bond with Rabbit, a bond that runs deeper than our moment-to-moment responses to his not always likable personality (Rabbit is, it must be said, entangled in racial and sexual prejudices). Indeed, this is a central paradox, and an indicator of Updike's achievement. That on one level Rabbit is but a shallow and reactionary male of his class and era, but that on another he is a sweet and watchful soul, as deep in his affectionate perceptiveness as the man who made his world:

> Rabbit feels betrayed. He was reared in a world where war was not strange but change was: the world stood still so you could grow up in it. He knows when the bottom fell out. When they closed down Kroll's, Kroll's that had stood in the center of Brewer all those years . . . with every Christmas those fantastic displays of circling trains and nodding dolls and twinkling stars in the corner windows as if God himself had put them there to light up this darkest time of the year. As a little kid he couldn't tell what God did from what people did; it all came from above somehow.

Rabbit at Rest. John Updike. 512 pp. Knopf. 1990. $21.95

SVEN BIRKERTS

Norman
Rush

Five years ago, Norman Rush made a serious literary splash with *Whites,* a slim collection of stories about expatriates living in Botswana. Anyone who has attempted to make a literary splash knows just how high the odds are against success. The writer must be very original, very good, or both. Rush was both. His stories were not only smart and engaging, they captured a larger sense of our historical moment. Rush got at our unease and cynicism—the easy part—but he also caught the private picture, the hands cupped around some flame of hope or desire. The locale was exotically specific, the resonances were universal.

With successful books, as with hit singles, there is always the question of the follow-up. Rush's response was to draw a deep breath and then slowly exhale a whole world onto the page. His new novel, *Mating,* is as thick as a metropolitan telephone directory. It is, depending on your angle of regard, a satire on sexual and cultural self-definition in postcolonial Botswana, an exploration of utopian fantasies, or an anatomy of love carried out with scalpels borrowed from Stendhal.

Rush's unnamed narrator—call her N—is a grad-school anthropologist in her early thirties. As she begins her story, she is adrift in Gaborone (or "Gabs"), recovering from a collapsed research project in the Kalahari. *Mating* is her chronicle—she calls it her "evagination," or turning-inside-out of the self—of her love affair with Nelson Denoon, an Ivan Illich–sized superstar of the international development circuit and the founding guru of Tsau, a utopian collective populated mainly by women.

The whole business was so overwhelming to N that she does not know how far back to go to set the stage. "I feel like someone after the deluge," she writes, "being asked to describe the way it was before the flood while I'm still picking seaweed out of my hair." But she does an admirable job, depicting her fizzled liaisons with available expatriates in Gaborone, evoking the incestuous ambience of their society and the adjacent otherness of the black culture.

N is just beginning to come to terms with her new life, its opportunistic maneuvering, when she goes to a party and meets Denoon. "Spare me is what I said to myself when I got my first look at Nelson. I meant, Spare me the heroic in all its guises." Denoon has it all. He is handsome, brilliant, visionary—and unattached. Indeed, it is Denoon's estranged wife who urges the meeting. The tugs and becks of fate are irresistible. N decides then and there to follow Denoon to his remote village, Tsau.

She undertakes the arduous overland journey by herself, with only a pair of donkeys to carry her supplies. It is a foolhardy move. The two-day trek across the Kalahari almost finishes her off. One of her pack animals runs off, she has to stab the other one repeatedly with a ballpoint pen to get it to move. But finally Tsau appears in the distance. "Internally I experienced something like a profound but subaudible chord being played," she reports. "And then I was alert. It was like falling back into my body from a height."

The three-hundred-plus pages that follow recount in scrupulous detail N's arrival, her acclimatization, and her conditional acceptance by the collective—which she understands to be "a brilliant machine intended to reroute social power to women." She is even more intent upon rendering every last psychological wrinkle of her deepening involvement with Denoon. At one point she remarks: "My story is turning into the map in Borges exactly the size of the country it represents," and the reader nods assent.

But not unhappily. For Rush deploys the narrative voice with such brio, such wit and perceptiveness, that even the sometimes lengthy accounts of arrangements in Utopia retard the progress only slightly. We keep turning pages for a very simple reason: these are two highly articulate and unique individuals, and we want to know what happens to them.

What happens? Sex, of course, happens. "I loved our early sex," writes N. "If it could be done I would drop down into reliving it over and over like those rats that press a pedal connected to their pleasure centers and press it until they die."

But dailiness happens as well. And it is in his presentation of the nondramatic backdrop, the slow and frictive rituals of accommodation any two people make, that Rush excels. The intricate faceting of N's intelligence, as capable of ironic detachment as of empathy, bends ordinary light in endlessly surprising ways:

> So he was different. Or was it just that I was dealing for the first time in my life with an actual mature male, a concept which up until then I had considered an essentially literary construct and a way of asking the question of whether or not in fact the real world reduced to a layer cake of differing grades of hysteria, with the hysteria of the ruling sex being simply more suppressed and expressing itself in ritualized forms like preparedness or memorizing lifetime batting averages . . .

The shimmer of rhetoric here conceals the strokes of a finely whetted blade.

There are two lines of tension that cross and spark in this relationship. One originates in N's own dividedness: her parrying defenses, honed by her earlier romances, keep getting in the way of her affections. She is like the tormented Christian who cries, "I believe, Lord—help Thou mine unbelief." The other tension lies in Denoon, whose passion for N begins to threaten the purity of his utopian vision. He tries to convince himself that societal perfection need not exclude private obsession.

For a time it all works. Denoon and N attain what feels to

her like a perfect intimacy. But she retains the slightest vestige of skepticism. Watching her lover as he holds a piece of glass up to the light, she realizes: "What I was suddenly afraid of was that this moment was our perihelion, the closest we would ever approach or be, and that everything after this would transpire between bodies farther apart."

She is prescient, though the problems that arise have less to do with personal discord than with troubles in Utopia. Rents begin to appear in the societal fabric: a group of disaffected insurgents, reports of a ring of young male prostitutes, and general flarings of repressed human orneriness. When the suspected instigator, one Raboupi, disappears, Denoon is accused of foul play. He sets off on a mysterious mission, ostensibly to clear things up. But then he is brought back to Tsau on an improvised stretcher. He recounts how he suffered an accident in the desert and while lying immobilized experienced a spiritual illumination. He now greets the world with what N calls "the Smile," an expression of beatitude that terrifies her.

The desert vision is a harbinger of Denoon's rededication to his mission. N realizes this and realizes too that his love and his calling are for him an either/or proposition. She cannot bear not being everything to him. Denoon's impersonal bliss is a cruel distancing. She finds herself thinking of an old torture method used by the Manchus, "in which an incision is made in the victim's stomach and a piece of the intestine is nailed to a tree and the victim is lashed and made to circle the tree, unwinding his entrails as he goes." Hyperbolic, yes—but so is her love.

N finally leaves Denoon to return to the States, where she takes a job on the fringes of academe. But being in Reagan's America, she finds, is a torture of a different kind. Life in our bland republic is "like being stabbed to death with a butter knife by a weakling." Before the intensities of her former life, everything pales. And when a cryptic telegram arrives from Botswana, she makes the rash decision to return. We don't know whether to be happy for her or not. Rush has alerted us to the transfiguring power of passion, but he has also pointed out the deadly traps that wait at every turn. We mark the end of N's story with a crossing of the fingers.

Mating is a brilliantly written and utterly sui generis work of fiction. It defies comparison with any of the usual woman-meets-

· · · ·

SVEN BIRKERTS

man novels. Rush has not merely *set* the book in Botswana, he has recreated the spirit of the place through his prose. The daily rhythms of village life, the social patterns, the quality of light after a storm— everything is freshly minted on the page. Nor is this an idyll away from the world. Denoon and the narrator have both been conjured from the turbulent air of the present. *Mating* is a freestanding structure. It is open on many sides, but holds at its center that wonderful nest of paradoxes: the human heart.

Mating. Norman Rush. 480 pp. Knopf. 1991. $23

.   .   .   .

Norman Rush

Philip
Roth

E very novel is, at root, an invasion of privacy—or, better yet, the illusion of such an invasion. The sensation of illicitness, faint or less faint, is the motor that moves the hand to turn the page. What is curious, though, is that this foraging among the precincts of the Other is most thrilling when it has a visual component. We don't so much want to get access to another's thoughts as to catch a glimpse of actual stocking—we want to know what people *do* behind closed doors.

Maybe this explains the odd sense of disengagement that arises while reading Philip Roth's *Deception*. While the hype surrounding the novel—including the *Esquire* teaser with its sex-kitten photo spread—suggests a no-holds-barred voyeuristic romp (". . . like eavesdropping on not just one illicit affair . . ." coos the flap), the real effect is very, *very* different. One feels an edgy sadness, a nostalgia for something that never quite was. The novel is not about sex at all, but about loneliness and the bridging—through talk—of separate solitudes. It is a slight but affecting work.

Deception is orchestrated almost entirely in voices. The premise is that we, as readers, are privy to the pre- and post-coital exchanges of a fiftyish American writer, Philip, and the married Englishwoman, in her thirties, who comes to visit him in his London studio. The exchanges between lovers often go something like this:

"It's five o'clock. Time you Gentiles start drinking, isn't it?"
"I think so."
"Very impressive."
"What?"
"You with your hair up."
"It doesn't suit me."
"It suits *me*."

And so on. Any brief excerpt is apt to sound bland, but in accumulation, and with the emergence of attributed identities, a certain credibility as well as situational interest develops.

Against the basic story of these lovers and what we come to suppose of their lives (we track their affair over a period of about five years), Roth cuts in counterpoint exchanges—imagined or recollected—between Philip and various young women, mostly Czech emigrées, with whom he has had relationships over the years. The purpose of these "insertions" is not clear, though they do bring variation into an account that has little in the way of naturally mounting tension.

Without benefit of traditional kinds of situations and descriptions, the reader must do some scrambling to get the scenario straight. But the basic circumstance is plain enough. The woman is drifting to and fro in a marriage gone stale. Philip loves to love her, but even more he loves to prod and listen. He wants a contact point with reality, and with a culture; and he wants to vent his spleen. As an American Jew, he reviles the closet anti-Semitism of the educated British. Every night, it seems, he attends another literary soiree—he can't get enough of the thing he despises. Rage opens the door of the inwardness that is the writer's prison.

Late in the novel, Roth springs a surprise. Philip's wife is brought forward from inconsequence: she has found her husband's writings and accuses him of having an affair. Philip quickly whirls the seven veils of his calling. He is a writer. The scenes are imagined. And to the degree that the wife is mollified, we are to be mystified. Or are

.   .   .

Philip Roth

we? It's not really clear whether Roth wants to do Pirandello here, bringing us to ponder the relative reality status of done deeds versus deeds in the mind. If this *is* his intent, then the section marks a major weakness. For our engagement does not depend, as it might in another kind of novel, upon an elaborated illusionism. Our expectations cannot be challenged, for we have none—at least not in the usual sense. We are simply listening to two people talking. Fortunately, the success of *Deception* does not hinge upon this authorial sleight-of-hand.

It is the Englishwoman, the mistress, who finally carries the book. She is moody and tart, anything but the obliging playmate. Her contradictions lift her off the flat of the page: she is quick but negligent, passionate but world-weary, interested but twice-shy. She stays on with Philip, we sense, partly out of inertia. Which is believable, too. And with so little around to block it, her voice pushes forward with a gritty independence: "And my husband says I've ruined his sex life. He says, 'You're so heavy, everything is so serious, awful, there's no joy, no fun, no humor in anything'—and it's true, I think. I think he exaggerates grossly, but it's truish. I don't enjoy sex at all. It's all rather lonely and hard. But it's like this, life, isn't it?"

Ultimately, though, the strict reliance on voices hobbles the book. We don't get the frisson of intimacy we might have expected at first. Neither is the aftereffect especially strong. We heed the talk with some interest, but when the voices finally die away, they're gone. There is no image left vibrating on the retina.

· · · ·

Philip Roth, who is now in the full flush of his literary maturity, has always openly mined his own experience in his work. He does not concoct scenarios too far removed from what he knows, but he does, in the etymological sense of the word, invent. That is, he discovers and shapes (the Latin *invenire* means "to come upon") that which is his. Indeed, to judge from his most recent books—*The Facts,* an account of his early years, and *Deception,* to all appearances an autobiographical novel—he is increasingly committed to the project of self-invention.

Patrimony: A True Story, the chronicle of the decline and death of his father, Herman Roth, is the latest, and perhaps the most

· · · ·

SVEN BIRKERTS

unguarded, of these personal forays. Success and the passing of time have done nothing to dull Roth's penetration. Slim though this volume appears, it cuts like a scalpel through the dense sheath of distraction and guile that encase our more tender sensibilities.

"My father had lost most of the sight in his right eye by the time he'd reached eighty-six," begins Roth, "but otherwise he seemed in phenomenal health for a man his age when he came down with what the Florida doctor diagnosed, incorrectly, as Bell's palsy, a viral infection that causes paralysis, usually temporary, to one side of the face."

He continues on in this largely uninflected reportorial vein for the next two-hundred-some pages, charting the ups and downs of the increasingly serious situation (the "infection" proves to be a huge, nearly inoperable tumor in the brain), staring, at times with a flinch, at every last indignity that old age and illness bring on, capturing with what feels like perfect accuracy the cycles of despondency and rage, as well as the interminable fussing and kvetching that otherwise prevail. Roth does not, surprisingly, avail himself of memories or anecdotes that might retrieve the younger man, and he uses none of the devices that might heighten tension or make his account more "artistic." We do not see here, at first glance, the recipe for a page-turner.

And yet the reader does turn the pages, scene to scene, start to finish, and does so for the oldest and least fashionable of reasons. Because Roth has looked in past all comfort and condolence to find the truth—about himself and his father; about death and the fear of it; and about the absolute vulnerability to which love condemns us all. *Patrimony* surpasses the coolness of its telling style to become a deeply resonant portrait of a father and son, and it gives proof, if proof were needed, that the straightforward exploration of what is can be as compelling as anything artifice might devise.

The discovery of the tumor, which is first concealed from the father, signals to Roth that the drama of death has begun. He does not say so directly, but we learn in the last pages that he began at this point to keep a written record of events. His father, when he hears the news, rejects the possibility that this may be the end, though he does betray himself in uncanny ways; at one point, in a most curious private leave-taking ceremony, he deposits his tefillin

.   .   .

Philip Roth

(small boxes containing biblical extracts) in a locker at the local Y. Mostly, of course, family and friends behave with bright resolve, debating the surgical options and making plans for the future. But the blackness encroaches anyway, and from the reader's vantage throws every least interchange and action into poignant relief.

Herman Roth is a retired insurance man, a widower, and from what we see in our first encounter—the paralytic drooling, the depressed introversion—it is easy enough to regard him as one of the bothersome old. Later, when he is in better form, he comes across as stubborn, opinionated, and sometimes, as with the woman who is his companion, inflexibly harsh. The better part of his intelligence appears to be his memory; like so many of the elderly, he is fixated upon the minutiae of decades past. The reader's reaction—and to a degree it must have been Roth's, too—is that the father's time has come and that he'd best get on with his dying.

Roth's great accomplishment in the succeeding pages is to undo that impression. He himself is drawn by the circumstance of caretaking to pay attention to the life, to grasp the ways in which it is still vital. Beneath the creaks and sputters he encounters an indomitable will. His discovery process is slow and hard; time and again Roth must push aside his irritation, or see past his own fear and discomfort. But once the prospect of loss takes hold of him and breaks his defenses, the revelations come. And though they often arise from the most trivial situations, their power to awaken is genuine.

At one point, for instance, Roth and his father are crossing a street. The old man has been complaining about his dentures, and he suddenly yanks them from his mouth. Roth takes them in exasperation. "To my astonishment, having them in my own hand was utterly satisfying. Far from feeling squeamish or repelled, as I continued along, guiding him by one arm up onto the curb, I was amused by the rightness of it, as though we'd now officially become partners in a comical duo . . . By taking the dentures, slimy saliva and all, and dumping them in my pocket, I had, quite inadvertently, stepped across the divide of physical estrangement that, not so unnaturally, had opened up between us once I'd stopped being a boy."

Herman Roth's decline is counterpointed at almost every turn by startled self-realization on the part of his son. The paradoxical twist comes late in the narrative, when Roth himself suffers a heart attack

.   .   .

SVEN BIRKERTS

and must go into the hospital for emergency surgery. The final distance, that between victim and watcher, is suddenly bridged. "Helpless at the center of this little medical hubbub," writes Roth, "I confronted, with a clarifying shock, the inevitability in which, for him, every second of existence was awash now." Though he recovers, he never forgets.

Eventually, after a long period of remission, the father succumbs to that inevitability. Roth, at his bedside, whispers: "Dad, I'm going to have to let you go." But his father is unconscious, unable to hear. Earlier this would have been tragic. Over the last months, however, both men have faced their pain and have, however haltingly, expressed their love. An unexpected radiance shines out in the final passages: Roth has lost his father but has taken in the meaning of the man's life.

Deception. Philip Roth. 208 pp. Simon & Schuster. 1990. $18.95
Patrimony. Philip Roth. 238 pp. Simon & Schuster. 1991. $19.95

.   .   .

Philip Roth

Don
DeLillo

Paranoia, they used to say in the waning days of the sixties, is just a heightened state of awareness. I don't know who first coined the phrase, but it may as well have been Don DeLillo. Certainly no American writer (except possibly Thomas Pynchon) has been so attuned to the implications of such a view. In novel after novel, he has explored the shrinking margin between reality and our worst imaginings. *Libra,* DeLillo's ninth, leads us further into the realm of edgy foreboding than anything thus far.

As the cover photo—of Lee Harvey Oswald with his rifle—reveals, the subject of *Libra* will be the events of the Kennedy assassination. But make sure you read the Author's Note at the back. "This," writes DeLillo, "is a work of imagination." He has based parts of his story upon unsubstantiated conspiracy theories; he has also availed himself of the author's prerogative of attending to the thoughts and emotions of his principal characters.

It is good that DeLillo gives us this reminder, for his telling is so psychologically convincing that readers might very easily accept it as the new gospel. And who could blame them—for the one thing hitherto missing from all accounts of the single most electrifying event in American history has been a coherent story with characters and motives.

Libra is that story. DeLillo has found a complex and dramatic pattern, and he has brought together a number of distinct narrative strands to make it all come vividly to life. At the core is the unfolding tale—the destiny—of Oswald himself. DeLillo stalks his man closely, animating the familiar accounts of a lonely childhood and confused adolescence. We are made to feel the confinement of the shabby rooms that Lee and his mother shared; we follow him through his frustrating stint in the marines, his short-lived defection to the USSR, his courtship of and marriage with the vulnerable young Marina Prusakova.

DeLillo gets us so close to Oswald—much of the time we are sharing his thoughts—that we begin to understand his situation, to feel for him. For he is the very prototype of the superfluous man, the societal zero. When he latches on to the radical philosophy of Marx, Lenin, and Castro, it is because he finds there an explanation and hope for his life. "History," he coaches himself, "means to merge. The purpose of history is to climb out of your own skin." His deeds will, in time, make a mockery of his belief.

DeLillo's other narrative picks up the plans and actions of a diverse group of players. Win Everett, one of the central figures, is a semiretired CIA operative. He is one of a number of anti-Castro activists outraged by the Bay of Pigs debacle and by Kennedy's softening stance toward the Cuban leader. He starts to shape an elaborate plan whereby a hired assassin will shoot at—and miss—the president during an upcoming visit to Miami. The idea is to alert the country to the Cuban menace. But as DeLillo writes, repeating almost verbatim an insight from his previous novel, *White Noise,* "Plots carry their own logic. There is a tendency of plots to move toward death . . ." Miami will become Dallas; the miss, murder.

After Everett has begun to formulate an identity and explanatory past for his gunman, he gets word of Oswald, recently returned from the USSR. One of his confederates, Mackey, has made contact. "Lee H. Oswald was real all right. What Mackey learned about him in a brief tour of his apartment made Everett feel displaced. It produced a sensation of the eeriest panic, gave him a glimpse of the fiction he'd been devising, a fiction living prematurely in the world."

The chilling effect of *Libra* derives from precisely this ambiguity—that we are never sure whether individuals are creating history, or whether history might not be moving of its own accord toward its own appointed resolutions. As Oswald's path crosses the paths of the conspirators, a terrifying (for Oswald *and* the reader) momentum of inevitability takes over. Oswald is convinced that he has a grand historical mission to fulfill. "Everything he heard and read these days," writes DeLillo, "was really about him. They were running messages into his skin." The reader, who knows the unavoidable outcome, experiences the full force of the man's delusions.

The assassination itself is handled with terse authority. DeLillo knows that the images of that day are stitched into the collective psyche—he has only to reactivate them. Indeed, the power of his finale, including the capture of Oswald and his murder by Jack Ruby, depends in part upon the triggering of the reader's own memories. The tactic would be risky with any other historic event, but with the Dallas tragedy it works. *Libra* neither falsifies nor trivializes its subject.

Why *Libra*? The title, we learn late in the book, refers to Oswald's astrological sign—the balancing pans. The suggestion is of trembling equipoise, of a character, or situation, that could tip in one of two directions. But what is DeLillo getting at? Certainly Oswald—oppressed, enraged, enthralled by images of violent retribution—was headed toward trouble from the start. If he had not shot Kennedy, he would have done something else.

Maybe the balance should be seen as the unresolved face-off between two ways of looking, not just at the assassination, but at history itself. The one view is expressed by conspirator David Ferrie, among others. For Ferrie, everything is set out, mystically determined. When he learns that the Kennedy motorcade will pass directly below the Book Depository Building where Oswald works, he exclaims: "There's no such *thing* as coincidence. We don't know what to call it, so we say coincidence."

The counterview is articulated by one Nicholas Branch, DeLillo's historian figure. Branch lives in the midst of an ever-growing pile of papers and reports; he has consecrated his life to figuring out exactly what happened in Dallas. As DeLillo says of Branch: "He has learned enough about the days and months preceding November 22, and enough about the twenty-second itself, to reach a determination that the conspiracy against the President was a rambling affair that succeeded in the short term mainly due to chance. Deft men and fools, ambivalence and fixed will and what the weather was like."

Odds are that we will never know what really happened. But that will not stop the interpretations and theories, the scholars and cranks. For if ever a culture caught a glimpse of its own dark core, it was on November 22, 1963. The idea persists that if we understand that day, we might also understand the twists and turns of our subsequent history. Don DeLillo has built his real-life tale around this longing to know—it is at once a satisfying and disturbing work.

. . . .

If Don DeLillo has not yet been canonized as the leading American novelist, then he is just a few quibbles short. It will happen. The man is brilliant and daring, tense with intuition. No one else can do the police in so many different voices. "It's just a feeling of there's something wrong," says a character, and it's dead-on. Never mind that his people are flat, or that his plots at times dissolve into vague patches of shimmer; DeLillo has something we cannot do without. Nerve. He stalks our atomic landscape like a human Geiger counter, and his books come at us clicking.

Mao II is DeLillo's tenth novel, and it is one of his best. The basic features will be familiar to his readers immediately: the terrorists and conspiracies, the obsession with media images, the off-kilter characters who act like survivors of a future that hasn't yet arrived, and the relentless one-sentence snapshots that tell us what we really think about our times. *Mao II* is also DeLillo's strongest statement yet about the crisis of crises. Namely: that we are living in the last violet twilight of the individual, and that "the future belongs to crowds."

"All plots tend to move deathward," quipped the author in his 1985 novel, *White Noise*. This plot is no exception. But death here carries a different weight. For Bill Gray, the protagonist, a writer of Pynchonesque reclusiveness, has already removed himself from the

. . . .

Don DeLillo

world out there. He lives in his circuit of words, writing and revising, and refusing to publish. A young man named Scott, an admirer of his two early books, takes care of Gray's earthly needs. The master is free to drink, smoke, and brood.

As the novel begins, however, Gray has granted permission to a photographer named Brita to visit his seclusion to do a "shoot." His explanation? "Well it's weariness really, to know that people make so much of this. When a writer doesn't show his face, he becomes a local symptom of God's famous reluctance to appear." Brita is herself a strange creature. Convinced that writers are an imperiled species, she jets from place to place gathering their images.

This one contact precipitates others, and before long Gray has agreed to his editor's request that he take part in a hush-hush hostage-release ploy. The writer is to appear at a press conference in London; at the same moment, in Beirut, a terrorist sect will release a Swiss UN worker who has been taken hostage. Publicity is the aim, but—as always in DeLillo—aims contort into disasters. Gray learns that Abu Rashid, the terrorist leader, wants the flesh-and-blood Bill Gray. And, with predictable unpredictability, he starts traveling eastward to his fate.

The plot is, of course, nowhere near so linear. Indeed, if there is a problem with this novel, it's formal. The tension that gathers around Gray dissipates when he unexpectedly dies, and the final pages feel unfocused. Still, DeLillo keeps busy with his secondary characters. He shuffles in scenes and subplots featuring Brita, Scott, and Scott's girlfriend, Karen. There is always a new angle, a new window onto a world in its paroxysms of transformation. Karen, for instance, is a former Moonie with a preternatural empathy for human suffering. She stares at the TV with the volume off. "She was thin-boundaried. She took it all in, she believed it all, pain, ecstasy, dogfood, all the seraphic matter . . . She carried the virus of the future."

And the future, we have learned, belongs to crowds. The crowd motif is threaded through the work in a hundred ingenious ways. We see the gathering masses in China, at soccer games, at a collective Moonie wedding, at Khomeini's funeral. . . . The images flow at us through TV screens, via photographs, in endless reproductions of faces by Warhol (the title refers to the artist's silkscreen of Chairman

. . .

Mao). The novel fills up with eerie intimations of masses in forma-
tion.

Gray himself emerges as the apotheosis of the dying breed—
the writer pledged to individuality. He and his kind are becoming
superfluous, and his perceptions of this truth ring with bitter irony.
"What terrorists gain," says Gray at one point, "novelists lose. The
degree to which they influence mass consciousness is the extent of
our decline as shapers of sensibility and thought. The danger they
represent equals our own failure to be dangerous." The making of
sentences has given way to the handing down of sentences; as individuality expires, morality becomes a chimera. This is not a happy
book, but since when do we read DeLillo to feel good about things?

Libra. Don DeLillo. 458 pp. Viking. 1988. $19.95
MAO II. Don DeLillo. 241 pp. Viking. 1991. $19.95.

· · · ·

Don DeLillo

Thomas
Pynchon

The Russian poet Osip Mandelstam once wrote about reading Dante: "One must traverse the full width of a river crammed with Chinese junks moving simultaneously in different directions. . . . The meaning, the itinerary, cannot be reconstructed by interrogating the boatmen."

The analogy proves unintentionally prophetic of the works of Thomas Pynchon. The man is elusive, a disappearing act, and the prose is his signature. *Vineland,* Pynchon's first novel since *Gravity's Rainbow* in 1973, is as slippery and brilliant as the novels that have made his reputation. Indeed, it is a kind of *Divine Comedy,* but with this small difference: hell, purgatory, and heaven are all here now, in 1980s America, jammed one atop the other. Confusing, yes. But also entirely original—a bulletin from our self-constituted one-man National Insecurity Council.

The novel opens in 1984, in Vineland, a northern California city where Zoyd Wheeler, odd-job man and itinerant bass player (his daughter, Prairie, considers him the "scroungy, usually slow-witted fringe element she'd been assigned, on this planet, for a father")

272

prepares to hurl himself through a plate-glass window at a local lounge. It is a staged event, enacted yearly, to qualify Zoyd for "mental disability" checks.

Zoyd's "transfenestration" may well be the reader's last moment of full command, for right after that Pynchon subverts his plot with half a hundred subplots and backdrop meanderings, thinning it into a cloudy dream. Which is precisely his intention. For *Vineland* is less about isolated lives than about the life of our times. The method, the race from junk to junk, triumphs.

Pynchon is a connoisseur of human oddity and black farce. *Vineland* abounds in perfectly improbable scenarios that somehow vaporize the reader's disbelief: assassination by finger-pressure in a Japanese brothel; a Mafia wedding where a punk band, disguised as Gino Baglione and the Paisans, belts out spaghetti standards; a sixties campus revolution at a Nixon-worshipping institution called College of the Surf. The cast of players could stroll into Terry Gilliam's *Brazil* without missing a beat.

A narrative eventually emerges, centering on Zoyd's ex-wife, Frenesi Gates. Frenesi passed her hippie days as lead camerawoman for a radical film collective, compiling footage on the war between the state and the people—until she got seduced by a slick prosecutor named Brock Vond and betrayed her cause. She has lived for years under deep cover, shielded by the Federal Witness Protection Program. Now, under Reagan, the funds have been cut, and Vond is heading an all-out drug war against Vineland and environs. Frenesi, suddenly a volatile element, must reencounter the principal figures from her past.

To say any more would be to undermine the potency of Pynchon's telling, which is full of odd surprises, pratfalls, and beautifully rendered illuminations. The payoff is not conventional—the ribbon does not get tied into a bright red bow. Instead, we have the joy of the voyage. We are confused, we grope for connection. Then come the turns in the road. We see: This *is* our America. There are our malls, our pols, our image-saturated wastelands; these frazzled drifters are our citizens—in hell, in heaven, in between.

Some have called Pynchon's imagination paranoic. Certainly in the darker pages of *Gravity's Rainbow* the sense of doom is corrosive. In *Vineland* we find darkness, too, but it is darkness zigzagged by

· · ·

Thomas Pynchon

sweep-lights. Pynchon has found a way to recount his legends of collapse while at the same time capturing the flash—the laugh, the spark of enterprise—in the survivor's soul. His wily misfits stand guard over the best energies and impulses of the sixties—there is a hint that all is not over for the contrary spirit that founded this land (the Vineland of the Vikings) and left its most recent tracks in the American West. *Vineland* is an essential novel of our *fin de siècle,* a finger pointing the way out of the 1980s.

Vineland. Thomas Pynchon. 385 pp. Little, Brown. 1990. $19.95

. . . .

Joyce Carol Oates

"The use of language," said Joyce Carol Oates, accepting the 1969 National Book Award for *them,* "is all we have to pit against death and silence." Readers who have expressed astonishment at this author's extraordinary productivity might find a clue about it in these words. Ms. Oates is a writer obsessed. Indeed, not only has she fought the specters of destruction with her unflagging verbal activity, but she has also, in a slightly different sense, made them her subject. Her oeuvre keeps moving forward in a landslide of psychic, physical, familial, and social catastrophe.

You Must Remember This, her eighteenth novel to date, marks no departure from the pattern. Here Oates plots the unhappy course of an American family—the Stevicks of Port Oriskany, New York (a fictitious city)—from an arbitrary beginning point in 1944 to a short-lived moment of surcease in 1956. The gradations of their malaise are exhaustively inventoried. And Oates proves that she is still without rival in creating atmospheres of futility and incipient violence—when we finally close the book, we feel as though we were stepping from a cramped, overheated apartment out into God's own fresh air.

Lyle Stevick is a superfluous man. He runs a perpetually faltering used-furniture store in a rough section of the city. The family lives in part of a rented duplex near the U.S. Steel and Swale Cyanamid factories. Lyle's wife, Hannah, is always taking to her bed with obscure ailments. Their kids grow up fast among the weedy back lots. Geraldine and Lizzie, the older daughters, swoon over hoods with D.A. haircuts; the one son, Warren, enlists to fight in Korea as soon as he is of age. And Enid, who will become the focus of the novel, spends the hours of childhood dreaming herself into the miniature worlds in the wallpaper pattern. She wants oblivion. Crossing a railway trestle near her home, she wishes she had the courage to throw herself off.

The trouble did not start with Lyle. His own father, a prominent local businessman, deserted Lyle's mother to take up with a flashy showgirl. He fathered another son, Felix, before shooting himself in a hospital bed. "Man hands on misery to man," wrote Philip Larkin. Lyle would not deny it. One night he goes so far as to hang a rope from the basement rafter of his store; he then sips Early Times and stares at the rope's shadow, "vague as a smudge on the damp stone."

No such brooding for Felix—not for a long time, anyway. A brash, quick-tempered punk he is the novel's most vital character. Felix's wretched childhood drove him out into the streets, then into the ring. He rose through Golden Gloves to become a middleweight champ and a local legend. (Oates has been a lifelong boxing aficionado, and her last book was the nonfictional *On Boxing*.) Felix knows a secret, which, from the perspective of this novel, strikes us as perfectly true: "The sport wasn't a sport at all. It was just life speeded up." Retired after a humiliating knockout, Felix now makes shady property deals and cruises around the city in pricey cars.

Enid has had a thrill for her uncle ever since Lyle took her to one of his fights. One day, when she is visiting Geraldine—Enid is now a precocious fourteen—Felix shows up. Uncle and niece begin a friendly outdoor scuffle. Felix dances, fends off her blows with a cigarillo clenched in his teeth. But Enid won't stop: "In a frenzy she sprang at him, flailing and kicking, her eyes maddened, teary, her hair in her face, and he saw he'd maybe gone too far, he said, 'Okay, sweetheart, that's it—enough for the first lesson'—he was laughing then startled, annoyed—'hey, you little bitch!' as Enid slipped through his guard, pummeling like a windmill, panting and feverish and using her nails and there at last went Felix's cigarillo flying— and everyone laughed."

From "sweetheart" to "bitch"—a key transition is registered. Not only has Felix recognized a nature as nervy as his own, but he has glimpsed the undercurrent of sexuality in her attack. Half-drunk now on beer and cheap wine, he invites Enid to come see an old resort hotel he has invested in. There, among the cavernous, dusty rooms, they play a game of hide-and-seek that quickly gets more serious. Ms. Oates paces the escalating tensions expertly. Though Felix stops short of taking Enid's virginity—she is, after all, his half brother's kid—his assault is rough and needy. "Don't tell anyone, Enid," he pleads afterward. But he has no reason to fear—the girl is in love.

Enid is a quicksilver character, cool and willful at one moment, utterly fragile the next. When Felix rebuffs her at their next encounter, the two strains collide: she methodically swallows a bottle of aspirins. For a second time, it seems, she has spoken in terms that Felix can understand. Partly out of guilt and fear, but more because her pure will to die magnetizes something in his own being, he is drawn back to her. When she leaves the hospital, their long love affair begins.

The trajectory of this affair—from its morbid inception through Enid's high school years to the final sundering—forms the structural arch around which Oates builds the rest of her novel. At first the architectonics works well; the urgency and pathos of their motel trysts support the less dramatic narrative interludes. The sex scenes are charged with the violence of Enid's and Felix's separate natures. But as time and habit begin to dissipate their fury, the book loses momentum.

Into her chronicle of *amour fou,* Oates has woven episodes from the lives of the Stevick males. Warren, who has returned from war with disfiguring wounds, leaves Port Oriskany to become a peace activist. Alas, for us he does not become anything more than a

. . .

Joyce Carol Oates

sentimentalized cutout. In his devotion to the teachings of Gandhi and Thoreau in his unalloyed goodness, he is too obviously a thematic counterweight, an idea from the author's planning chart.

Lyle is different. Though he has none of Felix's adrenaline or Enid's single-mindedness, he is memorable. For in Lyle, Oates has given failure a habitation and a name. We feel the punishing sameness of his routines; we sit with him through the beers and shots that blur them for a few hours. His decline begins when a McCarthy-ite zealot denounces him as a Communist sympathizer because he keeps books in his shop and knows where the Soviet Union is. Lyle's morale never fully recovers from the police interrogation. And later, when a pretty client rejects his attentions, he all but collapses.

Oates's works in period detail with a generous hand. Korea, Peggy Lee, the Adlai Stevenson campaign, Arthur Godfrey, the Army-McCarthy hearings, the bomb—she has overlooked nothing. However, the stage machinery creaks audibly when she has Lyle find salvation through the building of a backyard bomb shelter. We watch this confused, embittered man scurrying about like the ant in the old parable. But the pity we might expect to feel is undercut by the crude logic of compensation that Ms. Oates has set up.

The end of Enid and Felix's love affair brings the novel to its close. Oates unfortunately rushes the final episodes—we don't believe that the tangles of such a compulsive passion are so handily undone. Still, *You Must Remember This* has much to recommend it. The press of the action is in places relentless. And Ms. Oates has, if anything, sharpened her feel for gritty urban settings and the passions and despairs that flame up there. The inner voice of adolescence is convincingly intense—it plays effectively against the raging and choked-down voices of adulthood.

A few years back, in novels like *A Bloodsmoor Romance* and *Mysteries of Winterthurn*, Oates indulged the more gothic side of her sensibility. But with last year's *Marya* (which also depicted a young girl's coming-of-age in upstate New York) and the new novel, she has veered back onto the high road of realism. Perhaps the detour was an exorcism. For Oates is relying much less on the kind of violence that saturated early novels like *them* and *Wonderland*. The violence is now carried inward, where it has a chance of being countered by other psychic forces. The resulting prose is more complex and more tolerant of ambiguities, though the contest between tragic and redemptive forces has not yet been fought with the decisiveness that the highest art demands.

You Must Remember This. Joyce Carol Oates. 436 pp. William Abrahams / Dutton. 1987. $19.95

.   .   .   .

Joyce Carol Oates

Alan
Lelchuk

From the start of his career as a novelist, Alan Lelchuk has had a reputation as a bad boy, not a *real* bad boy of the old Burroughs/Genet stamp, more the kind who puts horns over the teacher's head in the class picture. His novels, *American Mischief, Shrinking, Miriam at Thirty-Four,* and *Miriam in Her Forties,* are brash. They all have something of that "prurience" that people went on about back when "Banned in Boston" was for real. Sexual interest aside, though, these works—the first three, certainly—are also valuable documents from the long-interred era of liberation and antiauthoritarian freethinking. The more recent Miriam novel (1989) is a brave effort at coming to terms with diminished cultural and personal expectations. It is a portrait from our time.

If Lelchuk has not stood forth in the first rank of novelists, it may be in part because the times have turned against his brand of outspokenness. It may also have to do with the fact that Philip Roth has always got to the same subjects first, writing of the guilt and sexual aggression of the emancipated Jew, and the half-comic, half-tragic involutions of the therapeutic process. Lelchuk has remained one row back, putting up horns.

What happens to bad boys as the years come on? Some, like Burroughs, get defanged by the media and their own cult status. Others, like Mailer, seem to mellow of their own accord. Lelchuk, if his novel/memoir *Brooklyn Boy* is any indication, has set out to reinvent himself from scratch: he has tried to rewrite his story as that of Jack Armstrong, all-American boy. Well, that's a slight exaggeration. No contortion of prose is going to make Jack Armstrong out of someone named Aaron Schlossberg. But the impulse to turn the son of a Russian immigrant into a baseball-loving, hot-dog-munching, gee-whiz American kid is very strong—so strong that it all but swamps the sharp tensions of assimilation that are this book's real subject.

Brooklyn Boy is a surprisingly conventional bildungsroman. Its unpredictable switches between the first and third person alert us to the extent to which this is the author's own story. The novel carries its hero, Aaron, from late boyhood through late adolescence. It leaves him, in the time-honored tradition of the genre, on the threshold of manhood. Aaron's growing up is rendered in distinct and mainly chronological episodes.

We first meet him as a boy living in cramped lower-middle-class circumstances in late 1940s Brooklyn. His father, Harry, is a staunchly unassimilated fellow traveler of indeterminate occupation and income. He lives for his weekly meetings with like-minded cronies, and for screenings of old Revolution-era Russian films. Except for a mysterious devotion to boxing matches, he despises the ways of his adopted country. Aaron's mother, soft, well-meaning, and fundamentally passive, is scarcely a presence.

Lelchuk's initial episodes center upon the immemorial struggle between the immigrant father and his willful son. Aaron is giddy with the desire to be one of the boys, to be "regular." He makes trouble at school, ogles pretty little girls, hangs out with the neighborhood gang. Mostly, though, he listens to, dreams, and plays baseball. Baseball is, for Aaron, the American code: to play the game and to master the lore of statistics is to gain admission to the real America. Baseball is his Ellis Island.

.   .   .

Alan Lelchuk

The heroes of Aaron's beloved Dodgers bestride the land like so many colossi. And the generational struggle, naturally enough, also revolves around baseball. To Harry Schlossberg, it is a nonsensical game. He is determined to raise the boy in his own image, and so long as he wields power, he drags Aaron to his meetings and his movies, and pressures him to play chess against his friends and their sons. Aaron must oblige. But one afternoon the power base abruptly shifts. Aaron goes for a match with a certain Sammy Goichberg and finds his father in bed with Sammy's mother. The days of Harry's rule—and his marriage—are over.

Here Lelchuk plays an unsettling trick with time. He narrates the dissolution of the marriage in a few sentences, and then, almost immediately, installs a live-in lover to replace the banished father. No sooner have we absorbed these rather large kernels of information, however, than we are back in a previous phase, with father and son warring over baseball. Aaron is skipping school to go to Ebbets Field with an older upstairs neighbor, and Harry is trying to lay down the law. Aaron keeps transgressing; he finally wins through sheer persistence. The inexplicable time shift, alas, checks the reader's momentum and reduces the effect of the victory.

Finally, Lelchuk's father-son material holds more in promise than it delivers in execution. He makes the confrontations, surely the main psychological fact of Aaron's existence, obvious and perfunctory. Rarely does he catch the racking ambivalence that lives at the core of these conflicts, ambivalence not only in the sense of love blending with hatred, but also of pride entwined with shame. Only once, really, does he break through the formulaic patter of their face-offs to root out the nerve of sensibility. In this one instance, Aaron and his father are walking home from a night at the ring. Aaron is elated, not by what happened at the fights, but by what he saw when he looked over at his father. He saw that odd, funny-looking man acting just like a normal red-blooded male, rooting and shouting. Just then, a rain shower breaks, and the two begin to run:

> Rain fell swiftly and hard, and to my surprise, Papa laughed and called over, "Come, silly boy, come!" And he was actually running. He ran funny, swaying his hips from side to side like a

girl, and sort of using his elbows, not arms, but his strength gave
him his speed.

A lovely moment, this, tender and excruciating. In the precision of
his description, Lelchuk has dared the hard kind of exposure.

Aaron's coming-of-age proceeds. After the struggles for autonomy, after the father is gone, the emphasis of the narrative changes.
Aaron is shown taking up sports reporting, the first hint of a future
vocation. He starts frequenting the school library, where he meets
and falls in love with the pretty West Indian librarian. She returns
the interest for a short time, and then—like Father—suddenly drops
out of Aaron's life. His heart is scored.

The next major phase comes in late high school when Aaron
takes a job in the city. He becomes "fiction boy" at Schulte's bookstore. Working deep in the basement stacks, he not only learns what
worlds are to be found between the covers of books, but he also gets
a schooling in another kind of sporting life. The elevator man, a
black wheeler-dealer named Jackson, runs a gaming and whoring
establishment right next to the bookstore basement. (Blacks are presented mainly by way of negative stereotypes throughout the book;
an earlier incident had Aaron robbed at knifepoint by a tough-talking
black from a rival school.) Aaron conquers what few inhibitions he
has and is soon an initiate in the major vices.

It is during this same bookstore period, a period of accelerated maturing, that Aaron decides that he must break free of Brooklyn and find
adventure. He takes a precipitous early leave from high school and
signs up as a deckhand on a Norwegian ship. He is transported, more
suddenly than he had thought possible, from the back streets of
Brooklyn to the open seas, then to the African coast. "Not bad," he
thinks, as the ship moves up the Congo River, "not bad at all." Privy
throughout to Aaron's flights of fancy, we know how to complete
the thought: not bad for a Brooklyn boy.

These words, we may also remember, are the recurrent tag line
in the books of another Brooklyn bad boy: Henry Miller. Time and
again in the course of his expatriated adventurings, Miller (or one
of his stand-in speakers) will rear back with a triumphant: "Not bad
for a Brooklyn boy!" And in that exclamation we hear a double note.

. . .

Alan Lelchuk

Pride of place, of origin, commingles with the sense that Brooklyn is also a burden that one can get free of only through tremendous exertion. It is a place to be *from,* a place to escape. The refrain itself, its recurrence, suggests that one never really does get away.

There is, incidentally, an interesting lineage that we might consider here—the lineage of Brooklyn-born (or reared) male writers, which is also, perhaps not coincidentally, a lineage of what might charitably be called youthful enthusiasts. First, naturally, there is Whitman, the original yea-saying American boy. Then, some years later, Miller, who incorporates Whitman, citing him throughout his books as a presiding figure of freedom and imagination. Then comes Mailer (born in New Jersey, but raised, and living, in Brooklyn)—he does for Miller what Miller did for Whitman. Finally, we have Lelchuk, singing Miller's awestruck refrain. All four writers uphold priapism and sexual frankness; all four tout, in their separate ways, the intensity and variousness of city life. Picture them packed one inside the other like so many Russian *katrinka* dolls—with Whitman, the grandest and most enduring, holding the others like a mother.

Within this grouping, the greatest similarity is to be found between Lelchuk and Miller. In both we see the same sharp split between the bravado of the emancipated male on the one hand, and the simplistic and sentimental reverence for the boyhood self on the other. When Miller turns from his "adult" exploits to write about his Brooklyn boyhood, his voice takes on a cloying good-boy sweetness: we long immediately for the return of the cynical philanderer. The same holds true for Lelchuk. The aggressions and the energies that a blocked and difficult childhood created in him, which can break out with such surprising verve in *his* adult novels, disappear when he looks back to track their source. The writing, instead of showing sinew and drive, turns pasteboard.

Listen to this snatch of dialogue between Aaron and his friends:

"Forget the Dodgers, come September and they'll blow it!" said Alan Kamph, diehard Yankee fan. "Yeah, the Cards look strong again," worried Ronald Tavel. "And don't forget 'Spahn and Sain and two days of rain,'" scholarly Jerry said, referring to the

Braves and their pitchers. "Aah, Brooklyn will murder those guys," asserted Morty Kassover, street bully and Dodger fanatic.

This sounds far too much like those boys' books that older relatives were always giving as presents, with the kind of decent "true-to-life" boyness that got promulgated in scouting manuals and *Boys' Life* magazine.

Alan Lelchuk's natural gifts find little room for play in this memoir. He has hobbled himself. I suspect that at some moment he recognized that he had a very representative story to tell, and decided to reach after the archetypal presentation. Unfortunately, Lelchuk cannot cut away the patina of the emblematic in order to get at the nastier and more hurtful life beneath: the very thing he does so effectively in his other books. This is the book to give your grandson if you are a well-meaning grandparent and he is a bright pip of a lad. Others may want to wait for the bad boy's return.

> *Brooklyn Boy*. Alan Lelchuk. 304 pp. McGraw-Hill. 1990. $19.95

.   .   .   .

Alan Lelchuk

Russell
Banks

B it by bit the inventory of the soul's dark holdings proceeds, if not in our sciences, then in our arts. We need look no further than the one-word titles of some of our novels: Sartre's *Nausea,* Robbe-Grillet's *Jealousy,* Rushdie's *Shame,* Nabokov's *Despair,* and Olesha's *Envy.* Each title is, in effect, the first word of its book; each seems to promise that we will find between the covers the last word on the subject. The draw is powerful; we want our darkness objectified in figures and situations and lit by the artist's understanding. Our happier selves concern us less in fiction—works about *Joy, Satisfaction, Contentment, Ease,* or *Bliss* are generally reserved for the how-to shelves.

To the remarkable former list we should now add Russell Banks's *Affliction,* the most sweepingly bleak label of all. It is Banks's intent to fix his sights on a place at the core of human unhappiness, and to trace the radial extensions from that core through the web of a single family. At the center of that web is Wade Whitehouse, in whom are gathered the various soul ailments itemized above, and a few others besides.

Wade Whitehouse's fictional lineage is a simple one. He is the son of Glenn and Sally Whitehouse, born and raised in the scrubby up-country of New Hampshire. His town is Catamount, which also happened to be the starting place of Bob Dubois, the protagonist of Banks's novel *Continental Drift,* which appeared in 1985. But if Wade's fictional origins are straightforward, the path leading to his creation is not. It has taken Banks a good long time to find the fusion of matter and manner that declares itself so forcefully here. His nine previous novels and story collections can be viewed as a painstaking—and in places, a very successful—progress toward *Affliction.*

Banks started out writing stories with one hand and novels with the other. His first novel, *Family Life* (1974), and his first collection, *Searching for Survivors* (1975), reflect a sensibility divided between the claim of the common life and the claim of the experimental or "artistic." An inclination toward the former often comes refracted through the aspiration toward the latter. In *Searching for Survivors,* for example, the stories of simple people are worked up in a variety of forms, many using oblique narration and unexpected elisions; and *Family Life* plays with its materials using fairy-tale conceits and a deliberately simplistic style. These works, skillful as they are in execution, share a kind of writerly self-consciousness that is the almost inevitable curse of the young writer with large ambitions. We feel the lives as fiction before we feel the lives themselves. The writer is still courting his subject matter from a distance.

With the stories in *The New World* (1978) and the novel *The Book of Jamaica* (1980), Banks veered resolutely onto the track of naturalistic narrative. *The Book of Jamaica* is a carefully written, almost documentarily faithful rendering of the stages of one man's immersion into the wholly alien culture of the Jamaican Maroons, descendants of African slaves brought to the island by the British colonists. Banks himself spent some time traveling and living in Jamaica, and the local detailings reflect an eye training itself to precise observation. Perhaps too much so: the book lags through long passages of description and historical documentation.

Still, Banks's next book, the novel/story-cycle *Trailerpark* (1981), plants us squarely in the country of his surest inspiration. In a sequence of thirteen linked stories, Banks unfolds the lives and relationships of the occupants of a gone-to-seed trailerpark in northern New Hampshire. The prose is vibrant, spirited; Banks has a natural way of presenting the peculiar and twisting drives of his characters, a drifter-druggie, a Jesus fanatic, a woman whose trailer (and life) gets overrun by the guinea pigs she keeps. These people are, in Nelson Algren's phrase, "lonesome monsters," and Banks knows their thoughts and doings, the scope of their daily concerns and the erratic inflation of their fantasy lives. If anything is missing from this book, it is perhaps some countervailing sense of normalcy, at very least the pretend normalcy that surrounds us in our day-to-day commerce.

Continental Drift was generally perceived to be Banks's breakthrough. Ambitious in reach, powered by the rage released from pent-up lives, the prose showed that Banks was ready to take up big themes and conflicts. *Continental Drift* was assertively complex in both its formal structure and its plot dynamics. Banks engineered the convergence of two very different lives: Bob Dubois, a refugee from dead-end Catamount, who winds up running a smuggling boat in Florida, and Vanise Dorsinville, a Haitian woman bent upon escaping the privations of her island life. In the catastrophic intersection of their fates we can read the legend of larger cultural forces, forces that drive the characters into actions that they blindly believe themselves to be choosing.

The book remains one of the more powerful achievements in recent American fiction. And one hesitates to quarrel over flaws and weaknesses where so much has been attempted, and with such success. God knows, our literature has little enough that reaches beyond the bedroom or nightclub wall. But it must be said that *Continental Drift* suffered from lopsidedness. The episodes featuring Bob Dubois are rendered with a confidence, a rightness of the kind we acknowledge when we say that a character is "inhabited"; the passages with Vanise, while sharply etched and outwardly penetrating, nonetheless lack this quality. The book belonged to its male lead, and the force of its final encounter is somewhat dissipated by the imbalance.

In many ways, *Affliction* pulls the concerns of *Continental Drift* inside out. Where Banks's earlier novel charted a grand scheme of cultural migration, seeking to isolate the larger as well as the human-sized circulations of malaise, *Affliction* stays rooted in place, hews to a single scale. Its study is the deeper ramifications of blood and kinship; it roots in to find the wellsprings of the will to violence.

The novel maps the flare-up of fate, tragic fate, in the life of Wade Whitehouse. We are told as much in the first sentence. "This," writes Rolfe Whitehouse, the narrator, "is the story of my older brother's strange criminal behavior and his disappearance." Rolfe is a history teacher living in Boston. He has long since fled family and place, and he soon convinces us that it is only the pressure of these extraordinary and sad events that brings him to speak. He has, he claims, pieced his account together from a great many sources, not least from Wade's own drunken telephone calls. The time frame is not large, given the extremity of the change in Wade. "Everything of importance," Rolfe informs us, "—that is, everything that gives rise to the telling of this story—occurred during a single deer-hunting season . . ."

Wade, as we meet him in the opening pages of his brother's narration, is an explosion waiting to happen. He is not different in kind from the other working people in Catamount, but the degrees of temperament and circumstance mark him as a man to be wary of. Wade is forty-one, divorced, living alone in the shambles of a trailer on the outskirts of town. His exwife, Lillian, and his daughter, Jill, are several hours away in Concord, where Lillian has remarried. Wade works two jobs, one as well-digger for Gordon LaRiviere, the town's one entrepreneur, the other as part-time policeman–crossing guard. He spends some of his nights with Margie, a waitress at the local diner, but most of his off-time is passed in bars or in solitary drinking bouts in his trailer. People tend to steer wide of Wade when he has been drinking; they recognize the intensity of the rage he has repressed, even if they don't understand its source.

Rolfe does not unfold Wade's tale as a causal sequence. Rather, he shows how disparate events come sheaving his way, moving him almost irresistibly onto his appointed track. Rolfe knows, too, that there are twists and turns of private circumstance that elude him, but he sets out with patient strokes the incidents he knows about. First, there is the unhappy night of Halloween. Jill has been sent against her wishes to spend the weekend with her father. Wade is awkward with her, his good intentions skewed by guilt and remorse.

· · · ·

Russell Banks

When he brings Jill to the town Halloween party, he pushes her to take part in the costume contest in progress. The abyss between them is immediately obvious, as is the volatility of the hurt Wade carries:

> The girl took a single step forward and stopped. Wade nudged her a second time. "Go on, Jill. Some of those kids you know." He looked down at the tiger's tail drooping to the floor and the child's blue sneakers peeking out from under the cuffs of the pathetic costume. Then he looked at the back of her head, her flax-colored hair creased by the string from the mask, and he suddenly wanted to weep.

Rolfe does not need to tell much more for us to know that Wade is not at heart a bad or callous man, and that we should consider closely the forces pressing at him. But Jill is miserable. She slips away during the party and calls her mother, who sets out immediately to bring her home. And several hours later, in the parking lot, Wade is made to suffer again the humiliation of his failure as a husband and a father. He vows at that moment to take legal steps to regain custody of Jill.

Other events press in. Late that same night Wade goes for a ride with his young co-worker Jack Hewitt, who brags to him that their boss, LaRiviere, has asked him to take an out-of-state union official deer hunting. The very next day the man is found shot to death in the woods—a victim, apparently, of a rifle accident. But Wade cannot rest with that explanation. He becomes obsessed with what he sees as the mystery of a backwoods murder. He is convinced of a setup. And for days he can think of little else. He replays the possibilities in his mind in every conceivable variation; he starts making late-night calls to Rolfe to air his theories. It is almost as if he believes that if he can solve the other man's death, then he can solve his own life as well.

As the novel gathers its first momentum, the reader has every reason to expect that the mystery of the shooting will form the propulsion, the core, of interest. But once he has planted this obsession in Wade, and, to an extent, in the reader, Banks steers away. While these circumstances will ultimately figure in Wade's tragedy, they will not be the main precipitants. Other factors—having to do with family bonds, and the warping of character through brutality—prove more important. These emerge as Banks begins to peel away at the carapace with which Wade has shielded himself for so many years.

Tracking Wade's movements over the next few days—his workaday trials, his consultation with a lawyer—Rolfe also starts to incorporate pieces of the background story. We get an inkling of how Wade came to be in his present situation. And with each bit of information, our picture of the man shifts; the closer Wade is brought to what will look to the outsider as senseless violence, the more we are able to see where the sense of it lies. As we learn the story of Wade and Lillian and Wade's father, we have to shed the preconceptions we were initially encouraged to hold.

As Auden wrote, "I and the public know/What all schoolchildren learn,/ Those to whom evil is done / Do evil in return." This physics of evil is what *Affliction* is finally about. For no person, of course, is born bearing hopelessness and rage; we are molded to shape by the people around us. Wade as a young man was very different from the scarred being we have beheld. He had plans; he had a powerful love for Lillian; he had a chance for sane happiness. In the beginning of their relationship, it seems, Lillian was a kind of angel for Wade, all tenderness and encouragement. "Without Lillian," Rolfe writes, "without her recognition and protection, Wade would have been forced to regard himself as no different from the boys and men who surrounded him. . . ."

Alas, her gift was not enough. For night after night Wade had to come home to a vicious, drunken father and a family scene of such helpless terror that damage was inevitable. "Pop" Whitehouse finds Wade's attempts at self-assertion a trigger to his fury. He tries to beat every last shred of independence out of him. Banks is very good at capturing the dulling repetition of these scenes, the rhythms of their intensification, the empty roaring of the aftermath. But what we register most keenly—it is impossible not to flinch—is the pitch of a young man's terror:

> There was no time to hide from the blow, no time to protect himself with his arms or even to turn away. Pop's huge fist descended and collided with the boy's cheekbone. Wade felt a terrible slow warmth wash thickly across his face, and then he

· · ·

Russell Banks

felt nothing at all. He was lying on his side, his face slammed against the couch, which smelled like cigarette smoke and sour milk, when there came a second blow, this one low on his back, and he heard his mother shout, "Glenn! Stop!" His body was behind him somewhere and felt hot and soft and bright, as if it had burst into flame. There was nothing before his eyes but blackness, and he realized that he was burrowing his face into the couch, showing his father his backside as he dug with his paws like a terrified animal into the earth.

Here is the root of damage, the source of the evil that later comes spilling forth from the boy grown up. When we learn that Wade may have beaten Lillian during their marriage, we are not surprised. When we see how he greets the oppressions in his life with fists, and alcoholic outbursts, and finally rifle fire, we are confirmed. It is the law of human nature that what enters as experience exits as behavior.

One Sunday, midway through the novel, Wade and Margie pay a visit to Wade's family and find Pop sitting in the kitchen in an alcoholic stupor. The stove has gone out, and Wade's mother is nowhere to be seen. Pop mumbles incoherent answers to their questions. They wait. But as the dreadful silence continues, Wade and Margie start exchanging glances. Finally they push into the bedroom, where they find that Wade's mother has frozen to death under the covers. Pop is too drunk to know what has happened; he is also too abject to draw down Wade's fury. There is no release, no explosion. The scene is as bleakly futile as any in recent literature.

From the time of the funeral on, Wade is in the grip of forces that he cannot command. He continues at his jobs, but he feels disengaged, as though he is walking in his sleep. He and Margie attempt to set up housekeeping with Pop, reckoning that he can no longer take care of himself. But Wade cannot begin to settle in. The atmospheric pressure around him intensifies by the hour. He cannot shake free of thinking about Evan Twombley, the union official. His paranoia is further fueled when he learns that LaRiviere is trying to buy Pop's land, that he has been covertly buying up every parcel on the mountain. Wade cannot figure out the connections, but he is sure they exist. On top of everything else, he has a rotting tooth that starts tormenting him to the point of madness.

I leave it to the reader to follow the skein of events that bring Wade to his final actions. The drive of the plot is intense through the final pages. Perhaps the last moment of any control that Wade has is when he lurches to the upstairs bathroom with a bottle of whiskey and a rusted pair of pliers. The pulpy horror of his tooth can be dealt with, even if the roots of his misery are too deep to be reached. Wade is finally without recourse; he cannot avoid the pull to violence.

This man's story is a tragedy in the Greek sense: at some point he surrendered a possible destiny and accepted a fate instead. Where the Greek heroes were driven to their ends by the implacable will of the gods, Wade is driven by the no less implacable imperatives of his mishapen character. Once that character has been formed, pressed out by blows and kicks, there is little hope that disaster will be averted. The reader's heart fills with pity and terror.

Banks controls the rush of his narrative with practiced skill. His device of refracting the story through Rolfe is a canny one, and it carries an added significance that occurs to us only later. Initially it seems a bit odd. Though Rolfe is giving us a scene-by-scene account of events he did not himself witness, he adopts the novelist's freedom to reconstruct these scenes down to the last detail and to enter into his brother's thoughts and feelings. Objectively, this is presumptuous, even though he claims to have interviewed everyone involved and to have listened for hours to Wade's drunken meanderings. But in fact we soon forget that Rolfe is doing the telling. We come to regard him as a stand-in novelist, a transparent screen through which we peer at the stages of the action. But there is a higher logic to Banks's setup. For Rolfe, too, is a Whitehouse. The novel is about blood ties and the handing on of legacies, and the blood that runs in his veins is Whitehouse blood. He knows the town, the country; he lived through the tension of those horrifying nights. And he is forced to write because of this—because he recognizes that he is, except by the grace of whatever powers, himself capable of every last dark deed. This echo of kinship within the book amplifies the message more persuasively than any of the chilling turns of the plot.

. . .

Russell Banks

Banks began his career divided between a common-life subject matter and an experimental style. Subject has obviously won out, and Banks's liberated energies have gone into the forging of a straight-on technique. Banks's idiom is now vigorous and gritty, perfectly suited to the life of his characters and place. With his last few books, but with *Affliction* especially, he joins that group of small-town realists—writers like William Kennedy, Andre Dubus, and Larry Woiwode—who have worked to sustain what may in time be seen as our dominant tradition. Like them, Banks unfolds the sufferings of the ordinary life, of those who must worry, who can't be happy.

Affliction. Russell Banks. 355 pp. Harper & Row. 1989. $18.95

· · · ·

SVEN BIRKERTS

Jack
Pulaski

There has been a great deal of back-and-forth in the last few
years about the state of the American short story. Optimistic
partisans insist that we are in the midst of a renaissance of the form.
They cite the proliferation of writing workshops—in which the short
story is the staple nutrient—and the incontrovertible evidence of the
marketplace. The reading public *is*, it seems, shelling out hard cash
for anthologies and collections, many of which bear the imprimatur
of major publishing houses. Not so long ago, you had to have a Nobel
Prize just to get a story manuscript over the transom. Things have
changed.

But not all critics have greeted this fiction with approbation. A
number of them have come out fiercely against what they perceive
as its stylish inconsequentiality and moral evasiveness (in the past
year alone, see Diane Johnson's "Hick Chic" in the *New York Review
of Books*, Madison Bell's "The Dwindling Short Story" in *Harper's*,
and Rosellen Brown's "The Emperor's New Clothes" in the *Boston
Review*). I have expressed similar sentiments more than once. Indeed,
in my worst moments, I fear that inconsequentiality and evasiveness

are the very source of this fiction's popular appeal—that the market-place is getting just what it wants. But no, the less cynical part of me believes that there *are* serious readers, and that they are arrayed like hungry travelers around a wayside table—when a real meal comes, they'll roll up their sleeves and have at it.

What a pleasure, then, to be able to throw off the doomy mantle of the naysayer and announce that an absolutely remarkable collection has fallen into my hands: *The St. Veronica Gig Stories,* by Jack Pulaski. The book has been beautifully produced by Zephyr Press, and it is available in more selective outlets. Promotion and supply budgets being what they are, though, you might have to pester your bookseller. Do so. For this is the rare real thing, the necessary infusion without which our literature would wither away.

Pulaski is, to judge from the jacket photo, a man with a few decades of hard knocks behind him. Although he was born and raised in Brooklyn (all of the stories take place within a five-mile radius of the home neighborhood), his biographical note hints at a peripatetic career of real-life employments. The stories have been squeezed drop by drop out of the pulp of experience. Pulaski does not appear to be prolific—for all I know, this is the sum of what he's written. But sparsity of output, as we know, is often a sign of uncompromising craft. Not one syllable in this book is gratuitous; every sentence has been weighed and assessed like a necklace in a jeweler's hand.

Pulaski's world—the Russian-Jewish and Hispanic immigrant neighborhoods in 1950s Brooklyn—will not be familiar to most readers. Neither would I say that the plot lines are especially gripping: the author likes to work a discursive narrative cluttered with sensation and oddly angled asides. "Don Juan, the Senior Citizen," for example, takes nearly forty pages to tell how an old man extricates himself from a birthday party thrown in his honor and goes home to dream about the beautiful Cuban woman he plans to marry. But then, most great stories—look at Chekhov, or Babel, or Welty—don't try to get us from Troy to Ithaca. Their aim is to give the reader an unforgettable glimpse of the world from behind another pair of eyes. This is no small accomplishment. The author must have a prodigious capacity for empathy as well as the courage to be idiosyn-

. . . .

cratic. Pulaski has both. What's more, he has a linguistic velocity that will leave you panting in his wake.

Reading only the enervated, tentative stuff that has been passing for fiction of late, you might easily forget the vitality and surprise that lie latent in the language. Try an experiment. Sit back for a few hours with some of the analgesic prose of Ann Beattie, or David Leavitt, or any one of a hundred other "hot" contemporary stylists. Then, when you start to feel as if you were bouncing around inside a cathode-ray tube, flip to the first paragraph of the first story in *The St. Veronica Gig Stories:*

> The merry-go-round truck came down the street, the calliope piping the overture to the *Barber of Seville.* Children leapt from their mothers' laps and shrieked for nickels. Hoodlums in their gabardine suits removed their hands from their testicles—the stance, dignified, stoic, their hands modestly cupped their balls; they contemplated the daily double and fished in their pockets, showering a largesse of nickels, as windows five stories up showered a consolation of apples. Below, the children snatched at the coins parachuted in knotted handkerchiefs, apples exploding on the sidewalk, a hubbub of knees and fists contesting apples and nickels.

The momentum is irresistible. A whole crowded street is brought to life, revealed to be a force field of vertical and horizontal energies. Apples are going off like champagne corks. And with the subtle disarming of the hoodlums' defensive postures, the ceremonies of innocence are ready to begin.

Pulaski is at his very best when he plunges the reader straight into the midst of action and milieu. And this is his strategy in most of the eight stories here. In "Music Story," the tour de force of the collection, he catches his principals, five young Jewish musicians, in the manic moments of their afternoon rehearsal. Jo-Jo, Manny, and Augie are noodling on their instruments. Artie, the piano player, is having a holy war with his mother, who is trying to force a lamb chop down his gullet. Practice for the evening gig is scotched completely when Artie's mother loses control and starts smashing the plaster busts of the great composers on the parquet floor.

. . . . .

Jack Pulaski

But this is just the prelude. The gig itself, a dance at St. Veronica's School, has been sponsored by the Sons of Calabria Fraternal Organization. The hosts seem to think they've hired a real Italian band, and the truth does not leak out right away. The boys get a long first set during which they show their stuff:

> The warm vibrato of my voice trailed off into a complicitous coda of the longing aboil in the blue air of St. Veronica's gymnasium. Bunny, Cookie, and Ginger answered with a soothing homophonic moan, joined by several of the modestly dressed, handkerchief-pinned-at-waists young ladies. When the dancers parted and the applause exploded I wondered if I might not be another Frank Sinatra and marry a movie star. Cookie said, "I'm Cookie," and tugged on my trouser leg. I felt the soft ding dong swing between my legs and looked down. Her red mouth cracked gum, and she said, "Ey-ey, you sing 'No Tomorra.' "

"No Tomorra" very nearly proves prophetic so far as the band is concerned. I won't spoil the prospective reader's pleasure by saying any more. Just this: by the time you've finished "Music Story," you will have gone through that nonpareil experience, complete engagement—you will have been in that decorated gym, mopping sweat, swigging cheap Chianti, and staring down with tremulous heart at the sharp-pointed shoes with their cubano heels.

Music is probably the best analogy for Pulaski's stylistic mode. Not melodic music, but fast jazz. A Pulaski story catches the beat with the very first word and within a sentence or two the various harmonic and rhythmic lines are jostling, streaming together. Story is not always central—at times it functions like an underlying chord pattern. What kindles you up is the moment-by-moment rush of the language, the fervid percolation of word sounds. A sentence will pause and hover . . . and the next thing you know, it's heading for the roof like a Charlie Parker solo.

Listen as the narrator of "Father of the Bride" pursues his wily antagonist down the street:

> He plunges on ahead of me. Stunned, I stand there, his hand waves goodbye, and the elegantly thin body in the white suit turns, the brown gnomic head turns, the tips of the moustachio

pointing up the gleeful eyes. I chase after him—past pushcarts and babylonian vendors in their bewildered hair, holding hysterical dominion over the ass end of the cornucopia; bobby-pins, canteloupes, pots, crockery, plaster saints, *halivah,* and mops; people, windows, a havoc of tongues, the little man in the white suit disappears behind me.

There is pleasure everywhere—in the staggered observation of the man turning, in the staging of words ("Stunned, I stand . . ."), in the descriptive inventiveness ("bewildered hair"), and, overwhelmingly, in the bob and weave of syllables. Read the passage aloud, hear the *b* and *p* and *h* sounds playing off the vowels, feel with your whole mouth the "havoc of tongues" that Pulaski is after.

In a sense, this havoc is what *The St. Veronica Gig Stories* is all about. Pulaski's people are immigrants moving about in a vast and mysterious new world. They are excessive and irregular; assimilation has not yet worn off their rough contours. In their myriad travails and excitements, all of which Pulaski has registered with the artist's adventurous senses, they release the buried energies of our speech. So long as you read, you inhabit a vital commotion-charged, all but forgotten America.

Ed Hogan, who operates Zephyr Press out of his Somerville, Massachusetts, home, first read "Father of the Bride" nearly a decade ago. "It was in the Pushcart Prize volume," he recalls, "and I put a check mark beside the title. That meant that I wanted to read it again." At the time, though, Hogan was busy publishing *Aspect,* a literary magazine that he had founded in 1969. He had no idea that Pulaski would one day be a keystone in a far more ambitious enterprise.

Aspect survived for eleven years, which is quite remarkable for a shoestring-budget journal. "Toward the end," says Hogan, "I was feeling more and more frustrated by the impermanence, by the fact that *Aspect* has no shelf life." He finally founded Zephyr Press in 1980, the same year he allowed *Aspect* to expire. One of Hogan's first moves was to publish a thick anthology of the best of the journal. Since then, Zephyr (which comprises Hogan and a staff of three volunteers), has issued three poetry chapbooks and three works of fiction: *I Brake for Delmore Schwartz,* by Richard Grayson; *Two Nov-*

. . . .

Jack Pulaski

els, by Philip Whalen (one of the more important West Coast "beat" writers); and Pulaski.

"I heard about Jack Pulaski through DeWitt Henry, the editor of *Ploughshares*," Hogan laughs. "I had forgotten all about that check mark." After reading everything he could find in old quarterlies, he was excited enough to contact the author immediately: "I was hoping he had a manuscript." As it turned out, Pulaski had been circulating *The St. Veronica Gig Stories* among trade houses, getting one regret-filled rejection letter after another. He agreed to let Hogan look at the collection. Two weeks later an agreement had been reached.

I'd like to say that the rest is history, but it's not. Not yet. Small publishers like Zephyr have to fight tremendous odds. They cannot afford to run big ads or to flood reviewers' desks with freebies. Booksellers seldom take a chance and order more than a copy or two. But if demand—fostered by word-of-mouth excitement—is strong enough, anything can happen. What can I say? Get the book and read it. And then shower copies on everyone you know who still enjoys moving his or her eyes from left to right.

The St. Veronica Gig Stories. Jack Pulaski. 170 pp. Zephyr Press. 1986. $15.95

·   ·   ·

SVEN BIRKERTS

Lynne Sharon Schwartz

A peculiar form, the novella. It isn't a long story, though many have called it such. Neither is it a short novel, though many more have erringly thought so. No, the novella does what it does as it would, obeying only its own subtle organic imperatives. It launches an arc—the line of story bending up, over and gracefully down—and then pulls up short before it threatens to become a circle, a whole big world.

Lynne Sharon Schwartz's *Leaving Brooklyn* can be seen as tracing just such a figure. An invention masked as a memory (Ms. Schwartz has confessed in an interview to blurring and changing real-life antecedents), the novella recounts the sexual initiation, at the hands of her ophthalmologist, of a fifteen-year-old Brooklyn girl named Audrey. But of course such a description is just a simple facade. The life of the book, the *real* story, has to do with the process whereby a self gets rid of its images and expectations and acts to make its own history. It is, in short, about growing up.

Audrey comes of age in the tight enclave of postwar Brooklyn, where rightness and decency reign and children are trained "to feel shame at every wayward emotion." But Audrey cannot quite make these injunctions her own. Because of an accident at birth, she sees things differently than others—literally. Through her left eye the world looks normal. But through the right that same world becomes "a tenuous place where the common, reasonable laws of physics did not apply, where a piece of face or the leg of a table or frame of a window might at any moment break off and drift away." Audrey's is, in a sense, the artist's wound, tipping her off from the start that life is not just a display of surfaces but a shifting, unstable place where depths and shadows and alternatives are forever pressing their claims.

When Audrey is fifteen, her parents take her into Manhattan to have her fitted for a special corrective lens. The office setting is blandly innocuous. Audrey sees "a tall fair-skinned man with thinning hair, a sandy mustache, and glasses"; she notices his professional aloofness. But then, at her next visit, a somewhat different awareness intrudes:

> He leaned over me, peering into my armored eye, his liquory breath dazing me and making me slightly sick, his right leg brushing against mine, producing an ellipse of warmth. I saw the pores of his cheeks, the dark of his nostrils; his gray pupils, enormous behind the thick glasses, seemed to vibrate. I was dizzy. His trousers felt rough against my thin cotton dress.

It is that last sentence that tips us off—the rubbing fabrics are already whispering about innocence and experience, submission and domination.

The expected happens, and happens again and again during subsequent visits. But the physical act of love is all that is predictable. Every other gesture and response of these ill-sorted lovers breaks free of type. What Schwartz ends up setting before us is fiction's most beautiful effect: we believe these moments to be unique; life has never been quite like this and will never be like this again, ever. For it is the distant doctor who exposes wells of tenderness, and Audrey, all naïveté and hesitancy, who discovers what powers are compacted in her soul.

Schwartz, who has published three novels and two story collections, writes with confidence and stylistic dash. Whether she is describing the hermetic milieu of her Brooklyn—its shops and living rooms and street-corner exchanges—or the edgy dreaminess of the adolescent psyche, she catches both the outer contours and the inner propulsions of her subject. The only creak in this otherwise stunning little book comes from Schwartz's way of working the good eye–bad eye motif. She comes perilously close to turning it into an actual *theme*, something students might be called upon to explicate. The suggestion is all we need; certain of Schwartz's more strenuously ruminative passages could be excised with profit.

But one can hardly hold stylistic grudges in the face of so much deftness and brio. Coming-of-age, one of the oldest of the ever-renewable subjects, is seldom registered as disarmingly as it is in *Leaving Brooklyn*. Here, as a tease and parting shot, is Audrey walking in on her parents' weekly card game:

> The card game men were Mr. Zelevansky, Mr. Tessler, Mr. Ribowitz, Mr. Singer, and Mr. Capaleggio, whom everyone called Cappy. Only I was expected to call them all Mr., and when for the first time—I was almost sixteen—I addressed Mr. Zelevansky, whom I had known all my life, as Lou, I felt as daring as if I had reached over and unzipped his fly.

Leaving Brooklyn. Lynne Sharon Schwartz. 146 pp. Houghton Mifflin. 1989. $15.95

Frederick Busch/
Elizabeth Spencer

From the point of view of our cultural life, a country that goes to war is like a python swallowing a jungle pig. An interminable peristalsis precedes digestion, as our Vietnam experience attests. While there has been no shortage of documentary writing or flashily disturbing films, that war has, with few exceptions, scarcely touched our literature. The reason is simple. The novel, which lives higher on the food chain than most other modes of expression, depends upon the writer's grasp of causes and effects; the psychological recoil within individuals happens in slow motion. Our decades-long silence is less likely the result of stupefaction or moral failure than a matter of necessary assimilation. We may now be ready to hear the speech that comes after long silence.

Frederick Busch and Elizabeth Spencer are both novelists and storytellers who have been suffering the curse—peculiar to America—of being very good but also very unread. They win prizes, accolades from fellow writers, and are stubbornly prolific (Busch has now published sixteen books of fiction, Spencer twelve), but neither has struck the magnesium flare of celebrity. They have remained subtle stylists in the mainstream realist tradition, focusing upon rites of maturity, love and the exactions of family life—the staples of most fiction. If we had a culture of serious readers, both would have name-brand recognition. Their new novels, concerned in different ways with Vietnam, might bring the attention they deserve.

Busch's *Closing Arguments* is a breathless unfolding of delayed trauma in the life of a former fighter pilot; Spencer's *The Night Travellers* sounds out the complex repercussions of one young man's antiwar activism. They are intelligent novels, edgy in their own ways. But how they fare will depend upon how ready we are to examine what happens when the stuff of headlines reaches hometown lives.

"Let's say I'm telling you the story of the upstate lawyer, the posttraumatic combat stress, the splendid wife, their solitudes and infidelities, their children, his client with her awkward affinities, the sense of impending recognition by which he is haunted." So begins Mark Brennan, Busch's protagonist, who is settling accounts with his life. Brennan was once "Goblin," hero of innumerable missions over jungles and rice paddies. Now he is a small-town attorney, a family man who is drifting out of touch with his family. His wife, Schelle, is distant and reproachful; his teenage son, Jack, has become a sullen troublemaker. Indeed, Brennan begins his story with an anguished memory of himself punching the boy. "We were standing up," he writes. "Upstairs in the hall, I think. I put a four-finger jab, the hand rigid and fingers locked, directly into his solar plexus. He started to double, and I said, Stand up."

It is a telling episode, harbinger of a truth that Brennan is not yet ready to understand. The realization that he carries a violence that is stronger than he is comes to him, and to the reader, gradually. First Busch must plait the two major strands of the plot. One is Brennan's recurrent memory from the war: the downing of his plane by enemy fire, his capture and torture at the hands of the Viet Cong, and his escape. The other begins to unfold in the present when Brennan is asked to take on, pro bono, the defense of Estella Pritchett, a young woman accused of strangling her lover in a motel bed during a bout of "rough sex."

Past and present form the rails of inevitability, and the novel careers forward. Busch deals out his tensely compressed chapters, letting implication gather. When Brennan finds himself getting involved with his client, he feels his repressed self waken; when their lovemaking edges toward violence, that self starts to take over.

Scenes from Brennan's captivity and torture are played off against Estella's accounts of incest and abuse in childhood. The lawyer understands all too well. He has his own memories: "He did smell his father, the yeasty, rich odors of beer . . . and the sweat of the day, and sometimes, when he raged, the stink, almost a bowel smell, that his father's body generated. It was oily and it clung to you after your father had seized and twisted your arm, or thrown you out of the way, or gone directly after you, maybe with open hands, maybe with fists."

Brennan and Estella recapitulate their sad histories in their lovemaking, moving ever closer to the danger zone. It is Freud's theory of repetition made flesh: the injured cope with psychic trauma by replaying it over and over. For Busch this works as a strong, if somewhat reductive, narrative engine. He may yield just a bit too readily to the Sophoclean urge—looking to spell tragedy with capital letters—but the message is powerful. We see that Brennan was not so much formed as *confirmed* by his war experience. Busch holds to the Hemingway doctrine about the American male—that he comes to manhood in a world deeply coded with violence and brutality. This climate makes for wars, not vice versa. There is no place of safety. "Dear Reader," writes Brennan at the end of the book, "the innocent are not protected." He means us.

Elizabeth Spencer is less concerned with trauma, and more with discovering the fate of moral idealism in a world riven by war and ideological hatreds. In *The Night Travellers,* we meet Mary Harbison, an introverted girl growing up in a small North Carolina city in the 1960s. Her father, whom she adores, dies of a sudden stroke, leaving her alone with her mother. Kate Harbison is narcissistic and cruel. She blames her daughter for the death—it was Mary's horsing around that killed "Poppy"—and from that point on there is no peace between them. Mary withdraws into her dreams of becoming a dancer, while Kate fills her nights with cocktails and men. When Mary is fifteen, away to spend the summer with relatives, she meets Jefferson Blaise—her fate.

Jeff Blaise is an idealistic radical of the sixties vintage. He is

SVEN BIRKERTS

utterly devoted to his activism and, when they later get involved, to Mary. And from the moment Mary sets eyes on Jeff, she is his. When fear and isolation eventually lead her to attempt suicide, she relives their first meeting: it was "as though a net had dropped over me, as though a segment of that net drawn about me was a fine-woven strong thread pressing against my throat. . . . When I finally got around in far-off Montreal to putting the bed sheet rope around my neck, it was that spot I thought most of, how it had first responded to the net of love." She then adds: "I had to learn more about that net: that it is woven with the history of the person who brings it, and that history descends on you along with it."

The descending of history—public and private—is what *The Night Travellers* is finally about. Mary gets pregnant, and she and Jeff are wed. Jeff, under the tutelage of his former teacher, Ethan Marbell, begins traveling around the country on the antiwar circuit. At first he speaks and organizes, then he drops from sight. Mary and her baby are shunted off to Montreal, away from the dangers of the radical's life. She gets mysterious envelopes stuffed with cash, sporadic letters, then nothing; rumors come that Jeff may have been involved in a bombing incident. Mary's unhappy exile, with its ever-constricting possibilities, allows Spencer to tally up some of the costs of Jeff's political engagement.

The author is especially good at manipulating foreground and background, presenting Mary's daily conflicts—with being a mother, making rent, keeping up her dance—in their full subjective momentousness, then shifting perspective to remind us of the tragedy of a society coming apart at the seams. Spencer switches among various narrators—all people who have some contact with Mary—and in the process catches sharp glimmers of the period without succumbing to counterculture parody.

Spencer's view of history is finally more like Chekhov's than Tolstoy's. For her, the mirage of public events dissolves into a dense composite of individual struggles—struggles defined not by clear oppositions of good and evil, but instead by what Simone de Beauvoir called "the ethics of ambiguity." But Spencer is on guard against the benedictions of moral relativism. Vietnam was a disease of the whole body politic, and it impinged upon even the most isolated of lives.

· · · ·

Frederick Busch/Elizabeth Spencer

There were moral lines to be drawn, stands to be taken. "All we did had to matter . . ." Ethan Marbell says. "If not for us, all of us, crying out together, they would have had carte blanche."

Yes, Vietnam was a disease, and it ravaged us. Since that time, there has been no center to our public life, and the spirit of the carpetbagger has ruled. Both *Closing Arguments* and *The Night Travellers* are responses to the malaise, each proposing a stern vision of moral accountability. When Brennan realizes how deeply he is meshed in violence, he owns it. He accepts the fatal embrace, hoping to expiate his accumulated sins. Jeff Blaise, wanted by the authorities, makes his own devil's bargain: he comes out of hiding and enlists— it is his only hope of one day returning to his wife and child. The reader must decide if this is a betrayal of ideals or a vindication of love, or both. The old easy answers are no longer possible. After idealism comes disillusionment, and after that come the long and painful inquisitions. Putting the house in order is hard work. These two novels tell us that we are just getting started.

Closing Arguments. Frederick Busch. 288 pp. Houghton Mifflin. 1991. $19.95

The Night Travellers. Elizabeth Spencer. 352 pp. Viking. 1991. $19.95

SVEN BIRKERTS

Larry
Woiwode

"This is the saddest story I have ever heard," announces John Dowell, Ford Madox Ford's narrator, at the beginning of *The Good Soldier*. Dowell turns out to be a dupe and a fool, more than a little unreliable in his judgments; but the opening gambit remains a stunning one. Indeed, my impulse is to steal it from Ford and pass it along to Larry Woiwode. His two linked novels, *Beyond the Bedroom Wall* (1975) and *Born Brothers*, are strong contenders for that same distinction. Certainly they are among the saddest—the most heart-breaking—of all American novels.

Beyond the Bedroom Wall is Woiwode's epic portrayal of midwest-ern life. Fitting together panels in different voices, from different perspectives, he depicts the evolving fates of three generations of the Neumiller family, from the early years of the century up into the 1960s. Landscape and atmosphere are deeply inscribed in the prose, first the dusty Dakota farms of their forebears, later the more hospita-ble climes of Illinois. At the core of the novel is the courtship and marriage of Martin Neumiller and Alpha Jones, their determined

309

forging of a life, the birth of their five children; later portions focus on the coming of age of the three boys, Jerome, Charles, and Tim.

But the book's real core—for this is not a plotted work so much as a chronicle of hearts and souls—is the unexpected death of Alpha. The tragedy takes place midway through the book. The rest of the narrative, spanning decades in the lives of Martin and his children, is the emotional equivalent of an explosion taking place in slow motion. The entire family is undermined. The loss not only envelops their every thought and action, but seems to penetrate the very floorboards of their house. Though Martin eventually remarries, and the children begin to find their own lives as adults, time cannot dissolve the sorrow. Our last impression of Martin, after his second wife has died, is of a man who has left his heart in the past.

Beyond the Bedroom Wall was in every sense a big novel, a swath-cutter. Grand in scope, ambitious in its organization, it was also prodigal with its prose. Scenes and descriptions were delivered with a kind of small-town garrulousness that threatened to go on and on, and sometimes did. But while the reader might not wish the work any longer, neither would he sacrifice any part of the achieved whole. Woiwode succeeded in bringing "sweep"—that adjective beloved of middle-brow page-turners—to the serious novel.

But what are we now to make of *Born Brothers*, another six-hundred-plus page leviathan that resumes the past of the Neumiller clan? To be sure, it's a different book. This time Woiwode has centered his narrative within the troubled psyche of the son Charles. Yet since the bulk of *Born Brothers* comprises Charles's memories of growing up—of his enmeshed relationship with his brother Jerome, of their mother's death, of his unhappy adolescence—much of the terrain is familiar. It may be that the author mined the heart of his subject the first time through.

The novel begins in New York in the early sixties, with Charles taking a room in a run-down doss-house. He is clearly a young man in distress, moving about without ties or means in the city of refugees. He has ambitions to act but can scarcely rouse himself to attend auditions. Only the price of a bed separates him from the Bowery. But if he has fled his family and his place, he nevertheless spends most of his time lying in bed brooding about the past. A full two

· · · ·

SVEN BIRKERTS

thirds of *Born Brothers* is an assemblage of Charles's recollections. These—some of them merest fragments of a scene—unfold as a kind of portrait of the artist as an evolving sensibility.

From the very first, even before we have begun to delve into Charles's past, we know that this will be, as the title suggests, a saga of brothers. Woiwode opens the novel with a letter from Jerome to Charles—a quick, casual bit of chatter about his medical school internship in Chicago. But it is enough to map the terms of their opposition: success versus failure, control versus chaos. Readers of *Beyond the Bedroom Wall* may remember something of the sort. There, characterizing Charles and Jerome, respectively, Woiwode wrote: "They'll be necessary to each other the rest of their lives, the one with his passionate need to know and be told what everything means, the other already serene in his knowledge, and living among elements that are invisible and his own."

Charles's earliest memories establish the ground of the relationship. Only a year apart, the brothers are, from the start, thrust together:

> A white windmill on wheels, with a blade that turns, rolls between my knees. Uncle Elling's gift. I spin the blade and it windmills away. I pull it back. It wheels away again. I reach for it and a hand like mine hits my reaching hand. I look into the same face I see when Mom holds me above the sink to show me a pouting child. It's my brother, so they say, and he is the missing half. I start hitting him back.

Their early years are marked by just such symbiosis: they sleep in one bed, fight and kick and vie for attention. At times all sense of boundaries disappears, leaving Charles with only a confused feeling of *odi et amo*. Here is how he remembers riding off for the first time on their shared bike: "I breeze by, so happy to be free of Jerome I wonder if I don't actually hate him. I'm never apart from him enough to even think this."

But bound up as they are, Charles and Jerome are very different. Though they are both schooled as Catholics, it is Charles who lives with a sense of sin and mystery. And when their mother dies, Charles is the brother who bears the wound. Worse still, he blames himself.

· · · ·

Larry Woiwode

"*If only I'd been different from the start,* he thinks, *this would never have happened to her.*" Try as he might, he never shakes off a residual guilt about her death. While Jerome manages the complex adjustments of growing up without a mother—finally deciding to become a doctor—Charles founders. The pain that originates in his boyhood will deepen until it finally finishes him off.

The crisis that seems to propel the brothers into their separate lives comes when they are in their teens. Jerome crashes the family car. But it is Charles, sitting beside him, who is gravely injured. In fact, he ends up spending a good part of his high school years confined to a wheelchair. Though he tries to carry on with his normal interests and appetites—studying, dating (hot-blooded girls named Dewey and Bobbie)—he is subject to enduring fits of moroseness and self-pity. A telling scene comes when the doctor finally saws the cast off. He is appalled by the near-gangrenous condition of Charles's leg. "I don't understand," he says. "I've put on hundreds of casts and never seen this! Chuck, did you stick something down there?" Charles admits to trying, but cries, "Nothing would reach!" To this the doctor can only add: "That's it. You went and screwed this up."

I don't think that Woiwode intends this to symbolize Charles's condition, but it's an apt figure all the same. Though he can't quite reach the source of his pain, neither can he leave off trying. The result, as the narrative progresses, is a continual exacerbation of his most conflicted emotions—about his mother, about Jerome—and a continued inability to come to terms with his life. Intercut episodes from a later period, after Charles has left New York, show him in an eroding marriage, struggling with alcoholism. But these glimpses are obscure in their chronology and are riddled with gaps. It's as if the real story ends when he leaves the Midwest to come East. Only those early years are drawn with any clarity.

The momentum of Charles's despair is ultimately toward suicide. Nothing—neither his love for his wife and children nor his devotion to Jerome—is enough to save him. Nor has his wound finally awakened in him the redemptive forces of art. The novel culminates with a long interior cadenza. Charles has slashed his wrists. His memories flash in bright confusion right up to the instant of death, whereupon comes a serene restorative coda, a poem which begins:

Oh, my brother, remember North Dakota,
The nights of angular snow, the drift of snow
That rose until it reached our windowsill
And then rose slowly up the glass; below
Its fuming surface, visible through the glass,
The quiet crystals, glittering, blue, serene.
Remember the trough of ice that guided
Our sled down past roots, stumps, stones,
A culvert, bumping—you on the bottom, me on the top,
Knocking your breath out—down the steep bank
To the uneven flatlands of the frozen lake below . . .

On the jacket flap of *Born Brothers,* Woiwode is quoted as saying: "I view this novel as more a companion to *Beyond the Bedroom Wall* than a sequel. . . . I don't believe you need to know the other one at all to completely participate in this one, and it's actually the book that *Beyond the Bedroom Wall* rose out of." How the prior world of the first novel could have arisen from the drama of consequences that is *Born Brothers* is a mystery that only their creator can explain. But I see no way that the downward spiral of Charles Neumiller can be understood without the dense layers of background—and massed feeling—provided in *Beyond the Bedroom Wall.* For even though Charles's memory bursts do cover much of the same material— including, but more obliquely, the death of Alpha—the reader needs to have experienced the full devastation of that death in order to follow the complex oscillations of Charles's psyche. Whether he admits it or not, Woiwode depends upon the prior narration—and so must we.

The truth of it is that the fragmented sections of *Born Brothers* cohere only around the magnetic center of *Beyond the Bedroom Wall.* Take that away and you have a scattering of bits. Many of these are interesting and intense in their evocation—and the writing is always of a high order—but they find no independent shape. But even *with* the organizing presence of the other book, there are problems. For one thing, the device of a confused, at times overwrought, narrator interferes with the presentation of a sustained account. Woiwode feels compelled to cut repeatedly into his telling in order to remind us of

• • • •

Larry Woiwode

the state of Charles's soul. The alternation feels willed and leaches away much of the dramatic tension.

What's more, as the novel moves to its close, the use of structural artifice is intensified. Woiwode jumps abruptly from one time frame to another, trying to weave the whole together. In a few places he even resorts to stream-of-consciousness narration to convey Charles's delirium. Chaos supervenes. At one moment we are in New York in the sixties, at the next in North Dakota with an older, married Charles. Jerome, so central to the earlier sections, is suddenly shown as married and practicing medicine out West. Since we've never got more than glimmers of the adult lives of the brothers, we feel uncentered, lost in someone else's dark wood without a compass.

Woiwode's problems with *Born Brothers* can finally be traced back to his conceptions of Charles and Jerome. The relationship between the two is just not a strong enough axis for the book—at least not as it has been drawn. For as Charles's memories are set out, in his own voice, Jerome never emerges as anything but a shadowy alter-ego. The same confusion of boundaries that afflicted Charles in childhood also hobbles his tale. Unable to see Jerome clearly, he resorts to what psychologists call "splitting"; he projects his own polarized feelings upon him. Jerome is a saint, a traitor. Charles sees him everywhere. Indeed, his first thought upon seeing his own newborn son is *Jerome*! But for all this attention, Jerome never becomes a freestanding character, and the book remains one man's monologue.

Born Brothers must be accounted a grand failure. A failure because of its excess and its mounting chaos, and because it cannot be fully grasped without the prior narration of *Beyond the Bedroom Wall.* Grand because for all his lapses Woiwode is a prodigiously gifted stylist. Very few writers can command a prose as responsive to the claims of the senses, or a lyricism as unstrained. His transcription of the inner world of the child—that profundity of perception—catches the full register of nuances:

> I get on my knees to look out the rear window, knowing I can do this now that I've been slapped, and see a sudden change. It's more than night coming down, though night has begun. Snow is descending grayly across a countryside that widens out so flat

behind the speeding car it feels we're flying, and the shifting flakes turn pastures here and there among the open fields so gray they start to rise to meet the snow, while yellow squares of stubble caught between them tremble: kites ready to lift off.

Passages like this—and there are many of them—make me think that the theme of fraternal bonding may just be a pretext for Woiwode, an excuse for returning to certain images and atmospheres. This can be the profoundest of all motivations—witness Proust. And Woiwode himself acknowledges it, albeit indirectly. Near the end of *Beyond the Bedroom Wall,* he has Jerome remember a visit from his childhood days. His two uncles, Conred and Elling, have dropped in to pass the time with their sister Alpha. Soon enough, the brothers get to talking about the past. Uncle Elling sums his views as follows:

> This reliving the past happens all the time. . . . Every time it happens, it's like I'm stepping out of what I don't want to be into who I really am. I have to stop myself and say "No, no, no, that's all over! Here's where you are now. You have a wife and kids. You have an important job to do." That's what I say and sometimes it helps, but it doesn't change things much. Old man McGough still means more to me than any millionaire client. . . . The smallest detail from then is clearer than what I did last year, or yesterday, or the day before that, and the older I grow and the farther I get from those days, the clearer and more important the details seem.

Elling's words may not add up to an aesthetic, but they do point out the wellspring of Woiwode's art. A certain confusion is here the price for a connection to a bygone world.

Born Brothers. Larry Woiwode. 611 pp. Farrar, Straus & Giroux. 1988. $19.95

· · ·

Larry Woiwode

Jonathan Strong /
Andre Dubus /
Alfred Alcorn

There was a lot of talk in the late sixties and early seventies about the "death of the novel," and my feeling at the time was that it would be a good thing. What was meant by "the novel," of course, was the *traditional* novel, that lumbering quadruped with its illusory fixities of character and narrative. It was the bourgeois art form par excellence—so said Georg Lukács—and no longer adequate to the social order that was trying to come into being. Far more promising, and certainly more interesting, were the new assaults and subversions: the experimental work coming out from New Directions and Grove Press (Beckett, Duras, Hawkes . . .), the metafictions of Barth, Coover, and others, the chic-sounding *nouveau roman* that Robbe-Grillet was trumpeting, the magic realism of the Latin Americans. The virtues of the well-written traditional novel were no longer self-evident.

But a decade has passed, and the fervor of those times is hard to reconstruct. Many of the fast-track talents have fizzled—unable, perhaps, to draw any sustenance from a thinning atmosphere. To question narrative seemed radical, and inevitable, when the whole social context was one of interrogation; but in a political vacuum it suddenly looks like just another form of academic aerobics. The traditional novel, on the other hand, has come through it all like someone's Yankee grandmother. Indeed, when so much cultural diffusion threatens the life of the mind, even illusory solidity starts to look good.

During this interval, however, another development has overtaken us, a new mode of fiction writing that—if it continues to be subsidized—may start us talking about the death of the novel all over again. I'm referring to the "Frank went to stand by the window" genre, the sort of thing practiced with varying intensity and success by writers like Raymond Carver, Bobbie Ann Mason, Ann Beattie, Frederick Barthelme, and a small army of *New Yorker*–sponsored epigones. Its distinguishing features are first-name-only characters, present-tense plotting devoid of depth or buildup, and a flattened, understated voice. We are given almost no sense of inward development, but we are presented—as if in compensation—with a great deal of supposedly "telling" bric-a-brac. Objects, settings, movements, and the inflections of everyday speech are orchestrated to tell us everything we need to know: that communication is difficult and modern life sterile, and that the lifeline to the certainties of the past has been cut.

The pedigree of this new fiction is curious. It preserves, to a degree, a stylistic bond to the laconic matter-of-factness of Hemingway. But there is also a distressing resemblance to television— the same episodic, relentlessly superficial kind of presentation, the same reliance on mannerisms and "common" speech. As different as Ann Beattie's baby boomers and Raymond Carver's embattled losers may seem at first glance, they are, in these respects, part of the same continuum, prime-time shows on different networks. (To be fair, Carver achieves a purchase on the real that is denied to Beattie and the others.)

In venturing neither the uncertainties of experiment nor the hard work of bringing the illusion of three-dimensional life to the page, this fiction opts for the middle path. And in so doing, it sacrifices any of the seductive qualities that the novel may have evolved over the centuries. We do not need to suspend our disbelief or work with our imagination; the surface yields to us instantly—and there is nothing *but* surface. We remember an Ann Beattie story for about as long as we remember an episode of *Hill Street Blues*.

Jonathan Strong's *Elsewhere* is a novel at once sincere and forgettable—an unfortunate combination for the reviewer, who would like to honor the former attribute more than the latter allows. Set in a place identical to Somerville, Massachusetts (Strong never explicitly names the locale), *Elsewhere* is a first-person account, a self-reckoning typed into a word processor (somehow fitting) by a onetime high school teacher named Burt. Burt is trying to sort out the events of the past few years, to process the emotional lacerations he's suffered through his complex, and ultimately incestuous, involvement with certain of his students. The events are of a kind that resist expeditious summary—a kidnapped baby, the suicide of a brilliant writing student, Burt's self-sacrificing marriage to the bereaved mother, his homosexual passion for a bratty young sprout named Liam—and it is to Strong's credit that they come to life at all. The pressure of his sincerity—he so obviously wants to put across the importance of these hedged-in lives—carries him some distance. But there is never the sense that these characters could move of their own accord. Their every action is willed into place. Move the sentences to one side, and you will find a void.

The problem—and it's not just Strong's, it's endemic to the whole approach—is flatness. The eviscerated narrative style puts an enormous burden on the writer. He must, if he is to win us, generate an impression of psychological depth. Described action, insofar as it displaces inner process, must function as an effective shorthand for that process. But this is as close as we get to subjective insight:

> When I come home from work tonight, will she be ready to talk again? I'm staying at work late again using the word processor. These late afternoons I find myself here after the others have left, and then I lock the disc away in my bottom desk drawer overnight. Tonight I want to stay even later than six-thirty.
>
> I called her at six, and she picked up the phone. I said, "Nell, it's me. Are you feeling all right?"

· · · ·

"Burt?" she asked.

"Do you want me to come home? If you're all right, I'll stay awhile and catch up on work. Are you all right? Are you watching television?" I heard it in the background.

I'm still hearing it.

Andre Dubus has been giving us visions of middle-class disenchantment for years now, telling the stories of generic "real people," shining his low beam at their family lives, jobs, affairs, divorces, drinking habits, and resolutions for self-betterment. The bittersweet taste of compromise—his people all learn to tailor their dreams down to fit unglamorous reality—pervades the work from first to last. *Voices from the Moon* is somewhat more "literary" in its conception, telling the story of one day in a family's life through alternating perspectives, but finally it's no exception. Indeed, whenever events come to center upon Greg, the rough-cut/honest/drinking/smoking/love-seeking paterfamilias, it is as if we'd walked back into *Separate Flights* or *Adultery and Other Choices* or one of Dubus's other previous offerings. But no matter. Ultimately it's the type, not the individual, that interests him. He is out to be the Homer of the working folk of the Merrimack Valley.

Which is not to say that Dubus has not worked hard at creating his characters. Twelve-year-old Richie, who is gentle, wise, and priesthood-bound, contrasts well with his embittered older brother, Larry; and both play nicely off Greg. This is fortunate, for the central tension—Greg admits at the outset that he has fallen in love with Larry's ex-wife, Brenda—would otherwise not have a prayer of rising above the level of soap opera. Strong as they are, however, the hormonal interactions are not enough to carry the book. Character development, constrained by the rotating point of view, remains superficial; Dubus is forced to fall back upon type psychology. We see Richie's piety warring with the sexual stirrings of puberty, but the real mysteries of adolescence are not illuminated. Larry hates his father yet cannot help identifying with him, but the opposition and resolution are far too conventional. There is no central action to bind the forces into a memorable figure. And the women—Brenda, Carol

(Greg's grown daughter), and Joan (his ex-wife)—stay trapped in two dimensions. We see them as cigarette-smoking shadows and tend to compress them in memory into a single image.

My complaint is that Dubus does not force our recognitions far enough out of the worn groove. Time and again we are given the expected perception, the easy chord change. Here, for example, is a snatch from one of Brenda's reveries:

> While the men Greg called friends were carpenters and electricians and cops and men who made telephone parts at Western Electric, and Greg only knew them because he liked drinking in the same places they did, stand-up bars where nearly everyone drank beer, and there was no blender and a bartender could work months without using a cocktail shaker, and only kept lemons and limes in the fruit bin, and not many of them, or they would soften and turn brown. Bartenders called them shot-and-a-beer bars. Brenda liked the ones Greg brought her to; she liked standing at the bar, and watching the men; and she liked the ceiling fans, and not having a juke-box or electronic games, and having the television on only for ball-games or hockey or boxing.

There's that damned TV again. Dubus's prose is tougher, more rhythmic, than the prose in *Elsewhere,* but the level of penetration is about the same. Although *Voices from the Moon* begins and ends inside the skin of Richie, the feeling you're left with has more to do with jaded adulthood.

I will not try to compare Alfred Alcorn's *The Pull of the Earth* with either of these novels. For here the life has been caught with all five senses; the emotions pierce, the images come at us through clear country air. From the first sentence it is obvious that we have escaped from the death-dealing aesthetic of flatness:

> Together, as if in prayer, the small hooves came first, glistening in the sunlight that stippled the floor of the pine grove. The cow arched her back and lowed. The caul-shrouded snout emerged, tucked along the forelegs like a cringing dog, then the rest of the head, slick as a seal's, the ears folded back. It stopped.

You see the event and hear it; through the skilled stacking of clauses, you feel the contractions. And with these few words, life starts pulsing through the lines of print.

The Pull of the Earth is set on a small working farm in Massachusetts in the 1950s. Bobby Dearborn, a twelve-year-old ward of the state, has been adopted by his distant relatives, Hedley and Janet Vaughn. He passes his days doing chores, tending the cows, and dreaming of an adventurous future as a fighter pilot. Hedley is tough, laconic, and a good deal older than Janet; hard work and responsibility sustain this marriage. The sense of inward distance that Edward Hopper rendered in his canvases suffuses the simple rooms of the house. Until one day a drifter, Lucien Quirk, arrives, bearing his own strange remoteness.

Described thus, the setup is not promising. There is nothing thrilling about the characters, the routines of farm life do not offer much variety or surprise, and you can guess right away that something will develop between Janet and Quirk. But you do read on, and you do get absorbed in these lives. Alcorn has the novelist's fundamental gift. He can take the most basic ingredients—setting, character relationships, and narrative sequence—and make a world that you believe and want to stay in. That that world is bleak and confining is all the more evidence of his talent.

The sexual tension between Janet and Quirk is handled with striking sureness. Quirk is at once brutal, low-minded, cowardly, and tender. He drinks cheap booze in his cramped quarters and stares at pinup girls. Janet is overworked, afraid that her youth and looks have fled; she has an enormous need to love. There is not a single false note in their complex coming together. To say any more would be to rob the prospective reader of the pleasures of suspense. I am not suggesting that the plot is perfect—Alcorn has a tendency to work toward the grand resolution—but the electricity between male and female poles is enough to light up a small country:

> The man and the woman were united momentarily in anger and in labor as they pushed and pulled the misplaced pile into a mow. But Janet Vaughn kept her distance. No small talk for the hired man as they sweated and struggled with the dry, neutral

hay that had begun to fill with surprising rapidity the cavernous emptiness of the loft. She kept her distance, but once, coming up late, she saw him silhouetted against the light from the windows ranged across the rear wall of the barn. He sat on a beam, head back against another beam, one knee up, pensive and handsome in profile. Another time he had the end of the handle of his fork coming out between his legs at a provocative angle.

The further we get from the natural sources of life, and the more we are inundated by the processed sensations of the media, the greater our need is for powerful and honest writing. *The Pull of the Earth* cuts the soil of the habitual with a polished share.

Elsewhere. Jonathan Strong. 167 pp. Available Press. 1985. $4.95 (paper)
Voices from the Moon. Andre Dubus. 162 pp. Crown. 1985. $6.95 (paper)
The Pull of the Earth. Alfred Alcorn. 298 pp. Houghton Mifflin. 1985. $15.95

J. California
Cooper

erhaps the biggest single difference between writing by blacks and writing by whites is that the former is overwhelmingly—in psychology as well as rendering of circumstance—about being black, while writing by white authors, though many things, is never explicitly about being white. This may seem like an obvious sort of recognition, but it is well worth pondering nonetheless. For not only does it tell us a great deal about what may be *the* fundamental dispositional difference between the races, but it also explains some of the ways in which our literary maps are being redrawn.

The reader's first impulse may be to suppose that African-American writers are working under a tremendous constraint, that in terms of both subject matter and vantage they have denied themselves access to some larger world. But this is a dangerous assumption—that if one is writing through a black identity, one cannot write fully about love, or politics, or spiritual aspiration, or any of the other things that form the preoccupation of literature. More likely the reverse is true: that not only does the black vantage *not* block the writer from the universal themes—it intensifies the engagement.

Indeed, in an age in which our literature is routinely scored for its thinness, its self-absorption, its divorce from vital subjects, it may be the black writer who stands the best chance of mattering. There are two main reasons for this. First, the history of the African-American, from slavery through civil-rights struggles and on into the embattled present, makes a tale of epic resonance. A writer could not ask for a greater subject—a subject, moreover, that has scarcely been mined. Second, the stylist is still within generational shouting distance of the oral tradition, and has for the taking, by natural right, a storytelling mode all but denied to the white artist.

Partly for these reasons, and partly for others—increased access to mainstream media, greater receptivity on the part of the white establishment—we are in the midst of what appears to be a flowering of black literature in all genres. A glance at the table of contents of Terry McMillan's recent *Breaking Ice: An Anthology of Contemporary African-American Fiction* offers one confirmation. Among the names: Toni Cade Bambara, David Bradley, Gayl Jones, James Alan McPherson, Gloria Naylor, Ishmael Reed, Ntozake Shange, Alice Walker, Charles Johnson, John Edgar Wideman, John A. Williams, and Al Young, not to mention the anthologist herself. And I'm just picking across the surface. Not included in the volume, but essential to the picture, are Jamaica Kinkaid, Toni Morrison, Maya Angelou, Paule Marshall, and doubtless others that I've overlooked. It is all one can do to keep up, but one must keep up, for these writers are producing some of the most arresting fiction of our time.

A vital portion of this literary outpouring deals in one way or another with slavery. This is hardly surprising. Scratch black America anywhere, and you find, just three generations removed from living memory, the shame of what has been called, with a frightful detachment, "the peculiar institution." James Baldwin long ago wrote of the African-American that "in every aspect of his living he betrays the memory of the auction block." Truly, if ever an experience has been known collectively, it has been that of slave labor. And however much the circumstances may have differed from one plantation to the next, the basic premise was fixed: human beings claimed to *own* other human beings.

Recent works of fiction give testimony. David Bradley's novel *The Chaneysville Incident* tracks a young black scholar's growing involvement with the lore of his own family's past. Out of notes and recollected stories there rises the figure of C. K. Washington, the charismatic leader of a series of slave escapes; in reliving his final martyrdom, the historian comes to understand his own mission. And Charles Johnson, in his 1990 National Book Award–winning novel, *Middle Passage,* gives us the brutal saga of Rutherford Calhoun, a freed slave who through misadventure finds himself aboard a slave ship plying between New Orleans and Guinea in 1830. Both works draw their main power from the dramatic staging of racial confrontations.

Toni Morrison's *Beloved,* by contrast, roots its action primarily within the four walls of a house in Ohio. Her heroine, Sethe, is also a recently escaped slave, but while Morrison in no way shirks the bloody particulars of Sethe's remembered past, her main concern is to trace how physical and emotional suffering have warped the woman's soul. Indeed, at the risk of generalizing, I would say that a similar vantage-split also characterizes male and female presentations of more contemporary aspects of black life. Men tend to write about men, often in stark adversarial situations; women—clichéd though the opposition may sound—are more intent upon the familial sphere and center their attention upon women's lives.

J. California Cooper's *Family* certainly fits to this rough typology. Cooper, a prolific playwright and author of three collections of stories, *A Piece of Mine, Homemade Love,* and *Some Soul to Keep,* tries in her first novel to give an account of one woman's long years of servitude and her eventual emancipation. A curious narrative strategy—telling the story through the dead mother of the protagonist, Always—allows her to locate events within a larger panorama. Cooper would like to convince us, I think, that Always's travails illuminate the universal plight of the black woman under slavery.

The unnamed narrator sets herself before us as one who has been unaccountably sprung from time—as a kind of muse of personal history—and she tells her tale in an easy and evocative dialect. She was herself, as she relates, the daughter of a slave who killed her master with a pitchfork and then took her own life. Orphaned early, she eventually found that she was no more willing than her mother to endure the abuses inflicted on herself and her children. She prepared poison for the lot of them, but through some odd stroke of Providence, she was the only one to succumb. The children—Always, Sun, Peach, and Plum—all survived. But the mother did not receive the mercy of complete extinction. "Somehow, I didn't go nowhere," she reports. "I saw them find my body, I heard what everybody said. I didn't really have to listen cause it seemed I knew what all was in everybody's mind before they spoke out."

Cooper has gone through considerable contortions to create what many another writer would assume as a natural prerogative— namely, an omniscient narrative voice. The revenant mother can read her children's thoughts and can move about in space and time. But we are neither shocked nor otherwise illuminated. In fact, she is so much akin to the invisible author of tradition that we forget for chapters on end that she is the one filtering the story.

This narrator, after dipping back into the generational memory to feature antecedents ("Came a time when the slave catchers came. Some of the couple's living children were taken. Stolen, separated and taken to many lands . . ."), and after telling her mother's and her own story, finally comes to focus upon her eldest daughter, Always.

Always is beautiful and light-skinned (she was fathered by the master), and when she is yet in her young teens, she is plucked away from her familiars and sold to a man named Doak Butler. Butler is crude and dissolute. He lives on a run-down farm with his crippled brother, and he wants Always to serve his bride-to-be. She will, it turns out, stay on his few acres of land for the rest of her long life. There she will practice, with great cunning and initiative, her arts of endurance.

Cooper's central plot device forces her into a precarious position. She is clearly trying to write the African-American *Everywoman,* but in the process she almost ends up doing soap opera, or its nineteenth-century equivalent. The pivotal coincidence smacks of Dickens at his most manipulative, or else Twain in *A Connecticut Yankee in King Arthur's Court.* The randy new master, Doak, forces himself on Always almost as soon as his wagon leaves the former master's yard. He then has his way with her several times during the week before his bride, Sue, comes to marry him. When, months later, Sue announces to her servant that she is expecting a baby, Always allows that she is in a similar situation. The two babies are born within hours of one another—*and* they look similar. Always, who sees Sue through her labor even as her own is coming on, finds a way to make the switch. And her son grows up to be Doak's heir, while his boy is christened Soon and grows up in her keeping.

Mercifully, Cooper doesn't work the coincidence too hard. She uses the reversal mainly as a way to reveal the utter capriciousness of racist assumptions of superiority. Her expedient reminds us that our identities are largely constituted by what others believe us to be. This explains, to a large degree, why Always's real son is overcome by enraged denial—*hatred*—when his mother finally tells him the truth. His self-conception is torn away at a stroke; the power of her knowledge unmans him. Explains the narrator: "He wanted to rid hisself of this ugliness that called itself his mother, who could ruin his life, his dreams." Doak, Jr., will never forgive Always.

Revelatory though Cooper's premise may be, it cannot by itself support the book. Nor do the episodic recountings of Always's steady resourcefulness quite suffice. The plot sags from the weight of too much summary. We are told that the Civil War begins and that the two boys go off to fight; that Doak Butler dies; and that with war's end comes Emancipation and the return of the sons. But whatever happens, Always is just yonder, in the middle distance, shouldering her load. Clairvoyant as the narrator may be, she doesn't give us much insight into Always's intimate thoughts. This, coupled with the meagerness of the sensory detail, keeps the reader removed from the life.

Cooper hobbles herself. She tries in a short novel to span the period from the early 1830s to late Reconstruction. To achieve the effect of the passing of many decades, she must jettison not only detail and episodic complexity, but the finer points of characterization as well. As a consequence, too many of the figures remain type-bound. We get the cruel master, his witless wife, his crippled brother, and the brother's kind but cowed servant—none of these characters ever steps forward into surprise. Nor do any of the males, the two sons included, ever break the shackle of negative stereotyping.

I suspect that Cooper had a specific intention in writing this novel as she has. That she did not so much set out to create a narrative about isolated and unique individuals—in the manner of, say, Morrison—but that she sought instead to activate certain basic archetypes. She very likely *wanted* her characters to act as types in

·   ·   ·

J. California Cooper

typical situations and her scenes to possess a genre quality. Such a
decision would have its justification. Since the subject is so rough
and monumental in aspect, why not work with a wide chisel? Alas,
the epic approach can only be effective where action drives the
plot. Cooper's saga is static in nature and requires credible character
development if it is to work. The long-suffering Always feels more
like an emblem than a living person, and she never takes on the
necessary psychological density. We heed the tale—the basic conception is powerful enough—and we remark the messages, but we
seldom register their true urgency.

To be fair, there are a few instances where Cooper's approach
generates scenes that do have a powerful tableau quality, where
instead of flatness we come upon evocative simplicity. Here, for
instance, is a description of Always in her surroundings just before
she is taken from her first home:

> It only took a minute to get her things.
>
> Then, she moved in dead silence to the square cut out of the
> wall for air. There she had stood many times lookin out toward
> where freedom might be. Where Sun might be. Where peace
> might be. The day was already hot with the late morning sun,
> when the heat thickens, grows heavy, and everything is caught
> in it. Through her tears and the hole-window, everything looked
> like it was burned in the minute, like time was standin still.
> Trees, bushes, vines could be seen through that hole back of the
> shack. A bush with flower buds grew up and through the crook-
> ed-cut window-hole, comin between some of the loose boards of
> the wall.

In this passage, we feel the contact points between language and
experience. Cooper has inscribed the moment so accurately—the
stasis brought on by inner numbness, the suddenly heightened perception of the commonplace—that the parting scene is charged with
significance. The challenge for the author would be to sustain such
a fusion of particular and universal throughout the novel.

It is in these passages where the power does shine through that
we discern not only Cooper's gifts as a writer, but also the enormous
possibilities of her subject matter. She has claimed essential terrain,
even if she has not yet managed to do it justice. Still, we should

applaud her for working to find a shape for the immense anguish of African-American history and, no less important, for reminding us all of the shame that is lodged at the heart of our national myth. Always may survive, even triumph, but the circumstances that fired her character cannot be explained away or redeemed. They can only be exposed and dramatized—and this will be the task of generations of writers.

Family. J. California Cooper. 233 pp. Doubleday. 1990. $18.95

· · ·

J. California Cooper

A Postscript on
Black American Fiction

his short piece on J. California Cooper's novel *Family* is essentially salvage—a chunk from the wreckage of a larger project. For a long time I had wanted to write a substantial essay assessing trends and tendencies in contemporary black American fiction. I spent months reading and making notes. I drew charts and more charts, looking for figures of likeness. How did male writers portray women? How did female writers deal with men? How did both depict white society? What about uses of language? Were there modes that were implicitly more black? And so on. Here and there I found correlations. I imagined I had got a "fix" on my subject. But no, what seemed clear one day was again obscure the next. I continued to fiddle with the material. I expected that at any moment I would find the vantage, or pose the key question—the question that would suddenly expose a pathway through the subject.

The vantage has not yet been found, nor has the one question. I have waited for a long time. Long enough to begin to believe that there is no such question, that the problem lies somewhere in my fundamental conception. Where did I get the idea that I could write about black American fiction in a single essay, as if black American fiction were a single thing, a topic to be bounded with a few stakes and some yards of string? Is there bias in the assumption itself? Perhaps. And perhaps I am being chastened by my own frustration and sense of obstacle.

In lieu of that essay, which I may or may not write someday, I offer a clutch of fragmented reflections. As their fragmentation directly reflects my own struggle, I have resisted the temptation to groom them into something more orderly. These are thoughts, nothing more. I do not flatter myself that their unkempt look confers upon them any modernist eloquence. No, these are the pulsing stars that surround the head of the cartoon character who has run headfirst into a brick wall.

Black American, or African-American, fiction can be viewed as a special case of a larger subject—that of black expression in a culture industry almost entirely controlled by whites. For this reason it may have illustrative value.

What do we mean when we say "black American fiction"? Are we talking just about the set that includes all stories and novels written by black Americans, or are we suggesting that there is some distinguishing trait shared by the works themselves that makes them black American?

The answer might depend upon who "we" is. Does "we" refer simply to all interested parties, black, white, and other? Or is it a "we" referring to a white establishment—a "we" that necessarily posits a "they"? Very likely it is the latter. And if this is so, then it means that there is, if not a problem, at very least a situation that must be addressed straightaway. The situation of two cultures.

As recently as twenty-five years ago, no one would have thought to question the fact that our society was racially two-tiered. Now things are more ambiguous. Our policymakers, our image industries, our public-relations operatives, and others all hustle before the general public a picture of the progressive integration of American society. Advertisements and commercials for everything from hamburgers to health plans paint the picture of the happy encroachment of black upon white—high-fives and easy amity.

But even as we are saturated down to our very cells with this sort of propaganda, we are all—black and white—aware that the ancient rupture has not really been healed, that racism, deep and virulent, survives our naive wish to have it be gone.

We do not have two cultures within a system of segregation as we did before. We have two cultures within a system that pays lip service to ideals of integration and equality.

The societal situation must have direct bearing on the literary situation—it could not be otherwise. And indeed, even a brief inspection discloses that even though books by black writers are published right alongside books by white writers—giving an outward appearance of marketplace democracy—the truth of things is nowhere near that simple.

For one thing, the literatures are profoundly different. They are apples and oranges. Or, to put it quite starkly: white fiction is fiction, while black fiction is black fiction.

This sounds useless and absurd, I realize. But I believe that there is a truth to be extracted from it—a defining truth. Let me try to phrase it thus: black fiction is about being black in a way that white fiction is not about being white. Or, to wriggle a bit further out onto the limb: being black is about being black in a way that being white is not about being white. Gertrude Stein would beam to hear this, but it is not altogether ridiculous.

What I'm trying to say is that black fiction is implicitly historical in a way that white fiction, even historical fiction, cannot be. That is, it reaches off the page, via the author himself or herself, to connect with actual circumstance—the circumstance of degradation inflicted by slavers and plantation bosses *and the perpetuation of that injury through societal racism*. This is likewise true, I would add, of the Jewish people and Native Americans. But they are the exceptions. Other historical markings—we all bear them in our own ways—have more to do with individual than racial circumstance.

Blackness refers, while whiteness does not. Blackness necessarily refers to the historical conditions that have shaped the fates of all black people. Blackness refers to white domination.

It is the assumption, often unstated, of the characters in black fiction—and they are nearly without exception black characters—that white culture was once, and may still be, the enemy. The pain of slavery is still alive in the consciousness of the American black; it will not go away just because certain legislation has been passed. The black, wrote James Baldwin, "in every aspect of his living . . . betrays the memory of the auction block." Being black is, at least in part, about having the cultural memory of slavery, just as being Jewish, now and henceforth, cannot be separated from the inherited memory of the Nazi genocide.

So far as literature is concerned, there is one positive consequence to this awareness. Every individual work, whatever its genre, carries a resonance of wholeness. No matter how partial the perspective, the expression still gestures toward the black culture that originated it. This is not to say that black culture itself is unitary—it is not. Indeed, it is torn by discords of every description. But this one historical link stands over and above all dividedness. And it marks the gulf between black and white literatures that uniform formatting conceals. White culture has no such intrinsic wholeness. Except, paradoxically, as it is perceived through the black lens, in which case it has the negative wholeness of being the Other.

A quick glance at the overall literary scene gives the impression that black fiction is in a healthy state (indeed, I wrote as much in the J. California Cooper essay). To be sure, black-to-white representation does not begin to be proportionate to the population, but one can at least point to a significant number of "name" authors and to the prizes and honors their work has garnered.

Underneath, however, I'm not so sure that all is well. The health of the literature cannot be considered apart from the question of audience. Sales are one thing, readers another. Is black literature thriving in spite of or because of white culture? I cannot answer this question, but I can perhaps illuminate it with an autobiographical aside.

I spent much of the seventies and eighties working in different bookstores in Ann Arbor and in the Boston area. I noticed a great many things about books and their buyers from my perch by the cash register. With respect to black fiction I observed that a) women of all races—but preponderantly white women—buy books of fiction by black women authors, and b) that almost no one buys fiction by black men, except students who are reading the books for courses. Maybe things have changed since the mid-eighties, when I left the business, and maybe I was getting a skewed sample by working only in college towns. But I must voice my suspicion.

Namely: that the black fiction "boom" of recent decades has really been a boom in the sales of a handful of black women authors—Toni Morrison, Alice Walker, Toni Cade Bambara, Maya Angelou (memoirs), Gloria Naylor, J. California Cooper, Terry McMillan, and a very few others. And that there is a good reason for this. For apart from their natural gifts as writers, these women have—to different degrees, of course—found a particularly powerful fusion-formula. In their work, the age-old hatred of the oppressed black for the white oppressor is projected through a second layer of rage, which is that of the black woman against the black man. In these works of fiction, he is (and I generalize): shiftless and cowardly, a shirker of familial responsibility, a sexual predator, a gambler, a rolling stone, a weakling gone seedy with booze and drugs. Against his baleful presence—or nonpresence—the community of women draws together. I think of *The Color Purple, Beloved,* and *The Women of Brewster Place,* to name three of the most popular books. Here we find the story of the black matriarchy as written with a poisoned pen.

These books hit a public nerve. More specifically, they hit a nerve with women, selling tens of thousands of copies. I have to wonder about the underlying reasons for their success. Was it just because of their excellence as works of fiction? Or was it because their anger—racial anger deflected and targeted upon men—made them such incendiary emblems for an emergent women's movement? I cannot answer.

From *!Click Song* by John A. Williams:

He was silent for a time and, still bent over, he seemed to be looking into an invisible glass ball, watching the past. He sighed. "America is a strange place for a black man to write in. We always found it so, but I suppose only Countee put it so succinctly—" He swung toward me, almost glaring. "You know the poem I mean?"

I quoted the last two lines:

"Yet do I marvel at this curious thing:
To make a poet black and bid him sing!"

Mr. Johnson's smile was warm and approving. "Ah, yes, Mr. Douglass, precisely. In America, even if you are writing about a thing as simple as feeling good on a bright, clear morning filled with fresh air—feeling as perhaps millions of others are, they will find it difficult, yes, white Americans will find it difficult to understand because the writer is black and they are white . . .

"On the other hand, should you write about their direct relationship to you, the only one they know, the correct, objective historical relationship, the one that needs improving on, they will understand. That is all they have been taught to understand, the inherent, basically unchanged state of hostility. That is why in so many words and deeds they deny that history in which we have both suffered and are suffering still. What they did is our mutual holocaust, together our passing through the Red Sea, the epicenter from which or to which the universality of the experience expands or contracts. It seems that we will always move at a fixed distance in relation to each other, but only from one place in space to another place in space.

The distance is fixed, and only the place in space will change. At a deeper level, that is. Beneath the surface of a propagandistic image-world which suggests progress. And if the distance remains fixed, then the rage, too, must exist undiminished. For the distance is the direct product of power relations, the fixed formula of white over black. But where is the rage? We see it erupt on the streets. We watch its hypnotic shimmer in films by Spike Lee. But what about fiction? Where has it found expression since Baldwin's "Going to Meet the Man," that grotesque parable of castration, lynching, and auto-da-fé? Or since the screeds of Black Power, since Soul on Ice? Where?

Women's fiction has, as I said, confronted racism—but in a curiously refracted way. The situation vis-à-vis whites is there, a given, but the emotions are not directed at the Enemy. White society is there like a weather system, and you cannot get mad at a weather system. The anger remains largely within the racial circuit, taking the black man for its object.

There are few generalizations to be made about fiction by black men. Perhaps one: that very few of the male writers—and there are only a few, it seems—address themselves to racism in our present-day society. Williams's *!Click Song* does—it gives a frank account of how things stand with blacks and publishing—but his outrage flares helplessly against what he perceives to be the monolithic indifference felt toward blacks by the white establishment. (Is it telling that his novel was published not by Random House or HarperCollins but by Thunder's Mouth Press?)

Williams is nearly alone in writing about racial matters in the present. Others are indirect or put their concerns elsewhere. Al Young is genial and sly, attuned to dailiness on the street level and just up: we must read for innuendo. Ishmael Reed scats, as he has been scatting for decades, somewhere outside the perimeters of naturalism. He makes a delightful pandemonium, a bubbling language-broth, but he does not take on the race question with any immediacy.

Two of the most powerful recent novels about the black experience happen to be historical. David Bradley's *The Chaneysville Incident* and Charles Johnson's *Middle Passage* both approach their subjects—runaway slaves and the slave trade, respectively—with a strong sense of their epical narrative potential. Both succeed—Bradley rather more—at prying open the historical dossiers. They ground us, but they don't help us see the present.

The only black male writer who is really looking to get a fix on the here and now is John Edgar Wideman. Wideman is not only prolific, but he is willing to approach his material from various perspectives, writing the "Homewood" novels, like *Reuben* and *Sent for You Yesterday,* about urban neighborhood life over the past few decades, as well as *Brothers and Keepers,* a tough and bitter documentary about his brother's imprisonment. His latest, *Philadelphia Fire,* is an anguished and ambitious collage. Insofar as it pretends to novelistic coherence, it fails. But it is a significant failure, a failure that is a direct consequence of Wideman's effort to answer the hardest of questions facing the African-American. What has happened to our struggle, our Movement, our vision? What he finds defeats him. The whole—a culture rising together to claim its rights—has become a scatter of parts. He faces so many failed initiatives, sees so many former allies at each other's throats, tastes so many different kinds of bitterness. He turns his narrator into a kind of Proteus figure, enabling him to inhabit one identity after another. But the center cannot hold—as in the culture, so in the book. *Philadelphia Fire* is a ruin raised as a monument to a community of spirit now disbanded. As such, it survives to haunt.

A Postscript on Black American Fiction

Paul
Auster

Paul Auster has been, until just now, the ghost at the banquet of contemporary American letters. Though unquestionably accomplished (in the last decade he has published a memoir, five novels, several collections of poetry, and a major compendium of modern French poetry, which he edited and partly translated), he has been curiously absent from the debates being waged at the far end of the table. There are reasons for this. For one thing, his work does not fit neatly into the currently active slots. While his prose has tended toward stylistic austerity, it has little in common with the water-and-wafer fare beloved of the minimalists. In the same way, Auster has narrowly escaped the "postmodernist" tag; for all his concern with the slipperiness of perception and identity, his writing has a solid modernist grounding. He has not given up on the idea that art can discover new meaning from experience.

This has really been the main cause of Auster's marginality: that he has favored the serious and "artistic"—the novel as epistemology—over the democratically accessible. His characters have been embodiments, players in philosophical puzzles (I'm thinking mainly of the three books of his *The New York Trilogy*), or test cases to be subjected to the pressure of extreme situations; his plots, coolly calculated. But now, quite suddenly, comes a change. *Moon Palace,* Auster's new novel, breaks the chrysalis of high seriousness and stretches out its colorful wings. And the retrospective gaze alters everything: we see that his career has been in fact a complex progress toward liberation.

Auster first announced himself with the publication of a two-part memoir titled *The Invention of Solitude* (1982). Section one, "Portrait of an Invisible Man," begins with the author receiving word of his father's death. The prose, as Auster searches himself for his reactions, is remarkably matter-of-fact. Distant. As if the deeper turmoils of life could only be handled with the gloves of intellect. Auster himself is surprised by his response:

> I had always imagined that death would numb me, immobilize me with grief. But now that it had happened, I did not shed any tears, I did not feel as though the world had collapsed around me. . . . What disturbed me was something else, something unrelated to death or my response to it: the realization that my father had left no traces.

We then partake of the sustained excavation of the life—of the apparent *non*life—of a man who was a stranger to himself. A man who hid from all emotion, all responsibility, who donned the proper masks of civility, who confided nothing, gave nothing. "Solitary. But not in the sense of being alone. . . . Solitary in the sense of retreat. In the sense of not having to see himself being seen by anyone else."

A coincidental encounter on an airplane (Auster is, throughout his work, a connoisseur of the serendipitous) eventually puts him on the track of the hidden horror in his family's past. He learns that sixty years before, in a small Wisconsin town, his grandmother shot her husband to death in their kitchen. His father, Sam, then a young boy, was present. The psychological clues begin to fall into place; the memoir becomes a kind of Freudian detective story. Auster steeps himself in ancient newspaper clippings, clarifying the web of circumstance for himself. Now all of the reticence, the blankness, that he remembers in his father can be explained. But explanation is cold comfort: a small compensation for a life with a man who gave nothing, and left nothing behind. Nothing, that is, but a permanent suspicion of appearances.

The Book of Memory, the second section, is a collage of meditations, memories, and quotations. Auster reflects upon his solitude, and upon his situation as a husband and a father. The piece is not satisfying as a narrative—the fragments gather no momentum—but we come away with a clear sense of the psychic imperatives that drive the writer. We feel the desolation of his small rooms in New York and Paris, as well as the nullifying glare of the empty page. The author struggles to find an expression that will be his own. His last sentences are tense with the effort of bringing a truth up out of the self:

> He finds a fresh sheet of paper. He lays it out on the table before him and writes these words with his pen.
> It was. It will never be again. Remember.

Auster's next three books, *City of Glass, Ghosts,* and *The Locked Room,* known collectively as *The New York Trilogy,* can be seen as detached, intellectual explorations of some of the core themes of the memoir. Each of these short, elegant books turns on a search of some kind—all of them feature detectives, missing persons, mistaken identities. The moods are of watching and waiting. Personalities and human crochets have no place here. Indeed, Auster seems bent upon pruning the urban detective novel (he has written in the genre under a pseudonym) of all extraneous particulars, in order to reveal the underlying paradigm: that all existence is, at root, a stalking of clues to the self, and to the true relation of that self to everything that is Other.

The premises in these novels are resoundingly French. Auster has absorbed a great deal from the hypervigilant and ultimately self-reflexive practice of the French modernists. (He has translated Mallarmé, Blanchot, and others.) The narration of the search, carried out in the simplest translucent prose, invariably reflects back upon the process of writing itself. Time and again, the characters come to feel that they are being scripted by some higher authority; their ventures come to seem coextensive with the movement of figments in an author's mind. Take, for instance, this passage from the climactic scene of *The Locked Room*. The narrator has just opened a notebook that he hopes will clarify something about his prolonged quest for a certain Fanshawe:

> I read steadily for almost an hour, flipping back and forth among the pages, trying to get a sense of what Fanshawe had written. If I say nothing about what I found there, it is because I understood very little. All the words were familiar to me, and yet they seemed to have been put together strangely, as though their final purpose was to cancel each other out. . . . Each sentence erased the sentence before it, each paragraph made the next paragraph impossible.

In some way, this response to the text is designed to mirror our response to the text that encloses it. The prose is thrilling in its reduced precision, its escalating sense of paradox, but it asks of the reader a powerful appetite for cerebration.

The problem with self-reflexive fictions is that they obey a law of diminishing returns. Unable to suspend his disbelief, the reader starts to find the revelations merely academic. Auster appears to have recognized this. In *In the Country of Last Things* (1987), he reasserted the traditional rights of the genre, exploring the "real" (here the word needs cautionary quotation marks) by way of the invented. This is not to say that Auster found his way back to naturalism—he's too much of a modernist for that—but he does allow us to forget that the story is the product of a superintending author.

In the Country of Last Things is a legend of postapocalypse. A young woman named Anna Blume (the book is her letter to a friend) arrives by ship at a large, unnamed port city. Its location, as well as the historical period, remain unspecified. Her mission is to locate her missing brother. But as she discovers that she has journeyed into a nightmare, the search is suspended; survival becomes her sole imperative.

The city is a place of worst fears. All municipal order has broken down. Gangs terrorize and pillage; those who would eat are forced to spend the entire day scavenging. Before long, Anna is pushing her own scavenger cart:

> Little by little, my hauls became almost adequate. Odds and ends, of course, but a few totally unexpected things as well: a collapsible telescope with one cracked lens; a rubber Frankenstein mask; a bicycle wheel; a Cyrillic typewriter missing only five keys and the space bar; the passport of a man named Quinn . . . but there were certain lines I drew within myself, limits I refused to step beyond. Touching the dead, for example.

Anna does eventually cross all of her inner boundaries, and with each transgression she discovers that she is less bound by her "human" ways than she had thought. Auster's aim is to find what remains after Anna has been systematically divested of the accretions of civilization. What she arrives at, paradoxically—and exaltingly—is an ideal of charity. Beneath brutishness a flame of goodness can live. In our extremity, Auster suggests, something like grace may flourish.

It is almost as if the author needed to put himself through a winnowing process—cutting away at narrative, peeling away the fabric of learned behavior—before he could find a way to begin writing. I don't mean that the prose of these novels is lacking in artistry. But what riches are there on the page have been carefully accumulated. The augmentation comes sentence by sentence, and is the product of great discipline. *Moon Palace* breaks free of such constraint with its opening lines:

> It was the summer that men first walked on the moon. I was very young then, but I did not believe there would ever be a future. I wanted to live dangerously, to push myself as far as I could go, and then see what happened to me when I got there. As it turned out, I nearly did not make it. Little by little, I saw my money dwindle to zero; I wound up living in the streets.

The paragraph continues. But one does not need to quote at great length to show that a change has taken place in Auster's prose. The forward motion is now kinetic; the language feels inhabited from within, is self-propelling. Gone is the studious bricklaying, the sense of mind controlling hand.

In *Moon Palace,* Auster sets out to write the fantastic destiny tale of Marco Stanley Fogg. In the manner of all good picaresques, Marco is presented as serious, noble-hearted, and (we might think of David Copperfield, Tom Jones, and Huck Finn) orphaned. Born illegitimate—he was never told about his father—Marco lost his mother in an accident while very young. He grew up in the care of his uncle Victor. (We can compute, by the way, that Marco was born in 1947, the same year as Auster.) Victor is something of an eccentric, an itinerant clarinetist with a love of books and chess. He treats the boy to his theories and obsessions, making little allowance for his years. Marco—small wonder—grows up a solitary misfit.

Victor uses the insurance payments from his sister's accident to set up a small trust for the boy. He sends him away to boarding school, and later provides tuition to Columbia. When Marco is ready to move to New York, Victor insists that he pack along the dozens and dozens of boxes that contain his library. Marco obliges, though the first use he finds for the books is peculiar; he uses the boxes to build a table, chairs, and bed for himself.

Auster begins the novel with energy and inventiveness, building in layers of allusiveness. There is, for instance, the matter of Marco's name:

> Uncle Victor loved to concoct elaborate, nonsensical theories about things, and he never tired of expounding on the glories hidden in my name. Marco Stanley Fogg. According to him, it proved that travel was in my blood, that life would carry me to places where no man had ever been before. Marco, naturally enough, was for Marco Polo, the first European to visit China. Stanley was for the American journalist who had tracked down Dr. Livingstone "in the heart of darkest Africa"; and Fogg was for Phileas, the man who had stormed around the globe in less than three months. It didn't matter that my mother had chosen Marco simply because she liked it, or that Stanley had been my grandfather's name, or that Fogg was a misnomer, the whim of some half-literate American functionary. Uncle Victor found

· · ·

Paul Auster

meanings where no one else would have found them, and then, very deftly, he turned them into a form of clandestine support.

Not only will Marco fulfill the promise of his moniker, but he will also become, like his uncle, a man who finds meanings and coincidental flashes wherever he turns. Auster obviously loves to sport with the possibilities. The mention of the moon landing in the first sentence is a case in point: Marco's wanderings will be accompanied at every step by lunar symbols. The word *moon,* the orb's painted image, and the orb itself are persistently recurrent in these pages. To what end? Perhaps just to place everything under the aspect of fancy and madness (lunacy). But Auster is also, to some extent, seeding the clouds to make sure that there will be rain. Though the references at times feel artificially planted, they help to promote an atmosphere of uncanniess that makes the myriad coincidences seem less impossible than common sense would judge.

Marco is studying at Columbia and living the fringe life of the late sixties when he learns that Uncle Victor has died. Soon after, compounding his grief, he discovers that his money is nearly gone—he will not be able to make his way through school as planned. Marco faces the problem with profound passivity. Little by little—reading them first—he sells off his uncle's books. When that money is gone, he starts to practice extraordinary economies, giving up one necessity after the next. He all but stops eating. Finally, inevitably, his landlord throws him out. But even when he reaches the street, Marco cannot take initiative. He can only react.

It is as if he must undergo this peculiar rite of passage—turning himself into a vagrant—before he can connect with his fate. Holderlin's lines are appropriate here: "Near, but hard to find, is the God / But where danger is, there the saving power grows." When Marco reaches the far extreme of destitution, everything changes. A beautiful young Chinese woman named Kitty Wu rescues him and becomes his lover. And very soon after, Marco answers a posted ad. The problem of making a living is solved as he signs on as amanuensis and scribe to a wealthy old cripple named Thomas Effing.

The first third of the book, which I have tried to summarize, is enormously compelling. We identify with Marco, share his confu-

. . . .

SVEN BIRKERTS

sions and pains. The voice is direct and winning. In addition, Auster is skillful in creating the ambience of the times: Marco's urban adventures are played against a backdrop of larger social malaise; change and violence are everywhere on these streets. Our hero is living, exaggeratedly, the life of his times. Alas, with the introduction of Effing comes a shift that weakens the strong surge of Marco's tale.

Effing wants Marco to write his obituary, as well as a lengthy essay that will explain his mysterious life to posterity. For months he retails his deeds and misdeeds: how he was once a promising painter, how he entangled himself in an unhappy marriage, how he traveled to the deserts of the West to paint. The story gets increasingly improbable. Effing is betrayed by his guide, left for dead; he engineers his own disappearance and returns under a new identity. The episodes are piled high. And Marco reports them all in faithful detail. The problem is, it has been Marco's book all along: *his* is the life that has won our attention, and he steps aside for too long. For the marvels of Effing's account come to us from a propped-up figure, and it gets harder and harder to care. Interestingly, Marco at one point makes an observation that inadvertently reflects upon Auster's own failing:

> The major turning points in Effing's life had all taken place in America, in the years before his departure for Utah and the accident in San Francisco, and once he arrived in Europe, the story became just another story. . . . Effing was aware of this, I felt, and though he didn't come out and say it directly, the manner of his telling began to change, to lose the precision and earnestness of the earlier episodes.

A metafictional prescience is expressed here: Auster has, likewise, begun to lose the precision and earnestness of his earlier pages.

I am circumspect about describing the developments in the second part of *Moon Palace,* because the drama hinges upon a series of recognitions as outlandish as anything in Dickens. I will not spoil the reader's pleasure by discharging the central tensions. I will say only that a player even stranger than Effing makes his way onto the stage, and that the discoveries that Marco subsequently makes tie a knot of lineage so bizarre that he ends up poised between madness and enlightenment. In contriving his kinds of resolutions, Auster takes a risk: the novel that began among portents and promises ends up ominously close to campy self-parody. Too many coincidences overwhelm the ground of plausibility that meaningful coincidences require. While *Moon Palace* never entirely surrenders its charm—the writing is engaging throughout—its animating force slackens at the halfway mark.

One would like to herald Auster's breakthrough without reservations. He has a rare combination of talent, scope, and audacity. And in the beginning of this novel, when all of the elements are working in concert, the narrative achieves an irresistible propulsion. The diminution, therefore, a consequence of overreaching, is doubly disappointing. Still, there is the good news. Auster has served out an exciting apprenticeship. He stands poised to write something momentous about our times.

Moon Palace. Paul Auster. 286 pp. Viking. 1989. $18.95

. . . .

SVEN BIRKERTS

Leslie Marmon
Silko

Leslie Marmon Silko is a Native American of the Lagunas tribe of the Southwest. Her 1977 novel, *Ceremony*, not only established her as one of the most gritty and imaginative Native American writers but also had considerable crossover appeal for the larger audience of serious readers. The novel, which charted the reentry struggles of a World War II veteran returning to his New Mexico reservation, brought together naturalistic narrative modes with the more startling mythopoeia of the indigenous storytelling tradition. Largely on the strength of that work, Silko was awarded a 1981 MacArthur Foundation fellowship.

Hefting Silko's new novel, *Almanac of the Dead*, one readily guesses how the writer passed her last decade. It is a megalith, a two-hander; certainly it is one of the most ambitious literary undertakings of the past quarter century. Silko has ventured nothing less than a paper apocalypse, a vivid enactment of the long-prophesied collapse of white European domination and the simultaneous resurgence of the Native American peoples of much of the continent.

347

The reader will have to bear with me as I chalk out the basic perimeters of the plot. There is simply no other way to take hold of the design, or to gauge the scope and implications—and, ultimately, the failure—of the vision that Silko has attempted.

The author has divided her seven hundred–some pages into six sections, as follows: "The United States of America," "Mexico," "Africa," "The Americas," "The Fifth World," and "One World, Many Tribes." Though the vast populations of characters cross from one section to another as readily as they cross the U.S.-Mexican border, each of the units has its own focal and thematic center. A look at the two principal sections—the first two—might begin to suggest the dynamics of the whole. To attempt any more would be like describing Rodin's *The Gates of Hell* figure by figure.

The main action originates from and returns to a heavily fortified ranch outside Tucson, Arizona. Lecha and Zeta, sixty-year-old twin sisters of Mexican-Indian extraction, rule the roost. Zeta, working with Lecha's estranged son, Ferro, directs a sizable smuggling operation, trading in drugs, illegal immigrants, and, later, arms.

Lecha, recently returned from years of wandering, is a psychic with a peculiar gift: She receives visions of the recently deceased. For some time she practiced her art on live TV, but one day her trance description sets her packing her bags:

> Lecha describes the gardens of Xochimilco, with the water lilies, yellow and pink blossoms, and the reeds and cattails parting gently to the prow of the small flat-bottomed boat. Then up ahead she sees a bright red and yellow woven-plastic shopping bag floating in the dark green water. There are two large objects visible through the plastic netting. But here the talk show host interrupts, afraid that the Indian woman is just killing time, setting him up with a dumb story about floating gardens and floating trash. "So far I don't see this one making next week's headlines," he says, and is gratified when the studio audience laughs at his cleverness. But Lecha does not hesitate. She repeats the sentence he interrupted and immediately there is silence, and Lecha has them on the canal as the little boat draws even with the brightly colored shopping bag. Inside the bag are two human heads, their eyes open wide, staring at the sky.

. . . .

SVEN BIRKERTS

The heads belong to the U.S. ambassador to Mexico and his aide, and Lecha is savvy enough to know that when ambassadors die, the CIA gets active. She returns to the ranch to work at transcribing the fragments of an ancient document, the Almanac of the Dead, sacred to her people, which has been bequeathed to her by her old Yaqui grandmother. Embedded in the text, in gnomic form, are prophecies about the second coming of the Indian peoples.

The first section—indeed, the first two thirds of the novel—is less concerned with plot development than with stage setting. For her design to work, Silko must populate an enormous canvas, and this means introducing characters, figuring the ever more complex relations among them, and eventually bringing them into position for action. Thus, in addition to the sisters, we meet Seese, a desperate young druggie who has come to Lecha for help in finding her abducted child; Sterling, the Indian caretaker who has been banished from his pueblo after he betrayed the whereabouts of a sacred stone snake to a Hollywood film crew; Paulie, Ferro's assistant and lover (*Almanac* is a veritable *Satyricon* of late-century sexual and narcotic practices); Calabazas, Zeta's onetime smuggling partner, who now supplies Lecha with her Demerol fixes. You get the idea. I have merely mentioned these players between semicolons—in the novel we get major excursions into their present lives and their pasts.

The second—"Mexico"—section revolves around one Menardo, a marvelous character who dominates the page with his appetites and his energetic, if foolish, scheming. Menardo is a mestizo from Chiapas. Mortified by his telltale flat nose, he flees from his origins, becoming in time the founder of an immensely successful insurance business. His claim to distinction is that he will insure against anything, even revolution. Menardo boasts his own army, air force (several planes), and arsenal, not to mention close contacts with the most powerful men in the state.

Menardo is also a married man, and when he decides to build a grand house for himself and his wife, he topples one of the many strands of narrative dominos around which *Almanac* is constructed. He falls promptly and passionately in love with Alegría, the architect assigned to the project. Their affair, at least from Menardo's side, begins in an almost uncontrollable anticipation:

.   .   .

Leslie Marmon Silko

She had talked almost non-stop to the hotel. Menardo could only watch her breathlessly, because when Alegría was talking about her vision of what the new house could be, her face and her hands—her whole body—were vibrant. Suddenly Menardo felt sweat rolling down his sides, sliding over his ribs and soaking the top of his shorts and trousers.

Alegría, whom he eventually marries, has links through her lover, Bartolomeo, to Marxist revolutionaries (draw the dotted lines to the two heads in the plastic bag). Meanwhile, his private driver, an Indian named Tacho, happens to be the keeper of the sacred macaw birds, which impart to him the secrets about the coming insurrection of the Indians. When the great day comes, it will be Tacho's twin brother, El Feo, who will march at the head of the rising masses.

In addition to the Tucson and Chiapas contingent, *Almanac* abounds in outlandish characters, each of whom is positioned to play a part. We meet any number of shady dealers and middlemen, brokers of arms, drugs, and pornography, who will line up behind anyone who holds enough cash. There is also Leah, wife of the powerful ex-Mafia figure Max Blue, who is quietly buying up immense tracts of Tucson real estate with the idea of building a Venice of the West, complete with canals and gondolas. And Trigg, *her* lover, the wheelchair-bound founder of Biomaterials, Inc., a company dealing in the international body-parts and plasma trade. And Roy, alias "Rambo," a Vietnam vet with plans to mobilize the legions of America's homeless into a people's army.

But enough. Let me say in Silko's praise that she has the storyteller's gift for weaving and interlocking anecdotes. Although little actually happens through the first two thirds of the book, apart from the dense exposition of deals, allegiances, and past histories, the narrative moves forward with the kind of incremental edginess we find in the novels of Robert Stone. The lines between private vice and political corruption cross and crisscross. There is a mounting sense of destinies converging, of great events taking shape just over the horizon line of the page. Alas, it is the events themselves that disappoint the (necessarily) dogged reader-accomplice. But since the novel is not a simple failure, some explanation is necessary.

· · · ·

SVEN BIRKERTS

For all of its Churrigueresque surface intricacy, the structural premise of *Almanac of the Dead* is fairly simple. Silko has spliced two types of narrative—two ways of seeing the world, really—into a DNA-like braid. One string is the naturalistic—the straight-on, if somewhat heightened, depiction of Western society in its declining phase (the novel is set in the unspecified present). We see our lost and ugly culture through the stories of some of its seedier representatives—Zeta, Ferro, Menardo, Max and Leah Blue, Trigg. They are the oppressed who are intent on wreaking vengeance, the fallout of late-period capitalism, foreshadowed in Marx. As one character, a Mexican revolutionary, puts it, Marx was "a storyteller who worked feverishly to gather together a magical assembly of stories to cure the suffering and evils of the world. . . . Stories of depravity and cruelty were the driving force of the revolution, not the other way around." Those stories come alive on every page of the novel.

The other narrative cable is the mystical-prophetic. Rooted in the sacred traditions of the Native American people, not anchored to simple chronology, this orientation is visionary. It is represented by Tacho and his macaws, who speak the prophecies of "The Reign of the Fire-Eye Macaw," as our era is known. And by Lecha with her second sight. And by the symbolic utterances inscribed in the fragments of the Almanac:

> There were the very poor people who did not escape when the oppressors appeared, when the anti-Christ had come to earth, the kinkajous of the towns, the coyotes of the towns, the blood-sucking insects of the towns, those who drained the poverty of the working people. But it shall come to pass that tears will fill the eyes of God. Justice shall descend from God to every part of the world, straight from God, justice shall smash the greedy hagglers of the world.

The last third of the book attempts to bring the naturalistic and prophetic modes together, to show how the fiery visions in the Almanac are borne out, but also to show just how the catastrophe is rooted in material necessity as well. Silko's ambition is enormous. She wants to have the governments and corrupted cities crumbling away from their own degeneracy and at the same time to convince

.   .   .   .

Leslie Marmon Silko

the reader that the sacred stone snake has bestirred itself and brought the hour of regeneration to hand.

To pull this off, Silko reverses narrative emphasis. The patiently assembled webwork of deals and conspiracies is overwhelmed by the rush of prophesied catastrophe. Silko tips all her dominos at once. In Mexico: El Feo gathers his army of disfranchised Indians and begins marching north. In Tucson: drug busts, bombings, and murders all coincide with a freakish gathering of shamans, shams, and would-be revolutionists at the International Holistic Healers Convention. And running like a jagged stitch through these chapters are the extracts—many of them nonsensical—from the Almanac: "Eight is the day called the Dog. Bloody pus pours from the ears of the dog," etc.

It should be as much work to untie a fictional knot as it has been to tie it. But Silko moves with such haste that she sacrifices much of the credibility she had amassed. Where before we had slow exposition, we now catch abrupt bulletins: "The Mexican president had declared a state of emergency as thousands and thousands of war refugees from the South were spilling over Mexico's southern borders." The novel ends in a welter of deaths and departures, all of them too sudden.

Silko's writerly gifts are such that one wishes she had found herself a better vehicle—or at very least had spent more time fine-tuning the present one. A novel can only achieve so much synthesis and remain readable. That the oppressed of the world should break their chains and retake what's theirs is not an unappealing idea (for some), but it is so contrary to what we know both of the structures of power and the psychology of the oppressed that the imagination simply balks. Similarly, while Silko's descriptions of the myriad ways that corruption chases cash are convincing enough (nothing could strain credulity on this score any longer), her premise of revolutionary insurrection is tethered to airy nothing. It is, frankly, naive to the point of silliness. The appeal to prophecy cannot make up the common-sense deficit. While it is true that a great deal of fiction is an enactment of wish-fulfillment scenarios, it is also true that little of it is of the first order.

Still, the subject is serious and the author is impassioned, and one must remark the enterprise. Native Americans *have* been violated and humiliated beyond belief. The figures that Silko quotes, as well as the snippets of the historical record she includes, tell of massacres that curdle the blood. Between 1500 and 1600, North, Central, and South America lost over sixty million people. Most of them were Indians. As Calabazas tells his friend Root:

> I have to laugh at all the talk about Hitler. Hitler got all he knew from the Spanish and Portuguese invaders. De Guzman was the first to make lampshades out of human skin. They just weren't electric lamps, that's all. De Guzman enjoyed sitting Indian women down on sharp-pointed sticks, then piling leather sacks of silver on their legs until the sticks poked right up through their guts. . . . In 1902, the federals are lining up Yaqui women, their little children, on the edge of an arroyo. The soldiers fire randomly. . . . Walk through those dry mountains. Right now. Today. I have seen it. Where the arroyo curves sharp. Caught, washed up against big boulders with broken branches and weeds. Human bones piled high. Skulls piled and stacked like melons for trail markers.

The tragedy and the rage at tragedy that underwrite *Almanac of the Dead* are very real. They have spawned in Silko's mind an epic of collapse and retribution—and implied regeneration. Unfortunately, her narrative proliferation—at which she excels—forces her to extremes of resolution. The reader grips the edges of the book as though they were the steering wheel of a vehicle careening out of control. Led into so many lives and fates, we are distressed to have them shorn from us so suddenly. Yet there would seem no other way, short of devising a denouement as comprehensive as the exposition. The answer for Silko might be to prune and prune until her tree of apocalypse stands in clear outline against the sky.

Almanac of the Dead. Leslie Marmon Silko. 832 pp. Simon & Schuster. 1991. $25

W. D. Wetherell

Tolstoy and Dostoyevski are, for most readers, the twin giants of nineteenth-century Russian literature—Tolstoy the chronicler of robust dramas and physical plenitude, Dostoyevski a medium transmitting darker spiritual conflicts. Their countryman Joseph Brodsky has posited them as the two options confronting Russian writers at the start of our century, the roads diverging in the yellow wood. That those writers took the more traveled road—from Tolstoy to the drabbest of social realism—has made all the difference for Russian literature.

Brodsky may well be right, both about the terms of the option and about the consequences of Tolstoy's influence. Our century has not been the golden age of Russian prose. What's interesting, though, is the fact that these alternatives—and the temperamental split that they represent—are local, not universal. For writers elsewhere—especially in England and America—it was not one or the other fork that proved the temptation. It was the slighter path that ran wavering through the woods between—the path represented by Anton Chekhov. Neither of the giants has exerted an effect remotely comparable upon fiction in English. The Tolstoyan panorama was too vast to be useful, and Dostoyevski's fevers of exacerbated consciousness have not been adaptable to the more arid Western soul. Chekhov, meanwhile, has taught his lessons to generations of stylists, influencing everyone from Frank O'Connor to Eudora Welty to V. S. Pritchett to Raymond Carver.

Next to Flaubert, Chekhov is probably the writer most compelling to other writers. Flaubert, who is not nearly so likable, wins his adherents through the sheer eloquence of his complaining: declaring his private agonies of composition, the tyrant of the *mot juste* is every writer's tortured and torturing superego. Chekhov, by contrast, makes the whole business look so easy—we are bewitched by the accumulating force of his "casual" details, by the surprise attack of his indirection. Like no one else, Chekhov creates moments that feel freshly plucked from life. They are everywhere—in "The Kiss," "Gooseberries," "The Lady with the Lapdog," to name only the better known of his stories. And where we find these moments, we find as well the inimitable and irresistible note of yearning. Chekhov knew by instinct the simple physics of the heart: to live is to yearn.

Apart from the stories and plays—the unique fracture line of each—is the image of the man himself. Writers seem to find in his life emblems of their own concerns and in his circumstances a template for their own. So many have mused over the impoverished medical student writing stories to support his family; the successful author, already ill with tuberculosis, journeying across the continent to the prison island of Sakhalin; the consumptive drinking a glass of champagne on his deathbed. Chekhov has become a kind of screen for the projections of his fellow writers: they would twine their lives with his in some way, assay themselves by looking to him. And Chekhov in some way abetted this; in his extreme self-effacement he all but relinquished claims to his own biography.

Thus James McConkey, exhausted by a long year of student uprisings at Cornell, retells the story of Chekhov's travels to Sakhalin (*To a Distant Island*, 1984) as a way of exploring a writer's relation to social injustice. And the Irish poet Seamus Heaney, in "Chekhov on Sakhalin," searches out the same elusive connection. What are the obligations—the chains—binding the artist to his society? When Heaney writes

.   .   .   .

W. D. Wetherell

> He who thought to squeeze
> His slave's blood out and waken the freeman
> Shadowed a convict guide through Sakhalin

we feel, behind the portraiture, the self-directed probe of an Irish conscience as well.

Probably the most poignant invocation of the Chekhov persona is to be found in "Errand," one of the very last stories that Raymond Carver wrote. Here, with a stilled attentiveness that prickles the skin, Carver writes of Chekhov's death at the Badenweiler spa in Germany, and of the postmortem vigil kept by his wife, the actress Olga Knipper, whom he had married only a few years before. The story, haunting in itself, becomes more haunting once the reader knows that Carver was dying of cancer at the time of writing, and that he, too, would be leaving a widow, the poet Tess Gallagher, after only a few years of marriage.

A somewhat different piece of Chekhoviana now comes to us from novelist and short-story writer W. D. Wetherell (winner of the 1985 Drue Heinz Literature Prize for his collection *The Man Who Loved Levittown*). His new novel, *Chekhov's Sister*, is a most peculiar summoning: though most of the events take place in Yalta in 1941, nearly forty years after Chekhov's death, the pages are as saturated with the master's presence as any of the other, more direct treatments. Indeed, Wetherell goes further. By incorporating portions of a staged performance of *The Seagull*, he sets Chekhov's phrases echoing among his own.

Chekhov's Sister opens with a document: a letter written from Chekhov to his sister Maria Pavlovna, bequeathing to her the house he had bought in the resort of Yalta late in his life. "You may sell the house if you so desire," he writes. The letter is dated 1901, three years before his death.

But as we see in the novel's first scene—at the Yalta house in 1941—Maria Pavlovna has done no such thing. On the contrary, she has made the house into the Chekhov Museum. Though she is in her late seventies, she presides vigorously over every detail of its running. Assisting her are her maid Varka, her servant Gerassim, a retired actor named Potapov, and Kunin, an ardent young man with literary ambitions—Maria Pavlovna believes that he may be her brother's successor.

The first scene, presented partly as a narrative and partly as a play (Wetherell switches between genres throughout), is quick with tension. The German Army is at the point of overrunning Yalta. Maria Pavlovna, who has sacrificed everything to this shrine to her brother, prepares for the new regime: portraits of Tolstoy and other Russians come down from the walls; Goethe and Hauptmann take their places. Chekhov's letters to German editors and literary figures are strategically placed. We sense that Maria Pavlovna would, if pressed, contend that her brother was not Russian at all, but German.

Already Wetherell has set out his first thematic skein. Is art a world unto itself, an end justifying all means? Should one lie, wheedle, and otherwise play false to oneself to preserve its sacred truths? Or are those truths, like all mortal clay, subject to the forces of historic change? For Maria Pavlovna there is no question—she bows before her brother's name as before an icon.

Kunin is less certain. Early on he finds himself buffeted by what seem to be the divergent claims of life and art. Sent to the Imperial Theater to recover a portrait, he has an epiphany about the eternal self-containment of art. Alone in the dark, abandoned theater, Kunin feels an enfolding sense of safety. "Regimes rose and fell," he reflects, "armies came and went, and yet this inarticulate thing latent in the theatre's amber light went on forever, and in its midst he could not be harmed."

A few minutes later, though, that idealization is abruptly shattered. Returning to the street, Kunin is confronted by a group of German soldiers with rifles. He finds that "in the moment of shame when the muscles of his arm had involuntarily tightened, he had been reaching for something after all—something inside himself that should have been there but wasn't." His affirmation of art's potency vanishes in a flash. In its place, he finds "the bewildered hollow of his faith's passing."

Wetherell investigates this most ancient of dilemmas from every possible angle. But he is cunning enough to avoid didacticism, and agile enough as a storyteller to keep the permutations of plot fresh and surprising. As in Chekhov, events are made to emerge from the imperatives of character, not characters from events.

•   •   •   •

W. D. Wetherell

What happens, briefly, is this. As the Germans are taking over Yalta, commandeering and requisitioning everything, a young man named Rene Diskau introduces himself to Maria Pavlovna. He is, it turns out, an officer with the Ministry of Culture; he is also a devotee of Chekhov. Diskau promptly proposes that the Imperial Theater be reopened for a staging of *The Seagull*. He will direct and play the role of Constantine. Maria Pavlovna agrees with enthusiasm—never mind that her brother would have reviled everything the Nazis represent.

The greater part of the novel revolves around the doings and interactions of the various players as they make ready to perform. Wetherell tenses the psychological webbing by incorporating flashbacks from the lives of the principal characters (he flashes forward, too, to show an aged Kunin living in Brezhnev-era Moscow). We learn, among other things, the childhood roots of Maria Pavlovna's devotion to her older brother. By the time the performance is ready to begin, we have begun to grasp the complexities of the story behind the story.

The major complications—romantic and moral—arise when Diskau (who is, we find out, in the grip of morphine addiction) unexpectedly produces a starving refugee actress to play Nina, one of the lead roles. This woman—she is called Nina throughout—is the lone survivor of a band of escapees. Her comrades all died horrible deaths at the hands of Diskau and his men. Nina herself was brutally violated. Yet here she stands, the actress unable to resist the siren call of the stage. Her speech to Kunin, who has fallen in love with her, bends the question of the relation of art and life through another facet of the prism. Says Nina (*passionately,* according to Wetherell's stage directions):

> All my career I've acted badly because I've never been able to forget my hates and loves and my own personality. I was never ruthless enough before. I never had the key. Now I throttle myself and it's only Nina that survives and nothing else matters. Diskau approaches me at lunch and I have to restrain myself from plunging the bread knife in his chest, but step onstage and I see in him only a boy named Constantine who is in love with me and half out of his mind from jealousy.

· · ·

SVEN BIRKERTS

Her passion, unlike the young Kunin's, bears all the scorch marks of experience.

As *Chekhov's Sister* ends, the battered troupe has weathered every calamity—illness, hysteria, curfew, threatened defections, not to mention the narcotic flare-ups of its director—and the show does go on. The first-night audience, sadly, is a bare-bones assortment of strays, nothing like the full house of actors' fantasies. But somehow that scarcely matters to the players. They have come to possess the play; they are transformed by the making of beauty from the materials of loss and desire:

> From out of the darkness someone throws a rose and it lands in tribute at her [Nina's] feet. She picks it up and holds it in front of her with both hands. She holds it in front of her with both hands and kisses it as if it were a chalice and brings it high over her head until the light surrounding her fades and all that is left is the heart-shaped rose there in the darkness, the one shining unquenchable thing, and when it is established there long enough for its memory to become eternal, the curtain falls again and the play ends.

A curious note, this. Indeed, it is a curious conception for a novel. We have gone such a long time without hearing art considered in such serious—no, *exalted*—terms. Throwaway wryness has been the order of the day—that, or else the deliberate flatness that would preempt any accusations of pretentiousness. But Wetherell has, with imagination and gumption, reanimated the questions about art and life that never get answered once and for all. To do this, he has had to travel, like some others before him, to meet the shade of Chekhov—the man who became one of art's highest servants by claiming to care nothing for artifice and everything for the life revealed.

Chekhov's Sister. W. D. Wetherell. 343 pp. Little, Brown. 1990. $17.95

· · ·

W. D. Wetherell

Rebecca
Goldstein

Until just a few decades ago, the mirror of American fiction was a glass half-empty. Present and much accounted for were men and their sagas; missing was a great deal else. But then came women's liberation and the consecutive waves of novels by women giving testimony about female sexuality, about marriage, and about the deeper currents of family life. This was the period that saw the emergence of novelists and storytellers like Anne Tyler, Gail Godwin, Sue Miller, Bobbie Ann Mason, Mary Gordon, Toni Morrison, and Alice Walker. For a while it felt as though a new golden age was upon us.

But what started out as an exciting telling of news and secrets has become its own genre, with all the attendant risks of stultification. Readers now expect that women writers will deliver certain goods. The electricity of suppressed lives is increasingly packaged as product—predictability has set in.

Novelist Rebecca Goldstein is a singular exception. She is a thinker in a world of feelers. Trained as a philosopher (she teaches the subject at Rutgers), she writes if not *like* a philosopher, then *as* one. Her first two novels, *The Mind-Body Problem* and *The Late Summer Passion of a Woman of Mind,* were, as the titles suggest, about intellectuals and the life of the mind. Her characters not only alluded to Spinoza and Wittgenstein, they discussed them for pages at a stretch. And if her plots were not the most inventive—in places, frankly, they creaked—the reader could nonetheless say, "So this is what it feels like to live in the world of ideas. . . ."

With her newest novel, *The Dark Sister,* Goldstein allows the formal architecture to take precedence over the cerebrations of her lead characters; in a sense, the structure itself generates the ideas. Goldstein not only contrives an intricate parallel plot, but she has her protagonist, a novelist named Hedda, do the same for the novel that *she* is writing. In nineteenth-century novels, such a strategy, Hedda observes, "was often the means by which moral points were made, the two stories played off against each other, so that the import of each emerges in the crack in between, as it were."

Goldstein builds *The Dark Sister* around this pair of echoing narratives, one contemporary, the other more in the vein of Charlotte Brontë. At the center, at once creation and creator, is Hedda. A successful author of contemporary novels about "angry" women, she has fled New York to set herself up in a lonely house on the New England coast—to write. No sooner does she arrive than she finds herself haunted by a strange array of characters from the previous century. She has only to stare into the mirror to find herself possessed by imaginings. Soon she is spinning out a dark and obsessive gothic tale, something altogether new for her.

In Hedda's book, a spinster named Alice Bonnet from the town of Willow Groves, Connecticut, pays a call on a Dr. Sloper. She professes concern for her younger sister, Vivianna. "We are to one another," she tells Sloper, "as the high noon is to midnight." The analogy is apt, for Vivianna is an astronomer and literally lives by night. She has posited the existence of what we now call a "black hole," and Alice fears that her drive to prove her hypothesis will unhinge her completely. "My sister suffers the awful burden of her genius, which her female frame cannot possibly support." Sloper refers the case to his old Harvard classmate philosopher William James; with James's first visit to the Bonnet home the narrative starts to gain momentum.

. . . .

Rebecca Goldstein

Meanwhile, the novelist Hedda is suffering a breakdown. As we watch her rattling around in her windy house, brooding into mirrors, we begin to realize to what extent the story of the Bonnet sisters is a transformation of her own family experience. Hedda is thirty-eight, and so is Alice (and so, I suspect, was Goldstein herself when she began working on this book). Where plain Alice is paired to vivid and brilliant Vivianna, Hedda—who stands over six feet and has a prognathous jaw—has Stella. Voluptuous, assertive, neurotic, and spoiled, Stella has been through four husbands and is, at the time of the story, deep in analysis. She is on the verge of stepping forth as a major character, but Goldstein holds her back. Her formidable presence can only emerge via her telephone calls to her sister.

Hedda and Stella were abandoned by their father while still young girls, and reared by their eccentric and tyrannical mother. As Goldstein writes: "They were enemies, Hedda and Stella; but they were enemies who confirmed one another's reality, and in this way they could keep out the craziness of the Mother. . . ." Needless to say, the family struggles find their way into Hedda's narrative in psychologically suggestive ways: the Freudian "romance" ultimately takes on the aspect of a dance of death.

Interestingly, Goldstein is at her best when she is dealing with William James. She inhabits the Cambridge philosopher less skittishly than she does her own Hedda. We get to know James as a man in midlife, at the center of the heady milieu that was the James family—corresponding with brother Henry in England, worrying about his delicate but triumphantly tough-minded sister Alice. We see him as he tries to forge a peace between the claims of reason and his ever more absorbing researches into psychic phenomena (from which would eventually result *The Varieties of Religious Experience*). This determination to bring together the rational and irrational, the intellect and the emotions, is what powers Goldstein's work throughout. Her decision to cast William James as a mediating figure is an inspired one.

Goldstein not only knows her way around the corridors of the House of James, but she skillfully recreates the leisurely and circumspect prose style of the period. Her rendering of James's first view of Vivianna conveys as much about the mores of the day as it does about the philosopher's sensuous disposition: "His artist's eye took in the natural curves in which she was arranged, which had none of the artfulness of the current strictures of fashion. Her waist filled out its natural circle. It was visibly and delightfully undeformed by stays."

But James's real attraction to the dark sister is intellectual, and their interchanges make up the most animated part of the novel. Vivianna's scientific and philosophical penetration astonishes him. In their first interview, she discourses with passionate focus about Giordano Bruno, Pierre Simon de Laplace, mathematical theory, not to mention the astrophysics of her "darkened stars." James listens, rapt, finally observing, "My own theories seek the hidden self, yours the hidden star"—a metaphoric relation that defines their special bond.

Alas, Vivianna's strengths are finally no match for the pressures of convention; she writes to James that she has decided to abandon her work. The news disturbs James deeply. He discerns in Vivianna's defeat not only the fate of gifted women but of originality itself.

The other characters, unfortunately, lack the density and detail conferred upon James. Goldstein cares less for the amassing of credible detail than for her Byzantine counterpointing of sisters and families. Just as the "import" of one or another parallel begins to emerge "in the crack in between," the author works up some new twist to distract her reader: a feminist diatribe delivered during a seance, or the sudden (and silly) incursion of a heroine from one of Hedda's earlier books.

When she is in her full stride, Goldstein tells an absorbing tale and sparks off all manner of intriguing ideas (about repression, female creativity, the expression of a collective unconscious in psychic phenomena . . .). Her core notion, of linking the split selves and doubled plots of the gothic novel to feminist preoccupations, may not be entirely new—Sandra Gilbert and Susan Gubar explored this in depth in *The Madwoman in the Attic*—but Goldstein has found inventive ways to create drama. She writes on behalf of the gifted woman, but her insights have a wider application. Societal emancipation, she affirms, is only a first step for liberation. The forces of repression have not disappeared; they have merely been internalized. Hedda must bring together the scattered selves that drive her to such desperate fabrication. Her writing will only matter if it is a path back to the world.

Rebecca Goldstein

In a way, Goldstein is still working on the mind/body problem that supplied the title for her first novel. As a thinker, and a writer writing about thinkers, she is most accomplished. But she still has a hard time connecting the mind component with the body, the nuts and bolts of the plot. Pairs and parallels are great sport to set into motion, but they pose serious problems of resolution. In the end, the author reaches for the grandly melodramatic wrap-up, and at that point, the novel gets simplified into self-parody, its promising seriousness undermined.

I don't know if philosophy has solved the age-old conundrum of the mind-body split. Goldstein certainly has the talent to solve hers. Already her appetite for difficult ideas and powerful conflicts sets her apart from most of her peers. She may yet lead the march away from the genre-bound woman's novel.

The Dark Sister. Rebecca Goldstein. 288 pp. Viking. 1991. $19.95

·   ·   ·   ·
SVEN BIRKERTS

Nicholson
Baker

"Anything becomes interesting if you look at it long enough." I have copied this quotation and have ascribed it to Flaubert, but I am no longer sure where I found it; nor do I know whether the master was being profoundly ironic or merely profound. Either way, though, it seems to me an adage useful to a writer. Certainly Nicholson Baker—*young* Nicholson Baker (born in 1957)—has made its wisdom work for him. His 1988 novel, *The Mezzanine,* was a largely comic tour de force, consisting entirely of the thoughts and observations of a young office worker on his lunch hour. The narrative constraint forced the author into veritable epics of magnification; he focused upon ordinary objects until they took on the proportions of Claes Oldenburg sculptures, and moved every least action through what felt like the slow syrup of a marijuana high. Even Leopold Bloom could get down the aisle of the local CVS faster than Baker's narrator.

Baker followed the critical success of *The Mezzanine* with *Room Temperature,* a not dissimilarly idiosyncratic novel wherein the narrator's thoughts and perceptions meld together over the course of a late-afternoon bottle-feeding of his six-month-old baby, Bug. Again, a blooming and buzzing prose of astonishing sensory attentiveness:

> Like a screech trumpet player, she held her bottle with one hand; her other hand roved in search of textures: my sweater's, of course, but also a wrinkle and the nipply bump of a snap on her own striped outfit, her hair and ear, and especially the raised ounce and cubic-centimeter demarcations that were molded into her Evenflo bottle's plastic, like the fractions of a cup that had once been molded into glass peanut butter jars, so useful for practicing your fingertip-reading skills on while you ate.

Even while enjoying Baker, however, I have sometimes been tempted to amend Flaubert slightly, to add that anything looked at *too* long may cease to be that thing, or else might cause the sensory receptors to calcify. Fortunately, Baker himself seems to have recognized that some shift was in order. His newest work, *U and I: A True Story*, breaks away from exterior microscopy to engage in a different sort of accounting—this time of his lifelong fascination with the writings, career, and personality of our master mandarin stylist, John Updike.

I take the adjective *mandarin* from Cyril Connolly's meditation on the literary vocation, *Enemies of Promise*, where Connolly uses it to designate writers of particularly aesthetic sensibility: writers, that is, who conquer their subjects through sheer force of style. Fittingly, Baker has taken his own epigraph from Connolly: "It may be *us* they want to meet but it's themselves they want to talk about." A perfect preemptive stroke, that. For once the vice has been admitted, we are free to find it charming—and we do.

Baker cues up his short memoir with great skill, presenting it, at least initially, as a serendipity. It is August 1989, and the author has just sent off his second novel. His writing momentum is still running high, so he sits with his keyboard in his lap and starts noodling. A mere few sentences in, however, a half-recollected bit from Updike's *Self-Consciousness* cuts across the flow of his reverie, and before long—after a divagation of several pages during which he contemplates writing an appreciation of his recently deceased former teacher Donald Barthelme—he succumbs. Baker then admits that he has long wanted to write about his Updike obsession. The time has come.

. . . .

SVEN BIRKERTS

And to demonstrate to himself that he is in earnest, he contracts to do the piece for *The Atlantic*.

The reader looking for the reassurance of a solid frame, or even the suasions of a good story, had better look elsewhere. *U and I* is just not that kind of book. Baker's agenda, loosely noted and no less loosely adhered to, is as follows:

> I was not writing an obituary or a traditional critical study, I was trying to record how one increasingly famous writer and his books, read and unread, really functioned in the fifteen or so years of my life since I had first become aware of his existence as I sat at the kitchen table on a Sunday afternoon, watching with envious puzzlement my mother laugh harder than I had ever seen her laugh before . . . as she read an Updike essay on golf in a special edition of *The New York Times Book Review*.

If Baker has set himself any constraint this time around, it is to *not* do the expected thing. He does not go back to read and annotate his Updike; he even forbids himself to look up any remembered passages. He will tell his reader's truth—however faulty—and nothing more. Consequently, Baker must bumble from one misremembered quotation to another (he later brackets in the correct citations), making up in passion and sharp self-scrutiny what he necessarily lacks in documentation. Another brilliant stroke! In his quirkily rambling way, Baker has given us an utterly sui generis chronicle of a reader's interior life. I know of nothing quite like it, though Julian Barnes's *Flaubert's Parrot* might rival it in *outré* eccentricity.

To get to what *U and I* is, I would first follow the way of negation and say what it is not. It is *not* in any sense a portrait of Updike as a man or writer or American legend; neither is it much of an accounting, except by inference, of Baker as a man, writer, or aspiring legend. Rather, Baker has shaken all of these possibilities together in a pressurized can and has sprayed the mixture free-form on the accommodating white of the page. The book is memory and reflection, sense and sensibility, exorbitant pride and no less exorbitant self-prejudice, all refracted through the supple and spontaneous-seeming medium of his prose. The categorizing reviewer shreds his sheaf of categories.

Baker idolizes Updike, sees him as the lord of contemporary

American literature. "How fortunate I was to be alive when he was alive!" he exclaims early on. His fixation extends not only to the variety and perfection of the writing itself, but also to the point-by-point trajectory of the career. Nor is there anything detached about his fascination. Baker confesses that he would like to *be* John Updike; as that is not possible, he must try to be as much like him as possible. Ideally, he concedes, he would surpass his hero (Baker is well aware of the son-slaying-father Freudian mythos, but he does not linger on it), but the almost supernatural velocity of Updike's early career has already scotched that option.

Baker knows this, but he cannot let the matter rest. At one point he asks his mother if she does not think that he is a better writer than Updike had been at his age. "There was a silence," writes Baker. Then came the mother's excruciatingly tactful reply: "I think you will *be* a better writer than John Updike—I have every faith that you will be a better writer than John Updike." Our author is crushed. And in his wounded abjectness, he starts a sympathetic vibration in the heart of anyone who writes or has even dreamed of being a writer. Baker plumbs himself, but the ferocious pride and will he discovers are universal.

But while Baker cannot resist measuring and comparing attainments, his book transcends the stroking/flaying of the private ego. Its distinctive appeal derives from its celebration of language and the life-giving currents that pass from writer to reader. Indeed, in an age of chaotic distraction and diminishing readerships, nothing could be more tonic than this young man's unapologetic bewitchment by the word. He is aggressive and outspoken in his appreciations, freeing strands of Updike's iridescence through his own iridescent enthusiasm. Pondering, for instance, whether the word *genius* could be applied as readily to Updike as to Nabokov, Baker finds himself wondering about his hero's own long-ago thoughts:

> And don't you have to admit, whatever your doubts are about the utility of the word, that it is pleasing, almost thrilling, to think of our very own living Updike at thirty-two or so writing "Her pointed yellow high-heeled shoes lay beside her feet as if dislodged by a sudden shift of momentum" and experiencing, when he looked at the words he had just so happily and casually

combined, that same puzzled, curious, surprised sensation—
"Maybe I am!"?

Or else, in what is to me a sublimely suggestive image, Baker
recalls for us Updike's own casual mention in an essay that his copy
of Moncrieff's translation of Proust is stained with drops of his ex-
wife's suntan oil. He writes:

> I envision the near transparency that the drops of lotion must
> have created in the paper as methylparaben portholes in Marcel's
> prose through which we glimpse for a moment the knowable,
> verifiable life we have now, in America, with spouses and deck
> chairs and healing sunlight, as opposed to the unknowable life of
> a homosexual genius in France before the First World War . . .

The suggestiveness owes as much to the conceptual concatena-
tion—from Proust to Moncrieff to Updike to Baker to ourselves,
reading—as it does to the lovely fusion of supposedly discrete realms,
those of literature and those of life. The image is a fitting emblem
for what Baker himself accomplishes through his ruminations.

U and I does build to an understated anecdotal climax. In the
last pages, Baker narrates, with winning self-deflation, his several
slight face-to-face encounters with his subject. I would spoil the fun
of the prospective reader if I were to paraphrase. I will only say that
anybody who has ever approached an admired individual in full fear
and trembling will feel the ticklish pleasure that another's mortifica-
tion can supply. But there is also in these scenes that exhilarating
sense—maybe I should call it "porthole consciousness"—that comes
when the wall dividing the word from the world is punched through.
I don't know whether the flesh-and-blood John Updike will laugh or
squirm when he reads Baker's peculiar paean. By now he must know
that young zealots are the toad that every successful author must
swallow with the morning tea. This particular toad just needs a pat
on the back to attain his princehood.

U and I. Nicholson Baker. 179 pp. Random House. 1991.
$18

. . .

Nicholson Baker

Allen Kurzweil

C lio, the muse of history, has been taking hits from all sides lately. In academe her story has undergone so much revision, deconstruction, and multiculturalization that even she is no longer sure what really happened and to whom. Nor are things any better in lay circles. As more and more of us succumb to the media spell, the shimmering and pulsing *now* of it, the sense of *then* further recedes. Educators are clutching their hair. The average high schooler believes that the War of the Roses is a Danny DeVito movie and that Vietnam lies somewhere off the coast of Africa. The past increasingly equals stuffy people in funny clothes, all speaking in the accents of *Masterpiece Theater*.

Against this uncertain background, the vision of Allen Kurzweil stands out in startling relief. In his debut novel, *A Case of Curiosities*, the thirty-year-old author has thrust himself headlong into the French eighteenth century. His energetic picaresque of the life and times of Claude Page, poor boy turned mechanical genius, suggests that what is a problem zone for the scholar and a *terra incognita* for the media generations could nonetheless become a romping ground for a new generation of fiction writers.

Kurzweil founds his novel on a clever conceit. In 1983, in a Paris auction house, the unnamed narrator makes a blind bid on a battered old trunk. An interested stranger informs him that he has just bought a *memento hominem,* or "life box." Each of its objects—including a jar, a button, a nautilus shell and an artist's lay figure—represents "a decisive moment or relationship in the personal history of the composer." The trunk also includes a text: *Claude Page: Chronicle of an Engineer.* Our narrator is intrigued—intrigued enough to spend six years researching and contemplating before writing the account we hold in our hands.

The story begins on September 10, 1780, in the French village of Tournay. Ten-year-old Claude Page and his widowed mother await the arrival of Adolphe Staemphli, noted Geneva surgeon, who is to remove an anomalous growth from Claude's finger—a birthmark that happens to resemble Louis XIV. They are joined by the Abbé, a good-hearted old apostate with an outsized passion for the natural sciences. He has come to buy herbs from Claude's mother, but after Staemphli ruthlessly removes the boy's finger (for his collection of medical curiosities), the Abbé takes a pitying interest in the boy, eventually making him his assistant. A paradoxical stroke of destiny: "Claude had lost a finger that night but acquired something much more valuable: a patron and a mentor. Amputation had brought about attachment."

Living at the Abbé's manor, Claude is soon infected with the man's encyclopedic enthusiasms. Master and student "spent hours hunched over a costly but inadequate screw-barrel microscope bought from Culpeper's of London, trying to find fault with Hook's study of the eye of the fly, the thorn of the nettle, and the stinger of the bee." The boy draws, copies, and tinkers with everything in sight; more unexpectedly, he helps the Abbé in his secret business by enameling pornographic scenes onto the pocket watches of aristocrats. His mentor is proud. And when he has taken Claude's measure, he announces: "We must all choose our metaphors. Mine is the nautilus. Your metaphor is that golden clam shell we call the watch."

As it turns out, what Claude witnesses one night—or *believes* he witnesses—in the hidden chamber of the Abbé's "nautilus" sends him fleeing to Paris and his prophesied future as an engineer. Paris proves to be the site of Claude's sentimental education. There he encounters the wisdom of the streets and the exactions of the worka-day grind, not to mention the first beckonings of lust. Degree by delicious degree, a once-renowned beauty named Madame Hugon leads the boy into her snares. The episodes are as comic as they are touching. Imagining that he is in love, Claude tells Madame Hugon that he would like to make something for her. "Watching Claude awkwardly eat his way through a cream pastry, she whispered, 'Keep delivering yourself to me, my little peasant boy. Nothing else is required.' " In due time, Madame Hugon will bear Claude's child, a daughter—but that is, as they say, another story.

Leaving his ill-paid apprenticeship behind, Claude sets up on his own as a maker of ingenious curios, including double-axle pinwheels that create intricate optical effects, and a trick drum: "When it was turned over, the simple passage of air through a thin tongue of hammered brass produced the sound of a cow." Kurzweil's precise but also poetic grasp of mechanisms and their functioning opens a window onto the obsessions of the Enlightenment. Claude's way of seeing gradually changes ours: "The pattern of the nautilus became the coil of mainspring. The sweep of the farmer's hay knife evoked the motion of a pendulum." We start to sense the laws of process and design that underlie appearances.

Claude's metaphor may be the watch, but his supreme achieve-ment will be a good deal more sophisticated. After all manner of ups and downs, including an emotional reconciliation with the Abbé, he realizes what he must do. He will devise nothing less than a talking automaton, the first of its kind, a machine even more wondrous than Vaucanson's infamous "defecating duck."

Kurzweil captures the full arc of the inventor's frenzy—the rushes of insight as well as the dead-end dejections. Helped along by his various cronies, Claude makes great headway, until it is time to invent the sound mechanism. The challenge almost finishes him. Try as he may, he cannot find the trick for reproducing human speech. Then, one day, while he is studying his sallow and stubbled face in a pocket mirror, Claude begins rubbing his neck, "and as he rubbed he started to cry. Suddenly he stopped. Not the rubbing. The rubbing continued, but the crying ended. He stared at the movement of his fingers on his throat. . . . For the first time in many months, Claude smiled."

He has extrapolated a simple friction into a solution. And before long his invention, the Talking Turk, is ready. Every detail has been fussed into perfection. A crowd gathers and the button is pushed. "Through the slightly parted lips emerged four distinct sounds. *Veeeeeee—vuhhh—luhh—Waaaaahhhhh!*" *Vive le roi*—the idea belongs to his principal funder, an aristocrat. "With those three words, the fame of Claude Page was secured, and so, too, was his fate." Right idea, wrong time. It is 1789—the Revolution. The Talking Turk is not talking turkey, but treason. Claude is lucky to escape with his head—the Turk is not so lucky.

With *A Case of Curiosities,* Kurzweil takes his place in the long and delightful picaresque tradition that reaches back to Fielding and earlier, but which also includes recent works like William Kennedy's *Quinn's Book* and Paul Auster's *Moon Palace.* Claude's dense explorations are not lore that has been swotted up to make a book—they represent an obsession that has found its voice. The book itself is a "time-piece" of sorts—the chapters, each oriented around an object in the life box, mesh to draw us deeper into the grappling of intelligence with physical law.

The narrator is a tricky fellow, quick with puns and sly connections. At one point, for instance, he mentions a certain Madame de Crayencour. This just happens to be the birth name of the brilliant historical novelist, Marguerite Yourcenar, who rearranged the letters into her nom de plume. A wink of homage, to be sure. But also a relevant point of reference for us. For like the author of *Hadrian's Memoirs* and *The Abyss,* Kurzweil gives vivid restoration to a lost time. Yourcenar was elegiac, and Kurzweil is more playful—but his engaging vision may be just what's needed to stimulate our atrophying historical sense.

A Case of Curiosities. Allen Kurzweil. 382 pp. Harcourt Brace Jovanovich. 1992. $19.95

. . . .

Allen Kurzweil

Ethan Canin/
Mona Simpson/
Brett Easton Ellis/
Jill Eisenstadt

According to a recent profile in *Publishers Weekly,* twenty-seven-year-old Ethan Canin has published every story he's written since the age of nineteen—most of them in prestigious journals like *Esquire, Atlantic,* and *Ploughshares.* Yet his debut volume, *Emperor of the Air,* contains only nine stories. Either Canin refused to republish everything he's written, or else he works very slowly.

I prefer the latter explanation, for it supports my sense that each separate work is an occasion, a rare and happy collaboration between craft and emotional imperative. Perspiration and inspiration, you might say, only not in the drab Protestant proportions of 99/1. These plums have a somewhat less predictable savor.

Canin has a highly honed, if cumulatively predictable, narrative procedure. Most of his stories begin, following Aristotle's advice, *in medias res.* They plant the hook straightaway with some beguilingly mysterious statement. "Pitch Memory," for instance, starts: "The day after Thanksgiving my mother was arrested outside the doors of J.C. Penney's, Los Angeles, and when I went to get her I considered leaving her at the security desk."

Once he has the reader on the line, Canin backtracks, introducing vignettes of character history, directing them toward the present, toward the crisis or mystery promised in the opening. When that point has been reached, he lets the narrative loose to find what is, invariably, an unexpected resolution. Indeed, I can't believe that Canin thinks out his endings; they have the rightness of something felt for and risked by the heart. The final revelations redeem what occasionally feels like a programmatic way of setting things up.

Canin works with contemporary settings and age-old dilemmas. His main subject is the American family. Nearly all of his characters are caught in the toils of some family dependency—daughters meshed with mothers, sons with fathers, siblings with one another. Canin calibrates degrees of entrapment and freedom. His special gift is for exposing tensions, rendering them volatile, and then slipping a slender lit filament into their midst. He is open-eyed and tender in his essential disposition, but he is not afraid of the harsher truths.

"The Year of Getting to Know Us," one of the shrewdest of the stories, begins with a grown-up son, Lenny, visiting his father in the hospital. There follow several scenes where Lenny remembers moments from childhood and adolescence, from the time before his parents divorced. A subnarrative unfolds. Lenny recounts how he once hid himself in the trunk of his father's Lincoln, beside his golf bag; how he trapped himself into hearing a backseat tryst with a mistress. Lenny cried out, bringing about this confrontation:

> His steps kicked up gravel. I heard jingling metal, the sound of his key in the trunk lock. He was standing over me in an explosion of light.
>
> He said, "Put back the club socks."
>
> I did and got out of the car to stand next to him. He rubbed his hands down the front of his shirt.
>
> "What the hell," he said.
>
> "I was in the trunk."
>
> "I know," he said. "What the goddam."

The episode is a triumph of minimalism. But Canin is not really a minimalist—he is after deeper, more varied resonances. Against these memories, therefore, he plays a countermemory. Lenny is led to recall the time that he discovered that his wife, Anne, was having an affair. The parallelism may seem too obvious at first, but it's not. For Canin is not interested in the dynamics of betrayal so much as in his evolving portrait of a man with strange kinds of distance in his heart. When Anne finally confesses, Lenny is unusually passive; there is even a hint of masochistic relish.

Everything is in place for the final twist. Near the end of the story, as we expect, Lenny gets word that his father has died. That night, unable to sleep, he eases the old Lincoln (the very same car) out from his father's garage. He drives through the night. At dawn, as he heads home in a drizzle, another memory surfaces. A family vacation, the year his mother designated as "The Year of Getting to Know Us." Lenny and his father stand overlooking the ocean; his father speaks.

> "Listen," he said. "We're here on this trip so we can get to know each other a little bit." A hundred yards below us waves broke on the rocks. He lowered his voice. "But I'm not sure about that. Anyway, you don't *have* to get to know me. You know why?"
>
> "Why?" I asked.
>
> "You don't have to get to know me," he said, "because one day you're going to grow up and then you're going to *be* me."

I got the old authentic chill when I read that. And it was by no means the only recognition in this superlative collection.

.   .   .   .

In the opening scene of Mona Simpson's *Anywhere But Here,* twelve-year-old Ann August stands at the edge of a flat western highway, watching with growing panic as her mother's white Continental turns into a dot on the horizon. Car and mother will reappear, but only after the girl is convinced that *this time* they are gone forever. For Adele, the mother, is an engineer of histrionic effects: she is willing to put Ann through the terrors of abandonment again and again in order to offer her the miracle of rescue.

Adele and Ann are on their way to California. Adele is in flight from a collapsed marriage and a constricting life in Bay City, Wisconsin. Young, pretty, dissatisfied—she pilots her Continental like a bus of dreams. Ann will be a child star in the movies; luxury and love will carry the day. In the meantime, they must do what they can to survive. Ann sweet-talks free produce from truck drivers; Adele charges meals and motels on a credit card filched from her ex.

A psychologist would probably describe the relations between mother and daughter as "symbiotic." In Adele's case, she would note a problem with boundaries; she does not know where she leaves off and her daughter begins.

Ann is shrewd, though, and no less a survivor than her mother. She recognizes the problem and the eventual solution:

> I must have looked pale standing there, because she pushed some lipstick over my lips. They were chapped and I wouldn't stand still, so she smeared a little and licked her finger to clean the edge of my mouth. I ran over to the sink and spit.
>
> "I felt something then, as I stood watching my spit twirl down the drain. I want to get away from her. There was nowhere I could go. I was twelve. She'd have me six more years.

Anywhere But Here is the story of those six years. But it is not a linear narrative. Ann's account is broken up by a series of digressions into the past, some in her own voice, others in the voices of Carol, Adele's older sister, and Lillian, their mother. Against the chronicle of Adele's scheming—for jobs, clothes, apartments, social connections, and men—and the nonstop friction between a deeply enmeshed mother and daughter, emerges a more substantive picture of the generations of August women. Adele's character, we see, did not emerge out of nowhere.

Simpson's novel achieves its force not so much through plotting as through the steady accumulation of sharply drawn scenes. In less skilled hands, such narration could easily become shapeless and repetitious. But Simpson has a sure instinct for the flash points of love and rage in her characters, and she soft-pedals nothing. Though *Anywhere But Here* is Simpson's first novel, she has already earned a place beside domestic pioneers like Anne Tyler and Alice Munro. She has not only shaken the family tree, she has plucked it from its soil to expose its tangled system of roots.

· · · ·

Ethan Canin /Mona Simpson /Brett Easton Ellis /Jill Eisenstadt

. . . .

From their short author biographies, we learn that Bret Easton Ellis and Jill Eisenstadt both attended Bennington College. From reading their novels, we can deduce that they're also friends, or at least collaborators of a sort. For Ellis has set his action at a place called Camden College, the very school that Eisenstadt's female protagonist, Alex, attends. Both novels have scenes at the same pub and at something called a Dress to Get Laid party; a dormitory drifter named Lars shows up in each.

This bit of cleverness almost guarantees *The Rules of Attraction* and *From Rockaway* will be discussed and, as here, reviewed together. Too bad for both authors. Ellis loses out, because next to *From Rockaway,* his novel looks like the clunker it is. Eisenstadt loses because her slight, skimming little sailboat has to tow the enormous anchor of association.

Ellis's first novel, *Less Than Zero,* became a kind of Baedeker guide for those who wanted to catch a glimpse of what today's disaffected, fast-lane kids were *really* up to. (Sex and coke, in case you didn't know.) It stood out, more for its nihilism than for any intrinsic merits. Ellis became a literary spokesman, a celebrity—he had barely finished driver's training.

How do you follow up a nihilistic *cause célèbre*? You either reverse yourself and start moving *toward* something, or you keep adding minus signs. Ellis has opted for the latter. From *Less Than Zero* to still less. Again, too bad. Whatever he has gained in the way of decadent negativity, he has sacrificed in reader interest. *The Rules of Attraction* is totally, *awesomely* worthless. No characters, no plot, execrable writing. Reading even a page of the prose feels like biting into an old boot.

The novel is narrated through various voices. Sean, Paul, and Lauren are the principals; other views are thrown in for sameness. Ellis's idea is to serve up a multifaceted stream-of-consciousness picture of daily life at Camden. But there's nothing in the stream except the toxic wastes of narcissism.

Next to this, Eisenstadt looks like Leo Tolstoy. Well, not quite. But she can at least create characters who are differentiated by more than just their names.

. . . .

SVEN BIRKERTS

Alex, Timothy, Chowder, and Peg are first introduced to us on the night of the senior prom. They are riding around in a chauffeured stretch limo; they are as drunk as can be. But they stand out.

The four meet up with the rest of their gang on the beach at Rockaway. There they greet the sunrise and chaff one another about the future.

Alex will be the only one to get away. The others will move on to wage jobs or the local junior college.

Breaking away and hanging on are what *From Rockaway* is finally all about. Plot complications are minimal. At the core of the novel is the reft relationship between Alex and Timothy. She leaves for college and breaks his heart. He has just enough intelligence and sensitivity to understand that the split is final and enough true passion to refuse the truth. He knows, too, with a bitterness that can erupt into fury, what the rest of his life will be.

From Rockaway is a slight, if engaging, novel. Perhaps its true fate is to end up on celluloid. (The book already has been optioned.) I can see it working. Like *Saturday Night Fever,* it pushes the energy of desire against the low ceiling of possibility. Subtle acting might round out some of the flatness in Eisenstadt's fashionably minimal prose. The basic human conflicts are all there.

Emperor of the Air. Ethan Canin. 179 pp. Houghton Mifflin. 1988. $15.95

Anywhere But Here. Mona Simpson. 480 pp. Knopf. 1987. $18.95

The Rules of Attraction. Brett Easton Ellis. 288 pp. Simon & Schuster. 1987.

From Rockaway. Jill Eisenstadt. 224 pp. Knopf. 1987. $15.95

.   .   .   .

Ethan Canin /Mona Simpson /Brett Easton Ellis /Jill Eisenstadt

Madison Smartt Bell/
Debra Spark

O n the desk in front of me are two books, *20 Under 30: Best Stories by America's New Young Writers,* edited by Debra Spark and *Straight Cut,* a novel by Madison Smartt Bell. The dust jacket of the latter features a cut-in color photograph of a handsome and brooding young man, and the author's biography begins: "Born in 1957 . . ." The note on the other book has me reaching for my cane: "Debra Spark was born in 1962 . . ." No doubt about it, the marketing mind has decided to locate the cutoff line between prodigy and ordinary adulthood at a round three-zero.

This is something new, and a quick retrospective glance will confirm it. Joyce had written *Dubliners* and most of *A Portrait of the Artist as a Young Man* before he was thirty, Lawrence published *Sons and Lovers* at twenty-eight, and when Hemingway affixed the date—September 21, 1925—to the manuscript of *The Sun Also Rises,* he was a mere twenty-six. Nobody exclaimed over their precocity, or flashed their numbers at the public. These were adult artists; they had long since put sweet youth behind them.

The changed perception, I'm certain, stems in part from the

demographics of what has come to be called a youth culture. But the real explanation goes deeper. Quite simply, it's become extraordinarily difficult for a writer—any writer—to give comprehensive expression to our times. The forces are too various and incalculable. The rate and magnitude of change have outstripped the integrating powers of the psyche. Even older, proven writers are at a loss. The *feel* of life out there in the present seems to elude their verbal net. With the possible exception of Don DeLillo's *White Noise,* I can't think of a single recent work that has managed to get a narrative frame around the ambient sensations of the cultural moment. And DeLillo is no beginner. The near impossibility of achieving significant art has raised the threshold—*any* literary attainment before the age of thirty starts to look remarkable.

Madison Bell touched on some aspects of this malaise in his essay "Less Is Less: The Dwindling American Short Story" in the April issue of *Harper's.* Although he deplored the "low-key noncommittal presentation" that characterizes the fiction of writers like Ann Beattie, David Leavitt, and Bobbie Ann Mason, Bell did not pay sufficient heed to the conditions that foster it. Against the engulfing insubstantiality, he raised the example of Peter Taylor, "arguably the best American short story writer of all time." But Taylor does not write toward the present, he turns against it; his work is an ongoing time capsule of Southern mores in the forties and fifties. Bell noted this, of course. Nevertheless, it was Taylor he invoked to bolster his final point: "Literature might as well undertake certain responsibilities abandoned by the rest of the entertainment industry." The syllables scarcely chime with conviction.

When I first ran up against that phrase yoking literature to "the rest of the entertainment industry," I assumed that Bell was being deliberately wry. But now, after reading *Straight Cut,* I realize that my impulse was too charitable. The book is a straightforward middle-brow page-turner that has been dressed up to look like something more: an existential thriller, an investigation of fast-lane morality. Forget the pretense. Starve it for a day, and it will reveal its true shape—a screenplay.

I have no problem with that. Entertainment is entertainment. What bothers me is that the idea of literature has got mixed in. I hear Bell touted in certain circles as a comer, a serious writer. And

· · · ·

Madison Smartt Bell / Debra Spark

then he goes public with big diagnostic pronouncements, raises a call for a responsible fiction. When a man takes the time to build his own gallows, we ought at least to do him the courtesy of hanging him.

Straight Cut is actually Bell's third novel. He won the terrifying moniker of "promising" (Cyril Connolly: "Whom the gods would destroy, they first call 'promising'") with *The Washington Square Ensemble* and *Waiting for the End of the World*. Both were praised for their energy and their openness to the edges of culture. Both were also criticized for their shapelessness and excess. Bell has evidently taken those reactions to heart—*Straight Cut* is pure narrative.

The plot begins simply enough. The protagonist, Tracy, who's living in numbed estrangement from his wife, Lauren, gets a call from his old moviemaking and drug-dealing partner, Kevin. Kevin wants him to fly to Rome immediately to edit a film. Tracy is suspicious—he knows just how duplicitous his "friend" can be, and he's being given far too much money up front—but he agrees anyway. Deadlocked souls love a promise of trouble. The project turns out to be small potatoes. Living in a borrowed apartment, Tracy falls into an automaton routine of work and sleep, hiding from everything. Until one day he comes back and finds Lauren in his room and a mysteriously locked briefcase parked by the door. As this is, ultimately, a genre novel, I dare not take away the sole reader incentive by divulging any more. The staples are all there: drugs, sex, guns, stakeouts, smuggling, betrayal, death . . . And yes, the usual gritty location shots in Brussels and London.

Take away the plot, and the critic has nothing left to bite into. Characterization is nonexistent. Whether this is by design or just a result of hasty execution I can't say. Possibly Bell wanted Tracy to be one of those hard-hurting iceberg narrators—he is given a drinking problem and a penchant for Kierkegaard. But there is an enormous, if superficially subtle, difference between an understated character like Jake Barnes and an undeveloped cutout like Tracy. And without a sense of who Tracy is, you can make nothing of the dark vibrations that he claims to feel for Kevin, or the wavering passion that Lauren seems to elicit.

I go on at this length only because *Straight Cut* is being sold to us as something that it's not. The back of the jacket features the *New Yorker* seal of approval: "Every sentence he writes is a joy." And other critics weigh in with phrases like "ennobled vision" and "Between your screams of delight are his overtures with death . . ." This is just blurbing, I know. But every so often we need to blow the whistle on it—after all, *you* might be the one tricked into buying the book. Bell's every sentence is *not* a joy. I open the book blind and find: "In Kevin's entryway I waited five minutes before I could stop shaking. Another drink would have gone down good but I didn't have one handy." The pages are filled with this kind of unshaven prose. Anyone capable of reading Kierkegaard ought to know that *good* should be *well*. For that matter any writer who can celebrate Peter Taylor as our living master should be well aware of how the line between literature and the entertainment industry gets drawn.

20 Under 30, though hardly an epoch-making collection, makes no promises that it cannot fulfill. John Register's cover painting—a row of empty tables rendered with photographic precision—sends a clear signal: poise and craft will be the virtues celebrated here. And Debra Spark is forthright about her principle of selection. "Any story I enjoyed well enough to wish I had written,' " she announces, "I included." (Can one enjoy something *well*?) But if she pats herself on the back for the variety of her choices, she draws back from making any larger proclamations. "Generalizations about the nature of a generation's literary tendencies do too much damage to the truth, so I will not make any."

Spark may desist, but I won't. The very fact that these stories are packaged as the products of a generation makes such generalizing a temptation. Neither is the task as daunting as it might appear at first reading. For though the settings and subjects reflect considerable diversity, the procedures do not. And these procedures—the ways that writers handle their subject matter—may tell us a good deal about the state of the art and its fitness for the future.

Basically, there are two-and-a-half kinds of story represented in this anthology, the traditional (plus the Carter/Beattie–derived) and what might be called the fragmented-associational. By "traditional" proper, I mean the kind of story that could just as well have been written in the 1950s or earlier. Most of the better stories fall into this category. Marjorie Sandor's "The Gittel," for example, builds a tense narrative around the tragic destiny of a young Jewish woman, playing off her blind momentum toward death against the survival of her legend in the present. Leigh Allison Wilson's "The Raising" and Ann Patchet's "All Little Colored Children Should Play the Harmonica," on the other hand, are wonderful manipulations of voice and character idiosyncrasy. But none of these could be said to advance the form. Sandor has drawn upon the traditionalist techniques of I. B. Singer and Cynthia Ozick; Wilson and Patchet move over terrain that Eudora Welty and Katherine Anne Porter first prospected decades ago.

I was relieved to find that only a handful of the selections conformed to the deadly Carver/Beattie pattern. (Although they're contemporary, workshop emulation has turned their kind of plotless-story-told-in-affectless-tone into something very like a tradition.) Brett Lott's "This Plumber" can stand in for the bunch. A grizzled, sweaty plumber arrives at a young man's apartment to track down the source of a leak. The young man watches him work. As the plumber pokes and mutters, the young man projects all sorts of fantasies onto him. He is "real," authentic; he probably hunts. The young man wants to tell him all about how his wife left him. The plumber finally says, "Don't ask me a goddam thing about anything other than plumbing." These pipes have been banged before.

The remaining stories—exactly ten of the twenty, as it happens—make use of a technique that has spread through workshops and writing programs like a prairie fire. The fragmented-associational story presents its insights in a series of discrete, obliquely related episodes. The idea is not to create character or narrative but to spin out an uncentered web of impressions and suggestions. Trademark features of this method include random-seeming jumps in time, a fixation on the minutiae of daily life, and, as often as not, a diaristic, present-tense telling style.

"Doug gave me the movies," states a young woman named Caroline at the outset of Ehud Havazelet's "Natalie Wood's Amazing Eyes." What she means is that Doug, her lover, introduced her to the movies as a world away from the world. One episode recounts their early days, how they spent every free hour together in a celluloid dream. Next we see Caroline going to the movies alone; Doug is always working. Presumably the relationship is disintegrating, though we don't know enough about either to grasp what that might mean. In the next sequence, a black man dressed all in pink sits down next to her and lifts up her skirt; she does nothing. Then she makes dinner for Doug's boss and his girlfriend—she serves heart. The girlfriend gets upset; Doug gets upset. The boss comes into the kitchen and rubs her breasts. In the last passage, Caroline is back in the theater. She has arrived hours early and is sitting in the stillness. She imagines the crowd of daylight desperadoes queuing up and thinks, Let them come to me. Finis.

The fragmented-associational mode is ideally suited to the beginning stylist, the stylist entranced by the shimmering surfaces of modern life but lacking the deeper grasp of how things work. Mysteries of time, place, and human motivation can be hinted at even where there is no real understanding. It is entirely possible to make a story that looks and feels modern and doesn't mean a thing.

I absorbed and enjoyed a number of these random exercises, but when I looked back at the book a few days later, I found that I had forgotten every one. That special feeling that a good story can give— that you have broken into the secret preserve of a life—did not exist. What I had kept, and this surprised me, were the sensations encountered in the more conventional stories; they alone attained to an afterlife.

Generalizations. All serious writers in our time confront a confoundingly complex and fluid outer reality. Representing it, much less interpreting it, requires not just talent and application, but a courage verging on hubris as well. To judge from the work collected in *20 Under 30* (Remember, I'm generalizing), younger writers are balking at the big job. They are falling back upon proven paths, or else contenting themselves with diffuse evocations. Needed: an anthology with a blazing cover, a gathering of writers who have some inkling of the terrible danger facing us. I don't mean extinction—I mean the encroaching blandness that will very likely swallow us all. Needed: blasts of energy and consequence, visions and vituperations.

Straight Cut. Madison Smartt Bell. 230 pp. Ticknor & Fields. 1986. $15.95

20 Under 30: Best Stories by America's New Young Writers. Debra Spark, ed. 272 pp. Scribner's. 1986. $7.95 (paper)

. . . .

Madison Smartt Bell / Debra Spark

David Foster Wallace

T om Wolfe, as we all know, has a positive genius for wetting his index finger and getting it up there into the weather. In his recent essay in *Harper's,* "Stalking the Billion-Footed Beast: A Literary Manifesto for the New Social Novel," he raised a call for a return to subject matter in fiction. Wolfe holds that in our postmodern and minimalist era the art has all but withered away. Novelists and story-tellers are busy with academic exercises; they are ceding the job of transcribing reality to journalists.

Wolfe, whose own grand social novel, *The Bonfire of the Vanities,* has achieved spectacular popular success, professes himself dumb-founded. Never in history has there been so much material. The big, gritty world is all but posing for the writer; our newspapers brim with outlandish and revelatory narratives. "American society today," Wolfe asserts, "is no more or less chaotic, random, discontinuous, or absurd than Russian society or French society or British society a hundred years ago, no matter how convenient it might be for a writer to think so."

Wolfe has proved himself often prescient—and always provocative—and at first his call appears to be just what we need. The serious novel is in crisis; bony tales of domestic trauma are the order of the day. But a more thoughtful reading of Wolfe's manifesto brings pause. His premise, that our society, while different in its particulars, is in its essentials unchanged, no more "chaotic" or "random" than the societies of Tolstoy's, Zola's, or Thackeray's day, is astonishing. It short-circuits modernity altogether, ignoring the catastrophic and all-transforming impacts of nuclear fission, the microchip, telecommunications, the multinational corporation, the all but total decimation of the farm economy. Wolfe is making a brash end run around modernism, attempting for fiction what he once attempted for architecture. His summons to a new social novel is, on closer inspection, a kind of retreat.

The success of *Bonfire* seems to have blinkered Wolfe's vision. Perhaps he interprets his sales figures as an endorsement of his literary principles. But he is confusing popularity with artistic attainment. *Bonfire* is a delightfully engaging popular novel—it is not great literature. It stands on a par with works by John O'Hara and Sinclair Lewis (whom Wolfe extols in his essay), and when its cultural moment has passed, it, too, will pass. Accurate as *Bonfire* is in capturing the social mores and commodity fetishism of late-twentieth-century urban America, its penetration of culture and human character is superficial. The novel, and Wolfe's proclamation, have little bearing on the deeper purposes of literature.

In the arts, as in human life, there is no going back to the past except in memory. We may deplore the triviality or aridity of current productions and long for the vigorous amplitude of an earlier day, but we cannot snap our fingers and will its recurrence. So-called "serious" literature is bound to both reflect and reflect *upon* the continuing evolution of the human; it must interrogate our meaning—individual and social—in the light of the history we keep making. Writers find their forms for this presentation not by reaching blindly into a grab bag of former modes but by extending or refuting the forms that their predecessors have used.

Let me try to illustrate the current dilemma. Picture two travelers. One is a man sitting at a table at a roadside inn in England in the late nineteenth century. The other is a man sitting under the crackling fluorescents of a mall cafeteria in late 1980s America. The first man, positioned naturally and comprehensibly in his environment, is a ready subject for the kind of novel Wolfe espouses; we recognize both man and inn from Hardy, Dickens, and Thackeray. Reading about him, we make a set of assumptions about the solidity and coherence of the world around him.

The man in the mall, however, presents a problem. The table in front of him is plastic; the food he eats is generic pulp. He sits not in silence or amid the low murmurs of others like him, but is enfolded in the ambient distraction of Muzak. He studies the napkin holder. Nearby a kid with an orange Mohawk bashes a video game. The swirl of energies around our subject all but erases him. The writer cannot simply plunk him down and get on with the business of narration. A thousand changed circumstances have combined to vaporize his human solidity—or its illusion.

Wolfe is on target in identifying subject matter as the greatest challenge facing the contemporary writer. But in proposing the panoramic approach, he has bypassed the underlying problem entirely. To work on the scale that Wolfe demands, to get at the big ironies and moral collisions of modern urban life, characters have to be flattened and typed until they are nearly cartoons; situations have to be heightened to tabloid contrast. Which is all very interesting but has little to do with the truth about how life is experienced by the individual in our time.

Yes, there is a crisis in the arts. The crisis is that the greater part of contemporary experience has fallen out of the reach of language—or very nearly so. We no longer till fields; most of us don't even make things—our attention is increasingly dispersed among inchoate signals. So much of our time is passed in talking on phones, driving on freeways, staring at terminals or TV screens, and waiting in lobbies. Larger and larger portions of what our lives are made up of cannot be encompassed in coherent narrative form. The writer must either distort or else work around the expanding blank spots.

The minimalists, pilloried by Wolfe, have at least recognized the nature of the problem. But their response (I'm thinking here of writers such as Ann Beattie, Amy Hempel, Frederick Barthelme, and

Mary Robison) is to retreat from the internal. These authors give us the descriptions of the places, the name brands, the clips of conversation, and we must infer what the innerscape is like.

Minimalism is ultimately a cul-de-sac, leaving the larger part of modern life untouched. The new social novel that Wolfe would sponsor is, by contrast, open to *stuff,* to big events and dramatic conflicts. It can incorporate in documentary fashion large masses of familiar material, including the brands and places beloved of the minimalists. But its scale and its hothouse sensationalism—its Dickensian ambition—forbid closer inspection of the conditions of our changed sensibilities.

What is the fiction writer—the writer who would try to catch us undistorted in our moment—to do? What prose will raise a mirror to our dispersed condition? One sort of answer is now offered in a collection of stories entitled *Girl with Curious Hair,* by David Foster Wallace. He is Wolfe's compass needle turned 180 degrees.

Wallace's stories are as startling and barometrically accurate as anything in recent decades. The author, still in his twenties (his novel, *The Broom of the System,* was published in 1987), writes what his adoring flap copy calls "*post*-postmodernism." Much as I revile flap copy, I have to say that the tag is right. We sense immediately that Wallace is beyond the calculated fiddle of the postmodernists. He is not announcing as news the irreparable fragmentation of our cultural life; he is not fastening upon TV and punk culture and airport lounges as if for the first time ever. Wallace comes toward us as a citizen of that new place, the place that the minimalists have only been able to point toward. The rhythms, disjunctions, and surreally beautiful—if terrifying—meldings of our present-day surround are fully his. Wallace is, for better or worse, the savvy and watchful voice of the *now*—and he is unburdened by any nostalgia for the old order.

Girl with Curious Hair collects ten of Wallace's stories, four or five of which are strong enough to inflict the scorpion's sting on the workshop verbiage that passes for fiction these days. The first piece, "Little Expressionless Animals," is one of these. In swift, artfully elided passages, Wallace tells the story of Julie Smith, for three years undefeated queen of the television quiz show *Jeopardy!* (She is, of course, an invention.) But the customary descriptions, I realize, will not work here. Wallace does not, in fact, *tell the story*. Instead, he inhabits for extended moments the airspace around Julie, her lover Faye (a researcher for the show), Faye's mother, Dee (the producer), and Alex Trebek (the host); or else he slips, as omniscient narrator, back into essential episodes from Julie's past. What emerges is a legend of real-life damage and media vampirism that dots the reader's flesh with goose bumps.

Here, as elsewhere, Wallace sets nearly all his scenes in the drab and untenanted places that writers avoid—in hallways, empty conference rooms, on the flashing plastic set of the show. And, episode by episode, there is little or no action. The reviewer butts against impossibility, for the whole effect of these fictions derives from the cumulation and cross echo of these elided moments. Citation would distort more than it would reveal.

I can, however, try to describe the effect. As readers, we feel we have made contact with a new dimension. We touch not the old illusion of reality that fiction has always traded in but the *irreality* that every day further obscures the recognizable. We enter a zone where signals flash across circuits; where faces balloon across monitors and voices slip in and out of clear sense; where media personnel work night and day to mask and stylize the merely personal; where Alex Trebek, master of poise, confesses to his psychiatrist that he's worried about his smile: "That it's starting to maybe be a tired smile. Which is *not* an inviting smile, which is professionally worrying."

"Girl with Curious Hair," the title story, reconnoiters adjacent terrain, but in a very different manner. A businessman by day, punk by night named Sick Puppy tells about an evening spent with friends at a Keith Jarrett concert. He sits with Big and Mr. Wonderful, and with his girlfriend, Gimlet, who wears her hair styled up to resemble an erect penis. The shock is less in the premise or the rude antics of the friends; it is in the idiom that Wallace has given his narrator. Tuning in on Sick Puppy at random, we hear:

> Her friend and confidante Tit sculptures Gimlet's hair and provides her with special haircare products from her career as a hair stylist which makes Gimlet's hair sculpture rigid and realistic at

. . . .

all times. I have my hair maintained at Julio's Unisex Fashion Cut Center in West Hollywood, with an attractive part on the right side of my hair.

By story's end precious little has happened, but we are reeling. The calculated pastiche of the prose, its phrasings drawn from TV, ad brochures, and commercial newspeak, forces the larger question: if we are as we speak, then where is Sick Puppy? He has put his expression together from everywhere; he is frighteningly, *awesomely,* nowhere.

Wallace's other stories, the best of them, set us straight into the heart of this newly seen present. In "My Appearance," a young woman worries for thirty pages about her guest spot on the David Letterman show. "Westward the Course of Empire Takes Its Way" recounts the journey through the Midwest of a group of former actors from McDonald's commercials; they are on their way to a grand reunion of all former players from McDonald's commercials. (Wallace's scenarios are as funny as they are uncanny or suggestive.) Again and again, nothing—or nearly nothing—happens. But the way that nothing happens, the eerie space it opens for stray turns and encounters, captures a feeling that often threatens to engulf us in our lives: the feeling that we are not fully hooked in, that the tide of distraction laps ever more forcefully at our boundaries and threatens to spill over one day soon.

To achieve this peculiar verisimilitude, Wallace is forced to steer away from the staple binding ingredient of most fiction: narrative drama. His stories go untensed by any overt conflicts or movements toward gratifying resolution. They are, like Pynchon's fictions, difficult to read over long stretches, and for many of the same reasons. Yet time and again we shake our heads to say, "It's true. That's what it's like out there."

Between Wolfe and Wallace, we find ourselves in a strange bind. If fiction is to win and hold a readership, it will probably have to move Wolfe's way. But the new social novel does not hold much of the truth about the changed conditions of our subjective lives, our feel for the contemporary, except in caricature. The other compass direction, which leads us closer to the man—or woman—hunched

. . .

David Foster Wallace

over coffee in the mall, cannot easily render that life and remain gratifying as narrative. Where shall we get the picture of who we are? It seems that the present keeps moving, with ever greater acceleration, out of the reach of language. It may take new geniuses and new genres to bring it back.

Girl with Curious Hair. David Foster Wallace. 373 pp. Norton. 1990. $17.95

. . . .

SVEN BIRKERTS

Index

A Note
About the Author . . .

Sven Birkerts attended Cranbrook School and The University of Michigan. After receiving his B.A. in 1973, he worked for many years as a bookseller in Ann Arbor, Michigan, and Cambridge, Massachusetts. His essays have appeared in *The New York Review of Books*, *The Nation*, *Partisan Review*, *Ploughshares*, and other publications. He is a recent recipient of a Lila Wallace–Reader's Digest Award. Sven Birkerts lives in Arlington, Massachusetts, with his wife, Lynn Focht, and his daughter, Mara, and teaches at Harvard University.